# THE UK AFTER BREXIT

# THE UK AFTER BREXIT

## Legal and Policy Challenges

*Edited by*
Michael DOUGAN

intersentia

Cambridge – Antwerp – Portland

Intersentia Ltd
Sheraton House | Castle Park
Cambridge | CB3 0AX | United Kingdom
Tel.: +44 1223 370 170 | Fax: +44 1223 370 169
Email: mail@intersentia.co.uk
www.intersentia.com | www.intersentia.co.uk

*Distribution for the UK and Ireland:*
NBN International
Airport Business Centre, 10 Thornbury Road
Plymouth, PL6 7 PP
United Kingdom
Tel.: +44 1752 202 301 | Fax: +44 1752 202 331
Email: orders@nbninternational.com

*Distribution for Europe and all other countries:*
Intersentia Publishing nv
Groenstraat 31
2640 Mortsel
Belgium
Tel.: +32 3 680 15 50 | Fax: +32 3 658 71 21
Email: mail@intersentia.be

*Distribution for the USA and Canada:*
International Specialized Book Services
920 NE 58th Ave. Suite 300
Portland, OR 97213
USA
Tel.: +1 800 944 6190 (toll free) | Fax: +1 503 280 8832
Email: info@isbs.com

The UK after Brexit. Legal and Policy Challenges
© The editor and contributors severally 2017

ISBN 978-1-78068-471-0
D/2017/7849/80
NUR 820

British Library Cataloguing in Publication Data. A catalogue record for this book is available from the British Library.

# CONTENTS

# LIST OF AUTHORS

Professor Catherine Barnard, University of Cambridge

Dr Aleksandra Čavoški, University of Birmingham

Professor Paul Craig, University of Oxford

Professor Marise Cremona, European University Institute

Professor Michael Dougan, University of Liverpool

Dr Michael Gordon, University of Liverpool

Professor Christian Henderson, University of Sussex

Dr Veerle Heyvaert, London School of Economics

Dr Thomas Horsley, University of Liverpool

Dr Joanne Hunt, Cardiff University

Dr Luke McDonagh, City University of London

Dr Gregory Messenger, University of Liverpool

Dr Marc Mimler, Bournemouth University

Professor Valsamis Mitsilegas, Queen Mary University of London

Professor Niamh Moloney, London School of Economics

Dr Stephanie Reynolds, University of Liverpool

Dr Mavluda Sattorova, University of Liverpool

# EDITOR'S INTRODUCTION

## Michael DOUGAN*

## 1. ABOUT THIS BOOK

The UK's decision to leave the European Union marks a fundamental reorientation in UK law and policy: both internally, when it comes to the structures, processes and outputs of our own domestic legal systems; and externally, as regards the UK's place in and relations with the broader European and international legal orders. Many of those who heartily championed and/or supported the 'Brexit' cause seem to have harboured only a limited comprehension of the scale and profundity of the changes they worked so hard to initiate. Many others positively delight in the prospect of being able, fundamentally, to rewrite the country's future direction, yet evince a comparable lack of understanding about the internal and external factors that will actually shape and constrain their grand revolutionary visions. This book seeks to offer its readers – be they students and postgraduate researchers, fellow academics and practitioners, policy-makers and NGOs, or indeed the interested public in the UK and abroad – a more informed and realistic basis upon which to understand the nature and importance of the challenges now facing the UK.

It goes almost without saying: this collection of essays is not intended to be either definitive or exhaustive of the legal and policy issues raised by the UK's withdrawal from the EU. The sheer range of fields which will be affected, combined with the general state of uncertainty about how events might now unfold, would militate against any such ambition. Instead, our aim is to highlight some of the key challenges which are likely to arise in selected areas of

---

\* Liverpool Law School, University of Liverpool. The views expressed in this introduction are my own and do not necessarily represent the views of any of the other contributors to this edited collection.

the UK legal system – thus providing a reference point for future discussion as the situation continues to develop, while also helping to identify parallel issues potentially affecting other policy sectors.

The essays are grouped into three main sections. Part I deals with some of the key constitutional issues arising from UK withdrawal. Michael Gordon addresses the fundamental question of how Brexit will affect relations between the UK Parliament and UK Government: not just in the short term, when it comes to execution of the decision to the leave the EU, particularly in the aftermath of the *Miller* judgment;[1] but also in the longer term, for example, as the regular democratic legitimacy of both Parliament and Government is challenged by the irregular democratic authority of popular referendums. Joanne Hunt then discusses some of the chief questions Brexit poses for the UK's devolution settlement – taking as her cue the tension between the 'unitary approach' towards the referendum result adopted by the UK Government versus the reality of 'remain' votes in Scotland and Northern Ireland; and highlighting how withdrawal from the EU might well demand a fundamental reform of the UK's entire devolution system. My own chapter focuses on the difficult challenges posed by Brexit for the land border between Northern Ireland and the Republic of Ireland: first, as regards the free movement of goods, once that border becomes a customs frontier between the UK and the EU; and secondly, as regards the free movement of persons, depending upon choices still to be made by the UK about its future immigration policies. Thomas Horsley analyses the potential impact of UK withdrawal from the EU upon the functions and powers of the domestic judges. What might be the effect of replacing the European Communities Act 1972 with a new (but as yet unclear) 'constitutional instruction' from Parliament about how the courts should interpret EU-derived legislation in the period after withdrawal? And how might this inform the judicial interpretation of future international agreements between the UK and the EU or indeed other international trade and cooperation partners?

Part II then considers a selection of substantive internal policy fields likely to be significantly affected by the UK's withdrawal from the EU. Catherine Barnard highlights the tension between the demands of many Leave campaigners to cut 'Brussels red tape' in the form of EU employment rights, the Prime Minister's promise (at least in the short term) to respect and build on existing worker protection legislation, and the potential longer-term consequences of leaving the EU for employment law in the UK. Veerle Heyvaert and Aleksandra Čavoški remind us that the UK may well be leaving the EU, but many of the most important challenges in environmental law and policy will still require the UK to cooperate closely with the EU and its Member States; while at home,

---

[1] *R (on the application of Miller and another) v Secretary of State for Exiting the European Union* [2017] UKSC 5.

those concerned with environmental protection need to be particularly vigilant about the removal of the EU's minimum regulatory standards as well as the loss of the EU's relatively effective environmental enforcement mechanisms. When it comes to the high-profile yet fiendishly complex field of financial services, Niamh Moloney argues that Brexit is unlikely to lead to any major upheavals in UK regulation, at least in the forseeable future: not only due to the need to maintain equivalence with EU legislation in order to minimise future trade barriers; but also (for example) because there is little evidence of significant industry or regulator pressure for extensive reform, while the UK will in any case remain bound to respect international standards for the sector. Luke McDonagh and Marc Mimler consider how, when it comes to intellectual property law, EU regulation affects the different categories of IP rights in very different ways, with some subject to more extensive regimes of coordination or harmonisation than others. UK withdrawal will therefore have significant but essentially variegated implications for different branches of intellectual property law.

Of all the policy fields certain to be affected by Brexit, arguably none has occupied a more prominent or controversial place in the public and political debate than the situation of existing migrants currently protected under EU citizenship law. Stephanie Reynolds offers a critical assessment of that debate – arguing that the UK Government's rejection of any unilateral protective action, in preference for seeking a high-priority reciprocal guarantee of residency rights with the rest of the EU, may well sit uneasily with the need to address a series of more complex issues (such as cross-border social security coordination) which actually make bare rights to residency meaningful in practice. Valsamis Mitsilegas addresses the prospects for future cross-border cooperation in criminal matters – a field where the utopian claims of the Leave campaign were starkly contradicted by academic experts and competent policy actors. The essential message is simple: the UK cannot hope for more effective cooperation from outside the EU than it enjoyed as a Member State; indeed, even to access a more limited degree of police and security cooperation, the UK may well be expected to respect yet more EU obligations as a third country than it did as a Member State.

Part III turns to consider the future of the UK's external relations in several crucial arenas. Gregory Messenger addresses the UK's membership of the World Trade Organization: not only the short-term challenges of 'regularising' the UK's terms of membership and ensuring effective British representation at various international decision-making and decision-influencing fora; but also the need to mainstream understanding of core WTO obligations into the UK's own policy-making processes and indeed to understand the very different legal and economic realities of (non-)compliance with WTO law. Marise Cremona discusses the main issues which will arise as the UK seeks to articulate an independent and effective trade policy: from coping with the immediate consequences of withdrawal for economic relations with the numerous countries with which the EU had already concluded trade agreements; to making decisions about the UK's preferences as regards the various elements – from preferential tariffs to regulatory barriers, trade-related policies and dispute settlement mechanisms – that go to make up an integrated trade policy. Mavluda Sattorova deals with the importance for the UK of international investment law: when it comes to securing the UK's future economic success, the Government has placed considerable emphasis on attracting foreign investment; yet the reality of many international investment treaties is that they are designed to protect the interests of foreign investors rather than respect the sovereignty of the host country or contribute to a balanced economic development across its population.

Christian Henderson considers the implications of UK withdrawal for the system of international peace and security. The impact upon both the UN and NATO may prove to be relatively limited, but when it comes to the EU's Common Security and Defence Policy, the picture is more complex and uncertain. On the one hand, the removal of the UK is a potentially significant loss in terms of military spending, hardware, personnel and leadership. On the other hand, the elimination of the UK's veto power over EU ambitions to develop an autonomous military capability might well provide opportunities for the EU27 to redefine the CSDP's aims and capacities. Finally, Paul Craig confronts the over-arching question which has been raised in so many previous chapters of this edited collection: what might the future hold for relations between the UK and the EU? His chapter discusses three keys issues: the withdrawal negotiations now governed by Article 50 TEU; the potential for future trade relations either under a bespoke trade agreement or defaulting to WTO terms; and non-trade issues, particularly concerning crime and security cooperation.

No editorial attempt to synthesise those diverse and rich contributions could possibly hope to do justice to their complex and multifaceted analyses and discussion. Perhaps it will suffice to highlight just several of the key points which emerge from across this collection. First, even if the future remains clouded in uncertainty, basic constitutional principles and legal frameworks do already allow us to identify many of the key issues which need to be addressed and many of the inherent parameters which will inevitably limit the available room for manoeuvre. Those observations can perhaps best be summed up in the concept of 'de-Europeanisation': what might it look like to undo 40 years of legal co-evolution between the UK and the EU? Secondly, such de-Europeanisation is inevitably going to affect different parts of the legal system in very different ways: some fields are likely to be impacted upon much more directly and strongly than others. But de-Europeanisation might also have effects which are more indirect and unexpected, as the reshaping of legal powers and relationships produces unintended or unforeseen consequences. Thirdly, although withdrawal from the EU will affect the basic legal framework of UK policy-making most obviously in those fields (such as agriculture, fisheries, immigration and customs) where the state will effectively need to design a new regulatory system, the impact may prove just as important and controversial in those sectors (such as employment or environmental protection) where EU law currently provides a safety net below which the Member States are not permitted to deregulate, but as regards which it may soon become open to future governments, if they so wish, to engage in more fundamental processes of deregulation. Fourthly, de-Europeanisation is not just about deciding which EU rules the UK should keep, amend or reject. It also implies important changes to the methodologies and cultures of our legal and political institutions; to the efficiency and effectiveness of our regulatory and problem-solving capacities; and at a more fundamental level, to the balance of power between our legal and political actors; as well as between concentrations of public and private power within our economy and society. Fifthly, all these questions about the future evolution of the UK legal system are inseparable from the issue of the UK's future external relations. For example: depending on the deal the UK eventually reaches with the EU about future trade and broader cooperation, we might well be obliged to adopt many of the EU's rules, in a whole series of policy fields, just as if the UK were still a member – though without having any real influence over the content of those rules any more. Or again: as the UK sets about designing its own independent trade policy, the balances struck by/imposed upon the UK in its external economic relations will have tangible and potentially significant effects upon its internal legal system – influencing the choices we make about not only economic regulation but also environmental protection, workers' rights and consumer protection.

In short: UK withdrawal is not just about finding a new relationship with the EU. It is also about opening our own legal and political systems to processes of far-reaching change. Much of that change will inevitably be a matter of deep contestation and division among politicians, stakeholders and citizens. But much of it will also be driven and/or constrained by our new place in the world and the new balances of power which emerge between the UK and our international partners.

The various chapters contained in this book were all completed during the period late March-early April 2017. Given the rapid pace of contemporary political developments, some contributions were therefore able to incorporate the most recent events – such as the UK's official notification of withdrawal under Article 50 TEU,[2] or the public release of the European Council's draft negotiating guidelines,[3] or publication of the UK Government's White Paper on the so-called Great Repeal Bill[4] – while other texts had already entered the

---

[2]   Letter from Theresa May to Donald Tusk, 29 March 2017.
[3]   European Council, *Draft guidelines following the United Kingdom's notification under Article 50 TEU* (published on 31 March 2017, expected to be adopted in late April 2017).
[4]   Department for Exiting the European Union, *Legislating for the United Kingdom's withdrawal from the European Union* (Cm 9446, March 2017).

publication process by the relevant time. Needless to say: besides being invited to focus on broader themes, rather than get too bogged down in technical details, our authors have enjoyed complete freedom in the conception and content of their own contributions. However, it is inevitable, given their sometimes complex and technical subject matter, that certain chapters will presuppose a substantial degree of prior knowledge about the specific field and will perhaps be less accessible to a general reader than some of the others.

## 2.  ON THE IMPORTANCE OF THE ACADEMIC CONTRIBUTION TO BETTER PUBLIC UNDERSTANDING

Besides seeking to inform its readers of some of the key issues in law and policy raised by the UK's withdrawal from the EU, this book serves another and perhaps even more important purpose: to vindicate and indeed celebrate the value of academic expertise as well as its potential to improve and enrich public understanding of the most pressing challenges facing our society.

I have had no hesitation in making and repeating the assertion that – taken together, since they were not one but several (often mutually contradictory) movements – the Leave alliance of 2016 conducted the most dishonest political campaign in modern British history.[5] In doing so, those responsible not only demeaned and debased our democracy. They also sought to inflict immeasurable damage upon some of the most important values which the academic profession is entrusted to represent and defend: the commitment to pragmatic, rational, evidence-based scientific investigation, which seeks to inform and better our society through the cultivation of expert skill, knowledge and experience, to be tested and refined through a process of objective and rigorous peer review. It is simply impossible to reconcile those values with a politics which is proudly ideological and, with it, indifferent to evidence, immune to persuasion, cynically selective and self-serving in its analysis, and ultimately anti-democratic in its intolerance of dissent.

That irreconcilable conflict perhaps helps to explain the ferocity of the attacks which so many Leave campaigners (in particular) launched against so many academics (including several contributors to this edited collection) who volunteered to perform the public service of participating in various debates surrounding the 2016 referendum.

---

[5]  See eg <https://www.youtube.com/watch?v=eyMcesYSLk8> and <https://www.youtube.com/watch?v=oHm9QOffpyE>.

Politically motivated hostility is one of the chief downsides of the otherwise important and positive 'impact agenda' that has strongly informed the direction of academic research in the UK since preparations for the Research Excellence Framework of 2014.[6] Universities could undoubtedly do more to prepare and support those staff whose academic work and public engagement exposes them to such hostility. But in the meantime, there can be real value in categorising then analysing the standard methods of abuse directed at academics – after all, the publication of abuse need cross no threshold of originality – as an important step in building up personal resilience as well as formulating an appropriate professional response.

My own experience might provide a useful example upon which to reflect. During the period from around June 2016 to March 2017, I received in excess of 20,000 personal messages (mostly by email but also sizeable numbers by more traditional post) from the general public – and that was besides the many tens of thousands of social media and other internet comments about my work, of which I remain largely ignorant, due to my own technical limitations and personal inclinations. Although those messages and comments included a great many expressions of gratitude or support, and myriad genuine questions and queries that their senders hoped I could help to answer, they also included vast amounts of abuse. For present purposes, the latter can conveniently be divided into four main strains.

Our first category consists of messages/comments which are best described as simple malice in the form of personal insults: from the straightforward (for example, 'I hope you watch your children die painfully of cancer before you die painfully of cancer yourself'); to those aggravated by racism or homophobia (such as 'fuck off back to paddyland you IRA cunt'); and those which sought to be threatening in a generically foreboding way (including 'watch out: we are about to go public with material about you that will ruin your life then maybe you'll learn to shut your fucking mouth'). It would be easy for me to say: this was all so much water off a duck's back. Growing up in working class Belfast in the late 1970s and early 1980s has apparently gifted me a rather thick skin. But I know too many colleagues whose personal and professional wellbeing were seriously adversely affected by precisely this sort of abuse – again, often aggravated by issues of gender or race – for nothing more than the crime of having dared to employ their expertise to help inform some important aspect of our current political debate about the very future of the UK. Unfortunately, there is perhaps little one can do against the army of cowards who use the distance and/or anonymity of the internet to vent the depths of their own spite against total strangers – apart from being prepared to involve the police in the case of

---

[6]    See further <http://www.ref.ac.uk>.

any potential criminal offence; and otherwise to remind oneself on a regular basis that such behaviour says an enormous amount about them, yet absolutely nothing about you.

Our second category also employs personal abuse with the primary intention of intimating its recipient into silence, but this time with a more specific focus: the allegation (mostly pre-referendum) of being an unpatriotic traitor and/or (mostly post-referendum) of being an anti-democratic subversive. Of course, such abuse was hardly unique to academics: we should neither forgive nor forget the comparable *Daily Mail* attack on members of our senior judiciary as 'enemies of the people';[7] or indeed the countless times that a fellow citizen was insulted and harangued as a 'remoaner' for daring to express their sincerely held and well-founded views and preferences. Here, our response surely needs to be significantly more proactive and robust: we cannot afford to allow any ideological movement cynically to self-appropriate fundamentally contested concepts such as 'patriotism' or 'democracy' and then seek to convert them into political weapons designed to suppress public freedom of expression in general, or hinder academic enquiry and debate in particular.

Screeching general abuse is one thing. Our third category was rather more targeted and also perhaps more sinister in nature: seeking to undermine public faith in the professional ethics and independence of academic researchers; usually by alleging some vested interest which rendered their work suspect if not altogether untrustworthy. Some such allegations were pitched at a level of abstraction and of such an irrational nature that it is difficult to believe anyone could take them seriously. Consider the argument that, since universities receive research funding from the EU, anyone who works at a university must therefore be biased in favour of the EU. It is rather bizarre to attack UK universities for succeeding (as they are actively encouraged to do by every UK Government) in securing public money from one of the largest funders of academic activity on earth. It is also curious that the allegation of bias only relates to EU money: apparently academics are capable of resisting the talismanic corruption of every other source of public funding for our work. And one would suppose that the same abstract allegation of bias should really apply also to anyone else who has ever indirectly benefited from some form of EU intervention: say, the entire populations of Scotland, Northern Ireland, Wales, Merseyside, Cornwall … Another personal favourite, in this category, was the oft-repeated argument that *of course* anyone doing work about the EU would be automatically biased in favour of 'remain' because otherwise they would be putting themselves out of a job. As if only someone living in America can work on American politics; or as if only an academic based in France is allowed to research French history; or

---

[7]     *Daily Mail* headline, 4 November 2016.

as if the UK will no longer have any need in the future to know and understand the law and policy of the European Union. Rest assured: we most certainly will. Indeed, the irony is: Brexit is any UK-EU legal researcher's lifetime gift.

But more pernicious than the abstract claims of academic bias were those that sought to undermine the credibility of particular researchers through false allegations of personal corruption. Let's take just one small yet influential example. In an internet story dated 21 June 2016, Leave campaigner Richard North claimed that '[Dougan's] post is supported by EU funds, typically worth €50,000 over three years. And, while post-holders deny bias, they are in effect paid agents of the EU'.[8] North's claim was (indeed, continues to be) circulated widely on social media – part of a widespread and no doubt partly successful attempt to undermine my own professional integrity and reputation. But if North had bothered to check even his most basic facts, he would have known – from information clearly and publicly available, not least on the University of Liverpool website – that the University was awarded a Jean Monnet Chair (a form of EU grant, not an academic position, despite its title) consisting of €36,000 (approximately £24,000 at the time) over the period from 2006 to 2009. For reference, that is estimated to account for significantly less than 0.0001 per cent of the institution's turnover since 2006. Under the terms of the grant, part of the money was spent on a major academic conference and publication (the latter undergoing the usual process of international peer review). The remaining funds were allocated to the department's general teaching resources and spent (to be precise) on enabling several PhD students to gain teaching experience in order to assist their academic career progression. My only obligation? To teach some EU law each year during the period 2006–09 – hardly very taxing for an EU lawyer teaching in a jurisdiction where EU law is compulsory for all law students seeking professional exemption: I teach some EU law every year. In accordance with the University's original contract, since my CV was included in the grant application, I may continue to refer to the 2006 award among my own professional distinctions. I am very happy and proud to do so, since such awards carry considerable prestige within my academic discipline.

Let's not even get so far as to query North's unsubstantiated and unwarranted allegation that anyone in receipt of EU funding through a long established and well respected scheme such as the Jean Monnet Chairs is to be dismissed as some 'paid agent' of the EU. Let's content ourselves with just the more specific query: was North correct to claim that my post is supported by EU funds? Not in the slightest. This was nothing more than an attempt to discredit someone who dared to express an opinion different from North – though as things turned out, his 21 June 2016 story proved only the first of several increasingly aggressive diatribes against 'Monnet Professor Dougan' or 'Dougan the

---

[8]     See <http://www.eureferendum.com/blogview.aspx?blogno=86112>.

Dishonest', some of which repeat the same fake claims about my non-existent EU funding. Several generous citizens have offered to fund a legal action on my behalf seeking substantial damages in defamation against North. I suggested they give the money instead to charity. By providing another example of the incompetent and mendacious abuse of academics, North has served his useful purpose. Though at this point, we should not let another example of ideological hypocrisy go past unmentioned: perhaps those academics so easily bribed into spreading pro-EU propaganda when their institutions received modest sums of EU funding for designated research and educational purposes, should have learned some of the moral fortitude of (say) UKIP, whose army of MEPs were never accused of pro-EU bias despite the fact that they took (and in some cases, allegedly misappropriated) far larger sums of public money from the very same EU cashcow.

Our fourth and final category of abuse – questioning the professional competence and abilities of academic researchers – also has its abstract as well as its more personalised variants. The 'ivory tower' jibe – attacking the capacity of those who work at universities to make any valuable contribution to public understanding and debate, on the curious grounds that we do not 'live in the real world' – is almost as commonplace as it is so obviously bankrupt. Yet how many times did one hear the apparently serious suggestion that, if you really wanted to know about UK or EU constitutional law, it was better to ask someone who had run their own small business (it being only a coincidence if they happened also to be a vocal Leave campaigner) rather than listen to some academic who has never had to worry about ordinary people's lives (it being immaterial that they happened to be a so-called 'expert' precisely on the topic of UK or EU constitutional law)? I have never got to the bottom of whether the same advice should apply if one needed to know about building a bridge (don't ask an engineer), or flying an airplane (no pilots, please) or performing heart surgery (anyone but a qualified doctor).

In its more personalised form, the attack on professional competence was – if anything – even more curious. I assumed that I knew (either personally or at least through their published work) the relatively small number of specialist EU lawyers (many internationally recognised, some of world leading stature) based here in the UK. I was rather surprised to find, during the course of the 2016 referendum campaign and now still afterwards, that the UK in fact boasts countless legions of legal commentators with a far superior understanding of the EU and its relationship to the UK legal system than any mere academic researcher. Those commentators may well lack any relevant qualifications, skills or experience in the field. Their rather idiosyncratic theories about EU law may not have made it through the process of international peer review for publication in any of the scientific legal journals. But none of that can deter them from directly questioning the competence of myself, or any number of my colleagues, to make even the most basic assertions of UK or EU law. Again, not that such challenges are in any way unique to the 2016 referendum experience: many colleagues will recognise the increasing importance of teaching undergraduate students how to discriminate effectively between reliable and unreliable sources of evidence, in an era when many people believe 'research' to be synonymous with 'typing something into Google'.

Allocating one's latest experience of anti-academic abuse to such a rough-and-ready system of categories-plus-variants provides a useful mechanism for both bursting the abuser's self-importance ('just another example of type 3 abuse, variant: personalised, to be put alongside its equally unoriginal peers in this little box …') and bringing to hand an effective response on those occasions when one is required ('could you please share, with myself and the rest of this audience, your evidence for the otherwise defamatory allegation that I am a "paid agent" of the EU …').

But the challenges are not just for academic researchers as individuals: such politically motivated abuse, systematic as well as diffuse, represents an attack on our entire profession and its fundamental scientific values. And nor does the responsibility for responding to those challenges lie solely with individual researchers: it is shared by every university, and the higher education sector as a whole, as well as those wider public institutions – not least the Government – that should be defending the importance of independent science in at least equal measure to touting its economic potential. This edited collection is very consciously intended as a symbol of how public engagement is among the most valuable and important responsibilities of our profession. Far from giving ground to personal intimidation or professional defamation, the experience of the 2016 referendum and its continuing aftermath should reinforce our collective determination to act as enthusiastic advocates for academic expertise and its invaluable contribution to public enlightenment.

## 3.   ACKNOWLEDGEMENTS

I will close with some thanks. First and foremost, sincere gratitude to my colleagues who gave freely and considerably of their time and expertise in order to contribute the chapters for this book – a task which was surely even more challenging than usual, thanks not only to the general state of upheaval and uncertainty surrounding the entire research field, but also to the need for a remarkably tight timescale between the original invitation to contribute and the final deadline for submission.

I am also extremely grateful to Intersentia Publishing – and above all to Ann-Christin Maak – for their unwavering support in both conceiving and executing this project. It has been an unqualified pleasure to work with Ann-Christin and her team: their professionalism, enthusiasm and experience cannot be too highly commended.

We also acknowledge the generosity of the School of Law and Social Justice at the University of Liverpool: together with Intersentia Publishing, the School's Research Development Fund supported a workshop in February 2017, at the University of Liverpool's campus in London, where many of the contributors were able to present and discuss their papers as work-in-progress. Particular thanks to my colleagues from the Liverpool Law School – Eleanor Drywood, Katy Sowery, Nikos Vogiatzis and Andrew Woodhouse – who acted as panel chairs at that workshop.

Finally, I am indebted to my fellow citizens who – in their many, many thousands – wrote to express their support for the importance of the academic contribution to our public debate and to call upon myself and my colleagues to continue sharing our work as researchers with a wider audience of political and social actors. Even if I was (and remain) unable to acknowledge let alone properly reply to each and every such message, I can nevertheless guarantee that their collective force provided the core inspiration to produce this book – and will carry on inspiring our efforts to inform and improve public understanding into the future, as the nature and consequences of the UK's decision to leave the EU continue to unfold.

17 April 2017
Liverpool

# PART I
# CONSTITUTIONAL ISSUES

# CHAPTER 1

# BREXIT: THE RELATIONSHIP BETWEEN THE UK PARLIAMENT AND THE UK GOVERNMENT

Michael GORDON[*]

## 1.  INTRODUCTION

The relationship between the UK Parliament and the UK Government is at the heart of the UK constitution. Between Parliament – the UK's legislature[1] – and the Government – understood here as the institution which sits at the head of the executive branch, and which has ultimate responsibility for the administration of the state[2] – the most crucial decisions as to the shape of law and policy in the UK are made. The decision to withdraw from the European Union (EU) is

---

[*]  Liverpool Law School, University of Liverpool. For helpful questions, comments and feedback, I am grateful to the participants at the workshop organised by the EU Law@Liverpool research unit in London on 17 April 2017.
[1]  The UK Parliament is split into 2 chambers – the elected House of Commons, and the unelected House of Lords, whose members may have obtained a right to sit in a number of ways, including nomination to a life peerage, election from within a group of peers holding hereditary titles, assuming office as a Bishop of the Church of England, or upon retirement as a senior judge.
[2]  'The Government' is sometimes an ambiguous term – it may refer to all institutions in a political system taken together (eg, 'the system of government'), the entire executive branch (comprising, among others, the civil service, police, army and Ministers, across local, regional and national levels), or the Ministers who are appointed by the Prime Minister

clearly one of the most profound governmental choices the UK has ever faced, and will have implications for law and policy of the very highest order. It is a position that has been reached as a direct result of a series of decisions made and actions taken by the UK Parliament and Government, albeit in a more complex fashion than is usually the case, given the constitutional significance of exiting the EU. But it is not only a decision which has been, in effect, taken by the UK Parliament and Government, acting in conjunction with others, most obviously the electorate which voted to leave the EU in the June 2016 referendum. Instead, the decision to exit the EU is also a decision that has the potential to test the boundaries of, and perhaps even alter, the relationship between the UK Parliament and Government.

In this sense, the decision to exit the EU is one which will be delivered by the UK Parliament and Government – with immense consequences throughout the UK's legal system, as is evident in the substantive chapters of this book – but also one which may come to impact on our understanding of the relationship between these institutions. Against this backdrop, this chapter has three aims: first, to explore how the process of Brexit is to be executed by the UK Parliament and Government, which itself depends on the way we conceive of the relationship between these institutions; second, to understand the complications for the domestic Brexit process that may result from the nature of that constitutional relationship; and third, to anticipate challenges that may be posed for both in the future.

The chapter will therefore initially outline the nature of the relationship between the UK Parliament and Government, and its constitutional significance. It will then move on to consider the domestic constitutional process by which the decision to exit the EU will be delivered, and the role(s) of Parliament and the Government within it. Next, the crucial complexities of the Brexit process – particularly as they affect the relationship between Parliament and the Government – will be examined. Finally, the chapter will reflect on some of the major challenges ahead, for both the UK Parliament and the UK Government, as they confront what is likely to be the major constitutional task of this era. At the outset of the process of withdrawal, while it is difficult to imagine the precise shape of the UK constitution after Brexit, or how the relationship between the UK Parliament and Government will be affected in the delivery of this decision, this chapter aims to demonstrate that the constitutional legacy of leaving the EU is certain to be profound.

---

(by convention, chosen from among Members of Parliament elected to the House of Commons, or peers entitled to sit in the House of Lords) to serve in Her Majesty's Government. It is with the Government in this latter sense that this chapter is concerned.

## 2. THE NATURE OF THE RELATIONSHIP BETWEEN THE UK PARLIAMENT AND THE UK GOVERNMENT

The relationship between the UK Parliament and the UK Government is the most significant in the UK's constitutional framework. There are other relationships of immense constitutional importance, of course, including the relationship between these political institutions and the courts, between the UK and the various devolved institutions operating in Scotland, Wales and Northern Ireland, and between all of these institutions of government and citizens. Yet none of these critical relationships has the centrality of that between Parliament and the Government, and while all shape and condition the relationship between Parliament and the Government in many important ways, they are all also ultimately subject to decisions taken between these two institutions.

The relationship between the UK Parliament and UK Government is an interactive one – these interactions may be positive or negative, reinforcing or challenging, complementary or conflicting, but the core functioning of these institutions is necessarily understood in terms of their engagement (or non-engagement) with one another. In this sense, the subject of the relationship between Parliament and the Government is huge – it is the fulcrum of constitutional decision-making, and permanently relevant to understanding the functioning of the UK system of government, but also potentially fluid, and concerns institutions which are themselves complex and multifaceted. This poses a number of challenges, when considering the impact of, and implications for, the relationship in the context of Brexit: how are we to break down the many and varied interactions, sub-relationships and processes, all occurring over a period of time? How can we understand what can be expected from the different branches? And how, if at all, can we begin to assess the performance of Parliament and the Government, individually and collectively?

Despite this complexity and these challenges, in a sense, there are at least some quite simple starting propositions which provide an essential structure to the constitutional relationship between the UK Parliament and Government. Parliament has a number of overlapping responsibilities: it is the sovereign legislative body, with constitutionally ultimate (and legally unlimited) power to make law in the UK; it is the forum from which a Government is established, and sustained, by virtue of possession of the continuing confidence of the House of Commons; it scrutinises official conduct, and holds the Government and its Ministers to account for their activity; and it represents the electorate, who elect constituency MPs to the House of Commons. The Government has related, intersecting functions to those of Parliament: it is generally responsible for drafting and promoting the Bills that the legislature will consider enacting as law; to retain office, it must retain the confidence of the legislature from which its authority is derived; it has a duty to account to Parliament for its administration of the state; and in making and implementing policy choices, it must seek to respect commitments made to the electorate. Ultimately, while the Government – crucially led by the Prime Minister – has the authority to take key decisions concerning policy, and implement those decisions within the law, it can only do so subject to the approval and oversight of Parliament.

A further distinction between the essential functions of Parliament and the Government is also of particular importance in the context of EU membership. The Government is the actor which represents the UK externally at the international – and in this case, European – level, whereas the responsibilities of Parliament are traditionally confined to the internal, domestic sphere. Membership of the EU complicates this classic division of responsibility to some extent, as Parliament is afforded some explicit functions as a matter of EU law, including a direct role in the scrutiny of European instruments, and the power to issue a 'yellow card', cautioning against the enactment of EU legislation, if acting in conjunction with sufficient other national legislatures in EU Member States.[3] UK law has also provided a more direct role for Parliament in authorising Government decision-making in a range of areas at EU level.[4] Yet despite these complexities, the Government remains the key external actor and primary decision-maker in relation to EU matters.

A final complication of relevance in this context relates to decision-making concerning matters of the highest constitutional and political significance. In some circumstances, despite the sovereignty and constitutional centrality of Parliament, and the political authority to lead the UK allocated to the Government, some decisions may be too important to be taken by these institutions acting together, without further input. Constitutional practice in the UK now recognises that a referendum may be required to obtain the direct popular support of the electorate for major change to the architecture of the state. This has been the case in particular in relation to the establishment of devolution in Scotland, Wales and Northern Ireland,[5] the possibility of independence for Scotland[6] or the reunification of Northern Ireland with the Republic of Ireland,[7] and potential change to the voting system to the House of Commons.[8] While there is no definitive prescription as to the character or extent of change which

---

[3]  For discussion of some relevant issues, see eg A WOODHOUSE, 'With Great Power, Comes no Responsibility? The "Political Exception" to Duties of Sincere Cooperation for National Parliaments' (2017) 54 *Common Market Law Review* 443–473.

[4]  See eg European Union (Amendment) Act 2008, and esp the European Union Act 2011.

[5]  See eg referendums held in Scotland in 1979 and 1997; Wales in 1979, 1997 and 2011; and Northern Ireland in 1998.

[6]  Scottish Independence Referendum Act 2013, section 1.

[7]  See eg the referendum held in Northern Ireland in 1973; also Northern Ireland Act 1998, section 1.

[8]  Parliamentary Constituencies and Voting System Act 2011, section 1.

can only be legitimised by a referendum,[9] it has long been clear that a decision to exit the EU would be a decision of such constitutional magnitude that popular approval would be politically essential. The decision to join the (then) EEC in 1972 was not subject to such a vote, but the question of the UK's continuing membership was put to a referendum in 1975,[10] effectively establishing a requirement widely accepted by the main political parties that withdrawal would only be possible subject to approval at a national referendum.

When these basic propositions are applied in combination to the decision to withdraw from the EU, an allocation of tasks between Parliament and the Government can be seen, in principle, to emerge. This is not a framework based on the idea of a separation of power – a model which is of questionable relevance to the UK's constitutional arrangements even as a matter of principle[11] – but instead one based on a 'close union, the nearly complete fusion' of powers between Parliament and the Government,[12] supplemented by the direct involvement of the electorate from which both institutions derive their democratic authority. It was for Parliament and the Government to decide to refer the question of the UK's ongoing membership of the EU to the electorate. In response to a decision to leave, the Government has a mandate to bring about our exit from the EU, in implementation of the referendum result, and at the international level, negotiate first the UK's withdrawal, and then begin to explore a future relationship. Parliament will be required to hold the Government to account during this process, and scrutinise its activity at the international level (as in general), while also legislating to make the necessary changes to domestic law in preparation for withdrawal, providing certainty and continuity as the authority of EU rules within the national legal order is removed.

As will be considered below, implementing the decision to leave the EU in this way creates complexities for the UK Parliament and the Government, and poses a number of challenges for the relationship between them. Before we consider them, however, we will first explore in further detail – and in light of the basic framework established above – the constitutional process of Brexit so far.

## 3.    BREXIT: THE UK CONSTITUTIONAL PROCESS

Withdrawal from the EU is very likely to be the major constitutional task of this era. The UK's political institutions face the challenge of attempting to unravel

---

9       See eg House of Lords Select Committee on the Constitution, *Referendums in the United Kingdom* (HL 2009–10, 99).
10     Referendum Act 1975.
11     See eg G MARSHALL, *Constitutional Theory*, Oxford University Press, Oxford 1971, Ch 5.
12     W BAGEHOT, *The English Constitution*, Oxford University Press, Oxford 2001, original 1867, p 11.

(and perhaps even before that, to understand) over four decades of legal integration, while establishing new economic, social and diplomatic relations with the rest of the continent. We have been led to this point by a series of decisions made and actions taken by the UK Parliament and Government(s) over a number of years. While the roots of the decision to exit the EU certainly run deep,[13] the core developments which have brought the UK to the point of withdrawal have occurred relatively quickly, and more activity will now be required in a very short space of time.

The formal starting point for Brexit was the manifesto commitment to hold an 'In/Out' referendum on EU membership of Prime Minister David Cameron's Government in the run-up to the 2015 general election.[14] That election delivered a surprise victory for Cameron, and a Conservative majority Government.[15] The manifesto referendum commitment was subsequently delivered, with Parliament enacting the European Union (Referendum) Act 2015 to allow for the national vote to be held. After a prolonged exercise in which the Government sought to renegotiate UK membership of the EU, Prime Minister Cameron backed the option of remaining in the EU.[16] The UK Government therefore campaigned on that basis, albeit with Cabinet collective responsibility suspended to allow some senior Ministers to support (some very actively) the 'Leave' campaign.[17] On 23 June 2016, the referendum was held and the electorate voted to leave the EU, by 51.9 per cent to 48.1 per cent on a turnout of 72.2 per cent of eligible voters.[18]

In the face of his defeat, David Cameron resigned as Prime Minister, and a new Conservative majority Government was formed under the leadership of Theresa May.[19] Despite also supporting the campaign to remain in the EU, the new Prime Minister enthusiastically affirmed her commitment to delivering

---

[13]   See eg A FORSTER, *Euroscepticism in Contemporary British Politics: Opposition to Europe in the British Conservative and Labour Parties since 1945*, Routledge, Abingdon 2002.

[14]   See *The Conservative Party Manifesto* (2015) pp 72–73 <https://www.conservatives.com/manifesto>.

[15]   See eg 'The 2015 General Election: A Voting System in Crisis', *Electoral Reform Society* (2015) p 8 <http://www.electoral-reform.org.uk/sites/default/files/2015%20General%20Election%20Report%20web.pdf>.

[16]   See 'Letter by President Donald Tusk to the Members of the European Council on his proposal for a new settlement for the United Kingdom within the European Union', 2 February 2016 <http://www.consilium.europa.eu/en/press/press-releases/2016/02/02-letter-tusk-proposal-new-settlement-uk/>. For comment, see M DOUGAN, 'The draft deal on UK membership of the EU', *The Liverpool View*, 3 February 2016 <https://news.liverpool.ac.uk/2016/02/03/the-liverpool-view-the-draft-deal-on-uk-membership-of-the-eu/>.

[17]   See 'EU vote: where the cabinet and other MPs stand', *BBC News*, 22 June 2016 <http://www.bbc.co.uk/news/uk-politics-eu-referendum-35616946>.

[18]   See The Electoral Commission, 'EU referendum results', <http://www.electoralcommission.org.uk/find-information-by-subject/elections-and-referendums/upcoming-elections-and-referendums/eu-referendum/electorate-and-count-information>.

[19]   See 'PM-in-waiting Theresa May promises "a better Britain"', *BBC News*, 11 July 2016 <http://www.bbc.co.uk/news/uk-politics-36768148>.

the referendum result, expressed in the empty circularity of the much repeated catchphrase 'Brexit means Brexit'.[20] A high-profile legal challenge was successful in establishing that an Act of Parliament was required, as a matter of domestic constitutional law, to authorise the formal notification by the Government to the European Council of an intention to withdraw from the EU.[21] On that basis, Parliament enacted the European Union (Notification of Withdrawal) Act 2017, and the Prime Minister – in accordance with the power conferred by that statute – duly issued notice of the UK's intention to withdraw as required under Article 50 of the Treaty on European Union on 29 March 2017.

Even a basic overview of the Brexit process to this point – in effect, covering the commencement of exiting the EU – demonstrates clearly the interactive nature of the constitutional relationship between the UK Parliament and Government. This will continue as we move into the core stages of delivery of the decision to withdraw from the EU. Yet now that notice of withdrawal has been given, this becomes more than simply a domestic constitutional process. Indeed, in many ways the process of withdrawal is critically framed by EU law, and in particular the terms of Article 50.[22] As well as setting out the manner in which a withdrawal agreement will be approved at the EU level,[23] Article 50 most significantly establishes a two-year time limit during which exit must be agreed, or it will occur automatically at the end of that period.[24] To avoid an abrupt and unmanaged exit, two parallel strands of activity must be completed within the two-year time period imposed by the Article 50 process.

First, at the international level, negotiation with the remaining EU Member States of a withdrawal agreement (and potentially a framework for a future relationship, or even, if the approach of the UK Government is accepted, a future free trade agreement). And second, at the domestic level, legislation to prepare the UK legal system for the withdrawal of the supremacy and effectiveness of EU law within the national order. This will principally involve the enactment of what the Government has described as a 'Great Repeal Bill'[25] – to deal more generally with

---

[20]  See 'Theresa May's Conservative conference speech: Key quotes', *BBC News*, 2 October 2016 <http://www.bbc.co.uk/news/uk-politics-37535527>.

[21]  *R (on the application of Miller and another) v Secretary of State for Exiting the European Union* [2017] UKSC 5; [2017] 2 WLR 583.

[22]  While there has been some debate about whether alternative ways of exiting the EU could be attempted, the Government has recognised that following the Article 50 process is the lawful way to withdraw: see Department for Exiting the European Union, *Legislating for the United Kingdom's withdrawal from the European Union* (Cm 9446, March 2017) para 1.9.

[23]  Article 50(2) and (4) TEU.

[24]  Article 50(3) TEU. The 2-year time limit can be extended in principle, but this is difficult – requiring unanimous consent of all remaining 27 EU Member States – and seems unlikely to be an option in practice: see HM Government, *The United Kingdom's exit from and new partnership with the European Union* (Cm 9417, February 2017) para 12.2.

[25]  See generally *Legislating for the United Kingdom's withdrawal from the European Union*, above n 22. See also House of Commons Library, 'Legislating for Brexit: the Great Repeal

---

the implications of the removal of EU law from the UK legal system, including the replacement of the European Communities Act 1972, the key legislation providing for the domestic effectiveness of EU law – along with other pieces of subject-specific legislation in areas which will see significant policy change as a consequence of Brexit, such as immigration law and customs regulation.[26] The delivery of these two strands of activity simultaneously, within a two-year timescale, will be an immense challenge to the capacity of both the UK Parliament and Government, and, in many ways, a test of the relationship between them.

The constitutional process to deliver the UK's exit from the EU has therefore already been complex and contentious, and further challenges inevitably lie ahead. The next section identifies some of the specific reasons for the complexity of the Brexit process for Parliament and the Government, and how we might seek to offset some of these difficulties. The section which follows then considers the major future challenges that the UK's central political institutions will have to confront.

## 4. COMPLEXITIES FOR PARLIAMENT AND THE GOVERNMENT

Implementing the UK's exit from the EU represents a near unprecedented constitutional challenge. There are a number of factors which combine to make the Brexit process extremely complex for both the UK Parliament and the Government: the scale and significance of EU law; the interlocking nature of supranational and domestic law which is a necessary consequence of EU membership; and the competition between the authority of the Brexit referendum and that of the representative political institutions themselves.

First, the scale and significance of EU law and administration, which has expanded during the UK's membership to cover a range of substantive areas from consumer and employment rights, to agriculture and fisheries policy, to environmental regulation and data protection. The precise number of EU laws which are applicable within the UK, or have influenced the development of domestic law, is a matter for debate, such is the scope of their impact.[27] Yet it

---

Bill' (Briefing Paper 7793, 23 February 2017) <http://researchbriefings.files.parliament.uk/documents/CBP-7793/CBP-7793.pdf>.

[26] *The United Kingdom's exit from and new partnership with the European Union*, above n 24, para 1.8.

[27] See eg House of Commons Library, 'Legislating for Brexit: directly applicable EU law' (Briefing Paper 7863, 12 January 2017) <http://researchbriefings.files.parliament.uk/documents/CBP-7863/CBP-7863.pdf>; House of Commons Library, 'Legislating for Brexit: Statutory Instruments implementing EU law' (Briefing Paper 7867, 16 January 2017) <http://researchbriefings.files.parliament.uk/documents/CBP-7867/CBP-7867.pdf>; *Legislating for the United Kingdom's withdrawal from the European Union*, above n 22, para 2.6.

is widely agreed that EU rules are broadly dispersed throughout the UK's legal system, and it will be a major job simply to map, let alone to unravel, their domestic application.

In removing the authority of EU rules, a variety of different difficult decisions will be required about how to fill the vacuums created. Some substantive rules or standards may more easily be domesticated, and simply converted into applicable UK legal norms. Others, however, depend on the existence of reciprocal arrangements with other EU Member States – such as rules concerning the free movement of people, or customs regulation – and so cannot simply be transposed into domestic law. Instead, such legal norms will need to be replaced; yet this may not be straightforward, since the law in these areas may be affected by whatever future trade relationship is agreed between the UK and EU, with customs rules or product safety standards being clear examples. Moreover, where substantive rules which can more readily be incorporated into UK law depend on implementation or administration by an EU agency, such as the European Medicines Agency, replacements for these arrangements will need to be designed. It is therefore clear that the very fundamental task of replacing EU law will be far from easy, for a diverse range of decisions will have to be taken to determine the way forward in a diverse range of areas of law.

Second, the UK's membership of the EU is necessarily premised on an interaction between supranational and domestic law: EU law exists at the supranational level, yet has effects in the national legal system, and the principle of supremacy requires that inconsistent national law must be disapplied to ensure conformity across the Member States.[28] This interlinking of supranational and domestic law will itself be a source of complexity for Parliament and the Government, because it means coordination is necessary as the connection between EU law and UK law is unlocked. That there will be two strands of activity – negotiating at the international level, legislating at the domestic level – has already been noted. Yet the nature of EU membership means that they cannot be approached in isolation; instead, the supranational and the domestic activity will be intrinsically linked. For example, the withdrawal agreement negotiated by the Government at the European level will be subject to approval by Parliament in the domestic sphere. Similarly, the legislation to be enacted by Parliament to replace EU law within the UK will need to be compatible (or at least not incompatible) with any future relationship agreed between the Government and the remaining 27 EU Member States.

Indeed, the potential for the connectivity between supranational and national law to cause complexity in the domestic constitutional process has already been made clear. This can be seen in the case of *R (on the application*

---

[28]    For recognition of this in the UK, see *R v Secretary of State for Transport, ex p Factortame (No 2)* [1991] 1 AC 603.

*of Miller and another) v Secretary of State for Exiting the European Union,*[29] in which the UK Supreme Court held by a majority of eight justices to three that an Act of Parliament was required to provide the Prime Minister with explicit authority to give notice of intention to withdraw from the EU, for the purposes of Article 50 TEU. The (in many ways unsubstantiated) basis for the majority decision was that EU law was constituted 'as an entirely new, independent and overriding source of domestic law',[30] and the potential for this source to be removed once notice had been given, potentially automatically, at the end of the Article 50 two-year time limit, was of such constitutional significance that it required express legislative authorisation: 'We cannot accept that a major change to UK constitutional arrangements can be achieved by ministers alone; it must be effected in the only way that the UK constitution recognises, namely by Parliamentary legislation'.[31] Yet this decision seemed to confound the well-established allocation of responsibilities between the Government and Parliament, in accordance with which the Government has the authority under its royal prerogative executive powers to take decisions at the international level concerning the making or unmaking of treaties, while Parliament is responsible for altering (or not altering, as it decides) any domestic law which is contingent on the operation of supranational agreements. That the European Communities Act 1972 did not seek to remove from the Government the power to withdraw from the EU treaties, nor would the terms or legal validity of that statute be in any way altered by issuing notice under the royal prerogative, provide reasons to doubt the conclusion reached by the majority.[32] Yet regardless of the correctness of the decision, the *Miller* case provides ample evidence of the kind of complexity that Parliament and the Government face in delivering Brexit, given the intersecting nature of UK and EU law which is a necessary consequence of EU membership.

Third, the manner in which the decision to leave the EU was reached also provides a further source of complexity for Parliament and the Government. Here, we see a competition between regular and irregular authority claims, in the form of the (related) representative democratic mandates of Parliament and the Government, and the direct democratic force of the referendum vote to leave the EU. The potential clash between these regular and irregular democratic claims is made more acute by the Government's advocacy of the defeated option of remaining in the EU, which also attracted overwhelming support among parliamentarians.[33] Moreover, the formal legal status of a referendum result is 'advisory', since it is the UK Parliament which is sovereign within the

---

29    [2017] UKSC 5; [2017] 2 WLR 583.
30    Ibid, [80].
31    Ibid, [82].
32    See esp the dissenting judgment of Lord Reed, ibid [179]–[204].
33    See above n 17.

constitution.[34] This creates difficulty for Parliament and the Government in that they are asked to deliver a policy of profound significance, but to which they were not committed, and which they may not be legally obliged to implement.

We have seen this complexity play out already in debates about the binding nature of the referendum result, and whether Parliament could have refused to accept it, an opportunity presented by the outcome of the *Miller* litigation.[35] It is also manifested in uncertainty about how exactly the Government should interpret the vote to leave the EU, especially given the multiplicity of reasons informing individual voter choices – whether control over immigration, sovereignty over law-making, or access to the single market should be prioritised is not determinable merely by reference to the referendum mandate. Of course, the simple juxtaposition of direct and representative democratic authority overlooks the fact that the representative institutions were the source of the resort to direct democratic decision-making: the Government through its election on a manifesto commitment to hold a referendum, and Parliament in enacting legislation to facilitate this. Yet if the true difficulty is therefore the competition between the irregular authority of the referendum and the regular authority of the UK's central political institutions, we may also see that the effect will be further attempts to use irregular authority to trigger constitutional change in the aftermath of Brexit. This may most obviously occur in Scotland and Northern Ireland – countries in which the national vote was in favour of remaining in the EU – if the consequence of Brexit is to provoke a (now-requested) second Scottish independence referendum,[36] or a border poll on the reunification of Ireland.[37]

How can we confront this complexity? While there is no sense in which it can be eliminated from the delivery of the decision to leave the EU, there are two things which may at least help us to respond appropriately.

First, we must seek to understand Brexit as a process, rather than as a series of unconnected momentary events (or crises). It is a constitutional process that, at least in principle, may be understood to occur in three phases: with the triggering of Article 50 Brexit has been commenced, it must now be executed by the UK's political institutions, and will ultimately (whether with or without a withdrawal agreement) reach a formal conclusion.[38] This is important because it

---

[34]   See eg *Miller* [2017] UKSC 5; [2017] 2 WLR 583, [116]–[125].

[35]   See eg G ROBERTSON, 'How to stop Brexit: get your MP to vote it down', *The Guardian*, 27 June 2016 <https://www.theguardian.com/commentisfree/2016/jun/27/stop-brexit-mp-vote-referendum-members-parliament-act-europe>.

[36]   First Minister of Scotland, 'Section 30 letter', 31 March 2017 <https://news.gov.scot/news/section-30-letter>.

[37]   For rejection of calls for a border poll, see Secretary of State for Northern Ireland, James Brokenshire MP, *Hansard*, HC Deb Vol 613, col 809 (20 July 2016).

[38]   See eg M GORDON, 'Brexit: A Challenge *for* the UK Constitution, *of* the UK Constitution?' (2016) 12(3) *European Constitutional Law Review* 409–444, 416–435.

demonstrates that the process of exiting the EU must be understood holistically, rather than considered in fragments.[39] It emphasises, crucially, that there will be different roles for different institutions at different times, and that some points will be more significant than others. Such an approach can help us to identify, in relative terms, what activity should be prioritised, and when, given the scale of the task, and the limited time available. For example, from this perspective we can appreciate that Parliament should be able to exert influence at some points more readily than others: dealing with the Great Repeal Bill, for instance, will present a far greater opportunity for the legislature to shape the Government's approach to the domestic change necessitated by Brexit than was realistic when enacting the Article 50 Bill designed simply to begin the formal process of negotiation.

Second, we must set expectations appropriately, in light of a clear understanding of the parameters of the relationship between the UK Parliament and the Government. There are significant and well-founded concerns about exit from the EU becoming an executive led and dominated process, given it will be the Government which is responsible for negotiating the terms on which we exit the EU, and (most likely subsequently) the parameters of a future relationship. Nonetheless, while frequently aired, suggestions that the UK constitution establishes an 'elective dictatorship' are in many ways based on a misunderstanding of the role of Parliament, and its ability to exert policy influence, often through activities which shape government action in ways which are difficult to measure, such as the power of the legislature's anticipated reactions and informal pressure.[40] Yet the thesis that Parliament is in contemporary decline has not only prospered because of misunderstanding of Parliament's role and capability, especially in comparison with the resources of even a shrinking executive, and a civil service subject to cost saving in an extended period of public sector funding cuts.[41] Instead, the decline thesis also prospers when the expectations of Parliament are inappropriately set – rhetoric of Brexit as a restoration of parliamentary sovereignty, exhibited throughout the referendum campaign and since,[42] is not helpful in this regard, in that it is

---

[39] For a dissenting judgment in the *Miller* case, recognising the importance of approaching Brexit as a process, see Lord Carnwath: [2017] UKSC 5; [2017] 2 WLR 583, esp [248]–[249], [264] and [274].

[40] See eg M RUSSELL and P COWLEY, 'The Policy Power of the Westminster Parliament: The "Parliamentary State" and the Empirical Evidence' (2016) 29 *Governance* 121–137.

[41] On the parliamentary decline thesis, see M FLINDERS and A KELSO, 'Mind the Gap: Political Analysis, Public Expectations and the Parliamentary Decline Thesis' (2011) 13 *British Journal of Politics and International Relations* 249–268.

[42] *The United Kingdom's exit from and new partnership with the European Union*, above n 24, para 2.1.

both a constitutionally flawed claim,[43] while also conjuring a mythical vision of parliamentary rule which did not exist prior to 1972, and cannot be revived now.[44] Parliament can be an effective actor in the UK constitution, and despite the complexity of withdrawal from the EU, there is the potential for it to influence very significantly the shape of the UK after Brexit. Yet for this to be possible, we must be clear about Parliament's role(s) in the process, recognise that it will inevitably have to interact with the Government, and set challenging but realistic expectations of what it might achieve.

We may therefore attempt to manage the complexities of the Brexit process, but it remains inevitable that withdrawal from the EU will pose major challenges for Parliament and the Government, and the functioning of the relationship between them. The final section of this chapter considers some of the key challenges which lie ahead.

## 5. MAJOR CHALLENGES AHEAD FOR PARLIAMENT AND THE GOVERNMENT

It is clear that the domestic constitutional process of exiting the EU will centrally involve the UK Parliament and Government, and will do so in complex ways. The pace of change is such that it is far from easy to anticipate the precise challenges which lie ahead. Nonetheless, we can identify some crucial future concerns. Perhaps the overwhelming constitutional danger for present purposes is that the relationship between Parliament and the Government could fail to function in an effective and legitimate way. Given the centrality of this relationship to delivering Brexit, the stakes are high: such a failure could have implications for the nature, quality and coherence of the UK's future domestic position and relationship with the EU, and potentially even undermine the authority of the domestic political institutions themselves. It would be an especially problematic time for the latter to occur, exactly at the moment the UK Parliament and Government are reacquiring very significant power and competence over the shape of the UK's legal system by virtue of exit from the EU.

---

[43]    In contrast, the better view is that Parliament remained sovereign throughout membership of the EU – and, indeed, the legislative facilitation of EU membership from 1972 onwards, and authorisation of a referendum leading to the decision to withdraw, provide very different examples of the flexibility of a constitution based on the legislative sovereignty of the UK Parliament: see eg M GORDON, *Parliamentary Sovereignty in the UK Constitution: Process, Politics and Democracy*, Hart Publishing, Oxford 2015, Ch 4. For a contrary view, see NW BARBER, 'The Afterlife of Parliamentary Sovereignty' (2011) *International Journal of Constitutional Law* 144, 152–153.

[44]    See eg M GORDON, 'The UK's Sovereignty Situation: Brexit, Bewilderment and Beyond ...' (2016) 27 *King's Law Journal* 333–343.

There are two areas in which risks of particular significance are present. First is an accountability challenge; second is a legislative challenge.

The accountability challenge concerns the way in which Parliament will hold the Government to account during the prolonged period of withdrawal negotiations with the EU. There are a number of areas of concern. The Government will be in a privileged position as the lead actor representing the UK at the international level, and may prioritise the confidentiality of the negotiations over the transparency necessary to facilitate meaningful parliamentary oversight. The Government has committed to ensure that the UK Parliament is at least as well informed as the European Parliament, although it is as yet unclear what this will amount to in practice.[45] Further, the scale of the negotiations means that the role of parliamentary select committee scrutiny in specialist substantive fields will be vital, and there has been a vast amount of activity already across a range of areas.[46] Yet there is also a danger of inadequate coordination of that scrutiny – competition between committees, political parties, and the Commons and Lords is inevitable and valuable if it raises the quality of oversight. But there is a need to avoid key messages getting lost in a morass of detail if they are to influence the Government (whether directly, or indirectly, by shaping public opinion).

Finally, there has been debate about what it means for Parliament to have a 'meaningful' vote on the final terms of the withdrawal agreement, now that the necessity of votes in both Houses of Parliament has been accepted by the Government (which represents an important upgrade on the already applicable treaty ratification rules contained in existing legislation).[47] The need for final votes on the terms of the agreement has a significant role to play in underpinning the Government's sustained engagement with Parliament: if the deal has to be sold to parliamentarians, the Government will need to interact constructively as Parliament scrutinises its ongoing diplomatic activity, while also anticipating the likely reaction(s) of the legislature to the shape of the withdrawal agreement, and attempting to mould its terms to address concerns where possible. Yet the limitations of a meaningful vote are also clear, insofar as the choice that faces Parliament will be highly constrained by external factors. For if Parliament

---

[45]   *The United Kingdom's exit from and new partnership with the European Union*, above n 24, para 1.11.

[46]   There has been too much select committee activity to cite in full; the Government estimated that there had so far been 36 inquiries commenced as of February 2017: see *The United Kingdom's exit from and new partnership with the European Union*, above n 24, para 1.10. Considerable work has been done in particular by the House of Commons Select Committee on Exiting the EU (which, at 21 members, is larger than a standard committee in light of the scale of work ahead of it) and the six sub-committees of the House of Lords EU Select Committee. Such has been the level of engagement with Brexit in all areas that, as of the end of March 2017, the House of Commons Transport Committee was conspicuous in *not* having commenced an inquiry relating to withdrawal from the EU.

[47]   Constitutional Reform and Governance Act 2010, sections 20–25.

rejects the deal on offer, it is not obvious that this will provide the Government with any scope for last minute renegotiation with the remaining EU Member States – instead, it may force the UK into the position of automatic exit without an agreement, in accordance with the operation of Article 50.

Parliament will therefore face a number of difficulties in holding the Government to account effectively. There is an obvious disparity between the capacity of the Government and a single legislature, although there may be ways to offset this – for example, coordination between the Parliaments and Assemblies of the UK (while not the core focus of this chapter),[48] could provide opportunities for an enhanced voice in areas of consensus with parliamentarians in Scotland, Wales and/or Northern Ireland. Similarly, the dispersal of power among parliamentarians, various select committees and between the two Houses, may give the impression of a lack of distinct leadership for Parliament – especially when compared to the European Parliament, with a very visible lead negotiator in Guy Verhofstadt. Yet we should not be too quick to underestimate Parliament – it is wrong, for example, to see the failure to amend the Article 50 Bill as a parliamentary failure, given the limited purpose of that legislation, and the difficulties in enforcing, in real terms, the kind of aspirational provisions guaranteeing the rights of EU nationals and 'meaningful' final votes that were most prominently debated. Indeed, rather than being constrained by legal provisions, we have seen Government concessions on final parliamentary votes and the production of a White Paper induced through the normal practices of the political constitution,[49] where pressure, the press and time combine to force changes in official policy or approach. Given the enormous public interest in the UK's exit from the EU, this kind of scrutiny, channelled by and through Parliament, is only likely to intensify.

The legislative challenge, in contrast, will be focused on the Great Repeal Bill, which will remove the authority and supremacy of EU law within the UK (by repealing the European Communities Act 1972), while preparing the legal system for exit by simultaneously transposing EU rules into the UK legal system, where practical and appropriate to ensure certainty and continuity. As has been discussed above, this will be an immensely complex task, requiring much technical work, and difficult decisions across a range of substantive areas. The capacity of Parliament will obviously be tested, and given the scale of work involved in a short timeframe, it is inevitable that much of the detailed work will need to be done by the Government, using subordinate law-making powers afforded to them by the legislature. There are obvious concerns attached to this, including those as to the possibility of overuse of secondary law-making

---

[48]     See the contribution by J Hunt (Ch 2) in this edited collection.
[49]     See eg JAG Griffith, 'The Political Constitution' (1979) 42 *Modern Law Review* 1.

powers by the Government,[50] that the Great Repeal Bill might include so-called 'Henry VIII' powers which allow the amendment of Parliament's primary Acts by secondary legislation made by the executive,[51] and that the entire process will include limited opportunities for parliamentary scrutiny, with the legislature bypassed and diminished at a crucial constitutional moment.

It is no doubt correct that there are real dangers here concerning the possibility of proper constitutional scrutiny of law-making and the level of democratic accountability for changes made under the Great Repeal Bill. Yet given the size of the challenge of preparing the UK legal system for exit from the EU, the use of secondary legislative power is not optional, but unavoidable. And this is no violation of the fundamental idea of the sovereignty of Parliament, which does not prohibit the allocation to the executive of delegated legislative powers – indeed to grant such powers is an exercise of legislative sovereignty in recognition of the scale and complexity of modern state activity. Parliament will retain responsibility for authorising (legally) and controlling (politically) all Government activity associated with preparing the domestic legal system for EU withdrawal. Yet in exercising its power and enacting a Great Repeal Bill, Parliament also has a constitutional responsibility to ensure these powers are appropriately constructed for effective completion of the stated purpose of ensuring legal certainty and continuity, and are limited to prevent the Government from obtaining powers to make significant policy changes as the authority of EU law is removed. In addition to clear and focused definition of the scope of the powers, conditions attaching to their use, such as requirements of impact assessment or explanatory statements, and time limits after which the powers expire, will also be critical to ensure that this task is executed in a constitutionally legitimate manner.[52] The design of the legislation will also, of course, need to be supplemented by a sustained desire from members of the House of Commons and Lords to scrutinise the detailed terms of delegated legislation made under the Great Repeal Bill – whether in specialist committees concerned in particular with statutory instruments,[53] or more generally – and give clear voice to any concerns arising.

---

[50] See generally, Lord Judge, 'Ceding Power to the Executive; the Resurrection of Henry VIII', *Lecture at King's College London*, 12 April 2016 <http://www.kcl.ac.uk/law/newsevents/newsrecords/2015-16/Ceding-Power-to-the-Executive---Lord-Judge---130416.pdf>.

[51] See generally NW BARBER and AL YOUNG, 'The Rise of Prospective Henry VIII Clauses and their Implications for Sovereignty' [2003] *Public Law* 112.

[52] For a case study of parliamentary engagement with a related challenge, see eg P DAVIS, 'The Significance of Parliamentary Procedures in Control of the Executive: A Case Study – the Passage of Part 1 of the Legislative and Regulatory Reform Act 2006' [2007] *Public Law* 677.

[53] Such as the Joint Committee on Statutory Instruments and the Secondary Legislation Committee of the House of Lords.

Whereas the accountability challenge will require persistent attention and activity from Parliament and the Government, and its tangible impact may often be unclear, the legislative challenge will be focused around more structured moments of activity, and the parliamentary impact may be more direct and discernible. Yet this does not mean that one is more important than the other – rather it demonstrates the variation in, and pervasiveness of, the challenge that the UK's central political institutions will face in delivering Brexit. There are genuine constitutional dangers to ward against as the process develops, and it would be wrong to fuel expectations of Parliament and the Government to a point beyond which they can be reached. This is already a risk, given the extensive, and simplistic, rhetoric about 'taking back control' and the 'restoration' of parliamentary sovereignty, which are unwelcome hangovers from the referendum campaign. That there will also be external constraints on what the UK can achieve in exiting the EU is clear, most obviously flowing from the positions taken by the EU27. There will also be a range of other internal dynamics in operation, with the potential to constrain both the Government and the UK Parliament – it will be essential, for example, for the views of the devolved governments and legislatures to be considered and acted upon within the process.

Nevertheless, the relationship between the UK Parliament and Government will be at the centre of the domestic constitutional process, and inevitably tested by Brexit. If the process of withdrawing from the EU is to be conducted in a way which is both effective and constitutionally legitimate, Parliament and the Government must ensure that their engagements are constructive and extensive, and that the account of their interactive relationship, set out at the start of this chapter, is not reduced to a formal constitutional nicety.

## 6.   CONCLUSION: TENSIONS IN THE CONSTITUTIONAL PROCESS OF BREXIT

Exiting the EU has been, and will continue to be, complex and challenging – it is impossible to underestimate the extent to which this task will test both the UK Parliament and Government, and the relationship between them, which will be central to the constitutional process of Brexit. Indeed, tensions are already emerging in (at least) three broad areas as Parliament and the Government deliver the UK's withdrawal from the EU, suggesting there is no room for complacency about the potentially dramatic constitutional implications of Brexit.

First, we see institutional tensions, generated by debate as to the proper roles of Parliament and the Government (and indeed, as a result of the *Miller*[54]

---

[54]    [2017] UKSC 5; [2017] 2 WLR 583.

case, the courts) in relation to the execution of Brexit. While there has been some genuine uncertainty in this area, there has also been a lot of simplistic and unhelpful rhetoric which has the potential to unsettle the process, distort the relationship between Parliament and the Government, and thereby foster false expectations about what exactly the UK can achieve from withdrawal from the EU. On all sides, there must now be awareness of the need for Parliament and the Government to interact, and do so effectively, in a sustained, open and critically constructive manner if the process and the aftermath of exiting the EU is to be navigated in a way which minimises division and maximises consensus.

Second, we have seen the emergence of tensions relating to legitimacy, most fundamentally in the potentially competing direct and representative democratic mandates of the referendum result and the MPs elected to the House of Commons respectively. While as a matter of constitutional practice, these mandates have been reconciled by the acceptance in Parliament of the authority of the referendum result, notwithstanding the overwhelming support for remaining in the EU among members of the legislature, again oversimplification has led to misunderstanding about the functioning of the UK constitution and its core political institutions. Perhaps more significant than the ostensible clash between direct and representative democracy will be the enduring difficulties that are likely to flow from the attempts to accommodate regular and irregular authority claims in the UK's uncodified constitution. The regular authority of the standing democratic institutions – including, but not only, Parliament and the Government – has very obviously been unsettled by the irregular authority flowing from the referendum decision, and the legacy of this could be long lasting. While some 'constitutional unsettlement' may be inevitable given the fluid fabric of our present framework,[55] there are broader questions here about how (if at all) the dissonance in views between the Brexit-voting majority and the Remain-supporting political establishment can be channelled into more effective regular constitutional engagements, rather than left to accumulate and deliver irregular, erratic systemic shocks. The planning of parliamentary and governmental reform may now be required, although the implications of the decision to exit the EU may be so far-reaching that further irregular shocks – perhaps most easily anticipated in the form of an independence referendum in Scotland and a border poll in Northern Ireland – may, in any event, be unavoidable. And while the general election to be held in June 2017 will provide the UK Government then elected with a new mandate, it will not resolve the underlying, ongoing tensions between competing claims to constitutional legitimacy.

Third, we may also see the development (or perhaps, for some, intensification) of constitutionalist tensions. While Brexit will obviously change the substantive

---

[55]    N WALKER, 'Our Constitutional Unsettlement' [2014] *Public Law* 529–548.

rules of the UK constitution in a very significant way, it may also have implications for the nature and dynamics of UK constitutionalism. Exiting the EU has the potential to change not just the powers of the UK Government, and the responsibility, authority and effectiveness of the UK Parliament (and the jurisdiction of the UK courts),[56] but also the way in which the constitution operates to empower and condition activities taken by, and interactions between, these core institutions. In particular, we may see continuing tension between visions of the constitution which emphasise its legal components and processes, and those which emphasise the political underpinnings and relationships.[57] How Brexit will affect this dynamic is unclear, yet that it has the potential to do so seems certain: existing debates about the authority of the referendum result and the triggering of Article 50 already reflect the differences in perspective from a legal and a political constitutionalist standpoint. Whether the influence of 'euro-legalism'[58] will now diminish, or the political constitution has facilitated a crisis which ultimately swallows it,[59] or some alternative, will be for the future. Yet we can be sure that this will not involve a reversion to the UK's pre-1972 condition. Instead, the constitutionalist tensions which Brexit has unleashed will surely lead to the development of some new model – for better or worse – because the impact on the UK constitution of EU membership, and its withdrawal, will be impossible to write out of what comes next.

---

[56]   See the contribution by T Horsley (Ch 4) in this edited collection.

[57]   See eg A Tomkins, 'In Defence of the Political Constitution' (2002) 22 *Oxford Journal of Legal Studies* 157; T Hickman, 'In Defence of the Legal Constitution' (2005) 55 *University of Toronto Law Journal* 981; G Gee and G Webber, 'What Is a Political Constitution?' (2010) 30 *Oxford Journal of Legal Studies* 273; M Goldoni and C McCorkindale, 'A Note from the Editors: The State of the Political Constitution' (2013) 14 *German Law Journal* 2103.

[58]   See generally RD Kelemen, *Eurolegalism: The Transformation of Law and Regulation in the European Union*, Harvard University Press, Cambridge MA 2011.

[59]   See eg Gordon, above n 38, pp 435–444.

# CHAPTER 2

# DEVOLUTION

Jo Hunt*

*'Because we voted in the referendum as one United Kingdom, we will negotiate as one United Kingdom, and we will leave the European Union as one United Kingdom'.*[1]

## 1.  INTRODUCTION

In the referendum vote on 23 June 2016, two of the four nations of the United Kingdom voted to remain,[2] and two to leave the European Union.[3] The combination of Scotland and Northern Ireland's votes to remain, along with the prospect of a centrally-driven 'hard Brexit' exacerbate political complexities internal to the UK at a time when its external relations are in such flux. The vision of the 'one United Kingdom' appealed to by the Prime Minister appears, constitutionally, to be that of a unitary state. But this vision of a unitary

---

\*       Cardiff University. This chapter was written during my Senior Fellowship under the ESRC *UK in a Changing Europe* initiative, Grant ES/N004523/1.

[1]      T May, *Britain after Brexit: A Vision of a Global Britain*, speech to Conservative Party Conference, Birmingham (2 October 2016).
[2]      Scotland voted to remain by 62% to 38%, on a turnout of 67%; Northern Ireland voted to remain by 56% to 44%, on a turnout of 63%.
[3]      England voted to leave by 53% to 47%, on a turnout of 73%; Wales voted to leave by 52.5% to 47.5%, on a turnout of 72%.

UK is profoundly out of step with the perception of the state not just by the independence-focused Government in Scotland, but in Wales too, where the forces for independence have less of an influence.

Indeed, the orthodoxy of the UK as a unitary state has been fundamentally challenged through the experiences of the past two decades of devolution.[4] The incoming 1997 Labour Government relaunched previous attempts to bring a degree of self-rule to Scotland, Wales and Northern Ireland, and was set to include the English regions in this too. Whilst devolution to the English regions has been a patchy, very limited affair to date,[5] devolution to the nations has appeared a more deeply profound and significant constitutional development. In a series of statutory steps, each different for each of the devolved nations, Edinburgh, Cardiff and Belfast have acquired their own governments, and their own parliaments with legislative powers, confirmed in the underpinning primary legislation[6] as permanent features of the UK constitutional order.[7] More recently, the first steps in fiscal powers for the devolved nations have been taken, coming into an established, though disputed, system of funding under a block grant for each devolved region.[8]

But the devolution settlements are creations of the Westminster Parliament, and each of the settlements contains a statutory acknowledgement of the Westminster Parliament's continuing legislative power,[9] which runs in parallel to those of the devolved parliaments and assemblies, and has the potential to override them. Unless and until understandings of sovereignty in the UK move on to allow the Westminster Parliament to dilute itself permanently, then the devolved institutions, their powers and the laws they make are as permanent as the Westminster Parliament decides them to be. However, not all players on the UK constitutional pitch would agree that the permanent limitation of Westminster sovereignty is impossible, or that it has not yet happened (politically,

---

[4]   J MITCHELL, *Devolution in the UK*, Manchester University Press, Manchester 2009; V BOGDANOR, *The New British Constitution*, Hart Publishing, Oxford 2009, Ch 4; R HAZELL and R RAWLINGS, *Devolution, Law Making and the Constitution*, Imprint Academic, Exeter 2005.

[5]   E COX, 'Devolution in England – Is the Genie out of the Lamp?' (2016) 87 *Political Quarterly* 565; M SANDFORD, 'Devolution to Local Government in England' (House of Commons Library Briefing Paper No 7029, 23 November 2016).

[6]   Scotland Act 1998, Northern Ireland Act 1998, Government of Wales Act 1998 and subsequently 2006 (all as amended).

[7]   Reflecting the profoundly asymmetric, though in part converging nature of the devolution process to date, this permanence of the institutions was contained in the Scotland Act 2016, as part of the post-independence referendum package of measures to further develop Scotland's place in the UK order. It was then repeated for Wales in the Wales Act 2017.

[8]   D BELL, 'Territorial Finance and the Future of Barnett' (2015) 86 *Political Quarterly* 209; T TRAVERS, 'Devolving Funding and Taxation in the UK: A Unique Challenge' (2015) 233 *National Institute Economic Review* R5.

[9]   Scotland Act 1998, section 28(7); Northern Ireland Act 1998, section 5(6); Government of Wales Act 2006, section 107(5).

if not legally) or indeed that such sovereignty may ever formally have stretched to all parts of the Kingdom.[10]

As the UK begins the process of detaching itself from the European Union, the UK's constitutional order is variously pitched somewhere on a continuum between a unitary state and a federation – where the powers held by the different levels of state are constitutionally entrenched. The labels used to describe the UK state, including the status and the relations between its parts, have included a union state,[11] a state of unions,[12] a quasi-federation,[13] and a voluntary association of nations.[14] These different perspectives on the place in the UK's constitutional order held by the devolved nations have been able to co-exist in the constitution's inchoate form, providing a pragmatic political fudge. No definitive fixing has been required – until now. The process of withdrawing from the EU places demands on the UK constitution which require a defining of elements otherwise indeterminate and evolving. Clashes over constitutional expectations are inevitable.

In fact, the first clash arose before the referendum had even taken place, over whether the rules by which the referendum would be run would require a veto power for the devolved nations. This would prevent the UK from withdrawing where a majority vote in any of the devolved nations was for remain. According to the Scottish Nationalist Party's Alex Salmond, such a step would be imperative as 'nations within a multi-national state should be recognised as more than regions, counties or areas and should not be counted by population; they are national entities in their own right, and that confers a relationship of respect'.[15] Such arguments were ultimately unsuccessful, and a unitary, UK-wide approach was adopted in the final Act.[16] Following the referendum, this has led to the Scottish Government presenting withdrawal as an undemocratic, illegitimate act, with Scotland being taken out of the EU against its wishes.[17]

---

[10] The Scottish 'Claim of Right' issued in 1989 by the Scottish Constitutional Convention, and signed by 58 of the then 72 Members of Parliament from Scotland, emphasised that sovereignty lay with the Scottish people.

[11] M KEATING, 'Reforging the Union: Devolution and Constitutional Change in the United Kingdom' (1998) 28 *Publius: The Journal of Federalism* 217, drawing on the work of S ROKKAN and D UNWIN, 'Introduction: Centres and Peripheries in Western Europe' in S ROKKAN and D UNWIN (eds), *The Politics of Territorial Identity*, Sage, London 1982. This usage reflects that the UK is formed of distinct nations/regions.

[12] MITCHELL, above n 4, p 15, emphasising the distinctive bilateral unions that England has with each of the devolved nations.

[13] BOGDANOR, above n 4. The continuing legislative competence of the Westminster Parliament to amend the constitutional settlements essentially unilaterally precludes the UK from being seen as a federation.

[14] This is the favoured definition used by the Welsh Government: see eg Welsh Government, *Written evidence to House of Lords Committee on the Constitution Inquiry on Devolution and the Union*, 2016.

[15] A SALMOND, *Hansard*, HC Deb Vol 597, col 192 (16 June 2015).

[16] European Union Referendum Act 2015.

[17] Scottish Government, *Scotland's Place in Europe*, White Paper (December 2016) para 174; N STURGEON, Scottish Parliament debate on motion S5M-04710 (21 March 2017).

Post-referendum, the devolved nations, with Scotland at the vanguard, are emphasising their separate political and legal identity. At the same time the UK Government is pursuing a 'whole UK' Brexit which affords the devolved nations little constitutional protection of their interests, or accommodation of the demands. This chapter will draw out two themes in particular, which both question the degree to which the devolved nations are separate legislative and political units, with autonomy from the UK Government, in the context of the different stages in the withdrawal process. The first looks at the relationships the devolved nations have had, and may prospectively have, with the EU even after withdrawal. Following an explanation of the ways in which the devolved nations have to date engaged with the EU's institutions and policy processes, consideration is given to the prospect for some form of continued engagement, through differentiated legally enforceable deals or softer forms of coordination and cooperation.

The second theme focuses on the repatriation of powers from the EU to the UK. Withdrawal from the EU is intended to lift the constraints on domestic legislative activity imposed by the requirements of EU law. Full competence will be 'returned' to the UK. Domestically, legislative competence is shared by both London (for the UK overall) and in certain policy areas, by the devolved nations as well. Devolution has taken place within the context of EU membership, and the return of powers may then bring about an expansion in devolved competence, in areas until now governed by EU frameworks. However, there is dispute over the way these powers coming back will be treated, and over the possible constraints that may be imposed on the devolved administrations' exercise of powers in these repatriated areas. In particular, the UK Government has indicated that common national frameworks may be required to ensure the functioning of a single economic market across the UK, previously ensured through EU law. What form these frameworks may take, and how decisions around their exercise will proceed, is as yet unclear. What is known is that the process will see starkly different positions taken in the different capitals of the UK on the separate political and legislative capacity of the devolved nations.

## 2. UK REGIONS AND THEIR RELATIONSHIPS WITH AND WITHIN THE EU

### 2.1. UK REGIONS IN THE EU SYSTEM OF GOVERNANCE

According to the EU's Committee of the Regions, roughly 70 per cent of all EU legislation falls to be implemented by local or regional authorities.[18]

---

[18]  Committee of the Regions, *A New Treaty: A New Role for Regional and Local Authorities* (Brussels, 2009).

The territorial dimension of certain policy areas, such as regional economic development, agriculture and the environment is obvious. As well as being heavily 'Europeanised' and subject to extensive EU regulatory activity, these policy areas also feature amongst those which have been devolved to the administrations in Cardiff, Edinburgh and Belfast under the UK's system of devolution.[19] The devolved administrations are key players in EU governance first owing to their important role in implementing and applying EU law. The ministerial power in the European Communities Act, section 2(2) to implement EU law by statutory instrument is extended to the Ministers of the devolved administrations,[20] and their primary legislative powers could also be used to implement EU obligations. This provides considerable 'downstream' regional involvement in EU policy. In addition, EU Directives and Regulations may also provide flexibility for the devolved administrations to adapt EU frameworks to reflect local factors. As a result, locally distinctive, differentiated interpretations in elements of environmental and agricultural law are part of the legal terrain.[21]

The scope for these distinctive policy relationships emerge more fully away from the regulatory policies, in respect of redistributive policies, and the various EU funding programmes that the nations and regions participate in, including regional development, education and research and culture.

In respect of 'upstream' involvement, in EU policy making, the opportunities for the devolved administrations might appear limited. The devolution settlements provide that foreign policy, including relations with the EU, are not within devolved competence, but lie with the UK Government.[22] However, there is recognition that the devolved administrations will have an interest in EU matters, and a role is foreseen for them in the development of the UK line to take to Brussels. As a supplement to the overarching (and non-binding) Memorandum of Understanding which sets out the principles by which the governments of the UK will work together (including good communication,

---

[19]   Devolution is under a 'reserved' powers model to Scotland and Northern Ireland, under which they can act on anything that has not been explicitly reserved (or for Northern Ireland, excepted) under the Schedules to the devolution legislation: see Scotland Act 1998, Schedule 5 and Northern Ireland Act 1998, Schedule 2.

[20]   Only the Welsh ministers have this power explicitly stated, in accordance with its conferred powers model, and this power is additionally subject to a relevant transfer of functions order having been made; Government of Wales Act 2006, section 59.

[21]   A Ross and H Nash, 'European Union Environmental Law – Who Legislates for Who in a Devolved Great Britain?' (2009) Public Law 564; J Hunt, 'Devolution and Differentiation: Regional Variation in EU Law (2010) 30 Legal Studies 421.

[22]   The different settlements again approach this differently, with foreign policy being a reserved matter under the Scotland Act 1998, Schedule 5; and an excepted matter under the Northern Ireland Act 1998, Schedules 2 and 3. Currently in Wales, a conferred powers model grants the administration the powers to act only where there has been explicit conferral under the devolution legislation, in areas set out in the Government of Wales Act 2006, Schedule 7. Under the Wales Act 2017, Wales will move to the reserved powers model.

consultation and cooperation), there is a specific Concordat on EU policy issues.[23] The Concordat provides that the UK Government will seek to involve the devolved administrations 'as directly and fully as possible in decision making on EU matters', and foresees early and comprehensive information provision, and involvement in the determination of the UK's line, through bilateral as well as multilateral discussions, which are facilitated through an institutional forum – the EU formation of the Joint Ministerial Committee (JMC(E)).[24] This meets regularly, and has proved more effective than other JMC formations. Finally, the Concordat provides that Ministers from devolved governments may attend Council of Ministers meetings. Developments in the EU's machinery of government have, over the years, created an environment more hospitable to the interests of regions and sub-states, in large part as a response to political pressures from German Länder and Belgian regions.[25] This has included an acknowledgement that regional Ministers may attend Council. In a UK context, this may be requested by the devolved administration, though it is at the discretion of the UK Government. The devolved Minister is there to represent the interests of the UK as a whole and not to advance an alternative regional line.

By and large, the assessments of the mechanisms for representing the interests of the devolved nations through this national channel are fairly positive, and situations where a coordinated, agreed line was not supported are few and far between.[26] That said, there are alternative, more direct routes that exist for the devolved nations to connect with and participate in the EU policy process, both formal and informal. These may see the devolved nations sidestep the gatekeeping of the central state, or at the very least, reinforce their visibility as separate actors in the EU system. Such activities can be brought together through the concept of 'paradiplomacy' – the exercise of international relations activities 'parallel to, often coordinated with, complementary to, and sometimes in conflict with centre-to-centre macro-diplomacy'.[27]

With the ongoing shift of policy competences to the EU level, many regions have turned to Brussels as a site for engagement. Regional governments, elected

---

[23]   <https://www.gov.uk/government/publications/devolution-memorandum-of-understanding-and-supplementary-agreement>.

[24]   This has now been supplemented by a specific formation to handle the withdrawal negotiations – JMC (European Negotiations).

[25]   F EGGERMONT, 'In the Name of Democracy: The External Representation of the Regions in the Council' in C PANARA and A DE BECKER (eds), *The Role of the Regions in EU Governance*, Springer, Heidelberg 2010.

[26]   M TATHAM, *With, Without or Against the State: How European Regions Play the Brussels Game*, Oxford University Press, Oxford 2016.

[27]   J MITCHELL, 'Lobbying "Brussels": The Case of Scotland Europa' (1995) 2 *European Urban and Regional Studies* 287; drawing on I DUCHACEK, 'Perforated Sovereignties: Towards a Typology of New Actors in International Relations' in H MICHELMANN and P SOLDATOS (eds), *Federalism and International Relations – The Role of Subnational Units*, Clarendon Press, Oxford 1990.

assemblies and interest groups (such as Higher Education groups and trade bodies) all operate offices in Brussels, for the varied purposes of intelligence-gathering, networking, interest promotion and policy lobbying. All of the UK nations have their own government outposts in Brussels, in addition to a parliamentary presence. UKRep is the UK's 'embassy' to the EU, and since devolution it has been joined by separate devolved offices for Wales, Scotland and Northern Ireland. Formally, these devolved offices are there to 'augment UKRep, to support the work of UKRep, to focus on issues of particular interest to the devolved executive and perhaps also to engage with the EU institutions, but always within the broad framework of a single UK "voice" on Brussels'.[28] However, evidence suggests this has not precluded more informal interactions from taking place with EU institutions to highlight areas of particular importance to the devolved administrations and advance their interests.[29] Other routes through which the devolved nations engage and seek to influence policy development include through connections with sympathetic MEPs. Scotland, Wales and Northern Ireland are each separate constituencies for the European Parliament elections, returning 'their' representatives. In addition, there is a role to be played by the Committee of the Regions,[30] which has a membership drawn from elected representatives in the devolved parliaments and assemblies, as well as local government level. Whilst the Committee itself has a limited role in EU governance processes compared with other institutions, it may nonetheless be a significant forum for developing networks for coordination and collaboration with other regions across the EU.

Other collaborative opportunities lie with initiatives such as the European Territorial Cooperation policy, with the potential for funding from the EU's structural and investment funds, and which provides a framework for regions to participate in cross-border and transnational partnerships.[31] Specific programmes involving the UK and its devolved nations include the INTERREG Atlantic Area, as well as the PEACE programmes – the special support programme for Peace and Reconciliation in Northern Ireland and the Border

---

[28] S Bulmer, M Burch, P Hogwood and A Scott, 'UK Devolution and the European Union: A Tale of Cooperative Assymetry?' (2006) 36 *Publius* 75, p 83.

[29] Tatham, above n 26; A Högenauer, 'The Limits of Territorial Representation in the European Union' (2015) 2 *Territory, Politics, Governance* 147; M Murphy, 'Regional Representation in Brussels and Multi-level Governance: Evidence from Northern Ireland' (2011) 13 *British Journal of Politics and International Relations* 551; A Cole and R Palmer, 'Europeanising Devolution: Wales and the European Union' (2011) 6 *British Politics* 379.

[30] S Piattoni and J Schonlau, *Shaping EU Policy from Below: EU Democracy and the Committee of the Regions*, Edward Elgar, Cheltenham 2015.

[31] S Gänzle, 'New Strategic Approaches to Territorial Cooperation in Europe: From Euro-regions to European Groupings for Territorial Cooperation (EGTCs) and Macro-regional Strategies' in S Piattoni and L Polverari (eds), *Handbook on Cohesion Policy in the EU*, Edward Elgar, Cheltenham 2016; LD Sousa, 'Understanding European Cross-Border Cooperation: A Framework for Analysis' (2013) *Journal of European Integration* 669.

Region of Ireland. Finally, there are other fora for regional collaboration and networking, outside the official EU framework, such as CALRE, the Conference of European Regional Legislature Assemblies; and CPMR, the Conference of Peripheral Maritime Regions – both of which see the regions and nations of the UK represented. Overall, whilst the central state as gatekeeper remains a critically important aspect of EU governance, mediating the interests of the devolved nations, it is clear that the latter have, alongside this, developed for themselves a separate identity within frameworks connected with EU governance. As will be seen, the devolved nations will seek to continue separate and distinct relations with the EU once UK withdrawal has taken place, though the prospect for these to be realised are mixed.

## 2.2. UK REGIONS AND THE EU – POSSIBLE FUTURES

According to Michael Keating, devolved governments generally are motivated to engage in external action for four main reasons: *functional*, reflecting the external dimension of internal competences, in areas such as economic development; *political*, seeking to cement the recognition of the nation as a distinctive actor and form alliances; *ethical*, involving policy action in the field of development, human rights and the environment; and finally, *policy learning*.[32] Such motives would support continued engagement by the devolved nations with EU policies, institutions and networks once the UK has left the EU. However, the devolved administrations in the UK do not have the external legal competence to be able to enter into international legal agreements on their own behalf – unlike some other sub-state entities, such as, most notably, the Belgian regions.[33] Calls from the devolved administrations to the UK Government for them to be empowered to be able to act effectively may be expected. Whether or not those powers are granted, we will expect to see the devolved nations continue to pursue paradiplomatic actions at the EU level, as well as seeking to have legal commitments entered into or endorsed by the UK Government on their behalf.

As Michael Dougan explores in his chapter in this volume, the UK Government's commitment to leaving the customs union and the single market pose particularly acute problems for the island of Ireland, which might be addressed through some form of differentiated solution for Northern Ireland. The EU Commission's chief negotiator Michel Barnier, is himself a former Commissioner with responsibility for regional policy and the PEACE

---

[32]     M Keating, 'The International Engagement of Sub-State Governments': *Report for Scottish Parliament* <http://www.parliament.scot/S4_EuropeanandExternalRelationsCommittee/Meeting %20Papers/Michael_Keating_report.pdf>.

[33]     D Criekemans (ed), *Regional Substate Diplomacy Today*, Martinus Nijhoff, Leiden 2010.

programme. Making reference to this in a speech to the Committee of the Regions in the week leading up to the formal notification of the UKs intention to withdraw from the EU, Barnier emphasised that 'I will be particularly attentive, in these negotiations, to the consequences of the UK's decision to leave the customs union, and to anything that may, in one way or another, weaken dialogue and peace'.[34] But any form of differentiated package for any part of the UK could only arise should the UK Government seek to negotiate and agree it. Nor, politically, would other Member State central governments be prepared to engage in discussions directly with any of the devolved administrations – a point made clear to the Scottish First Minister in her trip to Brussels in the week following the EU referendum result.[35]

In its White Paper *Scotland's Place in Europe*,[36] the Scottish Government first advanced the suggestion that the UK as a whole should seek continued participation in the single market through the route of the European Free Trade Association, the members of which, together with the EU have created the European Economic Area.[37] In the alternative, the White Paper submits that Scotland should have membership of EFTA/EEA. In the absence of Scottish independence, this might be through the UK having membership but disapplying it for the majority of its territory, through it entering into agreement for Scotland, or for Scotland to do so on its own behalf. Any of these alternatives, and especially the last would necessitate the devolution of appropriate legal competences on the Scottish Government and Parliament by the Westminster Parliament. These would need to be extensive, covering policy areas not already devolved (such as employment) to enable Scotland to give effect itself to EU obligations, as well as sufficient external competences. With EEA membership not extending to a customs union, the internal border between Scotland and the rest of the UK would not be a customs border, ostensibly sidestepping the difficulties that will be faced on the island of Ireland.[38] On the free movement of people, the Scottish Government envisages being part of a Common Travel Area covering the UK and Ireland, whilst at the same time being part of the EU's free movement of people regime. It calls for powers over immigration to be devolved, whether or not it remains in the single market, arguing that differentiated immigration

---

[34]  M BARNIER, 'The Conditions for Reaching an Agreement in the Negotiations with the United Kingdom', Speech at the Plenary Session of the European Committee of the Regions (22 March 2017).

[35]  'Brexit: Spain and France oppose Scotland EU Talks', *BBC News*, 29 June 2016 <http://www.bbc.co.uk/news/uk-scotland-scotland-politics-36656980>.

[36]  Scottish Government, *Scotland's Place in Europe*, White Paper (December 2016).

[37]  The EEA Agreement incorporates the provisions on the internal market, and flanking policies such as environmental law and employment law, but excludes the Common Agricultural Policy and Fisheries. The EEA is not a customs union.

[38]  See the contribution by M DOUGAN (Ch 3) in this edited collection.

rules, and the possibility of 'regional visas' would be welcomed in other parts of the UK.[39] Attempts to secure support for the proposal domestically have to date been even less successful than the international response. An expectation of its unwelcome reception may have been a factor in their proposal, with London's continued rejection of Scottish demands potentially strengthening public resolve in Scotland for further devolution and another independence referendum.

Wales, whilst supporting continued UK membership of the single market through the EEA, has not called for its own separate membership. The Welsh Government has had to reconcile its own support for EU membership with the majority 'no' vote in Wales. Its vision is set out in a document conceived together with Plaid Cymru, the nationalist Party of Wales.[40] Though it is clear in its belief that participation in the single market in goods and services is in Wales' best interests, it makes no case for a differentiated deal of the magnitude Scotland advances. The Welsh Government does though indicate that it wishes to continue to participate in various funding and collaborative programmes, highlighting the research funding programme Horizon2020, the education and skills focused Erasmus+, Creative Europe and the transnational Wales-Ireland Programme, as well as maintaining access to the European Investment Bank. That possibilities for this type of continuing relationship exist is reflected in the resolution from the Committee of the Regions on the implications for local and regional government of the UK's intention to withdraw from the European Union.[41] In it, it 'stresses that territorial cooperation programmes should remain open to all UK devolved administrations and local government beyond 2020, [and] highlights that the European Grouping of Territorial Cooperation (ETGC) could be a useful instrument in this regard'. Further, it 'considers that cooperation between local and regional government in the Irish Sea, Channel and North Sea areas, deserves particular attention'.[42] Formal participation would, in the absence of the grant of new external devolved competences, still require the endorsement of the UK Government, though more informal networking and collaborations could be done independently.

In the White Paper *Securing Wales' Future*, the commitment is also made to ensuring that withdrawal from the EU does not lead to a downward pressure on social and environmental standards in the UK. Whilst the UK Government has been quite vocal about maintaining the level of employment protection post-exit (if rather less so about environmental protections),[43] there is no legal

---

[39]   PWC (for City of London Corporation), *Regional Visas – A Unique Immigration Solution* (October 2016).

[40]   Welsh Government, *Securing Wales' Future: Transition from the European Union to a New Relationship with Europe* (2017).

[41]   Committee of the Regions, RESOL-V1/022, COR-2017-01049-00-00-RES-TRA.

[42]   Ibid, paras 12 and 13.

[43]   See further the contribution by V HEYVAERT and A ČAVOŠKI (Ch 6) in this edited collection.

guarantee that these will continue once the UK has withdrawn. From the EU side, continued common standards creating a level playing field in these areas have been flagged as an important aspect of future trade deals.[44] However, such rights would lose their EU law-derived enforceability in the UK order. To the extent that they fall within devolved competence – most obviously the case in respect of the environment – it might be expected that the devolved administrations could, post-UK exit, continue to pitch their own legislation at the EU level, reflecting their legal and political distinctiveness from the UK state. However, here too we witness a reassertion of the dominance of a UK unitary state approach in the management of competence repatriation, which sees the central government making moves to take the place of the EU regulator, and limit the scope of exercise of otherwise devolved powers.

## 3. THE DEVOLUTION SETTLEMENTS FOLLOWING EU WITHDRAWAL

### 3.1. SELF AND SHARED RULE UNDER THE UK CONSTITUTION

Countries which see the allocation of powers and responsibilities over multiple levels of the state will incorporate structures for self-rule and shared rule.[45] The first relates to the powers held by the regional unit, exercisable independently from the central state. Shared rule meanwhile refers to the systems for joint decision making in matters affecting the whole state. The UK's constitutional order also contains provisions for self and shared rule, though there are significant limitations from a devolved perspective. The development of self-rule is considered to have received greater attention than shared rule.[46] The former has seen the grant of devolved legislative and executive powers over ever wider fields and a 'degree of autonomy over its spending decisions exceeding that found in many other multilevel states'.[47] However, even here, self-rule runs up against that constant of the UK constitution: the sovereignty of the Westminster Parliament. The potential at least for Westminster to legislate in devolved areas is never fully excluded. This legal power is, however, constrained under the constitution by the Sewel Convention. This provides that Westminster will not normally legislate with regard to devolved matters without the prior consent of

---

[44] European Council, *Draft Guidelines Following the United Kingdom's Notification under Article 50 TEU* (31 March 2017) para 19; Committee of the Regions Resolution, above n 41, para 18.

[45] L Hooghe et al, *Measuring Regional Authority: A Postfunctionalist Theory of Governance, Volume 1*, Oxford University Press, Oxford 2016.

[46] N McEwen and W Swenden 'Between Autonomy and Interdependence: The Challenges of Shared Rule After the Scottish Referendum' (2015) 86 *Political Quarterly* 192.

[47] Ibid, p 196.

the devolved legislatures. Should the devolved Parliament or Assembly consider its consent is required, it will demonstrate it by passing a Legislative Consent Motion – or else (and exceptionally) refusing to pass it.[48]

Following the commitments made to enhance Scotland's devolution settlement in the wake of the 2014 independence referendum, the Sewel Convention was placed on a statutory footing in the Scotland Act.[49] This move was then repeated for Wales, with the adoption of the Wales Act 2017.[50] Days after the Welsh Assembly had voted to give its consent to the new Wales Act,[51] it learnt of the significance given to the Sewel Convention's new statutory status by the Supreme Court in the *Miller* judgment.[52] The Supreme Court did not rule on the scope of the Convention, or on whether it was engaged by UK legislation to endorse the triggering of Article 50 highlighted, but it did rule that it had not become legally enforceable through its statutory inclusion.[53] The Convention's constitutional importance was stressed, it having 'an important role in facilitating harmonious relationships between the UK Parliament and the devolved legislatures'.[54] However, it is politically enforceable, but not legally so, and failure to respect it will not lead to sanction from the courts.

In respect of shared governance meanwhile, the structures in place for cooperation when UK-wide legislation is being adopted are limited at best, regardless of whether the decision is being taken in a reserved area or one that is devolved. Unlike some federal states, the UK has no machinery for joint legislative decision-making bringing together the different legislatures and governments of the country. The Joint Ministerial Committee is not a decision-making body, and, apart from in its JMC(E) configuration, is widely criticised as an inadequate forum for effective intergovernmental cooperation that would

---

48  The Welsh Assembly has done this in respect of provisions of the Trade Union Bill, NDM5932 on UK Trade Union Bill, 21 January 2016. Welsh legislation has been tabled which will disapply the UK provisions adopted in the face of the rejected LCM. Whilst employment law and industrial relations are not conferred, the Assembly is claiming competence through its powers relating to public services, following an earlier successful, Supreme Court endorsed move to legislate on employment aspects of agriculture: *Agricultural Sector (Wages) Bill, Reference by the Attorney General for England and Wales* [2014] UKSC 43.

49  Scotland Act 1998, section 28(8), following the recommendations of the Smith Commission, *Report of the Smith Commission for the Future Devolution of Powers to the Scottish Parliament* (November 2014); C HIMSWORTH, 'Legislating for Permanence and a Statutory Footing' (2016) 20 *Edinburgh Law Review* 361.

50  This will also see Wales move from a conferred powers model to a reserved powers one. See D MOON and T EVANS, 'Welsh Devolution and the Problem of Legislative Competence' (2017) 12 *British Politics* (forthcoming); R RAWLINGS, 'Riders on the Storm: Wales, the Union and Territorial Constitutional Crisis' (2015) 42 *Journal of Law and Society* 471.

51  LCM-LD10888 – R-R (17 January 2017).

52  *R (on the application of Miller and another) v Secretary of State for Exiting the European Union* [2017] UKSC 5.

53  Ibid, [148] and [149].

54  Ibid, [151].

permit the devolved nations to feed in policy concerns and priorities that they would want to have reflected in UK-wide legislation.[55] In fact, the closest the UK gets to shared governance is in those areas which the EU legislates over. In these 'Europeanised' areas, as we have seen above, structures are in place which give the devolved assemblies and governments opportunities to participate in law-making, both directly in Brussels and indirectly through the channels of the UK Government. Furthermore, in respect of those areas covered by EU law, the principle of subsidiarity is woven through the fabric of multilevel governance.[56]

## 3.2. THE REPATRIATION OF COMPETENCES AND THE GREAT REPEAL BILL

In March 2017, the UK Government introduced its White Paper on the Great Repeal Bill.[57] In it, it proposes a three-pronged approach of Repeal, Convert, Correct. Repeal of the European Communities Act 1972 will end the formal supremacy of EU law over UK law, but existing EU law will be converted into UK domestic law, subject to such corrections as may be required to make it operative once the UK is outside the EU. In six short paragraphs, the White Paper deals with devolution issues,[58] and it does so without any reference to the subsidiarity principle. Instead, the dominant narrative is one of ensuring stability and consistency. At the same time, the White Paper provides that 'it is the expectation of the Government that the outcome of this process will be a significant increase in the decision-making power of each devolved administration'.[59] What is not clear is what new powers, if any, may be devolved, and how this fits with suggestions that have come from the Government that withdrawal from the EU provides the trigger to review where currently devolved powers should lie, which may be London, not Cardiff, Edinburgh or Belfast.

For the UK Government, withdrawal from the EU will see a return of powers to the UK. Even where these powers currently fall within policy areas which have been devolved domestically, such as agriculture and the environment, the process of their 'repatriation' foresees them coming back to Westminster before

---

[55]  MCEWEN and SWENDEN, above n 46; House of Lords Select Committee on the Constitution, *Intergovernmental Relations in the United Kingdom* (HL 2014–15, 146) Ch 2.
[56]  Since the Lisbon Treaty, the subsidiarity principle – which states that the EU should only act if the objectives cannot be effectively achieved by government closer to the citizen – recognises the regional and local level: see Article 5 TEU.
[57]  Department for Exiting the European Union, *Legislating for the United Kingdom's withdrawal from the European Union* (Cm 9446, March 2017). See also the contribution by M GORDON (Ch 1) in this edited collection.
[58]  *Legislating for the United Kingdom's Withdrawal from the European Union*, above n 57, Ch 4 (Interaction with the devolution settlements).
[59]  Ibid, para 4.5.

any decision is taken on whether they should return to the devolved level: 'as the powers to make these rules are repatriated to the UK from the EU, we have an opportunity to determine the level best placed to make new laws and policies on these issues'.[60] The view of the devolved administrations is quite different. These powers are not being 'returned', as they already lie at devolved level, albeit subject to constraints on their exercise. This was also the view of the Supreme Court in *Miller*: '[t]he removal of EU constraints on withdrawal from the EU Treaties will alter the competence of devolved institutions unless new legislative constraints are introduced. In the absence of such new restraints, withdrawal from the EU will enhance devolved competence'.[61]

The Great Repeal Bill's proposed approach to the devolution legislation markedly does not say that it will repeal the constraints that are currently imposed by EU law on the devolved administrations' exercise of competence, nor does it clearly specify at what level existing EU law will be converted into domestic law.[62] Instead, it says it will 'replicate the current frameworks provided by EU rules through UK legislation',[63] replacing the EU constraints for national, UK ones. This 'holding pattern'[64] would then continue until a decision can be reached on whether a centralised legislative framework is appropriate. The Great Repeal Bill White Paper says these decisions will be reached following 'intensive discussions with the devolved administrations', though it is silent on the issue of who the final decision lies with, and whether any new shared governance machinery will be developed.

The immediate response to the White Paper from the Scottish and Welsh devolved administrations was to be expected. The Scottish First Minister decried the prospect of a recentralising 'power grab' on the part of the UK Government.[65] In Wales, the First Minister stated in an Assembly Plenary debate that, 'to adapt a well-known phrase – devolution means devolution; what is already devolved stays devolved'.[66] Whilst the First Minister did not reject that common frameworks might be appropriate, he did reject them being imposed on the devolved nations, rather than agreed upon jointly.

The UK Government's proposed approach under the Great Repeal Bill prompted a further response from within the devolved administrations, to take

---

[60] HM Government, *The United Kingdom's exit from, and new partnership with the European Union* (Cm 9417, February 2017) para 3.5.
[61] *Miller*, above n 52, [130].
[62] It does, though, provide that devolved administrations will be granted competence to make corrections to EU-derived legislation falling within their competence: para 4.6.
[63] Ibid, para 4.4.
[64] Alun Cairns, Welsh Secretary, reported in 'Brexit holding pattern for EU Laws in Great Repeal Bill', *BBC News*, 30 March 2017 <http://www.bbc.co.uk/news/uk-wales-politics-39445547>.
[65] M Dickie, 'Great Repeal Bill Leaves Unanswered Questions on Devolution', *Financial Times*, 30 March 2017.
[66] National Assembly for Wales, Plenary of 4 April 2017.

steps to identify the different routes and mechanisms available for the devolved nations to advance and protect their interests during the passage of the Great Repeal Bill and into the future, in the absence of effective structures for shared governance, and insufficient protections for the realm of self-rule. One approach would be to withhold legislative consent to the Great Repeal Bill. However, this raises complexities, even if a broad reading of the Sewel Convention operates which covers changes to the scope of devolved competence, and not just the exercise of legislative powers within substantive fields of devolved competence. On one reading, if constraints imposed by EU law are being replaced by the same constraints though with a new authority standing in the EU's place, there has been no change to the devolved nations' competences that they would need to give their consent to. Such a technical reading is unlikely to win many over. But Sewel clearly has its limits, and leaving aside what is meant by core terms such as 'would not *normally* legislate', any transgression of the Convention will have as much or as little impact as the devolved administrations are able to generate political leverage.

Alternatively, and as was debated in and supported by the Welsh Assembly soon after the publication of the Great Repeal Bill White Paper, Continuation Bills may be introduced as a pre-emptive strike, before the UK Parliament passes the Repeal Bill. A local Continuation Act would convert all existing EU law within devolved competence into the body of Welsh law.[67] Subsequent UK legislation could of course, as a consequence of Westminster sovereignty, override this body of law, though in that case, the political message about the health of the UK's territorial constitution coming from both sides would be stark.

## 3.3.    THE DEMANDS OF A UK INTERNAL MARKET

In 1973, just as the UK was taking its place in the European Economic Community, the Royal Commission on the Constitution finally reported on the inquiry begun four years previously. By now under the chairmanship of Lord Kilbrandon, the Inquiry's terms of reference included examining 'the functions of the present legislature and government in relation to the several countries, nations and regions of the United Kingdom; and to consider, whether any changes are desirable in those functions or otherwise in present constitutional and economic relationships'.[68] Ultimately recommending a programme of legislative devolution[69] that would take 25 years to realise, the Report noted

---

[67]    Ibid, Motion NND6289.

[68]    *Royal Commission on the Constitution 1969-1973*, Vol 1 Report, HMSO, London 1973 (Cmnd 5460).

[69]    Not all Commission members were able to agree to the Report, and a minority Memorandum of Dissent was published.

that 'the UK is a unitary state in economic terms ... It has, for example, a single currency and a banking system responsible to a single central bank. Its people enjoy a right of freedom of movement of trade, labour and capital and of settlement and establishment anywhere within the UK'.[70] That the UK is amongst other things an economic Union has been repeatedly identified as one of its core characteristics,[71] though no explicit constitutional guarantees exist to underpin it. Of course, the opportunities for things to be done differently across the UK had not substantially arisen in 1973, and the UK could then more straightforwardly be defined as a unitary state.

By the time the 1998 devolution settlements had been put in place and competences allocated, the EU's own internal market was well established. The demands of this EU market have done much of the legwork of maintaining a single market within the UK. Its requirements have minimised the scope for regulatory divergence and have helped maintain a level playing field. That has not meant that EU law demands homogeneity within a Member State, any more than it requires strict uniformity of approach for all states across all policies. Space for local differentiation undoubtedly exists within the tolerances of EU law. Measures adopted by the devolved administrations have found themselves tested before the courts for their compliance with EU law, and have survived – including differential implementation of the CAP regulations, leading to differences in the regulatory burden on farmers in different parts of the UK,[72] bans on the use of electric shock dog collars covering one devolved territory,[73] and a separate regime for tobacco sale and promotion.[74]

Once the framework provided for EU law has been lifted, the requirement to legislate in accordance with the internal market principles will fall away. Without the introduction of a new common principle, hindrances to internal trade may emerge more sharply. Concern with these potential differences and the impact they may have on the UK's market and its economic union lies behind the call for replacement national level common frameworks. The Great Repeal Bill White Paper suggests that there are internal and external considerations which make the retention of common UK frameworks necessary: 'where they are necessary to protect the freedom of business to operate across the UK single

---

[70] *Royal Commission on the Constitution 1969–1973*, above n 68, para 57.
[71] House of Lords Select Committee on the Constitution, *The Union and Devolution* (HL 2015–16, 149) p 17 and evidence cited therein.
[72] Case C-428/07, *Horvath*, ECLI:EU:C:2009:458.
[73] *R (on the application of Petsafe Ltd and another) v Welsh Ministers* [2010] EWHC 2908 (Admin): an unsuccessful challenge to Animal Welfare (Electronic Collars) (Wales) Regulations 2010, SI 2010/943.
[74] *Imperial Tobacco Limited (Appellant) v The Lord Advocate (Respondent) (Scotland)* [2012] UKSC 61: an unsuccessful attempt to overturn the Tobacco and Primary Medical Service (Scotland) Act 2010.

market and to enable the UK to strike free trade deals with third countries'.[75] The internal market principle, previously assumed, looks as though it may become an important touchstone with a continuing constitutional significance for the allocation of powers and the policing of the exercise of devolved competences. To date though, there is little clarity about what this will look like and how it will work.

The UK is of course not the only multi-tiered state that has had to confront these issues. As Anderson observes, how this is handled is a political issue: 'there is always a judgment about the relative priority – and even legitimacy – to be assigned to the objective of an integrated internal market versus other objectives'.[76] A comparison with the approach adopted by other multi-tier states shows that there is a range of options for how a domestic internal market could be supported through law, shaped by considerations such as the balance of power between the centre and the constituent units, the existence of constitutional principles and the role foreseen for the courts.[77]

To the extent that an approach can be inferred, the UK Government does not appear to be considering any introduction of new institutional machinery or core justiciable 'free movement' principles to realise the UK's post-Brexit internal market. Instead, it appears set on operating through the conventional route of parliamentary sovereignty, with acts of the Westminster Parliament trumping all, and giving limited recognition to the separate legal and political forms of the devolved nations. Sectoral common frameworks will supplant devolved rules. Insufficiently developed systems of shared governance lying behind these top-down frameworks will lead to increased tensions, testing the limits of the territorial constitution yet further.

## 4. CONCLUSION

In facing withdrawal from the EU, the UK stands to lose the only frameworks which come close to providing opportunities for shared governance. The UK remains resolutely without effective mechanisms for shared governance of its own making. The Welsh Government, along with key Labour Party figures from across the UK, is now talking in terms of a constitutional convention for a resettlement of power along more federal lines.[78] However, as Roger Scully

---

[75]  *Legislating for the United Kingdom's withdrawal from the European Union*, above n 57, para 4.3.
[76]  G ANDERSON (ed), *Internal Markets and Multi-level Governance: The Experience of the European Union, Australia, Canada, Switzerland and the United States*, Oxford University Press, Oxford 2012, p 1.
[77]  G ANDERSON, 'Internal Markets in Federal or Multi-level Systems' in ANDERSON, above n 76.
[78]  Welsh Government, *Securing Wales' Future*, Ch 7: Constitutional and Devolution Issues.

observes, Wales is the only part of the UK which actively has an interest in bringing this about, and allies amongst the other devolved nations are unlikely to come forward: '[t]he Scottish Government, and half the Northern Irish one (when it is functioning) don't want to re-engineer the UK state, but to leave it'.[79]

The process of withdrawing from the EU has demanded a crystallisation of constitutional principles into a hard legal form. The indeterminacy in the political constitution which allowed for the accommodation of different perspectives on the degree of legal and political autonomy held by the devolved nations has been all but lost. Throughout the withdrawal process, the UK Government has pursued a unitary state strategy, which has seen repeated instances of it thwarting the expectations of the devolved administrations – over such matters as the date of the referendum vote; as well as opportunities to influence the UK Government's White Papers, to trigger Article 50 and to determine the key principles on which the UK will approach negotiations for 'the whole UK'. As the devolved nations are finding, there is no capacity for them to offer effective resistance to this resurgence of a unitary state perspective through legal channels. How effective political resistance may be remains to be seen.

---

[79]   R SCULLY, 'The Loneliness of the Devolutionist Unionist' published at <www.ukandeu. co.uk>.

# CHAPTER 3

# THE 'BREXIT' THREAT TO THE NORTHERN IRISH BORDER: CLARIFYING THE CONSTITUTIONAL FRAMEWORK

Michael Dougan[*]

## 1.   INTRODUCTION

Of all the regions of the United Kingdom, it is widely believed that Northern Ireland is likely to be most deeply affected by withdrawal from the European Union – notwithstanding the fact that 56 per cent of the electorate there who voted on 23 June 2016 expressed their desire to remain.[1] Equally, of all remaining Member States of the EU itself, it is widely accepted that the Republic of Ireland will be most deeply affected by the departure of the United Kingdom – even though the Republic's population obviously had no direct say in the UK

---

[*]   Liverpool Law School, University of Liverpool.
[1]   House of Lords European Union Committee, *Brexit: UK-Irish Relations* (HL 2016–17, 76) – hereafter simply referred to as *Brexit: UK-Irish Relations*.

Michael Dougan

referendum.[2] Indeed, as the House of Lords has observed: the whole network of tripartite relations, running north and south, east and west, that link together both past and future relations between the Republic, Northern Ireland and the rest of the UK now face significant challenges.[3]

To be fair, the salience of certain issues has perhaps been exaggerated: for example, it is difficult to see how UK withdrawal from the EU could, simply in and of itself, amount to a breach of either the Belfast (Good Friday) Agreement or the British-Irish Agreement.[4] Nevertheless, the causes for legitimate concern remain myriad: one need only consider the particular vulnerability of cross-border trade, supply chains and labour forces to the impact of imminent UK departure from the single market; the relative dependence of Northern Ireland's agricultural sector upon EU funding and indeed of its economy as a whole upon public sector employment; and the threats to maintaining strong cooperation in fields ranging from security to healthcare and energy supply.[5] The ultimate concern is that the cumulative effects of economic uncertainty and instability, fundamental changes to the longstanding constitutional framework which has underpinned the peace process, and the potential for one or both of the main communities to feel that important aspects of their identity are under pressure, will render even more difficult the task of securing political stability and promoting social cohesion.[6] Moreover, such concerns are exacerbated by the assumption that Northern Ireland's political representatives will struggle to ensure that the region's particular interests are accommodated within the overall negotiating objectives of the UK Government;[7] and that the Republic will also have to work hard to ensure that its strategic objectives are fairly reflected in the EU's deliberations, even allowing for the explicit recognition already afforded to Ireland's unique position by its European partners.[8]

---

[2]  Note that Irish nationals resident in the UK were entitled to vote in the 2016 referendum under section 2 of the European Union Referendum Act 2015.
[3]  *Brexit: UK-Irish Relations*, above n 1.
[4]  Agreement reached in the Multi-Party Negotiations; Agreement between the Government of the United Kingdom of Great Britain and Northern Ireland and the Government of Ireland.
[5]  See further, eg House of Commons Northern Ireland Affairs Committee, *Northern Ireland and the EU Referendum* (HC 2016–17, 48); *Brexit: UK-Irish Relations*, above n 1.
[6]  *Brexit: UK-Irish Relations*, above n 1, esp Ch 4.
[7]  Northern Ireland is represented at the Joint Ministerial Committee and the JMC Sub-Committee on EU Negotiations: see further HM Government, *The United Kingdom's exit from and new partnership with the European Union* (Cm 9417, February 2017) esp Section 3. Note that Northern Ireland (as with Scotland and Wales) held no right of veto over the UK decision to withdraw: see Supreme Court in *R (on the application of Miller and another) v Secretary of State for Exiting the European Union* [2017] UKSC 5. See further the contribution by J HUNT (Ch 2) in this edited collection.
[8]  See eg European Parliament, *Draft Resolution on negotiations with the United Kingdom following its notification that it intends to withdraw from the European Union* (dated 28 March 2017, published 29 March 2017, expected to be adopted in early April 2017) paras 8 and 20; European Council, *Draft guidelines following the United Kingdom's notification under*

Against that background, this chapter will focus on the legal dimension to one crucial aspect of the debate: the challenges facing the border between Northern Ireland and the Republic. Or to be more precise: the prospect of a hardening of the physical border between the two jurisdictions, capable of disrupting the smooth movement of goods and persons. After all, borders are legal constructs: they divide the earth into parcels of territory each subject to the regulatory power of a particular set of political institutions; to cross a border is to shift from one legislative environment and become subject to the authority of another. In that sense, there are as many 'borders' as there are different legal regimes governing every imaginable category of human activity: a 'border' for the manufacture and marketing of each tangible good; a 'border' for every possible provision of intangible services; a 'border' between each regulatory response to environmental degradation; a 'border' separating every attempt to protect public safety and security. But in the context of Northern Ireland, it is the border governing the physical exchange of goods and persons with the Republic which perhaps attracts most attention and causes greatest concern: there is no doubt whatsoever that any appreciable hardening of that particular frontier could have significant adverse economic, social and political implications. It is therefore unsurprising that maintaining (as far as possible) the current 'open border' arrangements has been recognised as a key objective by the main political actors in Northern Ireland,[9] by the UK Government,[10] and within the Republic;[11] and that that objective has received a sympathetic reception across the rest of the EU.[12]

However, there has sometimes been an unfortunate tendency in the public and political discourse before and after the 2016 referendum to treat even the specific issue of the physical frontier between Northern Ireland and the Republic as a single phenomenon, to be resolved in a single manner: 'the border' must remain open; or 'the border' risks beginning to close. In legal terms, such discourse is misleading and unhelpful. In fact, the applicable constitutional framework requires us to identify and address two distinct and separate physical

---

Article 50 TEU (published on 31 March 2017, expected to be adopted in late April 2017) para 11. On the formal process for negotiating and concluding a withdrawal agreement between the UK and the EU, see Article 50 TEU.

[9] See Letter to the Prime Minster from the First Minister and Deputy First Minister of the Northern Ireland Executive (10 August 2016).

[10] See *The United Kingdom's exit from and new partnership with the European Union*, above n 7, esp Section 4 and Annex B.

[11] eg 'Government statement on Brexit', *MerrionStreet*, 17 January 2017 <http://www.merrionstreet. ie/en/News-Room/News/Government_statement_on_Brexit.html> and 'Taoiseach says common travel area will be preserved', *RTE News*, 17 January 2017 <https://www.rte.ie/news/2017/0117/ 845587-theresa-may-brexit-speech-reaction/>.

[12] See eg *Draft Resolution on negotiations with the United Kingdom following its notification that it intends to withdraw from the European Union*, above n 8, para 20; *Draft guidelines following the United Kingdom's notification under Article 50 TEU*, above n 8, para 11.

borders: in the first place, the frontier for goods, which is bound up with the UK's intended departure from the EU customs union; and in the second place, the frontier for persons, which hinges upon the continuing existence of the Common Travel Area between the UK and Ireland.


## 2. THE PHYSICAL BORDER FOR GOODS: THE NORTHERN IRISH BORDER AS A CUSTOMS FRONTIER

The reason the physical frontier for goods demands its own constitutional analysis is that the customs union is one of the relatively unusual policy fields which is subject to the exclusive competence of the European Union: only the Union is entitled to exercise independent regulatory power in respect of the customs union; the Member States are obliged not to engage in autonomous action as regards customs affairs.[13] It is thus the EU that will determine (by unilateral measures as well as in potential agreement with the British) the legal nature of the physical border for goods between the Republic and Northern Ireland. Unless the EU were specifically to mandate otherwise, it will not be possible for Ireland and the UK to reach some separate bilateral settlement on this issue.

Of course, that is not to suggest that the potential burdens of any customs border between Northern Ireland and the Republic emanate solely from the needs or preferences of the EU and its customs union. After all, the land border will also be the frontier of the UK's newly constituted customs territory and as such become subject also to whatever customs policy the UK decides to create for itself in preparation for final withdrawal from the EU. However, given that we currently know almost nothing about the UK's intended customs policy, it seems more fruitful to concentrate our attention on the issues we can already be sure are bound to arise at least on the EU side of the equation.[14]

The EU customs union of course includes the traditional concern with import/export duties and charges having equivalent effect: the abolition of internal tariffs between Member States is accompanied by the imposition of a common tariff as regards third countries (in compliance with the rules of the WTO as well as the terms of any preferential trade agreements entered into

---

[13] See, in particular Articles 3(1)(a) and 2(1) TFEU.
[14] For the time being, we know only that the UK Government intends to bring forward primary legislation on a new UK customs policy: see *The United Kingdom's exit from and new partnership with the European Union*, above n 7; Department for Exiting the European Union, *Legislating for the United Kingdom's withdrawal from the European Union* (Cm 9446, March 2017).

between the EU and external parties).[15] But the customs frontier also serves a much broader function: assisting with the regulatory enforcement of a wide range of Union policies in fields such as trade, health and safety, environmental protection and countering illegal activities like smuggling and counterfeiting.[16]

For those twin reasons, it is inescapable that the EU customs union entails the erection of a physical frontier for goods in its relations with any third country. The real question is: what will be the nature and extent of the system of border controls, checks and surveillance applied at that external frontier? Here, we can make several key points based on past and current practice.[17] First, the EU aims in principle to adopt a single approach to customs enforcement across its entire territory, so as to avoid the creation of any 'soft underbellies' that would distort the cohesion of the customs union: national variations should be reduced; customs authorities should act as one. Secondly, the EU system seeks to reduce the need for and intrusive nature of physical inspections at the customs border through a variety of means: for example, widespread use of electronic systems for customs declarations; risk management strategies that identify potential problems and respond in a more targeted manner; a system of 'authorised economic operators' to facilitate ease of customs operations for reliable private actors; distinguishing between commercial transport (which might be required to use specific crossing points) and private traffic (which might be dealt with through more random searches). Thirdly, the EU has concluded a range of international agreements with third countries aimed at facilitating customs cooperation and mutual assistance. Some such arrangements are highly structured within the context of relatively close trading partnerships: for example, as with the EU's own (partial) customs union with Turkey;[18] or as in the case of relations between the EU customs union and the EFTA countries that participate also in the European Economic Area.[19] Other customs agreements between the EU and third countries are less advanced, tending to focus (for example) on the mutually beneficial exchange of relevant information.[20]

---

[15]  See, in particular, Article 28(1) TFEU. Also Articles 30–32 TFEU.

[16]  See eg European Commission, *The EU Customs Union: protecting people and facilitating trade* (2014).

[17]  See Regulation 952/2013 laying down the Union Customs Code [2013] OJ L269/1. See further, eg L GORMLEY, *EU Law of Free Movement of Goods and Customs Union*, Oxford University Press, Oxford 2009 – though note that this text is based upon the previous Community Customs Code as laid down in Regulation 2913/92 [1992] OJ L302/1 and Modernised Customs Code as laid down in Regulation 450/2008 [2008] OJ L145/1.

[18]  See, in particular, Decision No 1/95 of the EC-Turkey Association Council on implementing the final phase of the Customs Union. Note the evaluation of the EU-Turkey Customs Union carried out by the World Bank (Report No 85830-TR published on 28 March 2014).

[19]  See, in particular, Agreement on the European Economic Area [1994] OJ L1/3. Note the evaluation of the EEA Agreement conducted by Norway (*Outside and Inside: Norway's Agreements with the European Union*, Official Norwegian Reports NOU 2012:2).

[20]  The EU currently has customs cooperation agreements with countries including the US, Canada, China, India and Japan.

In short: the EU exercises its exclusive competence over the customs union in a way which seeks to limit the burdens and disruption inherent in customs procedures, and is prepared to cooperate with third countries in order to achieve the same ends, but the fact remains that 'customs' also mean 'borders'.

Turning more specifically to the position of the UK, the Government's White Paper of February 2017 indicated its intention to leave the EU customs union and instead seek some form of special customs relationship with the Union – no doubt providing for the total or near total elimination of customs duties and charges having equivalent effect in trade between the UK and the EU.[21] Of course, that aspiration leaves various basic issues to be resolved, even assuming a corresponding willingness to reach agreement on the part of the EU itself. What might be the scope of any special customs agreement (bearing in mind the need to comply with the WTO prohibition on sectoral tariff reductions): for example: will it cover all manufactured goods; agricultural goods (processed and unprocessed); fisheries products? What will the EU insist upon in return, as regards the alignment of broader regulatory standards and their effective enforcement, in order to ensure that its junior partner does not abuse its customs privileges in order to engage in unfair competition? What might be the applicable political and judicial institutions and processes required to operationalise any special customs agreement? In any case, even with an extensive customs agreement, the UK and the EU will still have to apply the usual 'rules of origin' requirements to their mutual trade – to make sure that third country products do not benefit from the special fiscal advantages that are meant to be reserved for each other's products. For those reasons, even if the UK does manage to secure some special relationship with the EU in the field of customs, it will not obviate the existence of some sort of physical frontier to trade in goods.

Indeed, as many commentators have already pointed out, the lessons from the EEA are highly instructive in this context. After all, the EEA already provides an example of a special customs relationship based upon the (extensive but not total) abolition of customs duties between the EU Member States and the EFTA-EEA states.[22] At the same time, the EFTA-EEA states are not part of the EU customs union, are not bound by the common customs tariff and do not otherwise participate in the EU's common commercial policy – thus limiting the benefits of the EEA's preferential tariff system to goods from the participating countries and necessitating the application of 'rules of origin' to ensure the appropriate customs treatment of third country products.[23] That said, the

---

[21] See further *The United Kingdom's exit from and new partnership with the European Union*, above n 7, esp paras 8.43–8.50. See also House of Lords European Union Committee, *Brexit: Trade in Goods* (HL 2016–17, 129).

[22] See, in particular, Articles 8 and 10 EEA.

[23] See, in particular, Articles 8 and 9 EEA as well as Protocol 4.

principle of 'dynamic homogeneity' which underpins the entire EEA system – ensuring that the EFTA-EEA states align their legislation to that of the EU itself across a wide range of policy fields – means that the Union's broader concern to ensure effective regulatory enforcement at its external customs frontier is less pressing in this particular context.[24] When it comes to border management, the EEA agreement provides for customs cooperation and mutual assistance, including detailed provisions on issues such as common standards and mutual recognition as regards customs security measures.[25] Specifically in the context of the land border between Norway and Sweden, a bilateral agreement dating from 1959 (and thus applicable even after subsequent Swedish accession to the EU) aims at reducing bureaucracy and duplication while still managing border crossings effectively: for example, providing for a common border zone where each country's customs authorities can operate freely across both territories.[26]

In short: an ambitious free trade agreement can reduce tariffs between the contracting parties, minimise regulatory discrepancies and provide for greater cooperation and mutual assistance. But even that will rarely succeed in eliminating all tariffs, or obviate the need to apply 'rules of origin', or extinguish concerns about the effective enforcement of broader regulatory policies – any or all of which still necessitate a customs border in order to safeguard the legitimate interests of the contracting parties.

When it comes to the physical border for goods between Northern Ireland and the Republic, the parameters set by EU law are therefore relatively clear: that border will become the external frontier of the EU customs union and will need to be enforced as such; it will then be for the EU and the UK (whether by mutual agreement or by unilateral action under their respective competences) to minimise the degree to which such enforcement leads to disruption on the land border between Northern Ireland and the Republic.[27] But no amount of tariff reductions, technological innovation, risk management or cross-border cooperation will eliminate the disruption entirely. Moreover, the adverse consequences are not only to be calculated in economic terms, based on the additional costs and inconvenience for businesses and consumers on both sides

---

[24]  See further on the principle of dynamic homogeneity within the legal framework and operation of the EEA since its inception, eg HH FREDRIKSEN and CNK FRANKLIN, 'Of Pragmatism and Principles: The EEA Agreement 20 Years on' (2015) 52 *Common Market Law Review* 629.

[25]  See, in particular, Article 21 EEA as well as Protocols 10 and 11.

[26]  See eg D SCALLY, 'Close Sweden-Norway ties despite EU border dividing them', *The Irish Times*, 13 June 2016.

[27]  On which, see *The United Kingdom's exit from and new partnership with the European Union*, above n 7, esp paras 8.49–8.50 and Annex B. Also: *Draft Resolution on negotiations with the United Kingdom following its notification that it intends to withdraw from the European Union*, above n 8, para 20; *Draft guidelines following the United Kingdom's notification under Article 50 TEU*, above n 8, para 11.

of the customs frontier, caused by having to pay any tariffs due on the cross-border movement of goods, as well as having to comply with all the applicable pre- and post-customs processes and formalities, in order for products from one jurisdiction to be treated as having entered free circulation in the other.[28] In addition, with a more closed physical border for goods will inevitably come a range of broader social and political challenges: for example, the creation of additional incentives to engage in cross-border smuggling and other forms of illegal activity; the risk that frontier points will once again become an easy target for violent attack by those directly opposed to the peace process; and the danger of undermining an important pillar of nationalist identity, which the current open border arrangements have without doubt come to express.[29]

## 3. THE PHYSICAL BORDER FOR PERSONS: MAINTAINING THE COMMON TRAVEL AREA?

Entirely separate from the question of the physical frontier for goods is the issue of the physical border for persons between Northern Ireland and the Republic and, in particular, the prospects for the survival of the Common Travel Area between the UK and Ireland after British withdrawal from the EU.[30] As is well known, the CTA is not enshrined in any international treaty between the two states. Rather, it is based upon a more informal understanding, which is then translated into the particular domestic legislative and administrative arrangements of each country.[31] Whilst one should acknowledge its limitations and weaknesses, the CTA has nevertheless led to the virtual elimination of border controls on persons between Northern Ireland and the Republic.[32] Throughout the 2016 referendum campaign, fears were expressed about the continued survival of the CTA in the event that the UK left the EU while Ireland remained a Member State.[33] The UK Government's White Paper from February 2017 sets out the aspiration that, whatever else may come to pass in terms of

---

[28]  See, in particular, Articles 28(2) and 29 TFEU. And that is besides the additional requirement of lawful marketing within the state of free circulation: see eg Case C-525/14, *Commission v Czech Republic*, ECLI:EU:C:2016:714.

[29]  See also *Brexit: UK-Irish Relations*, above n 1, esp Ch 3.

[30]  The CTA also extends to the Isle of Man and the Channel Islands.

[31]  See further B RYAN, 'The Common Travel Area between Britain and Ireland' (2001) 64 *Modern Law Review* 855. Also, eg House of Commons Library, 'The Common Travel Area and the Special Status of Irish Nationals in UK Law' (Briefing Paper No 7661, July 2016).

[32]  *Brexit: UK-Irish Relations*, above n 1, esp Ch 3.

[33]  Consider, eg HM Government, *The process for withdrawing from the European Union* (Cm 9216) p 19.

relations with the EU as a whole, the CTA with Ireland should in any event be preserved.[34] That aspiration is shared also by the Irish Government.[35] So what are the constitutional and legal hurdles that might stand in its way? There are two main challenges: one for Ireland, concerning the potential influence of the remaining EU Member States and institutions over Ireland's own border policy governing the entry of persons; and the other for the UK, concerning how far future changes in British immigration policy might undermine the conditions required for the smooth operation of the CTA.

## 3.1. THE BALANCE OF COMPETENCE BETWEEN IRELAND AND THE REST OF THE EU

Let's begin with the situation of Ireland. In contrast with the customs border for goods, the EU does not enjoy exclusive competence over the immigration border for persons. Rather, border policy is a shared competence between the EU and its Member States: both are entitled to regulate the entry of persons in accordance with their respective internal competences; though the Member States are required to respect whatever obligations are created for them at the EU level.[36] However, when it comes to identifying such obligations, the constitutional position of both the UK and Ireland is different under EU law from that of the great majority of other Member States.[37] Neither country fully

---

[34] See *The United Kingdom's exit from and new partnership with the European Union*, above n 7, esp para 4.8 and Annex B.

[35] See above n 11.

[36] See, in particular, Articles 4(2)(j) and 2(2) TFEU. See further, eg C GORTAZAR, 'Abolishing Border Controls: Individual Rights and Common Control of EU External Borders' in E GUILD and C HARLOW (eds), *Implementing Amsterdam: Immigration and Asylum Rights in EC Law*, Hart Publishing, Oxford 2001; F PASTORE, 'Visas, Borders, Immigration: Formation, Structure and Current Evolution of the EU Entry Control System' in N WALKER (ed), *Europe's Area of Freedom, Security and Justice*, Oxford University Press, Oxford 2004; S PEERS, *EU Justice and Home Affairs Law*, Oxford University Press, Oxford 2006, Chs 2 and 3.

[37] Note that Denmark also has a peculiar legal relationship to the AFSJ: see Protocol No 22 on the position of Denmark. See further on the legal framework for flexibility in relation to the AFSJ, eg J MONAR, 'Justice and Home Affairs in the Treaty of Amsterdam: Reform at the Price of Fragmentation' (1998) 23 *European Law Review* 320; M HEDEMANN-ROBINSON, 'The Area of Freedom, Security and Justice with Regard to the UK, Ireland and Denmark: The "Opt-in Opt-outs" under the Treaty of Amsterdam' in D O'KEEFFE and P TWOMEY (eds), *Legal Issues of the Amsterdam Treaty*, Hart Publishing, Oxford 1999; M FLETCHER, 'Schengen, the European Court of Justice and Flexibility under the Lisbon Treaty: Balancing the United Kingdom's "ins" and "outs"' (2009) 5 *European Constitutional Law Review* 71; E FAHEY, 'Swimming in a Sea of Law: Reflections on Water Borders, Irish(-British)-Euro Relations and Opting-out and Opting-in after the Treaty of Lisbon' (2010) 47 *Common Market Law Review* 673.

participates in the Area of Freedom, Security and Justice,[38] since both enjoy a complex system of opt-out/opt-in rights as regards the policy fields (borders, immigration, asylum, cooperation in civil and criminal matters) covered by the relevant Treaty provisions.[39] In particular, neither the UK nor Ireland has fully joined with the other Member States in the Schengen project of abolishing internal passport controls, and for that purpose, constructing a common external border regime.[40] Instead, EU law explicitly recognises the competence of both the UK and Ireland to retain their own border checks as well as to maintain the CTA in their mutual relations.[41]

Although the current legal position is thus clear and settled, questions have nevertheless arisen about Ireland's competence to continue exercising its own border policy – including the maintenance or renewal of the CTA itself – once the UK withdraws from the EU.

In the first place, there is an argument that the legal recognition afforded under the Treaties to Ireland's competence to exercise its own border controls, as well as to the existence of the CTA itself, is premised upon two facts: continuing EU membership by both the UK and Ireland; and the continuing maintenance of the CTA between the two countries. The key provision is to be found in Article 2 of Protocol No 20, which provides in effect that, as long as the UK and Ireland maintain the CTA arrangements, the right to exercise its own border controls which is recognised primarily in relation to the UK shall also apply to Ireland under the same terms and conditions as for the UK itself.[42] If either of those facts were to change – either the UK leaves the EU, or the CTA ceases to be a meaningful arrangement – then the relevant Treaty provisions should automatically cease to apply for the benefit of Ireland.[43]

In the second place, it has also been argued that Ireland should in any event require the agreement of the remaining Member States and/or EU institutions, in order to maintain or reach any agreement with the UK as regards border

[38] On the AFSJ, see Title V, Part Three TFEU. See also, specifically on criminal cooperation, the contribution by V MITSILEGAS (Ch 10) in this edited collection.
[39] See Protocol No 21 on the position of the United Kingdom and Ireland in respect of the Area of Freedom, Security and Justice. Recall also the UK's option under Protocol No 36 on transitional provisions to repudiate, then selectively opt back into, EU measures previously adopted under the ex-Third Pillar.
[40] The complex legal relationship of the UK and Ireland to the Schengen system under EU law is laid down in Protocol No 19 on the Schengen *acquis* integrated into the framework of the European Union.
[41] See Protocol No 20 on the application of certain aspects of Article 26 of the Treaty on the Functioning of the European Union to the United Kingdom and to Ireland.
[42] Note that Article 3 also nods towards the conditional nature of Ireland's benefits under Protocol No 20.
[43] This argument is hinted at in evidence cited by the House of Commons Northern Ireland Affairs Committee, *Northern Ireland and the EU Referendum*, above n 5, para 74.

controls between the two countries into the future.[44] Indeed, this particular suggestion has to some extent been endorsed even in official UK parliamentary reports.[45] It has to be said: no particular legal rationale is offered to back up this second line of argument, unless one counts the idea that the CTA happens to be explicitly referenced in EU law – as if that in itself should be considered enough to determine the constitutional balance of competence between the EU and a Member State.[46] One is tempted to suspect that this argument is just as often based upon a confused conflation of the EU's (admittedly exclusive) competence over the customs border for goods with the EU's (much more limited) competence in respect of Ireland's border policy on persons.[47]

Be that as it may, what is clear is that neither of those suggestions should be considered at all legally robust. To begin with, it surely cannot be the case that the UK's unilateral act of withdrawal from the EU may have the automatic effect of amending or abrogating Union primary law as regards the rights and obligations of another Member State. The particular wording of Article 2 of Protocol No 20 may be rather idiosyncratic, but its clear and unarguable effect is to grant legal respect under EU law for Ireland's power to conduct border checks as well as for its right of continuing participation in the CTA. To suggest that Ireland's own competences are somehow entirely derived from or contingent upon those of the UK, and only in the latter's capacity as a Member State, would not only be an inappropriate interpretation of Union law which seems difficult to reconcile with respect for Irish sovereignty.[48] It would also be tantamount to allowing the UK to rewrite Ireland's constitutional and substantive position under the Treaties, merely through the UK's own choices about membership, regardless of the views of Ireland itself, and altogether outside the ordinary procedure for amending Union primary law.

Perhaps more importantly: unilateral UK withdrawal from the EU can certainly have no effect whatsoever upon Ireland's entirely distinct prerogatives of opt-out/opt-in as regards the Area of Freedom, Security and Justice in general, and the system of Schengen cooperation in particular, which are also explicitly enshrined in the Treaties.[49] Entirely independently of the membership choices made by the UK, and even regardless of one's interpretation of Protocol No 20, Ireland does not have any obligation to participate in the EU system for abolishing internal borders as regards persons, creating common rules on

---

[44]    Again, see evidence cited by the House of Commons Northern Ireland Affairs Committee, *Northern Ireland and the EU Referendum*, ibid, para 74.
[45]    In particular: *Brexit: UK-Irish Relations*, above n 1, esp paras 110–114.
[46]    See *Brexit: UK-Irish Relations*, ibid, para 114.
[47]    eg consider Institute for Government, 'Four-Nation Brexit: How the UK and devolved governments should work together on leaving the EU' (Briefing Paper, October 2016) p 14.
[48]    Cp Article 4(2) TEU.
[49]    Precisely under Protocols No 21 and 19 (respectively).

passage through the external borders of the Schengen zone, or coordinating immigration policies as regards the residency and associated rights of third country nationals. Far from it: the Treaties leave no room to doubt that Ireland remains competent to exercise its own border controls in its relations with both the remaining Member States as well as third countries at large.[50] Ireland's proper duty is simply to comply with any specific EU law obligations it has assumed under the Treaties: for example, as regards the right of entry into Irish territory for EU nationals and their protected family members, in possession of the appropriate documentation, in accordance with Directive 2004/38.[51]

From a constitutional perspective, therefore, it is very difficult to see why UK withdrawal from the EU should change in any material respect the fundamental legal framework governing Ireland's own relationship to the Area of Freedom, Security and Justice.[52] In particular, UK withdrawal cannot deprive Ireland of the basic choice it currently enjoys under EU law: between deciding to abandon its special status and become a fully-fledged participant in the AFSJ, including even the Schengen policies on internal and external borders; or instead maintaining its existing national competence over its own border and immigration policies, including the possibilities for unilateral action or bilateral agreement with third countries, subject only to Ireland's specific EU law obligations.[53]

Obviously, if Ireland were to choose the former option, the physical border for persons with the UK in general, and Northern Ireland in particular, would become part of the external frontier of the Schengen area and the CTA would be dead in the water. But politically, there appears almost no prospect of the Republic making that choice.[54] Yet if Ireland chooses the latter option, it should be wary of finding the exercise of its national competence subjected to unnecessary constraints, precisely such as any supposed duty to obtain the consent of the remaining EU Member States and institutions to the future exercise of its own border prerogatives. Or at least: Ireland should only accept such external constraints consciously and voluntarily, for example, for the sake of maintaining

---

[50]  See, in particular, Article 2 of Protocol No 21. Note that, even as regards the great majority of Member States which fully participate in the AFSJ, Protocol No 23 provides that the Union's power to adopt measures concerning checks on persons crossing the external border shall be without prejudice to national competence to enter agreements with third countries (as long as they respect Union law).

[51]  Directive 2004/38 [2004] OJ L158/77. Note Articles 1 and 2 of Protocol No 20, which explicitly refer to these specific obligations. Note also Article 6 of Protocol No 21, as regards specific AFSJ measures that Ireland has chosen to participate in of its own volition.

[52]  See, in a similar sense, the written evidence cited in *Brexit: UK-Irish Relations*, above n 1, paras 112–113.

[53]  See, in particular, Article 8 of Protocol No 21: 'Ireland may notify the Council in writing that it no longer wishes to be covered by the terms of this Protocol' – in which case, the normal Treaty provisions will apply to Ireland.

[54]  Notwithstanding the apparently more open mind expressed by Ireland in Declaration No 56 at the time of the Lisbon Treaty.

an enhanced degree of unity between the EU27 during the defined period of their withdrawal negotiations with the UK. In that regard, there is already clear evidence of a political momentum to subsume discussions about the future of the CTA into the general multilateral framework for withdrawal negotiations under Article 50 TEU. Yet that essentially procedural choice need and should not involve also a blurring of the clear balance of constitutional competence between Ireland and the remainder of the Union when it comes to making substantive choices about border policy. It is noteworthy that, whereas the UK's withdrawal letter of 29 March 2017 refers generally to the maintenance of the CTA within the UK's proposed principles for the conduct of negotiations under Article 50 TEU,[55] the European Council's own draft negotiating guidelines are more carefully worded: on the one hand, 'there will be no separate negotiations between individual Member States and the United Kingdom on matters pertaining to the withdrawal of the United Kingdom from the Union'; on the other hand, the EU 'should … recognise existing bilateral agreements and arrangements between the United Kingdom and Ireland which are compatible with EU law'.[56]

## 3.2. THE IMPACT OF UK IMMIGRATION POLICY UPON THE FUTURE OF THE CTA

That brings us to our second main challenge: which border arrangements might Ireland and the UK make in the exercise of their respective national immigration competences (whether by formal mutual agreement, through some more informal understanding, or indeed by mere unilateral action)? The answer here depends largely upon the domestic choices that remain to be made by the UK concerning its future border and immigration policies.

Any cross-border system for the mutual suppression of border controls on persons, such as the CTA or indeed Schengen, is normally regarded as being dependent upon the participating states having closely aligned their external border and immigration systems, as well as establishing close cooperation between their national immigration authorities when it comes to border management and surveillance. Even if the CTA has never been fully aligned in the sense of having identical rules and procedures, the external border and immigration policies of the UK and Ireland were nevertheless regarded as sufficiently similar, and mutual cooperation between the competent national authorities functioned

---

55 See letter from Theresa May to Donald Tusk, 29 March 2017, p 5, point v.
56 See *Draft guidelines following the United Kingdom's notification under Article 50 TEU*, above n 8, paras 2 and 11 (respectively). Note that the Commission's subsequent recommendation for draft negotiating directives is even more explicit, identifying the CTA as an example of such bilateral agreements / arrangements: see COM(2017) 218 Final, Annex, para 14.

effectively enough, that any discrepancies or divergences were not considered so serious as to call into question the very existence of the CTA.[57]

After withdrawal from the EU, if the UK were to maintain border and immigration policies, as regards both EU and third country nationals, which are more or less equivalent to those which already exist today, then there seems no reason why the continued existence and smooth operation of the CTA itself should come under significant pressure. However, if the UK does eventually adopt an appreciably more restrictive border and/or immigration policy as regards either EU or third country nationals – and Ireland is unable (in the case of EU citizens) or unwilling (in the case of third country nationals) to follow suit – then the emergence of such discrepancies between the two countries' approaches to their common external frontier in respect of persons will surely put more considerable pressure upon the continued suppression of internal border checks in accordance with the existing CTA.

In that event, three main options would be available, as a matter of principle, to resolve the situation.[58] First, the CTA could be abandoned in its entirety, and border checks on persons introduced between Ireland and the UK, including at the land border with Northern Ireland, so as to enable the UK as a whole to enforce its new and more restrictive national border and/or immigration rules as regards EU citizens and/or third country nationals. However, this option raises obvious problems in terms of the sheer costs and practicability of attempting properly to instigate and enforce persons controls along the entire land border between Northern Ireland and the Republic; as well as the serious economic and social repercussions of closing the border; to say nothing of the implications for political stability, particularly having regard to the concerns of the nationalist community.[59]

Secondly, the land border between Northern Ireland and the Republic could be kept open and free of checks, at least when it comes to the movement of persons; but with border controls then introduced between the island of Ireland as a whole (on the one hand) and the rest of the UK (on the other hand) – so as to enable the latter territory to enforce its newfound border/immigration restrictions, also when it comes to sea and air transport from the former territories. However, this option again raises some obvious problems: it may well be more realistic in terms of costs and practicalities; but it would imply the need for Northern Ireland to accept (whether formally or informally) a border and/or immigration policy aligned more with that of the Republic than with the rest

---

[57] See further, eg House of Commons Library, 'The Common Travel Area and the Special Status of Irish Nationals in UK Law', above n 31.
[58] See, in a similar though not identical sense, House of Commons Northern Ireland Affairs Committee, *Northern Ireland and the EU Referendum* above n 5, paras 75–80.
[59] On which, see *Brexit: UK-Irish Relations*, above n 1, esp Ch 4.

of the UK; and again, there may be serious political implications, only this time stemming from unionist concerns.[60]

Thirdly, the CTA could be retained in its current form – no entry checks on persons between the Republic and the UK as a whole – notwithstanding the emergence of appreciable differences in Irish and UK border and/or immigration rules as regards EU and/or third country nationals. But in that event, the two countries would have to develop a range of policies – whether in cooperation or unilaterally – to ameliorate the adverse consequences which might arise in practice: for example, through more extensive data sharing between the competent national authorities as regards the movement of persons across the external frontiers of the CTA;[61] and by the UK in particular having to rely on more rigorous internal enforcement of its own immigration restrictions, including as regards access to employment, social security and public services.[62]

Obviously, none of those solutions can be considered ideal – but given the political commitment of both the UK and Ireland to maintaining the CTA, as well as the more extreme problems posed by the introduction of any border checks on persons between the two states, the third solution surely has much to commend it. However, the final choice will depend upon future circumstances and especially the degree to which UK border and/or immigration policies might become more restrictive than at present. At one extreme, if the UK continues to allow the entry of EU nationals without any visa requirements, and imposes only relatively marginal additional restrictions on their immigration rights (to reside, work or study) within the territory, it is difficult to see any justification for restricting the operation of the CTA. At the other extreme, if the UK were to impose visa entry requirements upon EU nationals, or to place significant additional limitations upon their immigration rights (as regards residence and employment etc) that could put much greater pressure on the future survival of the CTA.[63]

In any case, we should not forget that – even if Ireland and the UK reach some agreement or understanding that the CTA should continue to function in its current or some amended form – Ireland will still be obliged to respect any specific obligations imposed or accepted under EU law. For example: no

---

[60]　On which, see *Brexit: UK-Irish Relations*, ibid, paras 140–142.
[61]　On which, see *Brexit: UK-Irish Relations*, ibid, paras 134–139.
[62]　Ultimately, perhaps even some system of national identity cards – with all its attendant concerns about public costs and citizen privacy.
[63]　For the time being, we know only that the UK Government intends to bring forward primary legislation on UK immigration reform: see *The United Kingdom's exit from and new partnership with the European Union*, above n 7; *Legislating for the United Kingdom's withdrawal from the European Union*, above n 14. See further, eg House of Commons Exiting the European Union Committee, *The Government's Negotiating Objectives: The rights of UK and EU citizens* (HC 2016–17, 1125); House of Lords European Union Committee, *Brexit: UK-EU movement of people* (HL 2016–17, 121). And also the contribution by S REYNOLDS (Ch 9) in this edited collection.

matter what the UK decides in terms of its entry/immigration policies, Ireland must continue to respect the rights of entry and residency available to all EU nationals and their protected family members.[64] Similarly: if Ireland and the UK are minded to enhance their mutual cooperation as regards border surveillance and the exchange of information between national immigration authorities, Ireland would nevertheless have to respect its obligations under the relevant EU data protection legislation, including any applicable restrictions on transferring personal data to third countries.[65]

## 4. THE QUESTION OF MUTUAL RESIDENCY RIGHTS: A NON-PHYSICAL BORDER, BUT STILL A CRUCIAL ONE …

There is one final issue worth commenting on, since it is both relevant to and follows on from our discussion of the CTA, even though it does not involve any physical border of the sort we have already considered in relation to either goods or persons: the special immigration status of Irish nationals in the UK and of British nationals in the Republic. After all, even though EU law sets a minimum standard for the treatment of all EU migrants across the Member States, the UK and Ireland have in various respects afforded more favourable treatment to each other's citizens than is strictly required under the Treaties. Such more favourable treatment covers a variety of situations: for example, from basic rights to residency and protection from expulsion; to voting rights in national parliamentary elections and referendums.[66]

After British withdrawal from the EU – and regardless of any special agreement on the movement of persons that might be reached (or not) between the UK and the EU as a whole – Ireland and the UK will remain competent to decide or agree upon the immigration treatment of each other's nationals within their respective territories as regards issues such as residency, employment, social benefits and political participation. In that regard, it is important to note that the UK Government's White Paper from February 2017 explicitly states the desire to retain the current arrangements for reciprocal special treatment between the citizens of Ireland and of the UK.[67]

---

[64]    ie precisely in accordance with Directive 2004/38 [2004] OJ L158/77.

[65]    The EU's general data protection regime is now contained in Regulation 2016/679 [2016] OJ L119/1 and Directive 2016/680 [2016] OJ L119/89.

[66]    See further, eg House of Commons Library, 'The Common Travel Area and the Special Status of Irish Nationals in UK Law', above n 31; *Brexit: UK-Irish Relations*, above n 1, esp paras 126–131.

[67]    See HM Government, *The United Kingdom's exit from and new partnership with the European Union*, above n 7, esp paras 4.6–4.7 and Annex B.

Once again, however, the fact of UK withdrawal means that Ireland's future freedom of action to treat, or agree to treat, UK nationals just as it pleases, will be limited by certain specific obligations imposed under EU law, in ways which were perhaps less relevant or at least less obvious than in the past.[68]

Some such obligations would provide certain UK nationals with minimum standards of protection under Union law – regardless of what Ireland decides or agrees as a matter of its own immigration competence – even if the nature and extent of the reciprocal benefits agreed between the UK and Ireland mean that such protections are unlikely to be of much relevance in practice. For example, Ireland would be obliged to treat UK nationals who qualify as the protected family members of EU citizens in accordance with the minimum standards expected under Union law.[69] That includes the safeguards offered directly under Union primary law, in addition to the secondary legislation governing the free movement of Union citizens. Consider situations akin to *Ruiz Zambrano*: where the deportation of a UK national who is the primary carer of an Irish child would effectively oblige the latter also to leave the Union territory, that UK national may enjoy certain derived rights of residency and equal treatment within Ireland, notwithstanding that the situation would normally be considered wholly internal and outside the scope of protection afforded under Directive 2004/38.[70]

However, other EU law obligations could pull in the opposite direction – setting certain limits to, and creating certain costs consequent upon, the degree of favourable treatment that Ireland might be able or willing to provide for UK nationals. For example, Union law reserves the prerogative to scrutinise how far a Member State (such as Ireland) might allow certain third country nationals (such as UK citizens) to vote in elections to the European Parliament.[71] Perhaps more importantly: although there is no general obligation upon Member States always to grant preference to Union citizens over third country nationals in the ordinary exercise of their domestic competences,[72] various provisions of Union law do contain a more specific duty that Member States should not confer more favourable treatment upon third country nationals than they are prepared to offer other Union citizens in particular situations: that is typically the case, for example, when it comes to the power of existing Member States to impose

---

[68]   Note that the competence of both countries will, in these matters, also be restricted by the baseline of obligations imposed under the ECHR.

[69]   ie again in accordance with the provisions of Directive 2004/38 [2004] OJ L158/77.

[70]   Case C-34/09, *Ruiz Zambrano*, ECLI:EU:C:2011:124 (as interpreted in subsequent case law such as Case C-256/11, *Dereci*, ECLI:EU:C:2011:734).

[71]   See eg Case C-145/04, *Spain v United Kingdom*, ECLI:EU:C:2006:543.

[72]   See further, eg S ROBIN-OLIVIER, 'The Community Preference Principle in Labour Migration Policy in the European Union', *OECD Social, Employment and Migration Working Papers No 182*, OECD Publishing, Paris 2016.

transitional restrictions upon the free movement of workers from newly acceded Member States within the context of EU enlargement treaties.[73]

Another significant restriction upon Ireland's freedom of manoeuvre will be the principle that international agreements between a Member State and a third country are still required to comply with Union law.[74] That includes the general principle of equal treatment on grounds of nationality: where an international agreement seeks to confer certain benefits upon the nationals of the signatory Member State, the latter must extend those same benefits also to other EU citizens who find themselves in a comparable position.[75] For example: imagine that Ireland were to sign a bilateral agreement with the UK, providing for the coordination of social security contributions and payments between the two countries – something which may well be required in order to make the maintenance of reciprocal residency rights meaningful in practice.[76] Insofar as Ireland agrees to take into account periods of social security insurance within the UK, for the purposes of calculating entitlement to Irish benefits such as the state pension, the general principle of equal treatment on grounds of nationality would (in principle) oblige Ireland to do so for all migrant EU citizens, rather than just Irish (and UK) nationals alone.[77]

## 5. CONCLUSIONS

Just as Ireland finds itself thrust by the prospect of UK withdrawal from the EU into a uniquely vulnerable position among the remaining Member States, so

---

[73] eg Article 14, Part 1 (Freedom of Movement for Persons), Annex V (as regards the Czech Republic) to the Act concerning the conditions of accession of the Czech Republic, the Republic of Estonia, the Republic of Cyprus, the Republic of Latvia, the Republic of Lithuania, the Republic of Hungary, the Republic of Malta, the Republic of Poland, the Republic of Slovenia and the Slovak Republic and the adjustments to the Treaties on which the European Union is founded [2003] OJ L236/33. Similar provisions have applied to the accession of other Member States, eg consider Case C-15/11, *Sommer*, ECLI:EU:C:2012:371.

[74] Subject to Article 351 TFEU.

[75] eg Case C-55/00, *Gottardo*, ECLI:EU:C:2002:16. The fact that the relevant third country is not obliged to do the same is irrelevant.

[76] Assuming that the UK leaves the general system of cross-border social security coordination under Regulation 883/2004 [2004] OJ L200/1 without reaching agreement on any comparable replacement with the EU as a whole. See further, eg European Commission, *The External Dimension of EU Social Security Coordination*, COM(2012) 153 Final. On the importance of seeing residency as a part of bundle of broader social and economic rights, see the contribution by S REYNOLDS (Ch 9) in this edited collection.

[77] The full effects of the *Gottardo* principle assume that the issue falls within the scope of Union law, that the relevant situations are comparable, and there is no objective justification for the difference in treatment (such as respecting the balance and reciprocity of a bilateral agreement): see further, eg Case C-307/97, *Compagnie de Saint-Gobain*, ECLI:EU:C:1999:438; Case C-376/03, *D*, ECLI:EU:C:2005:424.

too Northern Ireland risks becoming the prime victim of the UK Government's hardline approach to implementing the result of the 2016 referendum. The only silver lining on those otherwise dark clouds is the political commitment of the UK and Ireland to seek to minimise the inevitable damage. For its part, the EU also has a clear and vested interest in actively seeking to cushion Northern Ireland, as well as the Republic, from the worst consequences of the UK's departure from the Union.[78] However, those worthy political aspirations must not only contend with the harsh realities of a complex and multifaceted set of international negotiations in which the interests of Northern Ireland will hardly play a decisive role. They must also tally with the constitutional principles and legal frameworks which govern relations between the EU and its Member States as well as their collective and separate relations with third countries.

This chapter has considered the relevance of such constitutional principles and legal frameworks to one crucial part of the Northern Irish question: the twofold manner in which the UK's withdrawal from the EU threatens the open border between Northern Ireland and the Republic.[79] In the first place, UK exit in accordance with the preferences set out by the British Government in its White Paper of February 2017 inevitably means that the Northern Irish land border will become the physical frontier for goods entering and leaving the EU customs union. Competence to regulate that border belongs to the EU itself. The challenge will be for the EU and the UK – by mutual agreement if possible, by unilateral action if necessary – to manage the land border in a manner which causes the least possible economic, social and political disruption on the island of Ireland, while still safeguarding the legitimate fiscal and regulatory interests of both the EU as a whole and the UK as a newly constituted customs territory. In the second place, UK exit has raised questions about the durability of the Common Travel Area which allows persons to cross the Northern Irish land border without being subject to entry or exit controls. From a constitutional perspective, the risk to the survival of the CTA should not be understood as relating to the balance of competence between Ireland and the rest of the EU. Instead, the main challenge facing the maintenance of the CTA emanates from the prospect of the UK adopting a more restrictive policy on border

---

[78] See eg *Draft Resolution on negotiations with the United Kingdom following its notification that it intends to withdraw from the European Union*, above n 8, paras 8 and 20; *Draft guidelines following the United Kingdom's notification under Article 50 TEU*, above n 8, para 11.

[79] Note that these lessons are also of potential relevance to debates about the border relationship between Scotland and England, in the event that Scotland either remains within the UK but secures a differentiated relationship with the EU; or becomes an independent state that then joins either the EU or EFTA plus the EEA. See Scottish Government, *Scotland's Place in Europe* (December 2016). Note also earlier discussion, eg B RYAN, 'At the Borders of Sovereignty: Nationality and Immigration Policy in an Independent Scotland' (2014) 28 *Journal of Immigration, Asylum and Nationality Law* 146.

controls and/or immigration rights than Ireland is legally able or politically willing to follow – and the UK then being unprepared to accept that stronger immigration cooperation with the Republic, combined with more effective internal enforcement of its own border policy, is a price worth paying to save the CTA and, indeed, to protect the interests of everyone living in Northern Ireland.

# CHAPTER 4

# BREXIT AND UK COURTS: AWAITING FRESH INSTRUCTION

Thomas Horsley\*

## 1. INTRODUCTION

The United Kingdom (UK) Government's decision to trigger Article 50 TEU to manage the UK's exit from the European Union (EU) has thrust its courts into the media spotlight. In particular, the English and Northern Irish High Courts and, subsequently, UK Supreme Court (UKSC), have been drawn into a series of legal disputes over the scope of the executive's prerogative powers and the competences of the devolved administrations.[1]

---

\* Senior Lecturer, University of Liverpool.
[1] *R (on the application of Miller and another) v Secretary of State for Exiting the European Union* [2016] EWHC 2768 (Admin); *McCord, Re Judicial Review* [2016] NIQB 85; and *R (on the application of Miller and another) v Secretary of State for Exiting the European Union* [2017] UKSC 5 (respectively).

This chapter looks ahead to changes to the institutional functions of UK courts[2] within the domestic legal order as a consequence of the UK's departure from the EU. More precisely, it forecasts potentially far-reaching changes to the nature of UK courts' institutional functions post-Brexit as a result of the anticipated repeal of the European Communities Act 1972 (ECA). For the duration of the UK's membership of the (now) EU, that Act has functioned as the source of the domestic 'constitutional instruction' to UK courts to give internal effect to EU law in proceedings falling within the scope of Union law. In summary, the ECA instructs UK courts, on their own reading thereof, to attribute direct effect and primacy to EU norms and, further, to interpret provisions of Union law in conformity with principles established by the Court of Justice.

The UK's exit from the European Union is tied domestically to an express political commitment to repeal the ECA through the enactment of the Great Repeal Bill (GRB).[3] The GRB (forthcoming, 2017) will be used, first, to 'nationalise' the body of law that currently falls within the scope of the EU Treaties – the EU *acquis*. It will also, secondly, establish new delegated powers to enable the repeal or subsequent amendment of specific aspects of the nationalised EU *acquis* post withdrawal. Both aspects are already attracting considerable parliamentary and academic scrutiny – with the spotlight on proposals to use the GRB to establish sweeping new executive competences to amend primary legislation.[4] By contrast, the impact of the repeal of the ECA on domestic courts and their institutional functions has received comparatively little attention. This chapter addresses that gap.

In summary, it is argued that the repeal of the ECA provides the UK Government, acting through Parliament, with the opportunity – but not obligation – to determine two related issues affecting the future institutional position of UK courts. First, and of greatest immediacy, how should domestic courts interpret the EU *acquis* that the UK Government intends to nationalise through the GRB at the point of withdrawal? Secondly, looking further ahead, what role should UK courts play in the interpretation and enforcement of future international treaty obligations (for example, provisions of any UK/EU withdrawal agreement and subsequent bilateral trade deals)?

Analysis in this chapter is focused on the first issue: the judicial development of the EU *acquis* post withdrawal. Section 2 outlines the current normative framework under the ECA. That Act, it is argued, functions within the UK

---

[2]   Unless otherwise noted, 'UK courts' is employed throughout this chapter to reference the courts of the UK's 3 distinct legal orders: England and Wales, Scotland and Northern Ireland.

[3]   HM Government, *The United Kingdom's exit from and new partnership with the European Union* (Cm 9417, February 2017) section 1.

[4]   For a summary, see JS CAIRD, 'Legislating for Brexit: The Great Repeal Bill' (House of Commons Briefing Paper No 7793, 23 February 2017).

legal order as a domestic 'constitutional instruction' to UK courts to attribute
internal effect to EU norms in accordance with the Court of Justice's case law.
It is also shown to have radically transformed the institutional position of UK
courts within the domestic legal order. Thereafter, Section 3 turns to consider
the potential options open to the UK Government when repealing the ECA
through the GRB. Through comparative analysis, this chapter constructs two
distinct models as the basis for reform and discusses their varying impact on the
future status of EU law within the UK legal order. Finally, Section 4 considers
the nature of the Brexit process and reflects on its potential to catalyse lasting
domestic institutional change. Brexit, it is argued, is a paradigm example of a
triangulated political process.[5] The stakes are high for UK courts – and those
who activate them.

## 2.  THE CURRENT FRAMEWORK: THE ECA AS 'CONSTITUTIONAL INSTRUCTION' TO UK COURTS

The Court of Justice has consistently maintained that EU law takes effect within
Member States solely on the basis of the EU Treaties as the foundation of a
'new legal order' that is independent of the normative framework of public
international law (*Van Gend en Loos*).[6] As far as that Court is concerned, national
courts give effect to EU law domestically as component institutions of the EU
legal order.[7] The relationship is one of agency, with national courts assuming
the functions and responsibilities of decentralised Union courts. As the Court
of Justice puts it,

> 'Every national court must, in a case within its jurisdiction, apply [Union] law in its
> entirety and protect rights which the latter confers on individuals and must accordingly
> set aside any provision of national law which may conflict with it, whether prior or
> subsequent to the [Union] rule.'[8]

In common with their counterparts in nearly all Member States, UK courts have
never accepted the Court of Justice's assertion that the domestic effect of EU law
is exclusively a matter for Union law. For UK courts, the obligation to attribute

---

5   On triangulation, see P ROTHBAUER, 'Triangulation' in L GIVEN (ed), *The SAGE Encyclopedia of Qualitative Research Methods*, Sage, California 2008, pp 892–894.
6   Case 26/62, *Van Gend en Loos*, ECLI:EU:C:1963:1. For a recent restatement, see *Opinion 2/13 on the Accession of the EU to the European Convention on Human Rights*, ECLI:EU:C:2014:2454 at para 157.
7   See I MAHER, 'National Courts as European Community Courts' (2000) 14 *Legal Studies* 226; M CLAES, *The National Courts' Mandate in the European Constitution*, Hart Publishing, Oxford 2006; and B DE WITTE ET AL (eds), *National Courts and EU Law: New Issues, Theories and Methods*, Edward Elgar, Cheltenham 2016.
8   Case 106/77, *Simmenthal*, ECLI:EU:C:1978:49 at para 21.

domestic effect to EU law in accordance with decisions of the Court of Justice derives exclusively from national law – and the ECA specifically.[9] In summary, the ECA, as interpreted by the UK judiciary, is read as the source of two basic instructions to UK courts.

First, the ECA instructs UK courts to attribute direct effect to EU norms within the UK legal order. Put another way, it mandates that provisions of EU law shall be enforceable *as national law* before domestic courts.[10] The requirement to attribute direct effect to Union law encompasses the obligation to afford primacy to EU norms that conflict with any national measure irrespective of its domestic constitutional status.[11] As the Supreme Court restated in *Miller*,

'The 1972 Act … authorises a dynamic process by which, without further primary legislation (and, in some cases, even without any domestic legislation), EU law not only becomes a source of UK law, but actually takes precedence over all domestic sources of UK law, including statutes.'[12]

Secondly, and in line with the Court of Justice's agency theory, the ECA instructs UK courts to act as 'European courts' when hearing disputes that engage questions of EU law. More specifically, section 3(1) prescribes that:

'For the purposes of all legal proceedings any question as to the meaning or effect of any of the Treaties, or as to the validity, meaning or effect of any [EU instrument], shall be treated as a question of law (and, if not referred to the European Court, be for determination as such in accordance with the principles laid down by and any relevant [decision of the European Court]).'

In combination, the key instructions set out in the ECA have had a fundamental impact on the position and functioning of UK courts. Exercising their European mandate, UK courts are directly responsible for the enforcement of EU legal norms;[13] contribute proactively to the further development of EU law through judicial interpretation;[14] and manage the administration of remedies – including,

---

9   See *R v Secretary of State for Transport, ex p Factortame Limited and others* [1991] 1 AC 603; *Thorburn v Sunderland City Council* [2002] EWHC (Admin) 195; *Pham v Secretary of State for the Home Department* [2015] UKSC 19; *Miller*, above n 1.

10  ECA, section 2(1). See also ECA, section 2(2) read in conjunction with section 2(4).

11  Case 6/64, *Costa v ENEL*, ECLI:EU:C:1964:66 and Case 11/70, *Internationale Handelsgesellschaft mbH*, ECLI:EU:C:1970:114.

12  *Miller*, above n 1 at [60].

13  See Case 244/80, *Foglia v Novello*, ECLI:EU:C:1981:302 at para 16 and Joined Cases C-422/93 to C-424/93, *Zabala Erasun and Others*, ECLI:EU:C:1995:183 at para 15.

14  For UK-specific examples, see eg Case 152/84, *Marshall v Southampton and South-West Hampshire Area Health Authority*, ECLI:EU:C:1986:84; Case C-200/02, *Zhu and Chen v Secretary of State for the Home Department*, ECLI:EU:C:2004:639; Case C-413/00, *Baumbast and R v Secretary of State for the Home Department*, ECLI:EU:C:2002:493; Case C-362/12, *Test Claimants in the FII Group Litigation v Commissioners of Inland Revenue*, ECLI:EU:C:2013:834.

most importantly, the *Francovich* action for damages.[15] In addition, the integration of the EU legal order into national law through the ECA has also shattered domestic judiciary hierarchies and affected key changes to entrenched approaches to judicial interpretation. Space precludes detailed analysis of each of these individual points. However, the following paragraphs précis the most significant constitutional changes to the position and function of UK courts under the ECA.

For UK courts, the most significant transformative impact as a direct result of the ECA instruction is the acquisition of competence to review primary domestic legislation. Under the doctrine of parliamentary sovereignty – the cornerstone of the UK constitutional order – national courts do not ordinarily enjoy jurisdiction to scrutinise Acts of Parliament.[16] Their powers of review extend only to include secondary instruments – including, of course, those enacted pursuant to section 2(2) of the ECA in order to implement obligations arising under the EU Treaties (for example, EU Directives). The exercise of judicial review functions over primary law as a consequence of the UK's membership of the EU remains a unique feature. Its closest equivalent is section 4 of the Human Rights Act 1998, which grants UK courts competence to issue 'declarations of incompatibility' against primary UK law for non-compliance with fundamental rights standards incorporated into domestic law through that Act. The effect of such declarations is, however, incomparable to that attaching to a finding that domestic law is incompatible with EU law. With respect to the latter, UK courts are directed (mandated) to *disapply* the incompatible national law to the extent that it conflicts with the demands of Union law.[17]

Secondly, the ECA has significantly enhanced the scope for UK courts to contribute directly to policy-making through judicial interpretation. This follows, first and foremost, as a consequence of the section 3 ECA obligation to 'adjudicate European' when hearing disputes that engage questions of EU law. The EU legal method, developed by the Court of Justice, differs markedly from the standard rules of statutory construction and methods of legal interpretation that operate domestically.[18] Pursuant to Parliament's instruction

---

[15] Joined Cases C-6/90 and 9/90, *Francovich and others v Italy*, ECLI:EU:C:1991:428.

[16] For analysis of the constitutional principle, see J GOLDSWORTHY, *The Sovereignty of Parliament: History and Philosophy*, Oxford University Press, Oxford 2001 and, recently, M GORDON, *Parliamentary Sovereignty in the UK Constitution: Process, Politics and Democracy*, Hart Publishing, Oxford 2015.

[17] *Simmenthal*, above n 8 at para 21.

[18] For detailed analysis of the approach under English law, see F BENNION, *Bennion on Statutory Interpretation*, 6th edn, Butterworths, Oxford 2013. Similarly for Scots law, see H MACQUEEN and I D WILLOCK, *The Scottish Legal System*, 5th edn, Bloomsbury, London 2013. On the Court of Justice and its legal method, see U NEERGAARD ET AL (eds), *European Legal Method*, DJØF, Copenhagen 2011.

in section 3 ECA, domestic judges have, for example, expressly referenced the fact that that:

'When interpreting national law transposing a Directive we must apply a teleological approach to interpretation – not the normal rules of statutory interpretation in English/UK law, which allow recourse to a linguistic "simple matter of language" approach.'[19]

The additional space opened up for domestic courts to contribute to the development of law through recourse to the more dynamic teleological method of interpretation applicable to Union law is further enhanced by the preliminary reference procedure.[20] That procedure places UK courts in direct conversation with the Court of Justice – one of the EU's most dynamic policy actors.[21] Through the ECA, UK courts are empowered to request binding interpretations of EU law (and also decisions on the validity of secondary Union law) by way of reference to the Luxembourg Court. Under Article 267 TFEU, lower courts may request such references whereas Member State courts of last instance are obliged to request preliminary references – subject to limited exceptions.[22]

The preliminary reference procedure has proven a powerful judicial tool in the development of the EU legal order.[23] Among other things, it has enabled domestic courts to contribute to the expansion and refinement of substantive Union law. In *Jessy St Prix*, for example, the UK Supreme Court recently made effective use of the preliminary reference procedure to provide the Court of Justice with an opportunity to extend the scope of protection afforded to EU nationals who are seeking to retain 'worker' status pursuant to Article 7(3) of Directive 2004/38 in circumstances where they have ceased employment.[24] The applicant, a French

---

[19]  *Aladeselu v Secretary of State for the Home Department* [2011] UKUT 253 (IAC); [2011] Imm AR 765; [2012] INLR 20 (UT (IAC)). See also, eg *PM (Turkey) v Secretary of State for the Home Department* [2011] UKUT 89 (IAC); [2011] Imm AR 413 (UT (IAC)).

[20]  For analysis, see M Bromber and N Fenger, *Preliminary References to the European Court of Justice*, Oxford University Press, Oxford 2014 and T Tridimas, 'Knocking on Heaven's Door: Fragmentation, Efficiency and Defiance in the Preliminary Reference Procedure' (2003) 41 *Common Market Law Review* 9.

[21]  On the dynamism of the Court of Justice, see M Adams et al (eds), *Judging Europe's Judges: The Legitimacy of the Case Law of the European Court of Justice*, Hart Publishing, Oxford 2013; G Conway, *The Limits of Legal Reasoning and the European Court of Justice*, Cambridge University Press, Cambridge 2013; M Dawson et al (eds), *Judicial Activism at the European Court of Justice*, Edward Elgar, Cheltenham 2013; T Horsley, 'Reflections on the Role of the Court of Justice as the "Motor" of European Integration: *Legal* Limits to Judicial Policymaking' (2013) 50 1 *Common Market Law Review* 931.

[22]  Article 267(2)/(3) TFEU (respectively). The Court of Justice has recognised a limited doctrine of *acte clair*: see Case 283/81, *CILFIT v Ministry of Health*, ECLI:EU:C:1982:335 at para 21.

[23]  For the classic account, see JHH Weiler, 'The Transformation of Europe' (1991) 100(8) *Yale Law Journal* 2403 and K Alter, *Establishing the Supremacy of European Law*, Oxford University Press, Oxford 2001.

[24]  *Jessy Saint Prix v Secretary of State for Work and Pensions* [2012] UKSC 49. Directive 2004/38/EC of the European Parliament and of the Council of 29 April 2004 on the right of citizens

national resident in the UK, had given up work owing to the stress of pregnancy and was refused income support on the grounds that she no longer qualified as a 'worker' for the purposes of EU law. That conclusion, however unfortunate for the applicant, was certainly consistent with Directive 2004/38 and the national implementing regulations. Nevertheless, the legal framework notwithstanding, the UK Supreme Court considered it desirable, using the preliminary reference procedure, to invite the Court of Justice to 'develop the concept of "worker" to meet this particular situation'.[25] The Luxembourg Court seized that opportunity and ruled that women who give up work because of the physical constraints of the late stages of pregnancy retain their status as 'workers' for the purposes of Union law, provided they return to employment within a reasonable period following childbirth.[26]

Thirdly, the availability of the preliminary reference procedure *to all domestic courts and tribunals* under the terms of the current ECA mandate has disrupted established domestic judicial hierarchies.[27] For lower UK courts, that procedure opens up space for direct dialogue with an external international court, the judgments of which are binding on all domestic courts – including the UK Supreme Court. Finally, and briefly, under the present ECA instruction, UK courts have also acquired an important role in the administration of remedies for breaches of EU law by (usually) state but also private action.[28] Importantly, national courts are not only obliged to apply existing domestic remedies to new legal situations engaging issues of Union law.[29] They are also required to apply *new* EU remedies established by the Court of Justice – specifically, the *Francovich* action for damages.[30]

## 3.    THE GRB AND UK COURTS: TWO MODELS FOR CHANGE

The repeal of the ECA through the GRB will terminate the legal framework that has defined the obligations of UK courts for the duration of the UK's membership of the (now) EU. What replaces that Act – and, more precisely, the terms of

---

of the Union and their family members to move and reside freely within the territory of the Member States [2005] OJ L197/4.

[25]    *Jessy Saint Prix*, above n 24 at [21].

[26]    Case C-507/12, *Jessy Saint Prix v Secretary of State for Work and Pensions*, ECLI:EU:C:2014:2007 at para 47.

[27]    On the empowerment thesis, see WEILER, above n 23 at p 2406.

[28]    On private action, see eg Case C-453/99, *Courage Ltd v Crehan and Crehan v Courage Ltd and Others*, ECLI:EU:C:2001:465. See M DOUGAN, *National Remedies before the Court of Justice: Issues of Harmonisation and Differentiation*, Hart Publishing, Oxford 2004.

[29]    See eg *ex p Factortame*, above n 9.

[30]    *Francovich*, above n 15.

Parliament's fresh instruction to national courts (where provided) – is absolutely critical to discussion of the impact of EU withdrawal on UK courts and their institutional functions within the domestic legal order post-Brexit.

This section uses comparative analysis to construct two alternative models that Parliament may select in order to manage the judicial development of the nationalised EU *acquis* post withdrawal. To a large extent, the two models available to Parliament apply *mutatis mutandis* to discussion of the second of the two issues highlighted in the Introduction (above). That issue addresses the future role of UK courts in the interpretation and enforcement of international obligations *outside the present EU context*; for example, pursuant to any new UK/non-EU bilateral trade deals. For the duration of its EU membership, the UK has not really been required to give much thought to that second issue. External trade policy is an exclusive EU competence and, moreover, the rules governing the domestic effect of external EU trade agreements remain a matter for Union, not Member State law.[31] That will likely change on both counts, post-Brexit.

## 3.1. MODEL 1: REPLACE THE CURRENT INSTRUCTION TO UK COURTS

For maximum continuity between the UK and EU legal orders post withdrawal, Parliament could include a so-called 'continuance clause' in the GRB as a replacement for the current instruction to UK courts set out in section 2 and section 3 ECA. By way of illustration, section 4(1) of the Jamaica (Constitution) Order in Council 1962 prescribes that:

'All laws which are in force in Jamaica immediately before the appointed day shall (subject to amendment or repeal by the authority having power to amend or repeal any such law) continue in force on and after that day, *and all [such] laws... shall, subject to the provisions of this section, be construed, in relation to any period beginning on or after the appointed day, with such adaptations and modifications as may be necessary to bring them into conformity with the provisions of this Order.*'[32]

With respect to the domestic interpretation of the nationalised EU *acquis*, a continuance clause of the above character in the GRB could be framed either statically or dynamically. Under the first alternative, Parliament would specify a cut-off date with respect to the future binding status of EU law and Court of Justice judgments within the UK legal order. Under the second prospective

---

[31]   See Article 3 TEU.
[32]   Emphasis added. See here also S Douglas-Scott, 'The 'Great Repeal Bill': Constitutional Chaos and Constitutional Crisis?', *UK Constitutional Law Blog* (10 October 2016) (available at <https://ukconstitutionallaw.org/>).

approach, a continuance clause would direct UK courts to continue to apply the nationalised EU *acquis* in accordance with EU law (and Court of Justice judgments) as it develops *subsequent* to the UK's withdrawal.

With respect to the static option, a number of key issues require careful consideration. In particular, what should UK courts do when faced with ambiguity in *existing* areas of EU law – including decisions of the Court of Justice that are to remain applicable domestically post withdrawal? If Parliament does not address this issue expressly in its replacement instruction in the GRB, it will ultimately fall to UK courts to resolve. The practical result of that omission may prove significant over time. In effect, UK courts would be left to determine the practical effect of the body of EU law declared 'binding' domestically at the point of withdrawal through a static continuance clause in the GRB. The repeal of the ECA will, of course, simultaneously also foreclose UK courts' access to the current legal mechanism for the resolution of disputes over the correct interpretation of EU norms: the preliminary reference procedure. The UK Government is committed to terminating the jurisdiction of the Court of Justice through the Article 50 TEU withdrawal process.[33]

Furthermore, a static continuance clause would also (ideally) need to instruct UK courts on the *ranking* of the nationalised EU *acquis* vis-à-vis ordinary domestic law. Specifically: should UK courts continue to attribute *primacy* to the nationalised EU *acquis* over all conflicting national law after withdrawal as before under the ECA? The repeal of the ECA will end the primacy of EU law within the UK legal order.[34] In the absence of any replacement legislative instruction in the GRB, there is no reason to expect UK courts to maintain the primacy of the nationalised EU *acquis* over ordinary national law as a matter of course. On the contrary, UK courts' express reference to the ECA as the specific source of the current direction to so do suggests otherwise. Accordingly, should Parliament wish to maintain the domestic application of the EU *acquis* to the same effect post withdrawal, it would be necessary (or at the very least desirable) to include an express instruction to that effect in any static continuance clause in the GRB.

A dynamic continuance clause presents additional challenges. First and foremost, Parliament would need to determine *how* it intends to 'lock' the UK and EU legal orders together prospectively – to the extent that it wishes to do so. One option would be to attribute direct effect to specific parts of the EU *acquis* that the UK has agreed to adhere to after withdrawal under the terms of the (expected) Article 50 TEU withdrawal agreement or, likewise, on a more permanent basis, under any subsequent UK/EU bilateral treaty(ies). The ECA is not the only precedent for this first option. Parliament has already legislated,

---

33    *The United Kingdom's exit from and new partnership with the European Union*, above n 3.
34    See *Miller*, above n 1 at [80] and Section 3.2 below.

for example, to provide for the direct effect of external international norms in other contexts. This includes, most comprehensively, the incorporation of ECHR rights into the domestic legal order through the Human Rights Act (HRA).[35]

Of course, it is important to stress that, with respect to ECHR rights, the manner in which Parliament has attributed direct effect to (incorporated) ECHR rights is very different from the approach under section 2 and section 3 of the ECA. With respect to ECHR obligations, Parliament has placed important limits on UK courts' powers to enforce the specific Convention rights incorporated into national law through the HRA. Under the HRA, for instance, UK courts do not enjoy any comparable competence to review primary legislation (ie Acts of Parliament) for compatibility with Convention rights (governed by section 4 HRA). Likewise, the instruction to interpret national law in line with ECHR rights – including ECtHR judgments – is far weaker than that which binds UK courts under the ECA (governed by section 3 HRA). Both these issues are discussed further below.

In any case, given the UK Government's political aversion to direct effect, the first option to structure a dynamic continuance clause – legislating to preserve the substance of the current instruction to UK courts under the ECA – is unlikely to find its way into the GRB. The Government's White Paper on Brexit makes no secret of its political hostility towards the direct effect of EU law and judgments of the Court of Justice, in particular.[36] Overall, the UK Government's current thinking on the structure of future links between the domestic and EU legal orders marks a clear departure from the present approach under the ECA. It strongly favours the introduction of weaker, state-managed dispute resolution mechanisms to manage the domestic enforcement of international norms. Such mechanisms would displace the current normative framework that provides – through the ECA – for the enforcement of EU law through private litigation before national courts using directly effective rights.[37]

A softer option would be to instruct UK courts to interpret the nationalised EU *acquis* in conformity with Union law as the latter develops post-Brexit. As a template for that instruction, a dynamic continuance clause in the GRB could seek to replicate the approach that is currently applied under section 3 HRA. That provision directs UK courts to interpret UK law (including primary legislation) in conformity with the ECHR rights incorporated into domestic law through the HRA.[38] It is worth noting that a similar interpretative obligation already binds

---

35    See J WADHAM ET AL (eds), *Blackstone's Guide to the Human Rights Act 1998*, 7th edn, Oxford University Press, Oxford 2015 and N KANG-RIOU ET AL (eds), *Confronting the Human Rights Act: Contemporary Themes and Perspectives*, Routledge, Abingdon 2012.
36    *The United Kingdom's exit from and new partnership with the European Union*, above n 3.
37    Ibid. See further Section 4 below.
38    For discussion, see H FENWICK ET AL (eds), *Judicial Reasoning under the UK Human Rights Act*, Cambridge University Press, Cambridge 2011 and B DICKSON, *Human Rights and the United Kingdom Supreme Court*, Oxford University Press, Oxford 2013.

UK courts pursuant to section 3 ECA. Under the doctrine of 'indirect effect' developed by the Court of Justice, UK courts are subject to a general obligation to interpret national law in line with EU law in disputes falling within the scope of the EU Treaties.[39] That obligation exists over and above the requirement to attribute primacy to directly effective EU norms in instances of conflict with provisions of national law.

Although 'softer' than direct effect, an interpretative obligation of the above kind would have the advantage of maintaining close links between the UK and EU legal orders post-Brexit. Specifically, it would instruct UK courts to continue to develop national law in harmony with future developments in Union law, whilst at the same time preserving space for national law to diverge as a matter of principle. In the hands of a willing court, a legislative instruction in the GRB to interpret UK law in conformity with, for instance, developments in EU case law, could be read to function in proxy for direct effect proper. That risk notwithstanding, an interpretative instruction of the above kind is, however, still arguably rather attractive politically: it satisfies the Government's 'take back control' headline narrative, whilst providing for the maintenance of practical links between the UK and EU legal orders post withdrawal.

Analysis of domestic case law on the strength of the interpretative obligation pursuant to section 3 HRA would provide useful insights into UK courts' likely approach to any similar instruction in the GRB.[40] Of course, it should not be forgotten that the approach of UK courts to section 3 HRA is itself the subject of separate and intense criticism within Government. In particular, the present Government maintains a longstanding aspiration to replace the HRA (including section 3 HRA) with a 'British Bill of Rights' the purpose of which is principally to weaken the impact of the ECHR and the Strasbourg Court's jurisprudence within domestic law. Thus, even as a softer and arguably rather appealing option, the introduction of an interpretative instruction in the GRB that is modelled on section 3 HRA may face just as much domestic political hostility as any proposal to maintain a legislative basis in the GRB for the continued direct effect of EU law post-Brexit.

## 3.2. MODEL 2: ISSUE NO REPLACEMENT INSTRUCTION TO UK COURTS

It is also open to Parliament to repeal the ECA without issuing any replacement instruction to UK courts with respect to the domestic effect of the EU *acquis*.

---

[39]  See eg Case 14/83, *Von Colson*, ECLI:EU:C:1984:153 and Case C-106/89, *Marleasing*, ECLI:EU:C:1990:395.

[40]  See eg *Ghaidan v Godin-Mendoza* [2004] UKHL 30 and *In re S (Minors)* [2002] UKHL 10. For analysis, see A KAVANAGH, *Constitutional Review under the UK Human Rights Act*, Cambridge University Press, Cambridge 2009 and also FENWICK ET AL, above n 38.

The GRB could simply seek to 'nationalise' that body of law without reference to its future domestic interpretation and/or enforcement. Should that be the case, UK courts can legitimately be expected to interpret the nationalised EU *acquis* in accordance with ordinary rules of domestic judicial interpretation.[41] It would arguably be rather bold for UK courts to conclude otherwise; for example, by asserting that the nationalised EU *acquis* should be attributed special status vis-à-vis ordinary domestic law in the absence of any replacement legislative instruction to that effect. As the UK Supreme Court reiterated forcefully in *Miller*, UK courts locate the current instruction to afford special treatment to the EU *acquis* expressly in the ECA and the doctrine of parliamentary sovereignty.[42]

Of course, UK courts could be bolder and see an opportunity to craft a new constitutional approach. In that connection, it is worth recalling that the terms of the current instruction to UK courts under the ECA were also shaped, in part, by the interpretative response of UK courts to the provisions of that Act. More precisely, it was left to domestic courts to reconcile the Court of Justice's case law on the direct effect and primacy of EU law with the cornerstone principle of parliamentary sovereignty. More likely, however, in the absence of any replacement instruction in the GRB, UK courts would continue to forge links between UK and EU law using established principles of domestic judicial interpretation.[43]

Over the last few decades, the English legal system has demonstrated its progressive openness to the use of external jurisprudence to aid statutory interpretation and support the development of the common law.[44] Within this environment, judgments of the Court of Justice would, in common with those from other jurisdictions, carry only persuasive authority domestically as 'foreign law.' The UK Supreme Court makes this point clear in *Miller* in anticipation of the repeal of the ECA. On its analysis:

> 'Upon the United Kingdom's withdrawal from the European Union, EU law will cease to be a source of domestic law for the future (even if the Great Repeal Bill provides that some legal rules derived from it should remain in force or continue to apply to accrued rights and liabilities), decisions of the Court of Justice will (again *depending on the precise terms of the Great Repeal Bill*) be of no more than persuasive authority.'[45]

It is difficult accurately to predict the degree to which UK courts would develop the nationalised EU *acquis* in conformity with future evolutions in EU law post

---

[41]    See *Miller*, above n 1 at [80]. See also above n 9 and the cases cited therein.
[42]    At [60].
[43]    See BENNION, above n 18 and MACQUEEN AND WILLOCK, above n 18.
[44]    See especially T BINGHAM, '"There is a World Elsewhere": The Changing Perspectives of English Law' (1992) 41 *International & Comparative Law Quarterly* 513 and *Fairchild v Glenhaven Funeral Services Ltd* [2002] UKHL 22.
[45]    At [80] (emphasis added).

withdrawal, should Union law transition to 'foreign law' following the repeal of the ECA. As a practical matter, UK courts would certainly not face any of the obstacles that judges and comparative law scholars traditionally associate with the use of foreign judgments in the development of national law.[46] The EU legal order has a single source of binding interpretations of Union law: the Court of Justice. The decisions of that Court are also readily available from a central online source and, moreover, invariably always published in English.

For UK courts, the key issues would not be practical, but more jurisprudential. In particular: what weight should be attached to the Court of Justice's future interpretations of EU law as a source of persuasive authority when developing the nationalised EU *acquis*? On the one hand, the pull towards conformity may be strong in particular substantive areas as a matter of practical expediency. On the other hand, however, UK courts may seek to exploit their new freedom to depart from or modify future evolutions in EU law in specific instances where these appear antagonistic to domestic legal principles or interpretative traditions. In any case, with established domestic hierarchies likely to be fully restored through the abolition of the preliminary reference procedure, it is the upper courts that would be expected to lead in determining the domestic judicial response to evolutions in EU law post-Brexit – and over time.

## 4. BREXIT AND UK COURTS: PROCESS AND INSTITUTIONAL IMPACT

As the preceding analysis has demonstrated, the UK Government, acting through Parliament, is able to select from two competing models (and the options within both) to manage the judicial development of the nationalised EU *acquis* post withdrawal. In so doing, it can also draw directly on its experience with existing templates – most notably under the HRA. Shifting the spotlight to broader issues, this section turns to consider, first, the nature of the Brexit process as a political exercise and, secondly, the potential institutional impact of changes to the current domestic role of UK courts post withdrawal. To what extent is the UK Government actually free to restructure unilaterally the terms of the current ECA instruction to UK courts through the GRB? And what is at stake for UK courts and, crucially, the individuals who activate them to protect their rights?

---

[46] For discussion, see M ANDEMAS AND D FAIRGRIEVE, 'Courts and Comparative Law: In Search of a Common Language for Open Legal Systems' in M ANDEMAS and D FAIRGRIEVE (eds), *Courts and Comparative Law*, Oxford University Press, Oxford 2015.

## 4.1.  MANAGING REFORM: TRIANGULATED DYNAMICS

The Government's White Paper on Brexit indicates that it presently favours radical change to the present constitutional instruction to UK courts under the ECA.[47] In particular, it is publicly opposed to the continued attribution of direct effect to international (EU) treaty norms and, moreover, the maintenance of any role for the Court of Justice in their interpretation. The preservation of these specific and fundamental aspects of the EU legal order under a new UK/EU institutional settlement is viewed as irreconcilable with what the Government has internalised as a strong domestic political mandate to 'take back control' of UK law-making following the outcome of the June 2016 referendum on EU membership. Unfortunately for the UK Government, the extent to which it will succeed in delivering on its aspirations for a new relationship with the EU27 on its preferred terms is not within its exclusive control. The final settlement will be not determined by the UK acting alone, but through a triangulated political process that is conditioned by two other key variables.[48]

First, and most significantly, the terms of any replacement instruction to UK courts in the GRB will necessarily reflect the extent to which domestic law is required both *legally* – as a matter of international law – and *practically* to maintain effective links with the EU legal order post withdrawal. That question will only be resolved in time through political negotiation and inevitable compromise. In large part, it will be conditioned by agreement on several headline issues. These include, inter alia, the terms of the UK's future relationship with (or possibly within) the EU internal market, its membership (or not) of the EU Customs Union, and its continued participation in the institutional framework of the EU.[49]

Secondly, and looking further ahead, the Government's preferences with respect to changes to the institutional role of UK courts post-Brexit will be shaped, in turn, by the reaction of national courts. Under the doctrine of parliamentary sovereignty, domestic courts can be expected faithfully to execute Parliament's instructions to them with respect to the internal effect of international treaty norms. This prediction applies with respect to both the internal interpretation and enforcement of past obligations (for example, the EU *acquis*) and any future international treaty commitments (for example, binding provisions of any UK/EU withdrawal agreement and subsequent bilateral treaties).

Given the triangulated nature of the Brexit process, the UK Government's announcement that it intends to prepare and enact the GRB in the next

---

[47]  *The United Kingdom's exit from and new partnership with the European Union*, above n 3, Section 2.

[48]  ROTHBAUER, above n 5.

[49]  See further the contribution by P CRAIG (Ch 15) in this edited collection.

parliamentary session (ie before any UK/EU withdrawal agreement is finalised under Article 50 TEU) is therefore rather striking. One would expect the detail of what is intended to replace the ECA – and, specifically, the terms of the current constitutional instruction to UK courts – to *follow*, not precede, agreement with the EU27 over the terms of the UK's exit. That is the usual sequencing with respect to the implementation of any adjustments to the domestic legal order to reflect changes to the UK's international commitments. The enactment of the ECA, for example, post-dated the UK's signature of the Treaty of Accession 1972 – the international treaty that paved the way for its accession to the (then) European Communities.

## 4.2. INSTITUTIONAL IMPACT: WHAT IS AT STAKE FOR UK COURTS AND LITIGANTS?

At the time of writing, it remains unclear where the Article 50 TEU exit process will ultimately position the UK – and its domestic courts. The withdrawal procedure has only just commenced (29 March 2017). Wherever the dust settles, it is beyond doubt, however, that the UK's departure from the EU is likely to precipitate potentially far-reaching changes to the role and functions of UK courts within the domestic legal order. And there is a lot at stake for domestic courts and, moreover, those who activate them to protect their rights.

With respect to UK courts, the current ECA mandate was shown to have significantly enhanced their institutional power within the domestic legal order. It has also done so on a far greater scale than is typical within most other EU Member States owing to the peculiar characteristics of the UK constitution with its doctrine of parliamentary sovereignty.[50] Under the ECA, UK courts have acquired (and now stand to lose) powers of judicial review the likes of which (certain) courts within other Member States have exercised domestically for years as designated guardians of their respective national constitutions.[51] For most other Member State courts, EU membership simply expanded the existing powers of domestic courts to monitor the constitutionality of national legislation through the integration of a new set of binding (EU) norms into those Member State legal systems.

Likewise, changes to the current ECA mandate have the potential significantly to reduce the institutional role of UK courts as policy innovators. As shown in Section 2, the present instruction under section 3 ECA to 'adjudicate European'

---

[50]   For an overview of the reception of EU law within Member States, see MAHER, above n 7, CLAES, above n 7 and DE WITTE ET AL, above n 7.

[51]   For analysis, see eg A STONE SWEET, *Governing with Judges: Constitution: Constitutional Politics in Europe*, Oxford University Press, Oxford 2000.

in disputes that fall within the scope of the EU Treaties has liberated UK courts from the normal rules of statutory interpretation, which, by comparison, restrict the scope for judicial law-making with their preference for the adoption of literal rather than teleological approaches to legal reasoning. Coupled with the preliminary reference procedure, the instruction to apply European law reasoning has empowered UK courts *at all levels* to play a pivotal role in advancement of EU law through judicial interpretation. Working together with the Court of Justice, UK courts and tribunals have contributed directly to some of the most significant developments in EU policy in the areas of employment law, equal treatment and the rights of EU citizenship.[52]

Separately, a decision to repeal the ECA without any replacement instruction to UK courts (Model 2) opens up the possibility that the nationalised EU *acquis* may evolve differently *within* the UK legal order. In particular, and over time, the upper tiers of the English, Northern Irish and (most likely) Scottish judiciaries may adopt different approaches to the development of the nationalised EU *acquis*. Under the terms of the ECA, the UK's three distinct legal systems have effectively been locked together through a shared legislative instruction to attribute direct effect and primacy to Union law. That instruction has functioned as a powerful force for *unification* across the UK's three legal systems in vast areas of substantive policy. Notably, the possible introduction of fragmentation *within* the UK legal order as a result of the Brexit process is a development that the UK Government is expressly seeking to avoid.[53] Its choices over the terms of any replacement constitutional instruction to UK courts are intimately connected with the achievement of that political objective.

Whichever of the two models is ultimately chosen for the GRB, the repeal of the ECA will not certainly extinguish the role of UK courts in the development of domestic law post-Brexit – including the nationalised EU *acquis*. However, the nature of that contribution can be expected to take shape under very different operating conditions. At the very least, it would seem likely that UK courts will, on current projections, no longer be able to scrutinise primary legislation for compliance with future evolutions in the scope of directly effective EU norms post withdrawal. At the same time, however, the expected abolition of the preliminary reference procedure as a mechanism to secure binding interpretations of Union law will restore established domestic judicial hierarchies. More precisely, upper courts will once again be empowered to impose discipline on (and demonstrate leadership to) inferior national courts and tribunals in all areas of domestic law presently within the scope of the EU Treaties.

---

[52] See n 14 above and the case law cited therein.
[53] *The United Kingdom's exit from and new partnership with the European Union*, above n 3. On devolution generally, see the contribution by J HUNT (Ch 2) in this edited collection.

The UK's withdrawal from the EU also has serious potential ramifications for those who activate UK courts to assert their rights. More precisely, it is submitted that individuals (whether based in the UK or elsewhere in the EU) should be particularly alert to the UK Government's aspiration to secure a new normative basis for the domestic enforcement of international treaty norms, including, for example, the provisions of any future UK/EU bilateral trade deal. The present approach, implemented within the UK level through the ECA, gives party litigants a direct stake in the enforcement of directly effective provisions of Union law throughout the EU.[54] As the Luxembourg Court ruled in *Van Gend en Loos*:

> 'The vigilance of individuals concern to protect their rights amounts to an effective supervision in addition to the supervision entrusted by Articles [258 and 259 TFEU] to the diligence of the Commission and of the Member States.'

The system of decentralised private enforcement is a remarkable feature of the EU legal order. It is also highly efficient. A UK national (or UK-based SME) faced with regulatory obstacles to the importation of her (its) products into France or refused access to the German services market can enforce her (its) rights directly before the French and German courts respectively – and even seek damages from those Member States under specific conditions.[55] The same applies with respect to the enforcement of directly effective EU norms within the UK.

The UK Government is committed to replacing the above system of decentralised private enforcement with weaker, state-managed dispute resolution mechanisms.[56] Such mechanisms are common features in international trade agreements, including the recently concluded EU/Canada Comprehensive Economic and Trade Agreement (CETA).[57] They typically provide for the public enforcement of international treaty obligations concluded between states as contracting parties.[58] Individual traders faced with obstacles to trade that are attributable to the activities of contracting states must look to (usually) their home state to enforce the relevant treaty obligations against the defaulting state.

---

[54]   *Van Gend en Loos*, above n 6.

[55]   *Francovich*, above n 14.

[56]   For discussion, see JD MERRILLS, *International Dispute Settlement*, 5th edn, Cambridge University Press, Cambridge 2011 and P VAN DEN BOSSCHE and W ZUDOC, *The Law and Policy of the World Trade Organization: Text, Cases and Materials*, 3rd edn, Cambridge University Press, Cambridge 2012, Ch 3.

[57]   Comprehensive Economic and Trade Agreement between Canada, of the one part, and the European Union and its Member States, of the other part, available at: <http://data.consilium.europa.eu/doc/document/ST-10973-2016-INIT/en/pdf>.

[58]   Likewise, states do not generally attribute direct effect to WTO obligations (with the exception of Mexico). See P VAN DEN BOSSCHE and D PRÉVOST, *Essentials of WTO Law*, Cambridge University Press, Cambridge 2016, p 12.

The decision to do so is a political one over which the individual ultimately has no direct control – all the more so if they wield little or no market power.

In addition, the UK national (or UK-based SME) that is faced with regulatory obstacles to the importation of her (its) products into France or refused access to the German services market cannot expect to receive damages for the economic impact of the treaty violation in question. Any sanctions are addressed to contracting parties and, where imposed, often bare little direct correlation to the violation in question.[59] Outside the EU legal framework, individuals enjoy specific protection in international trade law principally as investors in accordance with bi- and multilateral investment treaties and/or specific investor protection clauses included in international treaties.[60] These instruments and clauses are frequently criticised for operating primarily to favour the economic interests of powerful foreign investors.[61] Bad news for the next generation of Dutch chemical importers (*van Gend en Loos*), Belgian air stewards (*Defrenne v Sabena*) and British dieticians (*Marshall v Southampton Health Authority*) who seek to assert their rights under any UK/EU withdrawal and/or bilateral trade agreement that protects individual rights exclusively on that basis.[62]

## 5. CONCLUDING REMARKS

On 29 March 2017, the UK Government formally notified the European Council of its decision to activate Article 50 TEU. At the time of writing, it would challenge even Nostradamus to predict where the Article 50 TEU exit process will ultimately position the UK – and its domestic courts. For its part, the UK Government has initiated the process of change by outlining an ambitious 'wish list' of desired reforms to the current UK/EU relationship, framed by 12 overarching principles.[63] In summary, its narrative is one that would appear to seek principally *institutional* rather than substantive reform. With relatively few exceptions (immigration policy being the main one),[64] the UK's stated ambition is essentially to preserve much of the present substance of EU integration, albeit through the establishment of new institutional arrangements that would

---

[59]    Ibid, Ch 8.
[60]    See D COLLINS, *An Introduction to International Investment Law*, Cambridge University Press, Cambridge 2016 and R DOLZER and C SCHREUER, *Principles of International Investment Law*, 2nd edn, Oxford University Press, Oxford 2012. See also the contribution by M SATTOROVA (Ch 13) in this edited collection.
[61]    See SP SUBEDI, *International Investment Law: Reconciling Policy and Principle*, Hart Publishing, Oxford 2016.
[62]    *Van Gend en Loos*, above n 6; Case 149/77, *Defrenne v Sabena*, ECLI:EU:C:1978:130; *Marshall*, above n 14.
[63]    *The United Kingdom's exit from and new partnership with the European Union*, above n 3.
[64]    Ibid, Section 5.

effectively release the UK from the fundamental legal, political and financial obligations that attach to EU membership. The Government's thinking on precisely *how* it intends to achieve this ambitious, and some might say frankly audacious, objective remains as yet unclear.

This chapter has examined the implications for domestic courts of the UK's decision to withdraw from the EU. Its central claim is that future changes to UK courts' institutional functions post-Brexit are tied domestically to the Government's political commitment to repeal the ECA. For the duration of the UK's membership of the (now) EU, that Act, it is has been argued, has functioned as the source of a domestic constitutional instruction to UK courts to give internal effect to EU law in proceedings falling within the scope of Union law. What replaces that Act – and, more precisely, the terms of Parliament's fresh instruction to national courts (where provided) – is absolutely critical to discussion of the impact of EU withdrawal on UK courts and their future institutional functions within the domestic legal order post-Brexit.

Thus far, the impact of the repeal of the ECA on domestic courts and their present institutional functions has received comparatively little political and scholarly attention – in contrast to other aspects of the proposed GRB. This chapter has addressed that gap. In summary, it has been argued that the anticipated repeal of the ECA through the enactment of the GRB provides the UK Government, acting through Parliament, with the opportunity – but not obligation – to determine two related issues affecting the future institutional position of UK courts. First, and of greatest immediacy, how should domestic courts interpret the EU *acquis* that the UK Government intends to 'nationalise' through the GRB at the point of withdrawal? Secondly, looking further ahead, what role should UK courts play in the interpretation and enforcement of future international treaty obligations (for example, provisions of any UK/EU withdrawal agreement and subsequent bilateral trade deals)?

This chapter has focused principally on exploring potential responses to the first issue: the range of options that Parliament may select in order to manage the judicial development of the nationalised EU *acquis* post withdrawal. It employed comparative analysis to construct two alternative models for change. The first model anticipates the issue of a replacement constitutional instruction to UK courts in the GRB. The second model does not. Both models are flexible enough to accommodate the full spectrum of domestic political preferences. They can be used to preserve the substance of the current instruction on a new statutory basis, link the UK and EU legal systems through weaker interpretative obligations or, most dramatically, to relegate the status of Union law to 'foreign law'.

As a matter of domestic politics, the UK Government, acting through Parliament, enjoys considerable freedom to alter the institutional functions of national courts through the Brexit process. It has a free choice between the two competing models and the varying options that both offer. At present, its preferences favour more radical change. Most obviously, the UK Government is publicly opposed to the continued attribution of direct effect to international (EU) treaty norms and, moreover, the maintenance of any role for the Court of Justice in their interpretation. As this chapter has argued, should that view triumph, it will have far-reaching implications for courts and, crucially, those who activate them. In more specific terms, it has the potential to extinguish domestic courts' exceptional powers of judicial review over primary legislation, significantly curtail their role as direct policy-makers in vast areas of substantive policy, and even introduce new sites of legal fragmentation *within* the UK legal order.

The future role of UK courts post-Brexit will not, however, be determined by domestic political preferences alone. The decision to trigger Article 50 TEU has initiated a complex triangulated process, the outcome of which the UK Government does not exclusively control. On the contrary, as this chapter has argued, changes to the institutional role of UK courts as a result of the UK's departure from the EU will ultimately *and necessarily* reflect the extent to which domestic law is required both *legally* – as a matter of international law – and *practically* to maintain effective links with the EU legal order post withdrawal. Clarity on that fundamental issue will only emerge in time as a direct result of the Brexit negotiations. And the process of change does not end there. UK courts will, in turn, shape the impact of the UK's withdrawal from the EU through their institutional response to any replacement constitutional instruction included in the GRB – or absence thereof. Project Brexit begins.

## 6.  POSTSCRIPT[65]

Shortly after this chapter was completed, the UK Government published details of its draft Great Repeal Bill in its White Paper, *Legislating for the United Kingdom's withdrawal from the European Union*.[66] In summary, the White Paper sets out the Government's ambition to use the GRB to do three things: (1) repeal the ECA; (2) nationalise the EU *acquis* at the point of withdrawal; and (3) establish new powers to 'correct' that body of newly repatriated national law using secondary legislation.

With respect to UK courts, the White Paper announces the UK Government's intention to use the GRB to restore full domestic control over the interpretation and enforcement of the nationalised EU *acquis*– labelled 'EU-derived law' in the White Paper.[67] It leaves no doubt that, once the UK leaves the EU, domestic

---

[65]  Added 22 May 2017.
[66]  Department for Exiting the European Union, *Legislating for the United Kingdom's withdrawal from the European Union* (Cm 9446, March 2017).
[67]  Ibid, para 2.7.

courts shall enjoy exclusive competence to interpret EU-derived law with reference, where appropriate, to the EU Treaties and the case law of the Court of Justice as both exist at the moment of withdrawal.[68] In addition, the GRB will also be used to preserve the primacy of EU-derived law vis-à-vis ordinary domestic law.[69] However, where a conflict arises between EU-derived law and *new* primary legislation, the latter is to take precedence.[70] Accordingly, and over time, domestic courts – including the UKSC – can expect to see a significant reduction of their extraordinary competence to set aside primary UK legislation. That will profoundly restructure the institutional relationship between the judiciary and legislature established under the ECA.

Significantly, the White Paper proposes attributing pre-Brexit judgments of the Court of Justice equivalent domestic status to UKSC decisions.[71] That proposal goes some way to providing clarity on the ranking of EU-derived norms within the domestic legal order post-Brexit. In practical terms, it could also limit the scope for UK courts to adjust some of the most significant aspects of the nationalised EU *acquis* over time through judicial interpretation. This applies with respect to the activities of all domestic courts – including the UKSC. As the White Paper details, it is rare for the UKSC to depart from its previous decisions or those of its predecessor, the House of Lords.[72] In accordance with its Practice Statement, this occurs only exceptionally and 'when it appears right to do so.' The Government's White Paper states clearly that it would expect the UKSC to 'take a similar, sparing approach to departing from [nationalised] CJEU case law.'[73]

Overall, the UK Government's proposals fit neatly within the first of the two models constructed in this chapter (see Section 3.1). As its White Paper sets out, the UK Government intends to use the GRB, in part, to issue fresh instruction to domestic courts in place of sections 2 and 3 of the ECA. The precise wording of that revised instruction will be clarified when the draft GRB is presented to Parliament. It can, however, be reasonably expected to include fresh direction to UK courts in line with the White Paper's key statements on the status of EU-derived law within the UK legal order post withdrawal and, moreover, the principles that should govern its future domestic interpretation – summarised above.

What remains absent from the White Paper is a more realistic appreciation of the fundamentally triangulated nature of the Brexit process. The UK Government's proposals – with which it is committed to push ahead in the next

---

68    Ibid, paras 2.9–2.17.
69    Ibid, paras 2.18–2.20.
70    Ibid, para 2.20.
71    Ibid, para 2.16.
72    Ibid.
73    Ibid.

Parliament – continue to express domestic political preferences. As this chapter has argued, the Brexit process and, more specifically, the future role of UK courts within the domestic legal order will not be determined by the UK alone. Changes to the institutional role of UK courts as a result of the UK's departure from the EU will ultimately and necessarily reflect the extent to which domestic law is required both legally – as a matter of international law – and practically to maintain effective links with the EU legal order post withdrawal. Clarity on that fundamental issue will only emerge in time as a direct result of the Brexit negotiations

The Government's determination to detach the UK from the EU legal order – and the Court of Justice in particular – on the terms outlined in its White Paper is already subject to significant external pressure. For one thing, the EU27 are fully committed to maintaining a key role for the Court of Justice within the UK legal order post-Brexit – at the very least in order to guarantee the protection of specific categories of legal rights under the anticipated UK/EU withdrawal agreement. The Council Decision of 22 May 2017 adopting the EU Commission's draft Brexit negotiating directives formalised that commitment in clear terms.[74] Clearly something will have to give. The UK Government could very well find itself compelled to revisit some of the other reform options outlined in this chapter in order to secure a withdrawal agreement with the EU27 – whatever its domestic political preferences.

---

[74] ANNEX to Council decision (EU, Euratom) 2017/… authorising the opening of negotiations with the United Kingdom of Great Britain and Northern Ireland for an agreement setting out the arrangements for its withdrawal from the European Union XT 21016/17 ADD 1 REV 2.

# PART II
# SUBSTANTIVE POLICIES

# CHAPTER 5

# BREXIT AND EMPLOYMENT LAW

Catherine Barnard*

*'As we repeal the European Communities Act, we will convert the "acquis" … into British law. When the Great Repeal Bill is given Royal Assent, Parliament will be free – subject to international agreements and treaties with other countries and the EU on matters such as trade – to amend, repeal and improve any law it chooses. But by converting the acquis into British law, we will give businesses and workers maximum certainty as we leave the European Union. The same rules and laws will apply to them after Brexit as they did before. Any changes in the law will have to be subject to full scrutiny and proper Parliamentary debate. And let me be absolutely clear: existing workers' legal rights will continue to be guaranteed in law – and they will be guaranteed as long as I am Prime Minister.'*

British Prime Minister, Theresa May, party conference speech,
1 October 2016

## 1. INTRODUCTION

Priti Patel MP, one of the leading proponents of leaving the EU, said to the Institute of Directors that '[i]f we could just halve the burdens of the EU social and

---

* Trinity College, University of Cambridge.

employment legislation we could deliver a £4.3 billion boost to our economy and 60,000 new jobs'.[1] Liam Fox MP, who became Secretary of State for International Trade, had expressed similar sentiments prior to the referendum campaign: '[t]o restore international competitiveness we must begin by deregulating the labour market. Political objections must be overridden'.[2] His remarks re-emerged during the referendum campaign.

The Remain campaign, galvanised by these and other observations, responded. The StrongerIN website said:

'EU laws protect your rights in the workplace, meaning no government can scrap them.

Being in the EU protects your right to paid holiday leave, maximum working hours, equal treatment for men and women, rights for part-time workers, health and safety standards, parental leave, and protection from discrimination on the grounds of sex, race, religion, age disability and sexual orientation.

If we left the EU, your workers' rights would be up for debate and vulnerable to being scrapped. There could be years of uncertainty for you and your employers.'[3]

Francis O'Grady, General Secretary of the TUC, echoed these views:

'Leave the EU and lose your rights at work – that's the message that even Leave campaigners like Priti Patel are now giving. But which rights would go – your right to paid holidays, your right to parental leave, maybe protections for pregnant workers? The EU guarantees all these rights and more, and it's why Brexit is such a big risk for working people.'[4]

The vote to leave on 23 June 2016 therefore suggested a victory for those calling for a smaller state and less (employment) regulation.

But the Prime Minister, Theresa May, who came into office in July 2016, did not appear to share those views. This was made clear first, in her party conference speech cited in the opening lines of this chapter, and again in her Lancaster House speech on 17 January 2017, where she said:

'Indeed, under my leadership, not only will the government protect the rights of workers set out in European legislation, we will build on them. Because under this government,

---

[1]   Cited in <http://touchstoneblog.org.uk/2016/05/let-cats-priti-patel-suggests-lose-half-eu-work-rights-brexit/>.

[2]   <https://www.ft.com/content/2ee5b8de-5c8d-11e1-8f1f-00144feabdc0>. He continued: '[i]t is too difficult to hire and fire and too expensive to take on new employees. It is intellectually unsustainable to believe that workplace rights should remain untouchable while output and employment are clearly cyclical'.

[3]   <http://www.strongerin.co.uk/>.

[4]   <https://www.tuc.org.uk/international-issues/europe/eu-referendum/workplace-issues/priti-patel-reveals-leave-campaign-agenda>.

we will make sure legal protection for workers keeps pace with the changing labour market – and that the voices of workers are heard by the boards of publicly-listed companies for the first time.'[5]

She repeated those views in the House of Commons on 29 March 2017, the day Article 50 TEU was triggered. The White Paper on the Great Repeal Bill said much the same.[6]

Taking the Prime Minister's speech at face value, she has committed to maintain all of the EU-derived employment *acquis* so long as she is Prime Minister. So the Working Time, Fixed Term and Agency Work Regulations – widely regarded as doomed following Brexit – are safe, at least for now. There may be another reason, too, why workers' rights will have to be protected. Donald Tusk, President of the European Council, made clear in the draft Presidential Guidelines on negotiations over the UK's departure that any future free trade agreement between the EU and the UK should be 'balanced, ambitious and wide-ranging'. Further, such a deal must ensure 'a level playing field in terms of competition and state aid, and must encompass safeguards against unfair competitive advantages through, inter alia, fiscal, social and environmental dumping'.[7] The language was modified somewhat in the final version:[8] any free trade deal with the UK must 'encompass safeguards against unfair competitive advantages through, inter alia, tax, social, environmental and regulatory measures and practices'. But the intention is clear: the UK will have to respect workers' rights if there is to be a future trade deal, although at what level is not spelled out.

In this chapter, I want to consider the effect and implications of Theresa May's commitment to guarantee EU-derived employment rights. I will argue that there is reason for workers to be reassured but (1) only for so long as they are in work, and (2) only for so long as a future deal between the UK and the EU is reached. If these conditions are not satisfied, then the position of individuals could be very different for those in work and pretty catastrophic for those without work.

This chapter is structured around four questions. First, it asks: what does it mean that EU-derived workers' rights will continue to apply to the UK? Secondly, it considers what role decisions of the Court of Justice, so important in the employment field, will play post-Brexit.[9] Thirdly, it asks what opportunities

---

[5]   <https://www.gov.uk/government/speeches/the-governments-negotiating-objectives-for-exiting-the-eu-pm-speech>.
[6]   Department for Exiting the European Union, *Legislating for the United Kingdom's withdrawal from the European Union* (Cm 9446, March 2017) p 16.
[7]   European Council, *Draft guidelines following the United Kingdom's notification under Article 50 TEU* (published on 31 March 2017) para 19.
[8]   <http://www.consilium.europa.eu/en/press/press-releases/2017/04/29-euco-brexit-guidelines/>.
[9]   On which, see also the contribution by T HORSLEY (Ch 4) in this edited collection.

there may be in respect of the development of employment law for the UK post-Brexit. Fourthly, it raises the question what will happen to employment rights if there is no deal between the UK and the EU.

## 2. WHAT DOES IT MEAN THAT EU-DERIVED WORKERS' RIGHTS WILL CONTINUE TO APPLY TO THE UK?

### 2.1. INTRODUCTION

At one level, the maintenance in force of EU-derived workers' rights on Brexit day is no more than the Government has already committed itself to do for all EU-derived rights, whatever the field. The White Paper on Brexit said that the Great Repeal Bill (GRB) would have three primary elements:[10] what have subsequently become known as 'Repeal, Convert and Correct'. The 'Repeal' strand involves 'repeal[ing] the European Communities Act [ECA] 1972, and in so doing, return power to UK politicians and institutions'. This was the inevitable consequence of a vote to leave the EU.

Of more relevance for this chapter are the 'Convert' and 'Correct' strands. As far as 'Convert' is concerned, the Brexit White Paper says:

' … the Bill will preserve EU law where it stands at the moment before we leave the EU. Parliament (and, where appropriate, the devolved legislatures) will then be able to decide which elements of that law to keep, amend or repeal once we have left the EU. The UK courts will then apply those decisions of Parliament and the devolved legislatures.'[11]

In other words, the language of the 'Great *Repeal* Bill' is something of a misnomer: in fact it will be the Great Consistency Bill, freezing EU law on the date of Brexit and ensuring that it continues to operate post-Brexit. Specifically, the GRB will ensure that directly applicable EU rules (mainly EU Regulations) will continue to have effect in UK law. In fact, in the employment field, most EU measures come in the form of Directives, which have already been implemented in the UK. This legislation, including the important Equality Act 2010, will continue to stand, unaffected by the GRB. Where legislation has been adopted under powers in other Acts of Parliament, such as the Fixed Term Work Regulations 2002,[12]

---

[10] HM Government, *The United Kingdom's exit from and new partnership with the European Union* (Cm 9417, February 2017).
[11] Ibid, section 1.
[12] SI 2002/2034. These Regulations were adopted under the powers laid down in sections 45 and 51(1) of the Employment Act 2002.

this will also be unaffected by the GRB.[13] Where, as in the case of the Working Time Regulations 1998,[14] the legislation has been adopted under the (Henry VIII) powers in section 2(2) of the European Communities Act 1972, this legislation will be preserved by the GRB since the ECA itself will have been repealed.[15] So EU-derived employment law will be formally preserved.

As far as the 'Correct' strand is concerned, the Brexit White Paper says:

> 'Finally, the Bill will enable changes to be made by secondary legislation to the laws that would otherwise not function sensibly once we have left the EU, so that our legal system continues to function correctly outside the EU.'[16]

However, where the field of employment law differs is that, assuming the Prime Minister is as good as her word, it will not apparently be subject to the process of scrutiny and sifting to see whether those laws should be kept, amended or repealed.

## 2.2. WHAT ARE EU-DERIVED EMPLOYMENT LAWS?

So Theresa May's commitment raises the question as to what constitutes EU-derived employment law (see figure 1). It would certainly cover the legislation adopted under what is now Article 153 TFEU, the social policy legal basis, including the large number of Directives on health and safety at work, as well as the Directives covering working time, pregnant workers and young workers. More strikingly, the GRB White Paper indicates that Article 153 TFEU itself will continue to be relevant: 'our courts will continue to be able to look to the treaty provisions in interpreting EU laws that are preserved'.[17] The example given in the White Paper is how the Court of Justice used the legal basis of the Working Time Directive (what is now Article 153 TFEU) to steer the interpretation of the relevant provision in the *BECTU* case in favour of finding that a minimum period of employment with the same employer was not compatible with the Directive.[18] The UK courts will continue to be able to do the same.

---

[13]  For a full list of the range and sources of EU-derived UK legislation, see M FORD, Advice to the TUC prepared during the referendum campaign, <https://www.tuc.org.uk/international-issues/europe/eu-referendum/workers%E2%80%99-rights-europe-impact-brexit>.

[14]  SI 1998/1833.

[15]  *Legislating for the United Kingdom's withdrawal from the European Union*, above n 6, para 2.5.

[16]  *The United Kingdom's exit from and new partnership with the European Union*, above n 10, section 1.

[17]  *Legislating for the United Kingdom's withdrawal from the European Union*, above n 6, para 2.10.

[18]  Case C-173/99, *BECTU v Secretary of State for Trade and Industry*, ECLI:EU:C:2001:356.

Figure 1. The Range and Scope of EU Employment Rights

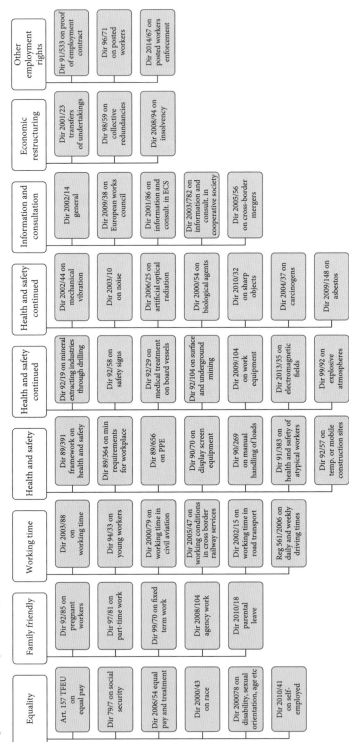

The principle of consistency of UK law pre- and post-Brexit would also cover the measures originally adopted under the more general legal bases contained in the EU Treaties but which were intended as social policy measures at a time when there was an absence of a distinct social policy legal basis. This would include the Directives on collective redundancies 98/59,[19] transfer of undertakings 2001/23[20] and protection of employees on insolvency 2008/94.[21]

Further, the principle of consistency means that the equality measures would be preserved, including Directive 2006/54 on equal pay and equal treatment for men and women[22] and the so-called 'Article 13 Directives'[23] extending the principle of equal treatment to other protected characteristics such as race, disability and age, through their incarnation in the Equality Act 2010. As the GRB White Paper says: '[t]his approach will give certainty to service providers and users, as well as employees and employers, creating stability in which the UK can grow and thrive'.[24]

Article 157 TFEU on equal pay for men and women, the only substantive provision on social policy found in the original Treaty of Rome, is also to be maintained. As the GRB White Paper says: '[w]here protections are provided by the EU Treaties as a final "backstop" – such as the right to rely on Article 157 … they will also be preserved'.[25] This is significant because Article 157 TFEU has played an important role in shaping the Equality Act 2010 and the UK's approach to eliminating discrimination in respect of, inter alia, occupational pension age. This will continue: as the White Paper says, 'there are rights in the EU Treaties that can be relied on directly in court by an individual, and the Great Repeal Bill will incorporate those rights into UK law'.[26]

In more recent years Article 157 TFEU has been used as a constitutional check on British legislation.[27] This will continue in respect of pre-Brexit UK adopted legislation:

'If, after exit, a conflict arises between two pre-exit laws, one of which is an EU-derived law and the other not, then the EU-derived law will continue to take precedence over

---

19    [1998] OJ L225/16.
20    [2001] OJ L82/16.
21    [2008] OJ L283/36.
22    [2006] OJ L204/23.
23    Directive 2000/43 [2000] OJ L180/22 and Directive 2000/78 [2000] OJ L303/16.
24    *Legislating for the United Kingdom's withdrawal from the European Union*, above n 6, 'Example 1' on p 16.
25    Ibid, p 19.
26    Ibid, para 2.11.
27    See eg *R v Secretary of State for Employment, ex p EOC* [1994] 2 WLR 409; [1994] IRLR 176; Case C-167/97, *R v Secretary of State for Employment, ex p Seymour-Smith*, ECLI:EU:C:1999:60; *R (Seymour-Smith) v Secretary of State for Employment* [2000] UKHL 12.

the other pre-exit law. Any other approach would change the law and create uncertainty as to its meaning.'[28]

Thus Article 157 TFEU will continue to enjoy supremacy over conflicting, pre-Brexit adopted UK legislation. However, post-Brexit, any ruling of the British courts which finds pre-Brexit legislation contrary to Article 157 TFEU can be overturned by the UK Parliament.

What about measures which are more on the margins of EU social policy, such as Article 56 TFEU and the Posted Workers Directive 96/71?[29] The core idea underpinning Article 56 TFEU is that, where a service provider wishes to use its own workforce to provide a service in another Member State, the labour law rules which apply to those 'posted' workers are those of the home state, not the host state. The Posted Workers Directive (PWD) has created an exception to that rule: in those areas of labour law listed in Articles 3(1)(a)–(g) PWD, host state law will apply. However, the *Laval* decision made clear that, as an exception to the principle of home state control, Articles 3(1)(a)–(g) had to be narrowly construed.[30] This has always sat uncomfortably with UK law, which has traditionally adopted a territorial approach to labour law: all of its labour law rules apply to all of those working in the UK provided they fall within the personal, temporal and material scope of the UK legislation. The UK has therefore never properly implemented the Posted Workers Directive and so has formally been in breach of EU law.[31] However, Article 56 TFEU itself, as well as the PWD, may both be removed as part of the UK's decision to take back control of immigration policy. On the other hand, the Public Procurement Regulations 2016 may continue to apply in the UK post-Brexit, and these envisage that services can be delivered by out-of-state service providers and their staff – so it may well be that the PWD will continue to have effect.

What about the Charter of Fundamental Rights? Labour lawyers have been somewhat ambivalent about the Charter.[32] While Title IV on Solidarity held

---

[28]    *Legislating for the United Kingdom's withdrawal from the European Union*, above n 6, para 2.20.

[29]    [1997] OJ L18/1. This Directive is now complemented by Directive 2014/67 [2014] OJ L159/11 on the enforcement of Directive 96/71/EC concerning the posting of workers in the framework of the provision of services. There is a proposal to amend Directive 96/71: see COM(2016) 128.

[30]    Case C-341/05, *Laval un Partneri*, ECLI:EU:C:2007:809; Case C-346/06, *Dirk Rüffert v Land Niedersachsen*, ECLI:EU:C:2008:189.

[31]    C BARNARD, 'The UK and Posted Workers: The Effect of *Commission v Luxembourg* on the Territorial Application of British Labour Law' (2009) 38 *Industrial Law Journal* 122.

[32]    C. BARNARD, 'The Silence of the Charter' in S DE VRIES, U BERNITZ and S WEATHERILL (eds), *The EU Charter of Fundamental Rights as a Binding Instrument: Five Years Old and Growing*, Hart Publishing, Oxford 2015.

much promise for improving workers' rights, in fact its content and application have been disappointing.[33] In perhaps the most controversial case, *Alemo-Herron*,[34] a reference from the UK courts about the interpretation of the UK's more generous implementation of the Transfer of Undertakings Directive, the Court used the Article 16 right to conduct a business to challenge and remove that higher protection since it was deemed to interfere with the employer's managerial freedom. At no stage did the Court consider the application of any of the provisions in the solidarity title as a counterweight to the employer's Article 16 right. The rights in the Equality Title have, however, offered more promise and been used to the greater benefit of workers.[35]

However, the GRB White Paper is clear:

'the Charter only applies to member states when acting within the scope of EU law, so its relevance is removed by our withdrawal from the EU. ... It cannot be right that the Charter could be used to bring challenges against the Government, or for UK legislation after our withdrawal to be struck down on the basis of the Charter. On that basis the Charter will not be converted into UK law by the Great Repeal Bill.'[36]

Nevertheless, the picture is more complicated than first appears. The GRB White Paper says that the Government's intention is that

'the removal of the Charter from UK law will not affect the substantive rights that individuals already benefit from in the UK. Many of these underlying rights exist elsewhere in the body of EU law which we will be converting into UK law. Others already exist in UK law, or in international agreements to which the UK is a party.'[37]

---

[33]  Case C-426/11, *Alemo-Herron v Parkwood Leisure*, ECLI:EU:C:2013:521; Case C-201/15, *AGET Iraklis*, ECLI:EU:C:2016:972.

[34]  *Alemo-Herron and Others v Parkwood Leisure Ltd*, ibid, paras 31–35:

'the interpretation of Article 3 of Directive 2001/23 must in any event comply with Article 16 of the Charter, laying down the freedom to conduct a business. [ ... ] In the light of Article 3 of Directive 2001/23, it is apparent that, by reason of the freedom to conduct a business, the transferee must be able to assert its interests effectively in a contractual process to which it is party and to negotiate the aspects determining changes in the working conditions of its employees with a view to its future economic activity. However, the transferee in the main proceedings is unable to participate in the collective bargaining body at issue. In those circumstances, the transferee can neither assert its interests effectively in a contractual process nor negotiate the aspects determining changes in working conditions for its employees with a view to its future economic activity. [ ... ] In those circumstances, the transferee's contractual freedom is seriously reduced to the point that such a limitation is liable to adversely affect the very essence of its freedom to conduct a business.'

[35]  Case C-176/12, *Association de médiation sociale*, ECLI:EU:C:2014:2.

[36]  *Legislating for the United Kingdom's withdrawal from the European Union*, above n 6, para 2.23.

[37]  Ibid, para 2.25.

It continues that,

'[a]s EU law is converted into UK law by the Great Repeal Bill, it will continue to be interpreted by UK courts in a way that is consistent with those underlying rights. Insofar as cases have been decided by reference to those underlying rights, that case law will continue to be relevant. In addition, insofar as such cases refer to the Charter, that element will have to be read as referring only to the underlying rights, rather than to the Charter itself.'[38]

This is a significant concession for employment rights, especially in the field of equality law. Even before the Charter, the principle of equal treatment was seen as a fundamental right and thus a general principle of EU law, and was influential in shaping the interpretation of EU equality Directives.[39] This will be preserved post-Brexit and it is these general principles which will do the heavy lifting now, rather than the Charter. So controversial decisions like *Mangold* and *Kücükdeveci*, on the horizontal application of the general principle of non-discrimination on the ground of age, are here to stay.[40] The language of *Kücükdeveci* is striking in this context – and useful for employment lawyers – since it contains an endorsement of equality as a general principle:

'It must be recalled here that ... Directive 2000/78 merely gives expression to, but does not lay down, the principle of equal treatment in employment and occupation, and that the principle of non-discrimination on grounds of age is a general principle of European Union law in that it constitutes a specific application of the *general principle of equal treatment*' (emphasis added).[41]

What about social partner agreements? Unsurprisingly, the role of the social partners (management and labour) is not mentioned in either White Paper. The agreements which they have entered into under the post-Maastricht Treaty collective route to legislation (for example: the agreements on part-time work, fixed-term work and parental leave), and which have been extended to all workers by means of EU Directives, have all been incorporated into UK law. Agreements which have not been negotiated via that route, such as the agreements on telework and on stress at work, already remain in the shadows of workers' rights. They have never been enforced in a UK court. However, there

---

38  Ibid, para 2.25.
39  See eg Case C-13/94, *P v S and Cornwall County Council*, ECLI:EU:C:1996:170.
40  Case C-144/04, *Mangold v Helm*, ECLI:EU:C:2005:709; Case C-555/07, *Kücükdeveci v Swedex GmbH & Co KG*, ECLI:EU:C:2010:21.
41  *Kücükdeveci v Swedex GmbH & Co KG*, ibid, para 50.

would be nothing to stop British trade unions from voluntarily adopting such measures; their legal effect will, however, remain limited.

In conclusion, EU-derived workers' rights will continue to apply in the UK. Employers are familiar with their obligations under EU law – under the rules on transfer of undertakings, under the health and safety legislation, and under the equality legislation. Many are sympathetic to the objectives of this legislation and respect their content. By contrast, the Regulations on information and consultation with workers' representatives[42] have never really taken root in the UK, in part because they are based on a Continental 'dual channel' model of industrial relations which has always sat uncomfortably with the British single channel approach.[43] Without the constant prodding of the EU Commission, these Regulations are likely to fall permanently into desuetude. They may not be repealed but they will become redundant in practice.

## 2.3.   REVISIONS TO THE EU DIRECTIVES

What happens when EU Directives and Regulations, which the UK has already implemented, get amended? If a future trade deal between the EU and the UK is adopted,[44] this might make it conditional on the UK keeping its laws up-to-date with EU obligations in the social policy field. In the absence of a trade deal, it may be that the UK will voluntarily opt to apply any new EU rules. Admittedly, in the field of workers' rights, change has, in recent years, been glacial. Some European officials have seen the UK as a drag on progress[45] towards developing a true European social policy and hope that Brexit might create space for a more enlightened approach under the European Pillar for Social Rights.[46] This seems unlikely. In the period when the UK had not signed up to the Social Chapter (1993–97) there were few signs that the then remaining 11 Member States had the appetite for proceeding with alacrity in the social policy field even in the absence of the UK. Since then, the EU has expanded to include Eastern European states who see their lower wages as a comparative advantage in the EU's single market. They would be reluctant to see that advantage eroded in the face of EU harmonisation.

---

[42]   See eg Information and Consultation (Employees) Regulations 2004, SI 2004/3426.

[43]   P Davies and C Kilpatrick, 'UK Worker Representation after the Single Channel' (2004) 34 *Industrial Law Journal* 121.

[44]   On which, see further the contribution by P Craig (Ch 15) in this edited collection.

[45]   See M Ford, 'The Impact of Brexit on UK Labour Law' (2016) 32 *International Journal of Comparative Labour Law and Industrial Relations* 473.

[46]   <https://ec.europa.eu/commission/priorities/deeper-and-fairer-economic-and-monetary-union/european-pillar-social-rights_en>.

## 3. WHAT ROLE WILL DECISIONS OF THE COURT OF JUSTICE PLAY POST-BREXIT?

It had been widely thought that decisions of the Court of Justice before Brexit day would continue to bind the UK courts after the UK's departure; decisions after Brexit day would be of persuasive authority only. This is broadly what the GRB White Paper proposed (but again subject to the terms of any future trade deal between the EU and the UK). The GRB White Paper says that to maximise certainty

> 'the Bill will provide that any question as to the meaning of EU-derived law will be determined in the UK courts by reference to the CJEU's case law as it exists on the day we leave the EU. Everyone will have been operating on the basis that the law means what the CJEU has already determined it does, and any other starting point would be to change the law.'[47]

By way of illustration, it offers the (contentious) example of CJEU case law on the calculation of holiday pay entitlements for UK workers. It says 'failure to carry across that case law would be to create uncertainty for workers and employers'.[48]

The GRB White Paper also addresses the mechanics of the process: historic CJEU case law will be given the same precedent status in UK courts as decisions of the UK Supreme Court. The Supreme Court can depart from that case law but only in the circumstances of the Practice Statement made by the House of Lords in 1966 and adopted by the Supreme Court in 2010.[49] The White Paper says: '[w]e would expect the Supreme Court to take a similar, sparing approach to departing from CJEU case law'.[50] Further, 'Parliament will be free to change the law, and therefore overturn case law, where it decides it is right to do so'.[51]

The GRB White Paper is less clear about the position of CJEU decisions post-Brexit. It is likely that the British courts will continue to give them much respect, particularly in the early years post-Brexit, since those decisions are interpreting the very EU legislation on which UK legislation is based. However, post-Brexit case law will present a number of challenges for UK courts. First, any new decisions of the Court post-Brexit will not have had the benefit of UK/common law input, whether it be through the intervention of British advocates before the Court, the British Advocate General or the British judge. Second, the interpretation of EU law will be carried out against the imperatives of the

---

[47] *Legislating for the United Kingdom's withdrawal from the European Union*, above n 6, para 2.14.
[48] Ibid, para 2.15.
[49] Ibid, para 2.16.
[50] Ibid, para 2.17.
[51] Ibid, para 2.17.

EU: market integration, the role of the Charter and possibly EU citizenship. These no longer will be the guiding principles of UK law.

But perhaps these concerns are overstated. British judges have never slavishly followed Court of Justice rulings, especially where they do not think them sensible. A good example is *ECM*,[52] where the Court of Appeal took a pragmatic line to managing the challenges of the much-criticised decision of the Court of Justice in *Süzen*[53] in determining whether a transfer of an undertaking had occurred in the case of a labour-intensive business. The Court of Justice's decision used the criteria of whether the majority of staff had been transferred to determine whether there was a transfer of an undertaking which would have triggered the transfer of those very staff. In other words, the reasoning was circular.[54] The Court of Appeal preferred the smorgasbord approach adopted by the Court of Justice in the earlier *Spijkers* decision,[55] which involved considering a range of factors, in determining whether a transfer of an undertaking had occurred and thus whether those staff should be transferred.

In *Govia*,[56] too, the Court of Appeal drew the teeth of the controversial Court of Justice decision in *Viking*.[57] *Viking* had had damaging consequences on the right to strike in the UK.[58] In *Govia*, the Court of Appeal had to consider whether the proposed strike action to be taken by trade unions over the introduction of Driver Only Operated passenger Trains (DOOP) would breach Article 49 TFEU, the argument being that a French company, Keolis, owned 35 per cent of Govia's shares and the strike action interfered with the exercise of its freedom of establishment rights. The Court of Appeal said:

> '39. … [I]t is the object or purpose of the industrial action and not the damage caused by the action itself which renders it potentially subject to the freedom of movement provisions. … In our judgment it is inconceivable that a rule which did not discriminate on grounds of nationality and which required a driver and a guard on all trains to ensure the safe closing of doors rather than just a driver, could be said to constitute a deterrent to freedom of establishment or to make it less attractive.'

The Court of Appeal then pointed out that, even where a measure operated to the detriment of a person, that would not justify an inference that its freedom

---

[52]   *ECM v Cox* [1999] IRLR 559.
[53]   Case C-13/95, *Süzen v Zehnacker Gebäudereinigung GmbH*, ECLI:EU:C:1997:141, para 15.
[54]   See eg <http://www.personneltoday.com/hr/tupe-in-turmoil-time-to-unravel-the-tangle-of-the-regulations/>.
[55]   Case 24/85, *Spijkers v Benedik*, ECLI:EU:C:1986:127.
[56]   *Govia v The Associated Society of Locomotive Engineers* [2016] EWCA (Civ) 1309.
[57]   Case C-438/05, *International Transport Workers' Federation and Finnish Seamen's Union v Viking Line ABP and OÜ Viking Line Eesti*, ECLI:EU:C:2007:772.
[58]   For a summary, see C Barnard, 'The Calm after the Storm. Time to Reflect on EU Scholarship after *Viking* and *Laval*' in A Bogg, C Costello and A Davies (eds), *Research Handbook on EU Labour Law*, Edward Elgar, Cheltenham 2016.

of movement had been infringed if the effect was either too uncertain, indirect or insignificant to have the requisite deterrent or dissuasive impact. The Court concluded, '[w]e have no doubt that it would be too insignificant here'.

So it may be that the British courts, post-Brexit, will feel more liberated and able to do more of the same, shaping the post-Brexit case law to better fit the circumstances of the UK labour market, including in respect of controversial matters such as rolled-up holiday pay[59] (where short-term contracts included a sum for holiday pay 'rolled up' in the hourly rate, a pragmatic solution which the Court of Justice found unlawful).[60] However, the Swiss experience is instructive. Officially, judgments of the Court of Justice are persuasive only. For a number of years, this meant that an equivalent Swiss judgment was needed to explain what effect the Court of Justice's judgment had in Switzerland. Because this became unmanageable, in 2009 the Swiss Supreme Court ruled that the judgments of the Court of Justice would apply unless there was a good reason why they should not.[61] In fact, the Swiss courts apply the judgments of the Court of Justice pretty faithfully. Failure to do so, they recognise, means that Swiss law will not keep up to date with EU law. Crucially, in the light of any future EU-UK trade deal, the Swiss recognise that non-compliance might also jeopardise the Swiss' trade relations with the EU.

Finally, what if there is genuine uncertainty as to what EU law means in the absence of the Article 267 TFEU reference procedure? Recourse to an EU-UK consultative council might be one solution, but this council might not have judges on its panel. Given the general reluctance of British courts to refer cases to the CJEU, it may be that British judges make the best of it and decide the cases for themselves. Decisions like *Govia* and *ECM* suggest that the outcomes may not necessarily be bad for employees.

## 4. WHAT ABOUT THE OPPORTUNITIES FOR WORKERS PROMISED BY THERESA MAY?

In her Lancaster House speech, Theresa May said that the UK Government will build on the rights laid down in European legislation. The Brexit White Paper elaborates on this, noting that the past few years have seen a number of independent actions by the Government to protect UK workers and ensure they are being treated fairly, and in many areas the UK Government has already

---

[59] <https://www.gov.uk/holiday-entitlement-rights/holiday-pay-the-basics>.
[60] Case C-131/04, *C D Robinson-Steele v R D Retail Services Ltd*, ECLI:EU:C:2006:177.
[61] Judgment of the Swiss Federal Tribunal (136 II 5), discussed in T Burri, 'Do Lawyers Knead the Dough? How Law, Chaos and Uncertainty Interact' (2010) 4 *European Journal of Risk Regulation* 371. See also T Burri, 'Brexit addendum: Why the "Great Repeal Bill" will not be so great', <https://papers.ssrn.com/sol3/papers.cfm?abstract_id=2966683>.

extended workers' rights beyond those set out in EU law. It cites, by way of example the fact that:

- UK domestic law already provides for 5.6 weeks of statutory annual leave, compared to the four weeks set out in EU law;
- in the UK, women who have had a child can enjoy 52 weeks of statutory maternity leave and 39 weeks of pay, not just the 14 weeks under EU law;
- the UK provides greater flexibility around shared parental leave, where, subject to certain conditions, parental leave can be shared by the father of a child, giving families choice as to how they balance their home and work responsibilities; and
- the UK offers 18 weeks' parental leave, and that provision goes beyond the EU Directive because it is available until the child's 18th birthday.[62]

The White Paper also notes that the Government is committed to 'strengthening rights when it is the right choice for UK workers and will continue to seek out opportunities to enhance protections'.[63] It pointed out that in

'April 2016 we introduced the National Living Wage and saw a 6.2 per cent pay increase for the lowest paid workers in our country over the previous year. We have complemented this measure with strong enforcement action, increasing the enforcement budget for the National Minimum and Living Wage to £20 million for 2016/17, up from £13 million in 2015/16. We have increased penalties for wilfully non-compliant employers and have set up a dedicated team to tackle the more serious cases. Furthermore, we are appointing a statutory Director of Labour Market Enforcement and Exploitation. These actions demonstrate our commitment to ensuring that hard working people are entitled to a fair wage and that they receive the pay to which they are entitled.'[64]

All of this is true; none of these developments have been required by EU law nor constrained by it. EU employment law lays down minimum standards, not maximum, and is in any event an incomplete legal regime. There are whole areas of social policy which are unaffected by EU law.[65] Member States have considerable freedom to do what they want in the social field, as the UK has already done while still a member of the EU. Brexit in and of itself will not create opportunities for developing social policy which were unavailable prior to the referendum.

---

[62]    *The United Kingdom's exit from and new partnership with the European Union*, above n 10, section 7.

[63]    Ibid, para 7.3.

[64]    Ibid, paras 7.4–7.5.

[65]    See generally J KENNER, *EU Employment Law. From Rome to Amsterdam and Beyond*, Hart Publishing, Oxford 2003.

More remarkable is the statement in the White Paper that '[w]e are committed to maintaining our status as a global leader on workers' rights and will make sure legal protection for workers keeps pace with the changing labour market'.[66] According to the OECD league tables, the UK is ranked third in its employment protection legislation table (with a score of 1.10 in 2013) for the *least* regulation in the field of individual and collective dismissal (after the US (0.26 in 2013) and Canada (0.92 in 2013)),[67] a point the UK has noted with some pride in its *Ending the Employment Relationship* Consultation.[68] Further, the UK continues to make its employment law more flexible, notably by lengthening the periods of service necessary to claim unfair dismissal, increasing the carve-outs from the right to claim unfair dismissal, and most significantly, imposing fees on access to employment tribunals. Claims have dropped by 70 per cent.[69] This is leadership of a sort but most trade union lawyers would not regard it as constituting global leadership in terms of the *protection* of employment rights.

Moreover, it is striking that these developments have occurred in areas in which the UK is not constrained by the floor of protection provided by EU law, namely unfair dismissal and the management of access to tribunals. This raises the question as to what will happen when Theresa May is no longer Prime Minister (or if the negotiations go badly). Will employment law, in the hands of a Conservative Government, mean in fact deregulation, as Liam Fox and Priti Patel have called for, or at least a continued process of salami slicing away of rights (eg reducing the personal scope of the protection from worker to employee or increasing the length of service requirement before an employee can take advantage of the right)?

---

[66] *The United Kingdom's exit from and new partnership with the European Union*, above n 10, para 7.6.
[67] <http://stats.oecd.org/Index.aspx?DataSetCode=EPL_OV>. The OECD average figure was 2.04.
[68] BIS, *Ending the Employment Relationship Consultation*, 2012: <https://www.gov.uk/government/uploads/system/uploads/attachment_data/file/32700/12-1037-ending-the-employment-relationship-consultation.pdf>.) See p 13:

> '[t]he OECD set out in its Indicators of Employment Protection 2008, that the UK labour market is one of the most lightly regulated amongst developed countries, with only the US and Canada having lighter overall regulation. Our system of employment regulation is an important element of the UK's comparative advantage. Nonetheless, we should never be complacent. We must be aware of steps being taken in other countries to increase flexibility of the labour market, and we also have to be conscious of concerns of employers that the potential cost of termination of employment puts them off taking on new employees'.

[69] See eg 'Unions blame 70% fall in employment tribunal cases on fees', *The Guardian*, 31 January 2017 <https://www.theguardian.com/money/2017/jan/31/employment-tribunal-cases-down-70-since-fees-introduced>. See further A ADAMS and J PRASSL, 'Vexatious Claims? Challenging the Case for Employment Tribunal Fees' (2017) 80 *Modern Law Review* (forthcoming) and the UNISON challenge to the introduction of tribunal fees in *R (on the application of UNISON) (Appellant) v Lord Chancellor*, UKSC 2015/0233, on appeal from [2015] EWCA (Civ) 935.

The Prime Minster, in her Lancaster House speech, also talked about legal protection for workers keeping pace with the changing labour market. She subsequently referred to worker representation on boards of companies. This suggests a more progressive approach to labour rights (although this proposal has already run into difficulties),[70] as does the subsequent reference to enhancing rights for workers. But what if the economy goes into recession following Brexit? Do such changes in the labour market mean in fact deregulation of workers' rights? This risk is exacerbated if no trade deal is reached with the EU.

## 5. WHAT IF THERE IS NO DEAL?

Theresa May's Lancaster House speech contained a threat. If the negotiations lead to a 'punitive deal' that 'punishes Britain', she said 'no deal for Britain is better than a bad deal for Britain', freeing the UK 'to set the competitive tax rates and embrace the policies that would attract the world's best companies and biggest investors to Britain'. Her Chancellor was more explicit. In his interview with *Die Welt*, he said that '[w]e are now objectively a European-style economy … with a social model that is recognizably the European social model that is recognizably in the mainstream of European norms, not US norms'.[71] He concluded: 'I personally hope we will be able to remain in the mainstream of European economic and social thinking. But if we are forced to be something different, then we will have to become something different'. Workers' rights may be less secure than first appears.

Such threats have not gone down well with the UK's European partners.[72] As we have already seen, any future EU-UK trade deal will be dependent on

---

[70] 'Plans to put workers on company boards falters', *Financial Times*, 31 October 2016 <https://www.ft.com/content/22128636-9ece-11e6-891e-abe238dee8e2>; although Sports Direct has decided to put workers on its board, *Financial Times*, <https://www.ft.com/content/d4d713ca-04ab-11e7-ace0-1ce02ef0def9>. However, the commitment is reiterated in the Conservative manifesto 2017 <https://s3.eu-west-2.amazonaws.com/manifesto2017/Manifesto2017.pdf>:

> 'To ensure employees' interests are represented at board level, we will change the law to ensure that listed companies will be required either to nominate a director from the workforce, create a formal employee advisory council or assign specific responsibility for employee representation to a designated non-executive director. Subject to sensible safeguards, we will introduce, for employees, a right to request information relating to the future direction of the company.'

[71] See 'Philip Hammond issues threat to EU partners', *Die Welt*, 15 January 2017 <https://www.welt.de/english-news/article161182946/Philip-Hammond-issues-threat-to-EU-partners.html>.

[72] D Boffey, 'Britain set to lose EU "crown jewels" of banking and medicine agencies', *The Observer*, 16 April 2017.

the UK respecting safeguards against unfair competitive advantages through, inter alia, social and environmental dumping. But that deal may be many years away, especially since the EU wants to see that there has been 'sufficient progress' towards reaching a satisfactory agreement on the arrangements for an orderly withdrawal (ie on the Article 50 (divorce) negotiations). In the meantime, workers must rely on Theresa May's statement of intent – and hope.

## 6. CONCLUSIONS

The Brexit process has thrown up numerous tensions, contradictions and inconsistencies. On the one hand, the Prime Minister wants to reach out to those who have been left behind by protecting jobs, improving training for British workers and even developing employment rights.[73] On the other hand, she is prepared to walk away from any 'bad' deal which, at least in the short term, would create terrible uncertainty in the UK. It will inevitably lead to price rises as tariffs are applied to imports into the UK from the EU, and other states with which the EU has a free trade agreement, and to exports from the UK to the EU. Jobs will be lost. Meanwhile, the uncertainty surrounding the UK's future trading arrangements with the EU is threatening jobs as firms start to relocate their operations to elsewhere in the EU.[74] Meanwhile, the health service is struggling (the promised £350 million has not materialised), as is social care. At least in the short to medium term the most vulnerable in society are likely to suffer. Brexit will come at a price. Many of those voting to leave recognised this and thought it was a price worth paying. For them control – of borders, of laws – was more important. Paradoxically, control over the laws may prove to be more apparent than real: good news for workers, bad news for sovereigntists. And if the individual is out of work, then even this protection is something of a chimera.

---

[73]  See also the launch of the Taylor Review, whose remit is to look at how employment practices need to change in order to keep pace with modern business models: <https://www.gov.uk/government/news/taylor-review-on-modern-employment-practices-launches>.

[74]  See eg 'Lloyd's of London will move jobs to new Brussels office', *The Guardian*, 29 March 2017 <https://www.theguardian.com/business/2017/mar/29/lloyds-of-london-will-move-jobs-to-new-brussels-office>; 'City banks warn of Brexit job moves', *BBC News*, 18 January 2017 <http://www.bbc.co.uk/news/business-38663537>; 'Goldman Sachs to move hundreds of jobs outs of London before Brexit deal is struck', *The Independent*, 31 March 2017 <http://www.independent.co.uk/news/business/news/goldman-sachs-brexit-bank-jobs-move-out-london-city-eu-deals-european-union-negotiations-a7641876.html>.

# CHAPTER 6

# UK ENVIRONMENTAL LAW POST-BREXIT

Veerle Heyvaert and Aleksandra Čavoški*

## 1.  INTRODUCTION

While much of the post referendum Brexit discussion focused on economic and constitutional issues, the future of environmental law and policies received much less attention. Environmental protection barely featured as a campaign issue on either side of the referendum debate, and it is notably overlooked in the Brexit White Paper.[1] Yet UK environmental law is deeply rooted in EU law and policies, and departure from the EU may herald significant changes within national law. Environmental law covers a broad range of public policies including biodiversity protection, air and water quality control, climate change and waste management, and deeply impacts on other key domestic policies such as agriculture, transport, industrial and energy policy. Moreover, uncertainty in environmental regulation

---

\*    London School of Economics and University of Birmingham (respectively).
[1]   HM Government, *The United Kingdom's exit from and new partnership with the European Union* (Cm 9417, February 2017).

significantly jeopardises its chance of effectiveness. Therefore, careful reflection on the impact of Brexit on environmental law is essential.

## 2. AREAS OF UK ENVIRONMENTAL LAW THAT WILL BE IMPACTED BY BREXIT

Environmental protection was not among the original European Economic Community policies. The first environmental measures were adopted in the early 1970s, initially to address the disruptive impact of different levels of national environmental protection on intra-EU competition.[2] It formally became an area of competence shared between the EU and Member States in 1987.[3] Despite its late start, EU environmental policy has undergone a major expansion: beyond traditional areas such as air, water, and nature protection, the EU environmental agenda covers waste, chemicals, climate change, marine protection, biodiversity and the urban environment. Moreover, EU law requires that environmental objectives and protection standards be integrated into other policy areas, notably agriculture, energy, industry and transport.

Much of the corpus of contemporary UK environmental law was either developed under the guidance of EU environmental law or is a direct application of EU law. Environmental law is an area densely populated with Directives, which for the most part have been transposed into national law and implemented domestically. For example, the bathing water standards, which the UK famously struggled to implement in the 1980s,[4] and the EU air quality provisions which more recently have proved to be a bone of contention between the UK Government and the European Court of Justice (CJEU),[5] are contained in Directives. Measures regarding the environmental quality of commercial products such as chemicals, pesticides and genetically modified food and feedstuffs,[6] on the other hand, are increasingly frequently found in Regulations, which do not call for transposition and are simply treated as part of domestic law after their entry into effect. In addition to the aforementioned sectors, EU law is the dominant source of UK environmental law on climate change abatement,

---

[2]    A good illustration is Directive 70/220/EEC of 20 March 1970 on the approximation of the laws of the Member States relating to measures to be taken against air pollution by gases from positive-ignition engines of motor vehicles [1970] OJ L76/1.

[3]    Single European Act [1987] OJ L169.

[4]    Case C-56/90, *Commission v United Kingdom*, ECLI:EU:C:1993:307.

[5]    *R v Secretary of State for the Environment, Food and Rural Affairs* [2015] UKSC 28.

[6]    Regulation 1829/2003 of the European Parliament and of the Council on genetically modified food and feed [2003] OL L268; Regulation 396/2005 of the European Parliament and of the Council on maximum residue levels of pesticides in or on food and feed of plant and animal origin and amending Council Directive 91/414/EEC [2005] OJ L70.

energy efficiency and renewable energy development; water quality; waste; environmental impact assessment; nature and biodiversity protection; industrial emissions; biocides, nanotechnology and other emerging technologies; access to environmental information, participation in decision-making and access to justice. Moreover, EU law must be interpreted in compliance with key environmental principles, such as the precautionary principle, the sustainable development and polluter-pays principles, as well as with certain *sui generis* EU environmental law principles such as the principle of proximity and self-sufficiency specific to individual areas of environmental law.

Areas of law that are still chiefly domestic include common law litigation in environmental damage claims; planning law; the law regarding the remediation of contaminated land; and environmental criminal law. Moreover, as environmental policy is a shared competence between the EU and the Member States, it is possible for the UK to adopt environmental legislation in areas that are not (yet) governed by EU environmental law, for example, because they fall below the relevant EU threshold. Thus, nature sites of European importance in the UK are governed by the EU Habitats and Birds Directive,[7] whereas English[8] sites of 'mere' national importance are governed by the Wildlife and Countryside Act 1981 (as amended). However, even within the domestic sphere the influence of EU environmental law is felt. The Environmental Liability Directive intersects with some aspects of the contaminated land remediation regime;[9] planning policy and law are affected by impact assessment requirements as well as designations under the EU's 'Natura 2000' nature protection project; and the EU has made attempts to criminalise certain behaviour in all Member States.[10]

In sum, when it comes to environmental matters, EU law and UK law are intimately entangled. Overall, it has been estimated that about 80 per cent of UK environmental law hails from the EU.[11] While the complexity of the subject matter cautions against taking any sweeping quantified estimates at face value, it is undeniable that UK law and policy on environmental protection has been fundamentally altered by 40 years of EU membership and, correspondingly, that it is one of the areas with the most potential for large-scale change (and disruption) in a post-Brexit world.

---

[7]     Implemented in UK law via the Conservation of Habitats and Species Regulations 2010, SI 2010/490 (as amended).

[8]     Domestically, nature conservation is a devolved matter.

[9]     Directive 2004/35/CE of the European Parliament and of the Council of 21 April 2004 on environmental liability with regard to the prevention and remedying of environmental damage [2004] OJ L143/56.

[10]    Directive 2008/99/EC of the European Parliament and of the Council on the protection of the environment through criminal law [2008] OJ L328.

[11]    Andrea Leadsom, speech on priorities for building world-leading food and farming industries at the National Farmers' Union Conference, 21 February 2017, <https://www.gov.uk/government/speeches/environment-secretary-speaks-at-nfu-conference>.

## 3. PROSPECTS FOR EU-UK LAW AND POLICY COOPERATION POST-BREXIT

Prospective studies inevitably rely on a degree of speculation, but the most plausible assumption at the time of writing is that the UK will exit the single market and, hence, will not remain subject to single market legislation after Article 50 negotiations have concluded. The current Government's preference seems to be for a full break with the EU legal regime and its institutions, and the separate negotiation of bespoke agreements that will set out the new relationship between the EU and its former Member State.[12] Although, to date, the UK Government has been silent on the question whether environmental protection would feature among the areas for which it would seek to negotiate a post-Brexit EU-UK agreement, there are several reasons why cooperation on environmental issues could and arguably should be continued. First, the 2014 Balance of Competences Review showed broad agreement that, in this policy area, the UK has benefited from EU membership.[13] It has pushed the UK to 'up its game' in areas such as water quality and waste management, and, conversely, enabled the country to exercise a formative influence on the development of a number of key EU environmental policies, such as climate change and integrated pollution prevention and control. It has afforded the UK a greater degree of control over the transboundary impact of pollution of foreign origin, and has helped to mitigate the potential anti-competitive effects of tighter environmental standards.

Secondly, the EU provides a robust institutional framework for addressing emerging environmental problems, which can facilitate the regulation of those issues at the national level. The EU has provided a forum for improving cooperation between states on transboundary challenges and put in place mechanisms to facilitate information exchange. The facilitating role of the EU as an environmental governance framework acquires even greater relevance when we consider the wealth of international environmental legal obligations to which the UK is subject, both as an individual signatory state and, currently, as part of the EU. The EU has positioned itself as a key environmental actor and raised the importance of EU and Member States' agendas at the international level, to mutually beneficial effect. The scientific knowledge provided by the UK scientific, academic and business communities, together with the experience and negotiating skills of UK civil servants, has been invaluable in this policy area.

---

[12] It should be noted that, after the June 2017 general election which saw the UK government retain its ranking as largest party but lose its overall majority in Parliament, this position is now less stable and may be subject to renegotiation. As further developments are extremely difficult to anticipate at the time of writing, this chapter continues to use the most recently communicated governmental position as point of reference.

[13] House of Lords European Union Committee, *Brexit: Environment and Climate Change* (HL 2016–17, 109). See also House of Commons Environmental Audit Committee, *EU and UK Environmental Policy* (HC 2015–16, 537) p 3.

At the same time, EU membership has enabled the UK to shore up its position in the international arena.

In the same vein, the EU actively fosters cooperation on research and development in environmental science, and enables the pooling of expertise via collaborative networks and EU institutions, such as the European Environment Agency. As its primary responsibility is to gather and disseminate information about the state of the environment to EU institutions and Member States, a continued relationship would be beneficial for the UK. The Agency has an impact on the environmental policy process by providing specific support to DG Environment. Thus, the maintenance of ties would assist the UK in continuing access to this knowledge community. Furthermore, it is important to recall that the EU's enforcement mechanisms also have facilitating aspects that the UK Government might be keen to retain. In the light of the prominent 'take back control' rhetoric that continues to colour the Government's Brexit strategy, the prospect of EU involvement in enforcement of environmental regulation may seem unlikely to whet the appetite for post-Brexit cooperation. However, the EU also supports effective implementation and enforcement through data-gathering, reporting and transnational networking. The key purpose of IMPEL, the European Union Network for the Implementation and Enforcement of Environmental Law, is not to police and punish Member State non-compliance, but instead to help countries comply, or comply in a more cost-effective manner, by sharing knowledge, skills and good practice. Post-Brexit, the mutual benefits of this form of enforcement facilitation may well persist for both parties.

Finally, a major reason for the UK Government to seek continued cooperation on environmental matters is its explicit desire to remain a main trading partner of the EU. As documented in decades of 'trade and environment' case law,[14] divergent environmental standards can constitute trade barriers. To avoid their resurgence in future EU-UK trade relations, either the UK would need to mimic new EU environmental standards on trade-related issues, or the EU would need to take its cue from the UK. Given respective market sizes, the latter scenario is less likely to materialise. In this context, the UK might prefer the prospect of sharing certain environmental competences with the EU over the alternative options of either becoming a 'policy taker' or facing trade barriers. Incentives for cooperation are all the more compelling in areas where manufacture and trade are conditioned on EU registration or approval. For example, any chemical substance produced or traded on the EU market in quantities of at least one tonne per manufacturer per year, must be registered with the European Chemicals Agency (ECHA).[15] If the UK drops out of this scheme, it will no longer have

---

[14]   eg Case C-302/86, *Commission v Denmark*, ECLI:EU:C:1988:421; Case C-28/09, *Commission v Austria*, ECLI:EU:C:2011:854.

[15]   Regulation 1907/2006 of the European Parliament and of the Council concerning the Registration, Evaluation, Authorisation and Restriction of Chemicals (REACH), establishing

any input in ECHA, yet any UK-based chemicals producer who wants to export to the EU still needs to comply with ECHA's registration requirements. Also, in order to retain control over the health and environmental quality of all chemical substances traded within the UK, a new domestic regulatory regime would need to be established. This would open space to tailor national chemicals regulation to fit the UK context, but would be a very costly endeavour. Moreover, given the intensity of EU-UK trade in this sector, the UK would be under fierce pressure from manufacturers and exporters to align new UK regulatory requirements closely with EU provisions. Hence, the sought-after freedom to make bespoke regulations may prove largely theoretical.

## 4. THE GREAT REPEAL ACT AND ITS LIKELY CONSEQUENCES FOR UK ENVIRONMENTAL LAW

For the purpose of this study, we assume that a Great Repeal Act (GRA)[16] which, according to the Secretary of State for Exiting the European Union, should 'ensure that there is no black hole in our statute book',[17] will indeed be adopted. The GRA is intended to be a multi-functional act. It will, first, repeal the European Communities Act 1972 (ECA) and abolish supremacy of EU law over national law.[18] Up to now, the ECA has provided the legal basis for the application of EU law in the UK, covering both law that was already in force at the time of UK accession to the EU and law enacted afterwards. To that effect, the ECA makes a distinction between section 2(1) which provides for EU law that does not require further enactment to be given legal effect, and section 2(2) which authorises the adoption of Orders in Council or departmental regulations necessary to implement EU law. The former category includes EU Treaties, Regulations and other directly effective EU law (including directly effective provisions in EU Directives). The latter category includes national measures transposing EU law, which predominantly relate to Directives and Decisions not directly effective. EU environmental law spans both categories, but is particularly rich in Directives.

Many EU environmental Directives have already been transposed into national law. Some were the subject of statutory adoption, but most have been introduced into domestic law via departmental regulations on the basis of

---

a European Chemicals Agency, amending Directive 1999/45/EC and repealing Council Regulation (EEC) No 793/93 and Commission Regulation (EC) No 1488/94 as well as Council Directive 76/769/EEC and Commission Directives 91/155/EEC, 93/67/EEC, 93/105/EC and 2000/21/EC [2006] OJ L396.

16    Theresa May announced the plans for the GRA on 2 October 2016.

17    'Exiting the EU: next steps': Ministerial statement of 10 October 2016, <https://www.gov.uk/government/speeches/exiting-the-eu-next-steps-ministerial-statement-10-october-2016>.

18    See further the contribution by T Horsley (Ch 4) in this edited collection.

section 2(2) ECA.[19] Once the ECA is repealed, their legal basis is invalidated. Hence, in order to avoid gaps in legal provision, the GRA will need to introduce a stipulation that restores the legality of instruments that were formerly rooted in the ECA. This could be fairly straightforwardly achieved, but the challenges of successfully disentangling EU from domestic environmental law run deeper. The Secretary of State for the Environment and Rural Affairs (DEFRA) pointed out that difficulties may arise 'where EU legislation is designed to organise cooperation between Member States, public authorities and businesses, as the relationship between these will fundamentally change'.[20] The UK's involvement in the EU Emissions Trading System (EU ETS), established by means of the 2003 Emissions Trading Directive, is a case in point.[21] In the absence of a special agreement between the EU and UK, after Brexit the UK will not be included in the Commission's calculation of the overall quota of emissions allowances per EU Member State, and emissions allowances held by UK companies will no longer be tradeable on the EU market. In a similar vein, Member State responsibilities under EU environmental Directives frequently include a requirement to report on implementation to the European Commission or another EU institution. It is difficult to imagine that such provisions, too, are intended to be repatriated upon the entry into effect of the GRA. Hence, the UK Government will need to identify which provisions in existing statutory instruments and domestic environmental regulations should be restored, and which modified or discarded.

Moreover, certain areas of environmental regulation, most notably environmental permitting rules, in recent years have relied increasingly heavily on 'legislation by reference', also known as the 'conveyor belt' approach to legal transposition.[22] Instead of fully transcribing the provisions of environmental Directives into departmental regulations, conveyor belt provisions simply refer to 'the Directive' and affirm that, in order to comply with the regulation, the parties affected must comply with the provisions of the Directive. This was greeted as a cost-effective approach to transposition which was warranted by the increasingly detailed and articulated nature of EU environmental Directive provisions. It also ensured that any amendments to environmental Directives could be swiftly incorporated. However, it is questionable whether a sheer

---

[19] See eg national regulations governing environmental impact assessment, industrial emissions and nature conservation.

[20] House of Commons Environmental Audit Committee Report, *The Future of Natural Environment after the EU Referendum* (HC 2016–17, 599) p 17.

[21] Directive 2003/87/EC of the European Parliament and of the Council of 13 October 2003 establishing a scheme for greenhouse gas emission allowance trading within the Community and amending Council Directive 96/61/EC [2003] OJ L275/32. See also Section 6.1 on climate change (below).

[22] *Brexit: Environment and Climate Change*, above n 13, pp 16–17; S Bell, D McGillivray and OW Pedersen, *Environmental Law*, Oxford University Press, Oxford 2013, p 518.

reference to the provisions in EU Directives will be deemed sufficient or acceptable once the UK ceases to be part of the EU legal regime. It is expected that such issues will be resolved independently of the GRA in a greater inquiry of EU law that will follow the passing of this Act. It is furthermore anticipated that the GRA will contain delegated powers which could be used, among other things, to make required amendments to existing national environmental provisions that implement EU Directives.[23]

Directly applicable EU environmental law, including Treaty provisions, EU Regulations, and directly applicable Decisions, will require active transposition into UK law in order not to become defunct upon the entry into effect of the GRA. Precisely how this transposition is going to happen is as yet unclear. One mooted option is for the GRA to contain a 'continuance clause'; a broadly framed provision which transfers all directly applicable EU law into domestic law on Brexit day.[24] Additionally, a Schedule listing all EU legal instruments that are excluded from the effect of the continuance clause could be attached. Which EU environmental measures ought to be transposed, and which should be excluded, will hinge upon the progress and outcome of the Brexit negotiations. In all likelihood, therefore, final determinations on transposition and exclusion will only be completed after the 'divorce settlement' component of the Brexit negotiations has concluded. To that effect, as the Secretary of State for Exiting the EU has pointed out, ministers will be vested with powers to 'make some changes by secondary legislation, giving the Government the flexibility to take account of the negotiations with the EU as they proceed'.[25]

Moreover, as with provisions in environmental Directives, a significant proportion of directly applicable EU environmental law cannot be transposed into national law without further intervention. Regulations will require careful reviewing to identify provisions that are unworkable outside the EU context, such as safeguard clauses that allow national competent authorities to take emergency health and safety measures on the condition that they notify the European Commission. In other cases, exit from the EU may strip away the entire institutional infrastructure upon which regulatory provisions are built. The REACH Regulation, for example, is administered by the European Chemicals Agency (ECHA), an institution in which the UK will no longer participate after Brexit, unless a bespoke agreement on the issue is reached. The fact that ECHA decisions would not be reviewable in accordance with national law, but instead

---

[23] House of Commons Library, 'Legislating for Brexit: The Great Repeal Bill' (Briefing Paper No 7793, 21 November 2016) p 35.
[24] Ibid, p 11.
[25] 'Government announces end of European Communities Act': Ministerial Statement of 2 October 2016, <https://www.gov.uk/government/news/government-announces-end-of-european-communities-act>.

fall under the jurisdiction of the CJEU, is a further complicating factor. The scope for transposition of the environmental principles contained in the Treaty on the Functioning of the EU (TFEU), too, raises a host of challenging questions. Beyond the questions of whether the UK would want to domestically transpose these principles after leaving the EU, and how such transposition should be achieved within the GRA, there is also the question of what the reach would be of a former EU environmental principle in a post-Brexit landscape. Would it apply only to measures of EU ancestry, or across the board of environmental legislation?

## 5. DEVOLUTION BEFORE AND AFTER THE GREAT REPEAL ACT

Environmental competencies are mostly devolved powers in the UK.[26] Hence, separate regimes secure the implementation of, for example, EU biodiversity protection, industrial permitting, waste and air quality law in England, Wales, Scotland and Northern Ireland respectively. Since much of EU environmental law is contained in Directives, which typically leave the addressees some flexibility in implementation, devolved administrations to a degree have been able to tailor implementing instruments to suit local conditions.[27] At the same time, however, EU environmental law acts as a cohesive force across administrations and limits the scope for regional differentiation. The UK's decision to leave the EU could lead to devolved administrations taking greater ownership of environmental policy and ultimately result in a higher degree of legal and regulatory differentiation. However, it also creates a new host of challenges for devolved administrations.[28]

A first set of challenges regards the involvement of devolved administrations in the process of converting EU environmental law into national laws. To date, their role remains unclear, beyond noting that devolved administrations will be consulted and included in the process.[29] According to the Sewel Convention, 'Westminster would not normally legislate with regard to devolved matters

---

[26]   See Scotland Act 1998, Government of Wales Act 1998 and Northern Ireland Act 1998. The legislative powers of the 3 devolved assemblies were further enhanced post-1998.

[27]   EA Kirk and KL Blackstock, 'Enhanced Decision Making: Balancing Public Participation against "Better Regulation" in British Environmental Permitting Regimes' (2011) 23 *Journal of Environmental Law* 97–116.

[28]   On devolution generally, see the contribution by J Hunt (Ch 2) in this edited collection.

[29]   'The Government's negotiating objectives for exiting the EU': PM speech of 17 January 2017, <https://www.gov.uk/government/speeches/the-governments-negotiating-objectives-for-exiting-the-eu-pm-speech>.

in Scotland without the consent of the Scottish parliament'.[30] Devolved administrations may well insist that this Convention be honoured with regard to the GRA, but the Supreme Court's recent ruling in *Miller* indicates that their consent is not formally required.[31] In his oral evidence on the impact of Brexit on the environment before the Welsh Parliament, Robert Lee asserted that whether the devolved administrations' consent is required would depend on the form of the GRA. If it simply features an open and general provision to repeal the ECA Act and retain EU law, consent would be unnecessary.[32]

Post-Brexit, devolved administrations should have the discretion to decide if they want to retain the corpus of EU environmental law that falls within devolved competences or to repeal or amend it. However, securing this will in all likelihood require further legal reform. Presently, any amendment to statutory environmental law cannot be incompatible with the EU law, as guaranteed by the Acts of devolved administrations. For example, section 29 of the Scotland Act 1998 provides that an Act of the Scottish Parliament is not law if outside the legislative competence of the Parliament, which includes instances of incompatibility with EU law. It is not inconceivable that Acts of devolved administrations would be amended simultaneously with the passing of the GRA.

The most likely scenario is that, initially, devolved administrations will by and large retain transposed EU environmental law. Over time, however, the environmental policies and laws of the various UK nations could drift further apart. Some devolved administrations could seize the opportunity of Brexit to develop a more ambitious environmental agenda that better responds to the particular needs and circumstances of the region. Others may want to repeal former EU provisions that are considered excessively costly or onerous. Further differentiation could foster the democratic legitimacy and effectiveness of environmental law, but it can also cause fragmentation and leave the country as a whole ill-equipped to confront transboundary environmental risks. Arguably, the short- and medium-term risk of fragmentation is modest. Moreover, the UK's membership of various international environmental agreements will continue to act as a convergent influence. Nevertheless, in the wake of Brexit, the UK will need to consider the development of additional coordination strategies to protect the compatibility and sustainability of environmental decision-making across devolved administrations.

---

30    Memorandum of Understanding and Supplementary Agreements between the United Kingdom Government, Scottish Ministers, the Cabinet of the National Assembly for Wales and the Northern Ireland Executive Committee (Cm 5240, December 2001).
31    *R (on the application of Miller and another) v Secretary of State for Exiting the European Union* [2017] UKSC 5.
32    Robert Lee in oral evidence to the External Affairs and Additional Legislation Committee on 31 October 2016, <http://www.senedd.tv/Meeting/Archive/bc4d752c-e33d-49db-bd28-1b86 1086e500?autostart=True#>.

# 6. UK ENVIRONMENTAL LAW AFTER BREXIT

The successful extrication of UK environmental law from the EU legal sphere undoubtedly will be a challenging, complex process. It is also fair to anticipate that, in spite of the desire to ensure full coverage, some gaps may emerge which will need to be addressed quickly to safeguard the integrity of UK environmental law. Moreover, it is important to remember that the activation of the GRA is only the first step in a programme of gradual repatriation. After EU environmental law has been relabelled as national law, it will be the responsibility of the UK Government and devolved administrations to scrutinise and, where appropriate, initiate the updating, amendment or repeal of environmental legal provisions in line with the present Government's aspiration to be 'the first generation to leave the environment in a better place than it found it'.[33] The extent to which the UK will develop an environmental legal arsenal capable of delivering on this promise, obviously depends on the executive's willingness to put their words into action. It is not the intention in this chapter to go into detailed speculation about the overall quality of future UK environmental law, but it must be acknowledged that current signs are worrying. The most recent ministerial reshuffle saw the abolishment of the Department of Energy and Climate Change (DECC); the Brexit White Paper does not mention the environment, and the answer to a recent parliamentary question indicates that, so far, the Department of Environment, Food and Rural Affairs (DEFRA) has not commissioned any research to inform UK agricultural and environmental policy after Brexit.[34]

Some areas of environmental law may not be changed significantly as it would be either detrimental for the UK or there is no incentive to change. For example, amending EU product quality regulation, which governs issues such as the permissible content of hazardous substances in certain products and vehicle emissions limits, would not only lower environmental protection but also impede the UK's ability to trade. In fact, in these areas the UK will have a clear incentive not only to retain EU standards, but also to follow and adopt future amendments to EU law. Failure to do so would saddle the UK with a range of technical regulations that are no longer up-to-date or capable of facilitating trade. Similarly, there are few incentives to change rules on environmental impact assessment (EIA) as they are firmly embedded in national law and any significant change would create unwelcome regulatory uncertainty for businesses and the legal profession. Other EU requirements, such as waste, air quality or renewable energy targets, are much more vulnerable to modification.

---

[33]    *The Future of Natural Environment after the EU Referendum*, above n 20, p 41.

[34]    Parliamentary Written Question 63096 of 6 February 2017 (by C Lucas), http://www.parliament.uk/business/publications/written-questions-answers-statements/written-question/Commons/2017-02-06/63096/.

Moreover, the UK enjoyed temporary derogations for the achievement of EU targets in certain areas, such as water quality standards under the Drinking Water Directive.[35] Post-Brexit, incentives to gradually push drinking water quality standards towards the EU level may wither, and the temporary state of exception may become the norm.

Alongside questions of the likely ambition of future UK environmental law, the full process of repatriation of environmental law will create a host of new challenges. The following sections review the anticipated impact of legal repatriation in key environmental policy areas and, in so doing, illustrate some of the most pressing dilemmas that law-makers, administrators and courts will face as UK environmental law moves beyond Brexit.

## 6.1. CLIMATE CHANGE

A large proportion of UK climate change law is either a direct application or implementation of EU legal measures on matters ranging from emissions trading, energy efficiency, fluorinated gases, transport fuel specifications and carbon capture and storage to the promotion of renewable energy.[36] However, the UK's core climate change text is a fully domestic product: the 2008 Climate Change Act (CCA). Vitally, the Act specifies the UK's long-term emissions reduction target: by 2050, the UK's net carbon account should be at least 80 per cent lower than the 1990 baseline. To structure this process, the CCA requires the UK Government to draw up five-yearly carbon budgets, which act as stepping stones toward the achievement of the overall 80 per cent goal. The most recently adopted carbon budget covers the period of 2028 to 2032 (Fifth Carbon Budget), and foresees a greenhouse gas emissions reduction of 57 per cent by 2030. The carbon budgets are drawn up in consultation with the Committee on Climate Change, an independent statutory body which also monitors progress towards the achievement of the CCA's main objectives.

The CCA thus anchors UK climate policy to a number of fixed targets, and as a law of national origin it is likely to provide much needed continuity during the Brexit transitional period. However, this does not mean the CCA is impervious to change: as an Act of Parliament it can, itself, be amended or repealed by subsequent parliamentary legislation. Indeed, former UK Environment Minister Owen Paterson has long been an advocate of precisely

---

[35] Council Directive 98/83/EC of 3 November 1998 on the quality of water intended for human consumption [1998] OJ L330.

[36] S KINGSTON, V HEYVAERT and A ČAVOŠKI, *European Environmental Law*, Cambridge University Press, Cambridge 2017, pp 273–275.

such a move.[37] Alternatively, the CCA allows the Secretary of State to alter either individual carbon budgets in the case of 'significant changes affecting the basis on which the previous decision was made' (CCA, section 22) or even the 2050 target itself if 'it appears that there have been significant developments in … scientific knowledge about climate change, or ( … ) European or international law or policy' (CCA, section 2). The anticipated scenario in drafting the latter provision was not, we submit, the UK's departure from the EU. Rather, it was primarily designed as a mechanism to ratchet up the UK's commitments should EU or international law demand a faster pace of change.[38] Yet, should the UK want to shift its targets downwards in coming years, it is not inconceivable that it would try to use the rather open-ended language of sections 2 and 22 to accomplish this. The CCA therefore provides reassurance of continuity, but not an iron-clad guarantee.

EU climate change abatement policy rests on three key pillars: carbon reduction through emissions trading; energy efficiency; and the promotion of renewable energy.[39] EU legal instruments adopted towards the latter two objectives mostly take a meta-regulatory approach to environmental governance: instead of prescribing specific technical interventions, they require Member States to develop, document and report on national policies that contribute effectively both towards individual Member State and collective EU emissions reduction targets. Post-Brexit, in the presumed absence of a specific agreement, the reporting duties will fall away, which reduces opportunities for accountability. Nevertheless, the UK has put a reasonably robust legal infrastructure in place and this has supported the implementation of energy efficiency and renewable energy policies in compliance with EU obligations. With the necessary amendments this infrastructure should be capable of delivering similar functions after Brexit. The same cannot be said, however, of the emissions trading component of UK climate change policy. Post-Brexit, the Commission will no longer have the competence to include a UK share in the calculation of overall allowances and, correspondingly, the UK will no longer be able to issue or auction EU allowances to the approximately 1000 UK facilities that are currently subject to the scheme. The UK's continued participation in the EU ETS would require a special agreement involving mutual recognition of EU- and UK-issued allowances. Such arrangements could however be complicated by the EU's legal restrictions on offsetting, which tightly limit the number of

---

[37] Owen Paterson, 'Why we have to scrap the Climate Change Act', *Daily Telegraph*, 12 December 2015 <http://www.telegraph.co.uk/news/earth/environment/climatechange/12046531/Why-we-have-to-scrap-the-Climate-Change-Act.html>.

[38] As the UK's emission reduction targets at the time of adopting the CCA were considerably more stringent than the EU's, it is very unlikely that the provisions were intended to respond to a future lowering of EU standards.

[39] S KINGSTON, V HEYVAERT and A ČAVOŠKI, above n 36, p 273.

externally generated credits that can be converted into EU allowances.[40] Also, a linking agreement would subject the UK's management of emissions trading to a degree of Commission and, potentially, CJEU scrutiny. This may not be politically feasible. On the other hand, supplanting the EU ETS with a domestic emissions trading regime, or introducing alternative abatement obligations for ETS participant industries, could be a high-cost, high-risk endeavour with much weaker prospects for efficiency gains, as UK facilities would no longer be able to trade, or would be compelled to trade on a much smaller market. A third option would be for the UK to seek access to an alternative emissions market in, for instance, the US or Asia. The California Regional Greenhouse Gas Initiative, or the nascent Chinese carbon market, could be plausible candidates. However, linking agreements with non-EU trading schemes may also expose the UK emissions market to both greater trading risks and external scrutiny.

A final point to consider regards Brexit's consequences for the UK's position in international climate change law. Currently, the UK's Nationally Determined Contributions (NDCs) under the Paris Agreement to the United Nations Framework Convention on Climate Change (UNFCCC) are subsumed within the EU NDC submission. Post-Brexit, the UK will need to prepare an individual NDC instead. One intriguing question is whether this submission would already be subject to the Paris Agreement's 'ratcheting expectation',[41] which requires successive NDCs to be more environmentally ambitious than their predecessors. More generally, Brexit will have a profound impact on the UK's ability to affect future negotiations and, correspondingly, the direction of international climate change law. As an EU Member State, the UK is represented by the European Commission in most international environmental negotiations. The loss of membership may strengthen the UK's position, in that the UK gets to distinguish itself and represent its direct interests on the world stage, yet there is a significant risk that in climate change negotiations, as in other international contexts, the UK will be a weaker player than as part of the EU. As climate change negotiations are characterised by a particularly high level of coalition-building and negotiation in distinctive 'blocs', the UK is likely to lose influence as a sole operator. It could either join the EU as a negotiation partner, which might constrain the extent of future divergence between EU and UK climate change law and policy, or build a coalition with other states, such as Australia, the US and Canada. The latter choice could cause a fundamental shift in UK external and internal climate change strategy, and could potentially put the achievement of existing targets at risk.

---

[40]  Regulation 1123/2013 on Determining International Credit Entitlements pursuant to Directive 2003/87/EC of the European Parliament and of the Council [2013] OJ L299/32.
[41]  Article 4(3) Paris Agreement, available at <http://unfccc.int>.

## 6.2. BIODIVERSITY

Like climate change, nature and biodiversity protection are multilevel governance issues, pursued at the international, European Union and national level. Internationally, the UK is signatory to the landmark multilateral conservation and biodiversity protection agreements, including the World Heritage Convention, the Ramsar Convention on Wetlands, the Biodiversity Convention and the Convention on International Trade in Endangered Species. The chief instruments of the EU legal regime on nature and biodiversity protection, in turn, are the Birds and Habitats Directives,[42] both of which have been transposed into national law via delegated legislation. Moreover, nature and biodiversity protection are mostly devolved matters in the UK, which adds a further layer of regional decision-making to the dense governance network in place.

This area of environmental protection is distinctive in that European and domestic conservation regimes do not only overlap in terms of shared competences, but also geographically. In England and Wales, a key instrument through which nature and biodiversity protection is organised is the designation of sites of special scientific interest (SSSIs). Where the government's advisory body for nature protection, Natural England (or the Natural Resources Council for Wales), considers an area of special interest for reasons of fauna or flora or for its geological or physiographical qualities, it should notify local authorities, owners and occupiers, and the Secretary of State that the area constitutes a SSSI. Importantly, this notification should include a management regime for the SSSI, identifying both actions likely to damage and to enhance the specialness of the area, which should be observed by the notified parties including owners and occupiers. Under EU law, the British regions have furthermore been required to identify special protection areas (SPAs), which are migratory bird habitats, and special areas of conservation (SACs), which are environmentally important habitats for species other than wild birds. Together, SPAs and SACs across the EU constitute Natura 2000, an integrated network of core breeding and resting sites for rare and threatened species, as well as some rare natural habitat types.[43] Member States must take steps to avoid the deterioration of SPAs and SACs, and must establish 'appropriate management plans'. In England and Wales, these requirements are typically met through the notification of a SSSI.[44] Hence, the overwhelming majority of SPAs and SACs are also SSSIs. However, compared

---

[42]   Directive 2009/147/EC of the European Parliament and of the Council of 30 November 2009 on the conservation of wild birds [2010] OJ L20/7; Council Directive 92/43/EEC on the conservation of natural habits and of wild fauna and flora [1992] OJ L206/7.

[43]   KINGSTON, HEYVAERT and ČAVOŠKI, above n 36, pp 416–420.

[44]   J HOLDER and M LEE, *Environmental Protection: Law and Policy*, Cambridge University Press, Cambridge 2007, p 648.

to SSSIs of purely national importance, SPAs and SACs are subject to additional regulatory constraints. Most importantly, EU law requires that any development likely to significantly affect the site must be environmentally assessed, and in in principle prohibits any development that is determined likely to negatively affect the integrity of the site.

The EU assessment requirement and development restrictions should be incorporated into national law by virtue of the GRA. Moreover, national courts are expected to continue to interpret former EU law provisions in accordance with EU case law on the subject, which is famously precautionary and known to err on the side of biodiversity over development.[45] Hence, theoretically SACs and SPAs should remain subject to a higher standard of protection than 'pure' SSSIs. However, once the EU context falls away, and particularly if funding for biodiversity enhancement via the EU LIFE Programme dries up,[46] this distinction may become difficult to justify. Conceivably, this could fuel a drive to extend the assessment and development conditions to non-EU SSSIs, but a swing in the opposite direction is arguably more plausible. If so, this would result in the removal of environmental safeguards to protect many of the country's most precious habitats against the eroding force of unchecked development. Alternatively, the provisions might remain on the books, but their weaker legitimacy could negatively impact on developers and public authorities' willingness diligently to observe regulatory conditions. At worst, the assessment and development conditions could devolve into 'zombie legislation' – corporeally present, but stripped of its essence.

A reduced willingness to enforce the EU aspects of nature and biodiversity conservation would place a greater onus on concerned citizens to act as watchdogs and avert the decline of legal provisions into zombie legislation, for example, by judicially challenging planning permissions granted in the absence of an appropriate assessment. However, as will be discussed in the section below, the disappearance of the EU legal framework may make it harder for third parties to fight and win such legal battles.

## 6.3. AIR AND WATER

The UK is famously the birthplace of the world's first air pollution agency, the Alkali Inspectorate. In the past 40 years, however, the EU has been the main driving force in both air and water regulation. This is one of the most comprehensively developed parts of the EU environmental law. It regulates

---

[45]  Case C-127/02, *Waddenzee*, ECLI:EU:C:2004:482; Case C-258/11, *Sweetman*, ECLI:EU:
C:2013:220.

[46]  See <http://ec.europa.eu/environment/life/index.htm>.

polluting activities, ranging from air pollution from mobile and stationary sources to singular and diffuse sources of water pollution, and deploys a similar 'belt and braces' approach in both fields: it imposes emissions and environmental quality standards in combination with product and process standards. Member States are required to produce plans and programmes and to regularly monitor and assess air and water quality. Public involvement is an important feature in both areas and information on ambient air quality and water quality has to be made available to the public.

EU water and air law is mainly in the form of Directives which have been transposed nationally via primary and secondary legislation. There is a broad consensus that EU law had a particularly positive impact on water quality in the UK. The quality of bathing water has continuously improved over the years and this was largely due to advances in infrastructure, including sewerage and treatment facilities, imposed by the Waste Water Directive.[47] There is obviously room for improvement. For instance, too few water bodies within river basins districts under the Water Framework Directive have achieved 'good quality' status.[48] However, its track record of delivering a high level of environmental protection with regard to air quality is unfortunately much less encouraging. The UK's emissions rates persistently exceed EU-determined maxima for several air pollutants, in particular nitrogen oxide and particulate matter. The UK's large-scale failings to meet ambient air standards were recently exposed in *Client Earth,*[49] in which the UK Supreme Court ruled that the Government had breached its air quality protection obligations under EU law. The case highlighted that, in 2010, 40 of out 43 zones or agglomerations in the UK significantly exceeded several limit values for nitrogen dioxide prescribed in the EU Ambient Air Quality Directive.[50] In the following five years, levels of compliance deteriorated further, especially in urban areas.[51] In 2016 and 2017, London reached and breached its annual nitrogen dioxide limit, which provides that hourly maximum levels may be exceeded at most 18 times per year, in the first weeks of January.[52]

As air and water pollution are textbook transboundary environmental issues, it is expected that post-Brexit UK-EU relations will be marked by at least some

---

[47]   In 2016, 287 bathing waters in England (69.5%) met the excellent standard of the Bathing Water Directive. See more in Statistics on English Coastal and Inland Bathing Waters: A Summary of Compliance with the 2006 Bathing Water Directive, <https://www.gov.uk/government/statistics/bathing-water-quality-statistics>.

[48]   <https://www.gov.uk/government/collections/river-basin-management-plans-2015>.

[49]   See above n 5.

[50]   Directive 2008/50/EC of the European Parliament and of the Council of 21 May 2008 on ambient air quality and cleaner air for Europe [2008] OJ L152/1.

[51]   See above n 5, [30].

[52]   D CARRINGTON, 'London Breaches annual air pollution limit for 2017 in just five days', *The Guardian*, 6 January 2017.

degree of cooperation. This is particularly pertinent to Northern Ireland and the Republic of Ireland, which are interconnected terrestrially, atmospherically and aquatically.[53] Cooperation could partner the UK's environment agencies with the European Environment Agency and could secure the sharing of environmental information and scientific knowledge related to air and water. Industry representatives also expressed an interest in continuing cooperation with European networks and counterparts in EU Member States.[54]

The key challenge for the UK after Brexit will be to maintain water standards, enhance air quality and ensure the effective enforcement of national legislation. The latter will be especially challenging since the UK's departure from the EU severely curtails the range of enforcement mechanisms available to civil society and countries affected by transboundary pollution. With the unavailability of the management and enforcement mechanisms under Articles 258, 259 and 260 TFEU, a critical layer of accountability will be lost. The Commission, as a supervisory authority, effectively uses both mechanisms to ensure Member State compliance in the environmental policy area. Moreover, in the past decade it has made a concerted effort to embed citizens' concerns into its approach to environmental compliance and address the negative perception of the EU as an elite organisation. The Commission's invigilation is further backed up by the disciplining force of the CJEU, which has the authority to identify non-compliance and impose financial sanctions on Member States. The UK has been on the receiving end of this disciplining force on the very question of water regulation: in 1992 the CJEU found the UK in breach of its obligations to respect the 'maximum admissible concentrations' under the 1980 Drinking Water Directive.[55] Recently, the Commission again exercised its supervisory powers and issued a final warning to the UK over continued air pollution breaches, in particular repeated breaches of air pollution limits for nitrogen dioxide, before taking the matter before the CJEU.[56]

In the absence of the EU's enforcement machinery, the burden of monitoring Government compliance with legal air and water quality standards will increasingly rest on the shoulders of civil society organisations. However, the channels through which NGOs and other concerned citizens can voice their concerns are limited: the remit for intervention by the Local Government Ombudsman is extremely restricted, as is the scope for judicial review of public policy decisions, especially when the cause of complaint is a lack of government action, rather than an allegedly disproportionate or unlawful action. Moreover, even if the option of judicial review were available, UK courts will no longer

---

[53]    *Brexit: Environment and Climate Change*, above n 13, p 37.
[54]    Ibid, p 42.
[55]    Case C-340/96, *Commission v United Kingdom*, ECLI:EU:C:1999:192.
[56]    <http://europa.eu/rapid/press-release_IP-17-238_en.htm>.

have recourse to the preliminary reference procedure to pass on potentially controversial decisions to the CJEU. Without this mechanism, national courts may become more conservative in the interpretation of environmental provisions that have not yet been clarified through CJEU case law, and might adopt a more deferential attitude towards UK governmental authority.

## 7. CONCLUSION: POST-BREXIT CHALLENGES FOR ENVIRONMENTAL LAW

The current UK Government likes to assert that the UK may be leaving the European Union, but it is not leaving Europe. In the case of environmental protection, this is not only a political slogan but also an inescapable physical reality. The effective regulation of local and global environmental problems will continue to require concerted action throughout the European region. Thus, the challenge for the UK is to ensure continued cooperation, as its absence would jeopardise the state of the environment in the UK and would moreover expose the country to significant potential trade barriers. The lack of any meaningful discussion on environmental protection in the light of Brexit to date is, therefore, greatly worrying.

Governmental reticence and the pervasive uncertainties surrounding the details of the GRA and its consequences complicate an informed, level-headed assessment of the extent to which Brexit will affect, and possibly impair, environmental legal protection in the UK. At best, post-Brexit environmental quality standards could go beyond EU ambitions, and UK product standards could remain compatible with EU counterparts. At worst, Brexit could become an opportunity to perform an environmental 'regulatory roll-back', especially in those areas where the UK is already performing badly, such as air quality.

The future of enforcement of environmental law in the UK, too, hangs in the balance. The loss of the EU's enforcement machinery removes a vital layer of accountability and an important environmental safeguard. This will put greater pressure on civil society and national courts to scrutinise and, if needed, challenge the adequacy of domestic accountability mechanisms.

# CHAPTER 7

# EXTRACTING THE UK FROM EU FINANCIAL SERVICES GOVERNANCE: REGULATORY RECASTING OR SHADOWING FROM A DISTANCE?

Niamh MOLONEY[*]

## 1. INTRODUCTION

Much of UK policy, political and industry discourse since the 23 June 2016 Brexit decision has been framed in terms of the implications for financial services.[1] The stakes are high. The UK hosts some 35 per cent of the wholesale financial market activities (including trading, asset management and derivatives-related risk management services) provided in the EU[2] and which are essential to the liquidity, stability and efficiency of the EU financial system; and in the region of 25 per cent of UK financial services revenue derives from EU-related business.[3]

---

[*]    London School of Economics and Political Science.
[1]    For a policy/political example, see House of Lords European Union Committee, *Brexit: Financial Services* (HL 2016–17, 81) and for an industry view, see FINANCIAL SERVICES NEGOTIATION FORUM and NORTON ROSE FULBRIGHT, *Examining Regulatory Equivalence* (12 January 2017).
[2]    THECITYUK, *The UK: Europe's Financial Centre* (August 2016).
[3]    O WYMAN, *The Impact of the UK's Exit from the EU on the UK-based Financial Services Sector* (2016) <http://www.oliverwyman.com/content/dam/oliver-wyman/global/en/2016/oct/OW%20report_Brexit%20impact%20on%20Uk-based%20FS.pdf>.

The interdependencies between the UK and the EU are many and deep; the potential for significant market dislocation and economic disruption if EU/UK market access arrangements are not secure (or if a workable transitional arrangement is not in place) when the UK leaves the EU is real.[4] How the negotiations treat the technicalities of market access, whether through bespoke arrangements in a free trade agreement, changes to the EU rules which currently govern 'third country' access to the EU financial market, or the current third country access mechanisms, is of signal importance for the EU and UK financial systems.[5]

The discussions thus far have not focused closely on how Brexit might shape UK financial governance – or the regulatory, supervisory and enforcement arrangements which protect the public interest in a stable and secure UK financial system and which also manage how the UK engages with the international market beyond the EU. This chapter speculates on the impact Brexit may have on UK financial governance and on whether major, re-setting change is likely to follow or whether the UK regime can be expected to shadow EU financial governance. Section 2 examines the relationship between UK and EU financial governance, the extent to which both systems are intertwined and whether there is 'pent up' demand for UK governance change. Section 3 considers how UK financial governance might evolve in relation to the risks and challenges which Brexit poses. Section 4 considers the potential for re-setting change. Section 5 briefly concludes.

## 2. EU FINANCIAL GOVERNANCE AND THE UK: A CLAMP ON AUTONOMY OR ROOM TO INNOVATE?

The institutional setting of UK financial governance has (in broad terms) two main locations: conduct governance – which is oriented to client/consumer protection and the support of market efficiency and integrity – is the responsibility of the Financial Conduct Authority (FCA); while prudential or stability-oriented governance is located with the Bank of England and the Prudential Regulation Authority (PRA) which forms part of the Bank.[6] The regulatory governance

---

[4]    For an analysis of potential economic and fiscal risks to the UK economy, see ibid.

[5]    See J ARMOUR, 'Brexit and Financial Services' (2017) 33 (Supp 1) *Oxford Journal of Economic Policy* S54; N MOLONEY, 'The EU and its Investment Banker: Rethinking Equivalence for the EU Capital Market', *LSE Law Society and Economy Working Paper Series* WP No 5/2017 (2017) <https://ssrn.com/abstract=2929229>; and E FERRAN, 'The UK as a Third Country in EU Financial Services Regulation' (2017) 3(1) *Journal of Financial Regulation* 40.

[6]    The distinction is not a bright-line one. The FCA is responsible for the prudential supervision of certain regulated institutions, including smaller firms, while the Bank is increasingly extending its policy reach over conduct in the financial markets, notably through its 2015

regime is framed by legislation, primarily but not only the Financial Services and Markets Act 2000, as frequently amended,[7] which inter alia sets out the objectives and powers of the FCA and PRA in relation to financial governance. But its main constituent is a dense and intertwined thicket of administrative rules, guidance and other forms of soft law, the main sources for which are the immensely detailed and often highly complex administrative 'rulebooks' (the PRA term) or 'handbooks' (the FCA term) of the FCA and the PRA. The FCA and PRA rulebooks are based on a hierarchy of norms approach as they also include two similar sets of over-arching principles which are designed to express the FCA's and PRA's general objectives and to set high-level (and enforceable) requirements for the financial services industry.[8] Supervision and enforcement is carried out by the FCA and PRA in relation to their respective populations of regulated actors, albeit that ex post enforcement is associated much more strongly with conduct regulation and the FCA; prudential regulation is traditionally policed by ex ante supervisory controls, mainly risk-oriented capital-related requirements, which are primarily the concern of the PRA.

The financial services sector is among the most intensely regulated sectors of the modern economy, reflecting the scale of the costs which failures and abuses can wreak on the economy and on households, as the global financial crisis – only the most recent and severe of the scandals and crises which have shaped modern financial regulation – made clear.[9] The governance of the UK financial sector is no different from the financial governance arrangements of any other major economy globally in this regard. But it differs in one significant respect. Although the UK financial market is in many respects distinct from other EU27

---

Fair and Effective Markets Review. In addition, the Bank has a distinct financial stability mandate in relation to which it: acts as 'lender of last resort'; is responsible for removing/reducing systemic risk (through its Financial Policy Committee); acts as the UK's resolution authority for failing firms; supervises certain financial market infrastructures, notably central clearing counterparties (CCPs); and supports financial sector continuity and resilience.

[7] Most significantly by the crisis-era Financial Services Act 2012 which created the PRA and FCA (from the previously unitary Financial Services Authority (FSA)) and which enhanced the financial stability powers of the Bank. Other key legislative measures include the 2009 Banking Act which conferred a statutory objective to protect and enhance financial stability on the Bank.

[8] The PRA's 8 'Fundamental Rules and Principles for Businesses' are 'high level rules which collectively act as an expression of the PRA's general objective of promoting the safety and soundness of regulated firms' (PRA, *Fundamental Rules and Principles for Businesses*). The FCA similarly deploys 11 'Principles for Business' which are a 'general statement of the fundamental obligations of firms under the regulatory system' (FCA, *Principles for Businesses Handbook*, para 1.1.2).

[9] For an examination of the relationship between crisis and the evolution of financial governance, see F PARTNOY, 'Financial Systems, Crises and Regulation' in N MOLONEY, E FERRAN and J PAYNE (eds), *The Oxford Handbook of Financial Regulation*, Oxford University Press, Oxford 2015, p 68.

markets, being significantly larger and hosting the deepest wholesale market,[10] many of its governing rules are set by the EU and the EU is also increasingly shaping how supervision is carried out.[11]

Since the financial crisis, the scale of EU financial regulation has increased exponentially in response to a range of drivers, including the G20 crisis-era reform agenda which the EU committed to implementing; the need to repair the EU financial system and address the EU-specific and significant regulatory and supervisory weaknesses exposed by the spread of risk cross-border over the financial crisis; and the emergence of a more sceptical approach – in certain EU quarters – to intense levels of financial market activity (or financial intermediation).[12] A harmonised 'single rulebook' of vast scope and immense granularity now governs national financial systems in the EU and has been the defining influence on UK financial governance in recent years, particularly with respect to wholesale market regulation. The single rulebook has multiple components, being based on often highly detailed EU legislation, increasingly in the form of Regulations; a behemoth administrative rulebook; and tracts of soft law guidance to the market and regulators. The scale of the single rulebook is in part a function of the rise of administrative governance in EU financial governance since the financial crisis. The three European Supervisory Authorities (ESAs) (the European Banking Authority (EBA) – banking; the European Securities and Markets Authority (ESMA) – securities; and the European Insurance and Occupational Pensions Authority (EIOPA) – insurance and pensions), which were established in 2011 as part of the EU's crisis-era governance reforms, are, inter alia, charged with proposing certain forms of administrative rule (Binding Technical Standards); advising the Commission on others (Delegated Acts); and adopting Guidelines and other soft law measures. The administrative capacity which they have brought to EU financial regulatory governance has led to an exponential increase in the breadth and depth of the single rulebook. To take only one example, the Capital Requirements Directive IV/Capital Requirements Regulation (2013),[13] the leviathan of EU banking regulation, has been amplified

---

10   See recently European Commission, *European Financial Stability and Integration Review*, SWD (2016) 146.

11   For accounts of EU financial governance, see eg R VEIL (ed), *European Capital Markets Law*, 2nd edn, Hart Publishing, Oxford 2017 and N MOLONEY, *EU Securities and Financial Markets Regulation*, Oxford University Press, Oxford 2014.

12   See E FERRAN, 'Crisis-driven Regulatory Reform: Where in the World is the EU Going?' and N MOLONEY, 'The Legacy Effects of the Financial Crisis on Regulatory Design in the EU' in E FERRAN, N MOLONEY, J HILL and JC COFFEE (eds), *The Regulatory Aftermath of the Global Financial Crisis*, Cambridge University Press, Cambridge 2012, p 1 and p 111 (respectively).

13   Directive 2013/2013/36/EU of the European Parliament and of the Council of 26 June 2013 on access to the activity of credit institutions and the prudential supervision of credit institutions and investment firms, and amending Directive 2002/87/EC and repealing Directives 2006/48/EC and 2006/49 [2013] OJ L176/338 (CRD IV); and Regulation (EU) No 575/2013 of the European Parliament and of the Council of 26 June 2013 on prudential

by some 47 separate Binding Technical Standards, a number of which are of immense length and complexity.[14]

EU financial governance also extends to supervision, albeit not to the same extent. Distinct arrangements apply in the Banking Union zone where supervision and rescue/resolution of banks is now managed within the Single Supervisory Mechanism (overseen by the ECB) and the Single Resolution Mechanism. The UK is not a member of Banking Union (participation is mandatory only for euro area Member States), regarding Banking Union as a euro area stability project, being concerned to protect its national supervisory autonomy and control over financial stability, and being opposed to risk sharing. But supervisory governance in the single financial market generally, while located with national regulators, is coordinated through the three ESAs and is increasingly being subject to harmonised requirements and following standard operational templates. In parallel with the many arrangements which govern cross-border supervisory cooperation and coordination between national regulators (and which include colleges of supervisors, information exchange requirements and investigation cooperation), legislative and administrative rules are coming to govern the granular business of operational supervision. Chief among these are the rules which apply to the 'SREP,' or the annual Supervisory Review and Evaluation Process of banks which EU supervisors are required to carry out of EU banks under their jurisdiction,[15] and to the related stress testing of EU banks.[16] The SREP is unusual in its degree of operational harmonisation. But supervisory requirements also apply elsewhere. In the markets sphere, detailed rules govern, for example, how regulators should intervene in the commodity derivatives markets and in relation to the practice of short selling.[17] In some (very limited) cases, the ESAs exercise direct supervisory jurisdiction over certain EU actors. ESMA is the most advanced of the ESAs in this regard, having exclusive

---

requirements for credit institutions and investment firms and amending Regulation (EU) No 648/2012 [2013] OJ L176/1 (CRR).

[14] One administrative rule, which sets out the technical reporting template to be used by banks for supervisory reporting and which includes a series of data cells, runs to some 1,861 pages in the Official Journal.

[15] Legislative rules, administrative rules and EBA guidance govern how the SREP should be organised and carried out; the internal data-gathering required of banks before the SREP; and how supervisory remediation measures (such as extra capital requirements) should be designed and used. For 1 example, see EBA, *Guidelines on Common Procedures and Methodologies for the Supervisory Review and Evaluation Process* (EBA/GL/2014/13).

[16] On the 2016 stress test, see EBA, *2016 EU-Wide Stress Test Results*, 29 July 2016.

[17] Under the Markets in Financial Instruments Regulation 2014 (Regulation (EU) No 600/2014 of the European Parliament and of the Council of 15 May 2014 on markets in financial instruments and amending Regulation (EU) No 648/2012 [2014] OJ L173/84) and the Short Selling Regulation (Regulation (EU) No 236/2012 of the European Parliament and of the Council of 14 March 2012 on short selling and certain aspects of credit default swaps [2012] OJ L86/1).

jurisdiction over authorisation, supervision and enforcement in relation to credit rating agencies and trade repositories (the latter being 'data warehouses' for the derivatives markets). ESMA additionally has intervention powers in relation to short selling practices and carries out the operationally critical function of reviewing the risk models used by the central clearing counterparties (CCPs) which support the stability of the EU derivatives market. ESMA and EBA also have powers to intervene to prohibit the sale of investment products. More generally the ESAs may compel regulators (and regulated actors) to act in three unusual cases (in relation to a regulator's breach of EU law; in the case of a binding ESA mediation; and in emergency conditions) – although these powers have yet to be used. Less intrusively, a host of increasingly ambitious 'supervisory convergence' strategies are being deployed through the ESAs, including peer review and oversight of supervisory practices, to achieve greater convergence in supervision.[18] The operationalisation and standardisation of supervision at EU level extends to the collection, centralisation and interrogation of data. ESMA, for example, collects, collates and interrogates a vast data-set on market trading from national markets through its 'FIRDS' data system.[19] This centralised data system informs a host of domestic supervisory activities, including in relation to the control of market abuse and insider trading and the management of market liquidity risks, across the EU.

Enforcement remains a national competence, but here also the grip of the EU is tightening. The crisis-era reforms are notable for the extent to which they prescribe the forms of administrative sanctions which national regulators should have at their disposal and how and when they should be used, including in relation to the quantum of penalties.

UK financial governance is therefore deeply embedded within EU governance, particularly in relation to the governance of the wholesale markets. The immense FCA and PRA administrative rulebooks in many cases simply link through to relevant EU rules. The recent coming into force of the 2014 Market Abuse Regulation[20] and its related administrative rules required a large-scale recasting and editing of the FCA's long-established 'MAR' (the rulebook governing the control of market abuse) and the related removal of extensive and longstanding FCA guidance for the UK market which could no longer sit alongside the directly applicable and highly detailed EU regime.[21] Similarly

---

[18]   For examples, see ESMA, *Supervisory Convergence Work Programme 2017* and EBA, *Report on the Convergence of Supervisory Practices* (EBA-Op-2016-11).

[19]   For discussion, see ESMA, *Risk Assessment Work Programme 2017*.

[20]   Regulation (EU) No 596/2014 of the European Parliament and of the Council of 16 April 2014 on market abuse and repealing Directive 2003/6/EC and Commission Directives 2003/124/EC, 2003/125/EC and 2004/72/EC [2014] OJ L173/1.

[21]   FCA, Policy Statement PS16/13, *Implementation of the Market Abuse Regulation* (2016).

the Markets in Financial Instruments Directive IV[22]/Markets in Financial Instruments Regulation 2014 (MiFID II/MiFIR), a massive legislative measure of great reach which is recasting how investment services and trading venues are regulated across the EU, and which is of signal importance to the UK capital market, is currently being implemented in the UK through a light-touch process which reflects the granularity of much of the regime, as well as the location of many of the rules in the MiFIR Regulation or in administrative rules in the form of Regulations. The UK FCA has noted that while certain of the new measures are significant for the UK market, it would not consult on their implementation given their location in directly applicable Regulations.[23]

Nonetheless, this embedding of UK financial governance within EU financial governance should not be read as prejudicial to the UK. The UK has supported the drive to harmonisation under the single rulebook, in part given the benefits it brings in terms of UK regulated actors being permitted to 'passport' into national markets across the EU on the basis of home (UK) authorisation and supervision.[24] The UK has also been highly effective in bending EU financial governance to its specific preferences, and has had a significant competitive advantage in this regard given its deep technical expertise and long experience in regulating the EU's largest financial market. Most recently, it has brought this technical capacity to bear on the development of administrative rules at the ESA level (the UK sits as a supervisor on the Boards of Supervisors which govern the ESAs and has regularly staffed the technical working groups through which the ESAs often work). Technical quality assurance aside, the UK has often been successful in ensuring that EU harmonising measures have contained exemptions, derogations and calibrations designed to protect UK interests and market features.[25] The many exemptions and calibrations in MiFID II/MiFIR which are designed to protect liquidity in the professional, wholesale trading markets, for example, were driven by the UK and its interest in achieving distinct treatment for the sophisticated trading markets in the City of London.[26] Much of EU financial regulation has also been shaped by the UK experience, with the UK regulatory regime often acting as something of an incubator for the

---

[22] Directive 2014/56/EU of the European Parliament and of the Council of 15 May 2014 on markets in financial instruments and amending Directive 2002/92/EC and Directive 2011/61/EU [2014] OJ L173/349.

[23] FCA, Consultation Paper CP15/43, *Markets in Financial Instruments Directive II Implementation – Consultation Paper I* (2016).

[24] It made clear its support for 'more Europe' over 'less Europe' at an early stage of the crisis-era reforms: FSA, *The Turner Review: A Regulatory Response to the Global Banking Crisis* (2007) pp 100–02.

[25] For analysis of the preferences which shaped the main crisis-era measures and the role of the UK, see FERRAN, above n 12.

[26] See House of Lords European Union Committee, *MiFID II: Getting it Right for the City and EU Financial Services Industry* (HL 2012–13, 28).

EU. For example, the new MiFID II/MiFIR regime governing investment advice which prohibits payment by commission where investment advice is labelled as 'independent' is based on the reforms earlier introduced by the UK's wide-ranging 'Retail Distribution Review' which brought extensive structural reform to the UK investment advice industry.[27]

There have, of course, been flashpoints, particularly as a coalition of more interventionist/dirigiste 'market-shaping' Member States came into the ascendant in the Council over the crisis-era, often trumping the preferences of the more liberal 'market-making' coalition.[28] The UK struggled to protect its fund management industry under the Alternative Investment Fund Managers Directive 2011[29] and, in probably the most high-profile example, was left isolated in attempting to oppose the cap on bonus remuneration (now within CRD IV/CRR).

The UK has arguably been most successful in imposing its preferences in limiting the transfer of supervisory powers to the EU and opposing the related mutualisation and sharing of fiscal risk outside Banking Union. It has been a fierce opponent of Banking Union/euro area measures shaping single market financial governance and has advocated for a multi-currency form of integration and governance.[30] This is evident most recently in the UK's negotiating stance on the upcoming reforms to the CRD IV/CRR banking rulebook. Although the UK will have limited (or no) political influence in these negotiations as it leaves the EU, it has argued that the reforms must in no way lead to the imposition of euro area preferences or interests on the single banking market.[31] The UK has similarly opposed the conferral of direct supervisory powers on the ESAs, often deploying in aid the *Meroni* ruling[32] which prohibits the exercise of wide-ranging discretion by EU agencies.[33]

---

[27]  The large-scale UK reforms, which experienced years of consultation and market testing, were expressly acknowledged during MiFID II's development: European Commission, *MiFID II Proposal Impact Assessment* (SEC (2011) 1226) eg at pp 193, 256 and 260.

[28]  L QUAGLIA, 'The "Old" and "New" Politics of Financial Services Regulation in the EU' (2012) 17(4) *New Political Economy* 15; and L QUAGLIA, 'Completing the Single Market in Financial Services: the Politics of Competing Advocacy Coalitions' (2010) 17 *Journal of European Public Policy* 1007.

[29]  Directive 2011/61/EU of the European Parliament and of the Council of 8 June 2011 on Alternative Investment Fund Managers and amending Directives 2003/41/EC and 2009/65/EC and Regulations (EC) No 1060/2009 and (EU) No 1095/2010 [2011] OJ L174/1.

[30]  The protection of the single market from euro area caucusing and preferences was a major theme of the 'New Settlement' which David Cameron agreed with the European Council prior to the Brexit referendum: Decision of the Heads of State or Government Meeting Within the European Council, Concerning a New Settlement for the United Kingdom with the European Union, European Council Meeting, 18 and 19 February 2016, EUCO 1/16 (Annex 1).

[31]  Department for Exiting the European Union, *Explanatory Memorandum for EU Legislation and Documents*, 14 December 2016.

[32]  Case C-9/56, *Meroni v Haute Autorité*, ECLI:EU:C:1958:7.

[33]  See HM Treasury, *Response to the Commission Services Consultation on the Review of the European System of Financial Supervision* (2013) and HM Government, *Review of the Balance*

It should not accordingly be assumed that the UK lost all sovereignty over financial regulation and that a period of 'grand designs' in regulatory governance, leading to a refreshing and recasting of UK financial governance to reflect previously subjugated UK interests and preferences, can be expected after Brexit. Further, while the UK has often been successful in imposing its preferences, it is also the case that EU financial regulatory governance is not, notwithstanding the single rulebook, monolithic. Much of consumer financial protection regulation remains a domestic competence, for example. In addition, the EU is often a rule-taker from the Member States, borrowing from domestic regulatory incubators, the UK often chief among them, when addressing new areas of regulation, particularly in the area of conduct regulation.

The UK has also repeatedly experimented with and reshaped its regulatory governance over its period of EU membership. This has been particularly marked in relation to consumer protection regulation. The UK has engaged in repeated cycles of reforms to investment product distribution and advice, attempting to get at the root causes of the recurring cycles of mis-selling in the UK,[34] and has been able to do so given either the more limited coverage of EU law, or the availability of exemptions or possibilities for 'gold-plating' (or imposing additional and higher standards on UK actors above the EU minimum). The Retail Distribution Review (RDR), as noted above, led to a series of highly contested and wide-ranging reforms to investment advice and production distribution which came into force at the end of 2012. This reform process has continued. The ongoing review of the RDR[35] is leading to related reforms and assessments of the investment advice industry in the UK, including the joint FCA/HM Treasury Financial Advice Market Review,[36] which are independent of related EU law developments. The Financial Advice Market Review addresses, for example, the affordability of financial advice, access to advice, and redress – areas which are, by and large, outside the reach of EU consumer financial protection regulation and the related reforms to which reflect the distinct structural features and risks of the UK financial advice market. The UK has also innovated in other areas, typically where the EU has adopted a minimum harmonisation approach. The minimum standards adopted in the EU's 'listing regime', which governs the

---

of Competences between the United Kingdom and the European Union: The Single Market: Financial Services and the Free Movement of Capital (2013). The UK took an unsuccessful action against the validity of the Short Selling Regulation which conferred certain direct intervention powers on ESMA, based in part on breach of the Meroni ruling: Case C-270/12, UK v Parliament and Council, ECLI:EU:C:2014:18.

[34] N MOLONEY, How to Protect Investors, Lessons from the EU and the UK, Cambridge University Press, Cambridge 2010, pp 269–273.

[35] See eg FCA, Post Implementation Review of the Retail Distribution Review (2014).

[36] HM Treasury and FCA, Financial Advice Market Review (2016).

admission by firms of their securities to trading venues,[37] have allowed the UK to develop a sophisticated, graduated listing system, which is designed to attract different forms of firm to UK trading venues, and to design the FCA's 'Official List' as a badge of high quality which attracts global listing business to UK trading venues.[38]

Beyond regulatory governance, the UK has also frequently deployed novel and domestically-oriented supervisory strategies to achieve outcomes for the domestic market. Most attention has focused on the ill-fated 'principles-based regulation' (PBR) approach followed by the then-unitary Financial Services Authority (FSA), which has since been replaced by the more nuanced 'outcomes-based' approach to supervision.[39] With more success, the FSA built a sophisticated supervisory strategy to enhance consumer outcomes, which defined most of its consumer market engagement prior to the financial crisis, on one of the 11 Principles which now frame the FCA rulebook – the 'Treating Customers Fairly' (TCF) strategy.[40] As noted in Section 4, approaches to enforcement have also evolved.

While the extent to which the UK could innovate has been a function of the room left by the EU, the drivers for UK change and experimentation have typically been independent of the EU. Regulatory mandates and institutional redesigns, for example, have been determinative. The Financial Services Act 2012, which established the FCA and PRA, set out distinct objectives for both authorities which have shaped their activities. Of particular note is the conferral of a distinct competition objective on the FCA by the 2012 Act which requires the FCA to promote effective competition in the interests of consumers in the markets for regulated financial services and in relation to trading venues (Financial Services and Markets Act 2000, section 1E); specific competition enforcement powers were subsequently conferred on the FCA by the Banking Act 2013.[41]

---

[37] Set out in Directive 2001/34/EC of the European Parliament and of the Council of 28 May 2001 on the admission of securities to official stock exchange listing and on the information to be published on those securities [2001] OJ L184/1.

[38] The listing regime is almost continually reviewed and reformed, reflecting its importance to the competitiveness of the UK capital market. The Brexit decision, and related risk to the competitive position of the UK capital market, has, not unexpectedly, not led to any loss of appetite for reform. Early 2017 saw a series of reforms being proposed by the FCA to the listing and capital-raising process (including FCA, Discussion Paper DP17/2, *Review of the Effectiveness of Primary Markets: the UK Primary Market Landscape* (2017)).

[39] J BLACK, 'Regulatory Styles and Supervisory Strategies' in MOLONEY, FERRAN and PAYNE, above n 9, p 217.

[40] On the TCF strategy and how it deployed supervisory strategies to drive better consumer outcomes, see MOLONEY, above n 34, pp 219–224 and A GEORGOSOULI, 'The FSA's "Treating Customers Fairly" (TCF) Initiative: What is So Good About It and Why It May Not Work' (2011) 38(3) *Journal of Law and Society* 405.

[41] The new powers empower the FCA to enforce against breaches of the Competition Act 1998 in the financial services sector. The PRA similarly has a competition objective and powers in relation to the entities it supervises.

The imposition of a competition-related objective on a financial regulator was at the time and remains a novelty.[42] But it has had a significant influence on how the FCA operates, driving, for example, the production of a series of market studies into how competition is working in inter alia the credit card and asset management sectors; the credit card study led to a series of reforms directed to how firms deal with credit card indebtedness.[43] The FCA's current work on its 'mission' has highlighted the centrality of its competition objective and of its related mandate to identify and address competition-related problems, including by means of requiring greater firm transparency; intervening in such a way that provides a proxy for competition; using its regulatory tools to incentivise appropriate firm behaviour; specific market interventions (such as capping prices for payday loans);[44] targeted product interventions; and extensive behavioural studies designed to deepen the FCA's understanding of firm and consumer behaviour.[45] All the indications suggest that the competition mandate is likely to be a major influence on the FCA's future work and to lead to a series of interventionist actions, beyond the regulatory/conduct standards traditionally associated with FCA action.[46]

Market forces have also been relevant. As new challenges for regulation have emerged as the market innovates, the UK has often been an early responder. The emergence of 'fintech'[47] has been a prominent driver of recent FCA initiatives. The FCA was, for example, an innovator in relation to the regulation of crowdfunding, which has yet to be governed by EU rules.[48] It has also recently developed, as part of its 'Innovation Hub' the much-examined 'regulatory sandbox' which is designed to support innovative, fintech companies in accessing the regulated space.[49] The growth of 'robo-advice' has similarly led to reforms and a rethink of how investment advice is regulated in the UK.

---

[42] On the challenges which a competition mandate brings to a financial regulator, particularly in relation to ensuring that consumer protection is not prejudiced by incentives to follow a more light-touch approach, see E FERRAN, 'The New Mandate for the Supervision of Financial Services Conduct' (2011) 65(1) *Current Legal Problems* 411.

[43] FCA, Market Study MS14/6.3, *Credit Card Market Study: Final Findings Report* (2016).

[44] FCA, Policy Statement PS 14/16, *Detailed Rules for the Price Cap on High-Cost Short-Term Credit* (2014).

[45] FCA, *Our Future Mission* (2016) pp 37–39.

[46] In late 2016 eg it announced a series of actions to improve competition in the current account market, particularly in relation to the overdraft market: FCA, *Our Response to the CMA's Final Report on its Investigation into Competition in the Retail Banking Market* (2016).

[47] See D ARNER, JN BARBERIS and R BUCKLEY, 'Fintech, Regtech and the Reconceptualization of Financial Regulation' (2017) *Northwestern Journal of International Law & Business*, forthcoming.

[48] The FCA issued its first set of rules in 2014 and has since carried out a post-implementation review: FCA, *Interim Feedback to the Call for Input to the Post Implementation Review of the FCA's Crowdfunding Rules* (2016).

[49] The 'sandbox' is designed to support firms in getting innovative ideas and business models to market and allows eligible firms to test innovation without being subject to the full range

It is axiomatic that prevailing political and societal concerns have mattered. Financial sector accountability provides a useful example. The EU banking rulebook is not granular in relation to the authorisation of key individuals or in relation to accountability mechanisms, reflecting the different approaches to corporate governance and structure across the EU. But following a series of reviews into accountability in the UK banking sector in the wake of the financial crisis and other failures,[50] wide-ranging reforms have been made at the legislative level,[51] a new Banking Standards Board has been established[52] and the FCA and PRA have put in place a new accountability regime for senior managers and related reforms designed to enhance accountability more generally.[53]

UK financial governance can therefore, over the period of the UK's EU membership, and certainly since the turn of the century when EU financial governance first began to intensify, be characterised as dynamic and frequently experimental, and as responding to local conditions, notwithstanding the reach of EU financial governance. It is unlikely accordingly that there is a pent-up demand for governance innovation.

Nonetheless, the interconnection between UK and EU financial governance is deep and entrenched. The need to minimise the costs and risks associated with the disentangling of the UK from EU financial governance is likely to frame UK financial governance in the short to medium term – assuming there is no major market dislocation which calls for a more radical governance response.


## 3.   RISKS TO UK FINANCIAL GOVERNANCE AND THE POST-BREXIT UK GOVERNANCE AGENDA

The disentangling of UK financial governance from the EU, which is likely to take several years, generates risks and costs which will require nuanced and

---

of regulatory requirements which would otherwise apply. See FCA, *Business Plan 2016/17* (2016) p 33 and FCA, *Regulatory Sandbox* (2015).

[50]   Chief among them the work of the Parliamentary Commission on Banking Standards. See esp PCBS, Fifth Report, *Changing Banking for Good*, 12 June 2013.

[51]   Primarily the Banking Reform Act 2013 which put in place a new oversight system for individuals composed of a senior managers regime, certification regime (for less senior staff) and banking standards rules, to be amplified and implemented by the FCA and PRA. The Act also provides for a new criminal offence (applicable to senior managers) relating to the taking of a decision which causes a financial institution to fail.

[52]   The new Banking Standard Board, established in 2015, is a private sector 'soft' body which seeks to promote high standards of behaviour and competence across UK banks and building societies and restore trust in the banking sector. Its establishment was recommended by the Parliamentary Commission on Banking and the industry-initiated Banking Standards Review (2014) led by Sir Richard Lambert.

[53]   The FCA and PRA regimes are multifaceted but are based on imposing new certification, conduct and accountability requirements on individuals, including senior managers but also other individuals.

careful legal and policy responses. The management of these risks and costs can be expected to preoccupy UK financial governance for some time.

The UK Government's commitment to carrying over the corpus of EU law through the proposed Great Repeal Bill removes the risk that the UK financial industry will be largely unregulated on 'Brexit Day One'; this risk derives from the direct applicability of the many legislative and administrative Regulations within EU financial regulation. But the Act alone is unlikely to resolve the legal uncertainty risks or to remove the need for governance action. Multiple and fine judgements will be needed concerning the 'carry over' of the massive body of EU financial administrative law and soft law which shapes UK firms' business models and practices.

In addition, EU financial regulatory governance is highly dynamic. Granular changes are frequently made to administrative rules which have implications for firms and their business models. Technical but material changes of this nature are likely to intensify and accelerate given the current EU policy and political commitment to enhancing and reforming EU financial regulatory governance, in part to ensure growth is not obstructed.[54] Reforms are also likely to be made to the technical capacity of the ESAs in relation to rule-making which raise the prospect of the ESAs driving further technical change.[55] If UK financial regulatory governance does not respond as EU regulation evolves difficulties will arise in relation to UK law being 'equivalent' to EU law, which may, depending on how the Brexit negotiations proceed, have implications for market access, as noted in Section 4 (below). But a failure to follow EU developments may also mean that UK rules – particularly at the administrative level – become uncompetitive for UK firms competing with EU actors, embed overlooked errors and carry the wider opportunity costs associated with failures to refresh regulation.

Particular risks and costs which will require a response follow from the extent to which EU financial governance now drills deep into the business models and internal risk structures of financial institutions. Two current examples are illustrative. The EU banking sector is currently grappling with two major sets of reforms which have significant implications for business model and internal risk governance design. First, the implementation of the new 'IFRS 9' financial reporting standard, which changes how banks account for impaired loans and which is designed to ensure that credit losses are reported and responded to by banks at an earlier stage, is generating material transaction costs and internal

---

[54]    The Commission has recently committed to related reforms following the 2015–16 'stocktake' of the crisis-era reforms: European Commission, *Communication on Call for Evidence – EU Regulatory Framework for Financial Services*, COM(2016) 855.

[55]    EBA eg has proposed reforms which would facilitate it in adopting technical reporting-related rules: EBA, *Opinion on Improving the Decision-Making Framework for Supervisory Reporting Requirements under Regulation (EU) No 575/2013* (EBA/Op/2017/03).

risk management changes for EU banks, and may lead to significantly higher levels of capital being required across the banking sector.[56] The onerous industry implementation process is being steered by EU-level guidance from EBA,[57] and some attempt to mitigate the costs of the transition to the new reporting standard is being made by the Commission's related proposals to provide for a transitional regime over which the impact of IFRS 9 on banks' capital requirements will be moderated.[58] IFRS 9 must be implemented by January 2018, at which point the UK will be in the EU. But the calibration and refining process is likely to go on for some time. UK firms are unlikely to welcome any new arrangements or supervisory changes in emphasis which do not reflect the EU approach. Similarly, the UK regime will need to ensure that UK firms benefit from any ameliorations/ relaxations which the EU provides for EU firms if distortions to competition are to be avoided. Second, the EU banking sector is now and will be for some time preoccupied with the wide-ranging, multi-year and intrusive internal model review being led by EBA and the SSM (within the Banking Union zone) and which is designed to reduce the extent to which internal risk models, and particularly models for assessing capital requirements, diverge within banks.[59] While much of the operational management of this process is located at national level, UK firms can be expected to resist any major change of direction by the UK authorities which negates earlier preparatory work at EU level. Similarly, efforts will need to be made to ensure that UK firms are not disadvantaged by any divergences between the UK and EU approaches to model review.

The solutions to this difficulty of how to achieve some degree of alignment between UK and EU financial governance, particularly at the granular, internal risk management level, are not straightforward. Any attempt to move in lockstep with the EU is likely to raise significant political difficulties. It also raises governance difficulties in terms of how such technical developments, which are primarily driven by the ESAs, should be monitored and assessed – as the UK will no longer be a member of the ESAs – and implemented – given that EU rule implementation is currently shared between the Treasury and the Bank/PRA/ FCA (the Government's March 2017 White Paper on the Great Repeal Bill does not clarify the extent to which (if at all) additional rule-making powers will be conferred on the Bank, PRA or FCA in relation to the rollover of the EU *acquis*).[60]

---

[56] See BARCLAYS, *Equity Research, European Banks. IFRS 9 – Bigger than Basel IV*, 9 January 2017.

[57] eg EBA, *Report on Results from the EBA Impact Assessment of IFRS 9* (2016).

[58] The Commission's November 2016 proposal to revise CRD IV/CRR contains a phase-in arrangement for capital requirements to moderate the impact of IFRS 9: COM(2016) 850.

[59] See eg EBA, *Opinion on the Implementation of the Regulatory Review of the IRB Approach* (EBA/Op/2016/01).

[60] Department for Exiting the European Union, *Legislating for the United Kingdom's withdrawal from the European Union* (Cm 9446, March 2017). Ch 3 covers delegated powers but does not expressly address the financial regulators.

Challenges also arise in relation to ensuring the effectiveness of supervision in the UK. One of the main lessons from the epochal crisis-era reform period has been the need for regulatory reform to be accompanied by nimble and responsive supervision.[61] The extraction of the UK from the EU financial governance raises distinct risks in this regard. The UK is currently embedded within the increasingly sophisticated structures which support cross-border cooperation and coordination within the EU. These include the colleges of supervisors which coordinate the supervision of financial subsidiaries and their groups across the UK; the home/host coordination arrangements which govern cross-border supply of financial services from the home state to the host, through services or a branch; and the array of supervisory coordination and cooperation measures adopted or provided by the ESAs (including templates for cooperation and information exchange and ESA-based mediation channels). On Brexit, the UK will no longer have access to these now well-tested arrangements which operate under single market governance arrangements. Its ability to assess and manage risks to the UK financial system may be compromised as a result. Alternative forms of cooperation, and in particular information exchange channels, will need to be constructed to ensure the UK can protect the stability of the UK market, and that the FCA and PRA can meet their regulatory mandates, particularly in relation to risks arising from cross-border EU business and from the interconnections more generally between the UK and EU27 markets. For example, any weakness in a major EU market infrastructure, such as a CCP, is likely to have consequences for the UK. Similarly, market integrity risks to the UK could follow from EU-based abusive trading behaviour, particularly where derivatives are deployed to hide manipulation on different trading venues. It may be that the current arrangement can provide some form of basic template on which new mechanisms can be built. But the current EU arrangements are located within single market legislative measures, overseen by the Court of Justice of the EU, and supported by the ESAs and so are not readily transportable.

Data collection is a particular risk. Data is the lifeblood of supervision; much of the G20 crisis-era reform programme globally was directed to ensuring that 'dark' corners of the financial system became transparent so that effective supervision could be deployed and precautionary ex ante measures taken against risks. At present, the UK forms part of an intricate data-sharing and collection network, organised and governed by EU law and managed through the ESAs. ESMA hosts the massive 'FIRDs' market/trading data system, for example, while EBA hosts the vast 'FINREP' and 'COREP' data-streams which flow from EU banks and which contain a wealth of data on the health of the EU banking system and on emerging risks. Some form of alternative means for ensuring access to

---

[61]   As was acknowledged by the UK Government: HM Treasury, *A New Approach to Financial Regulation: judgment, focus and stability* (2010) p 28.

data will be required if the UK is to have adequate access to the market data needed for supervisory purposes.

Specific supervisory functions will also need to be replicated. ESMA, for example, currently has exclusive jurisdiction over rating agencies, including those based in the UK; a new regulatory and supervisory governance regime will be required if rating agencies – currently a major component of the City of London's infrastructure for supporting financial markets – are to remain based in the UK.[62]

Finally, new means for engaging with international financial governance and with the coalitions which shape it will be required. Since the financial crisis, regulatory regimes globally, particularly in relation to stability-oriented prudential regulation, have come to be shaped by the standards adopted by the International Standard Setting Bodies (ISSBs) of global financial governance, chief among them the Basel Committee (banking), the International Association of Insurance Supervisors (IAS, insurance), the International Organization of Securities Commissions (IOSCO, securities), and the Financial Stability Board (the senior ISSB which monitors and adopts standards to support global financial stability).[63] The ISSBs have adopted a raft of standards, the implementation of which is policed through the FSB. These standards have come to have a decisive influence on domestic/regional regulatory regimes,[64] often leading to the construction of new domestic/regional coalitions of regulators and policy-makers which drive the national implementation of international standards whose application may otherwise be contested.[65] The EU has, particularly since the financial crisis, come to exert significant influence on international financial governance, becoming increasingly effective in imposing its preferences.[66] The UK sits alongside the EU, holding separate membership in the key ISSBs. It has

---

[62]   Some industry anxiety as to the UK's preparedness for supervising UK-based rating agencies has been reported: C Binham, 'Brexit Casts Doubt over Rating Agencies' Future in London' *Financial Times*, 21 February 2017.

[63]   See generally M Barr, 'Who's in Charge of Global Finance?' (2014) 45(4) *Georgetown Journal of International Law* 971.

[64]   D Mugge, *Europe and the Governance of Global Finance*, Oxford University Press, Oxford 2014; and E Helleiner, S Pagliari and H Zimmerman (eds), *Global Finance in Crisis*, Routledge, London 2010.

[65]   A Newman and E Posner, 'Structuring Transnational Interests: the Second Order Effect of Soft Law in the Politics of Global Finance' (2016) 23(5) *Review of International Political Economy* 768.

[66]   N Moloney, 'International Financial Governance, the EU, and Brexit: the Agencification of EU Financial Governance and the Implications' (2016) 17 *European Business Organization Law Review* 451; A Newman and E Posner, 'Putting the EU in its Place: Policy Strategies and the Global Regulatory Context' (2015) 22(9) *Journal of European Public Policy* 1316; and L Quaglia, *The European Union & Global Financial Regulation*, Oxford University Press, Oxford 2014.

at times held different views from the EU and advocated for different interests,[67] but it has also benefited from the EU's ability to represent a distinct set of preferences, where such can be formed. The EU's preferences are organised and imposed through a range of EU actors, including the Commission and the ESAs, on which the UK will not be represented following its exit from the EU. Functional substitutes for formal membership of these bodies, and related dialogue and communication channels, will be important to ensuring the UK's preferences are given maximum heft in international discussions. Effective engagement with the EU is likely to be all the more important given current indications (noted below) of the US adopting a more antagonistic posture to international financial governance and a deregulatory stance which may prejudice the City of London.

## 4.  RECASTING UK FINANCIAL GOVERNANCE – AND RELATED FRICTIONS

Governance changes directed to shadowing EU financial governance in some way can therefore be expected. Others will also likely follow – it is unlikely that Brexit will not lead to some recasting of the current governance regime. But not all elements of UK financial governance are likely to experience Brexit-associated change.

The enforcement component of UK financial governance, in particular, has long operated outside EU financial governance, and the forces which have shaped change have been largely independent of EU financial governance; for example, while EU financial governance has become increasingly prescriptive in relation to how administrative sanctions are used, UK financial governance has long deployed administrative sanctions and has adopted a sophisticated procedural regime and practice in this regard.[68] As has been well documented,[69] the financial crisis era led to a shift within what is now the FCA towards 'credible deterrence' – or a conscious institutional shift towards more intensive enforcement of rules.[70] This shift has led to higher administrative sanctions and penalties but also to greater recourse to the criminal law, particularly in relation

---

[67] On the crisis-era Basel III negotiations on bank capital reforms and the UK's position, see D HOWARTH and L QUAGLIA, 'The Comparative Political Economy of Basel III in Europe' (2017) 35(3) *Policy and Society* 205.

[68] Set out in, eg, the FCA's DEPP (or Decision Procedure and Penalties Manual) and in its Enforcement Guide.

[69] See I MACNEIL, 'Enforcement and Sanctioning' in MOLONEY, FERRAN and PAYNE, above n 9, p 280.

[70] Outlined in, eg, M COLE (then FSA Director of Enforcement), Speech on 'Delivering Credible Deterrence', 27 April 2009. The increasing reliance on enforcement can be traced through the FCA's Enforcement Annual Performance Account.

to market abuse (as illustrated by the high-profile series of criminal prosecutions taken by the FCA following the major 'Operation Tabernula' investigation into a suspected insider dealing ring). The change in the FCA's approach to enforcement has significant empirical support: an extensive literature shows that rule enforcement, and not rule adoption, leads to positive market outcomes, including with respect to domestic growth.[71] The FCA was also following other major regulatory systems globally in enhancing enforcement.[72] But other factors were also at play, notably the (then) FSA's incentives to strengthen its credibility and capacity as a regulator in the aftermath of the crisis when it came under close political scrutiny (following which it was ultimately broken up into what are now the FCA and PRA).[73] The FCA's approach to enforcement is continuing to evolve, reflecting sometimes conflicting environmental factors. The highly critical 2011 Green Report into the crisis-era failures at HBOS, for example, identified failures in how the FSA carried out investigations.[74] But changes to enforcement posture can be uncomfortable for a regulator, given the increased costs (reputational and financial) to the industry which usually follow a lower regulatory tolerance for rule breach.[75] As the financial crisis period receded, HM Treasury, following a review, issued recommendations to the FCA and PRA designed to improve transparency, fairness, effectiveness and speed of enforcement decision-making.[76] While the reforms proposed (and since enacted) are reasonable, it is not hard to read a cautionary tone in the Treasury review. The review supported credible deterrence and the taking of tough enforcement action where warranted, but it also noted that prompt, robust supervisory action could be the better immediate course in some circumstances and called for increased reporting on supervisory action as a means for changing behaviour across the financial sector. While credible deterrence continues to

---

[71] See eg J ARMOUR, C MAYER and A POLO, 'Regulatory Sanctions and Reputation Damage in Financial Markets', *Oxford Legal Studies Research Paper No 62/2015* (2015) <https://ssrn.com/abstract=1678028>; H CHRISTENSEN, L HAIL and C LEUZ, 'Capital-Market Effects of Securities Regulation: Prior Conditions, Implementation and Enforcement', *ECGI Finance Working Paper No 407* (2014) <https:ssrn.com/abstract=1745105>; and U BHATTACHARYA and H DAOUK, 'The World Price of Insider Trading' (2002) 57 *Journal of Finance* 5.

[72] On the crisis-era enhancement of enforcement in the US, see M BARR, 'Financial Reform: Making the System Safer and Fairer' (2017) 3(1) *Russell Sage Foundation Journal of the Social Sciences* 2.

[73] E FERRAN, 'The Break-Up of the Financial Services Authority' (2011) *Oxford Journal of Legal Studies* 455.

[74] A GREEN, *Report into the FSA's Enforcement Actions Following the Failure of HBOS* (2011).

[75] On the evidence of political cycles effecting regulator behaviour in the EU, see J LAWRENCE, 'Political Cycles in Regulatory Enforcement', *MIT Political Science Department Research Paper No 2013-35* (2013) <https://ssrn.com/abstract=2303321>.

[76] HM Treasury, *Review of Enforcement Decision-Making at the Financial Services Regulators* (Final Report, 2014).

define UK enforcement practices,[77] early 2017 saw the FCA and PRA adopt significant changes to their enforcement procedures which include a new 'focused resolution procedure' designed to facilitate the settlement process, as well as a mechanism for facilitating the referral of contested enforcement cases to the Upper Tribunal (which hears appeals from FCA/PRA decisions).[78] On Brexit, the competitive pressure which the UK financial sector will likely face may lead to a softer posture on enforcement and to further reforms. But the future direction of enforcement policy is more likely to be shaped by myriad domestic factors, including the political environment, as indicated by the recent evolution of enforcement policy

Similarly, dramatic Brexit-related changes to supervisory governance – the granular day-to-day business of regulators which can have material effects on firms' business models and practices – are unlikely. Outside the banking sphere, the supervision of markets and of the consumer markets has not been subject to significant operational harmonisation at EU-level, although the EU is becoming increasingly intrusive, as noted above. But while ESMA is increasingly strengthening its supervisory convergence and peer review activities, styles of supervision remain a national competence. Changes to UK supervisory governance have accordingly generally reflected UK interests and preferences. The UK's well-known 'risk-based approach' to supervision,[79] for example, which assumes that it is not possible to prevent all failures and that supervision should be informed by the related risks to the regulator's objectives,[80] has never been required as a matter of EU law, although national supervisors have been encouraged to follow such an approach.[81] Supervisory change has tended to be a function of domestic drivers. The then FSA's supervisory approach was changed over the financial crisis era, for example, through the 'Supervisory Enhancement Programme' to a more interventionist 'Intensive Supervision' model. The style of supervisory intervention in the UK shifted from being 'principles-based' (associated with a more 'light-touch' approach which deferred to management and to internal processes) to an 'outcomes-based' approach (associated with a close focus on how the outcomes sought by regulation could be achieved through

---

[77]  See FCA, *Business Plan 2016/17* (2016) p 42.
[78]  FCA and PRA, Policy Statement, *Implementation of the Enforcement Review and the Green Report* (2017).
[79]  The FCA has described its approach to supervision as being 'delivered through a risk-based and proportionate supervisory approach': FCA, *Supervision Manual*, Ch 1A, para 1A.3.1.
[80]  On risk-based supervision, see J BLACK, 'Paradoxes and Failures: New Governance Techniques and the Financial Crisis' (2012) 75(6) *Modern Law Review* 1037.
[81]  The ESAs have, eg, encouraged a risk-based approach to supervision in the context of anti-money-laundering and terrorist financing rules: ESAs, *The Risk-Based Supervision Guidelines* (ESAs 2016 72).

rules, supervision and related enforcement).[82] This change in approach was particularly marked in the consumer protection sphere. Supervisory approaches to the consumer markets have gone through repeated cycles of change in the UK as solutions have been sought to the persistence of repeated cycles of investment product mis-selling. Prior to the financial crisis, the then FSA was adopting an increasingly intrusive approach, built on its flagship 'TCF' strategy, and deploying a variety of tools, including thematic reviews of particular industry segments and sectors and related supervisory guidance. Following the crisis-era deconstruction of the FSA, the then newly-minted FCA announced that its tolerance level for detriment to consumers had changed (becoming lower) and that its administrative tools would be deployed in a more interventionist manner.[83] Supervision already has, accordingly, a dynamic quality and responds to the distinct risks and features of the UK market.

In those areas where the EU has dictated the nature of supervision more closely (notably the banking sphere), radical change is unlikely. Once outside the EU, the PRA will no longer be required to follow the EU 'SREP' when supervising banks. But it is unlikely that the UK's experience with the SREP (which has been informed by UK expertise through the UK's participation on EBA which adopts guidelines for the SREP) will be jettisoned (not least as the Basel Agreements require some form of SREP process) or that the industry will be required to adopt new reporting and supervisory practices which are disruptive and costly.

Regulatory governance is the most likely arena in which change may occur. Cycles of regulation and deregulation are common in financial governance. Regulation tends to follow a sine curve – intensifying and receding in response to political and societal attitudes which are typically shaped by crisis and its aftermath.[84] Up to now, this cycle has been shaped by EU dynamics which have included but have not been limited to UK preferences. When the UK leaves the EU it will have significantly greater autonomy (formally at least) in relation to regulatory governance, and the sine curve will be a function of UK dynamics (albeit shaped by Brexit). Calls for deregulation are emerging,[85] although there is no evidence yet of a clamour for major change and little sense of an institutional appetite.[86] Deregulation could, however, become a means for strengthening the

---

82 Discussed in N MOLONEY, 'Monitoring Regulation: the Difficulties of Achieving "Law in Action" and the EU Challenge' in G FERRARINI, K HOPT and E WYMEERSCH (eds), *Financial Regulation and Supervision: A Post Crisis Analysis*, Oxford University Press, Oxford 2012, p 71.
83 Financial Conduct Authority, *Approach to Regulation* (2011).
84 JC COFFEE, 'The Political Economy of Dodd-Frank: Why Financial Reform Tends to be Frustrated and Systemic Risk Perpetrated' (2012) 97 *Cornell Law Review* 1019.
85 See eg, B REYNOLDS, *A Blueprint for Brexit, The Future of Global Financial Services and Markets in the UK*, Politeia 2016 < http://www.politeia.co.uk/wp-content/uploads/2016/11/Barnabas-Reynolds-A-Blueprint-for-Brexit-2.pdf>.
86 The chief executive of the FCA, eg, has ruled out a 'bonfire of regulation': EA HUGHES, 'Regulator Rules Out Brexit 'Bonfire of Regulation', *FT Adviser*, 19 July 2016.

competitive position of the UK market post-Brexit, particularly if the US engages in significant deregulation in the financial services sector, as has been signalled by the Trump administration, and if UK firms are placed at a competitive disadvantage. Current indications suggest that the Dodd Frank Act, the major crisis-era measure adopted in the US, may be subject to significant revision and repeal following President Trump's Executive Order of 3 February 2017.[87] The UK has long been careful to signal its openness to the international market and been conscious of the disincentives which perceptions of burdensome regulation can generate. For example, in the mid-2000s, when concerns were growing in the US that a series of regulatory reforms might be diminishing the international attractiveness of the US capital market,[88] the UK took action under the Investment Exchanges and Clearing Houses Act 2006 to prevent the adoption by any UK trading venue of 'excessive' regulation and to support the competitiveness of the UK market. The Act, which was directed to the risk of burdensome rules being applied by a UK trading venue were it to be taken into foreign (in particular US) ownership, empowered the then FSA to prohibit any excessive regulatory provision being adopted by a trading venue, having regard to, inter alia, the global character of financial services and markets and the international mobility of activity.[89] Similarly, the UK has adopted a relatively facilitative approach to UK market access by third country actors. It permits, for example, certain banking activities to be carried out through (authorised) branches, rather than more costly subsidiaries, as long as certain stability-related conditions are met,[90] while cross-border investment services can, in certain circumstances, be provided without authorisation.[91] Deregulation could also be used to address the complexity risks which can be associated with the crisis-era rulebook.[92] The UK could, for example, place the regulatory system on a more

---

[87]   The Executive Order sets out core principles for regulating the US financial system, which include that regulation be efficient, effective and appropriately tailored, and calls on all relevant agencies to report on the extent to which current laws and international obligations promote and support the core principles. President Trump has singled out the Dodd Frank Act for reform stating, in the context of the Order, that cuts to Dodd Frank could be expected: B JOPSON and B MCLANNAHAN, 'Trump Prepares to take Axe to Wall St Regulation', *Financial Times*, 3 February 2017.

[88]   J COFFEE, 'Law and the Market: the Impact of Enforcement' (2007) 156 *University of Pennsylvania Law Review* 229.

[89]   Under section 300A of the Financial Services and Markets Act 2000.

[90]   PRA, Supervisory Statement SS10/14, *Supervising International Banks: the PRA's Approach to Branch Supervision* (2014).

[91]   Under the Regulated Activities Order 2001 (Article 72).

[92]   Which were examined in a much-commented-on paper: A HALDANE and V MADOUROS, 'The Dog and the Frisbee', speech at Federal Reserve Bank of Kansas City, 366th Economic Policy Symposium, Jackson Hole, Wyoming, 31 August 2012.

principles-based footing or simplify bank regulation by relying more heavily on capital-based requirements.[93]

There are, however, material countering frictions. Traditionally, UK regulators have not adopted a minimalist approach to regulatory governance; the tendency of the UK authorities to 'gold-plate' EU standards has long been a complaint of the City. And while the UK can be expected to be sensitive to the need to protect the position of the City of London globally, Brexit-driven radical deregulatory action is unlikely to be called for. Major financial centres do not easily lose their position, in part because of the very strong network effects which attract capital and liquidity to major established financial centres with tested and mature infrastructures. In addition, since the financial crisis and the related crystallisation of the fiscal risks of weak regulation and supervision, global financial governance has been framed in terms of regulatory convergence and not regulatory competition or arbitrage: the G20 reform agenda has led to an intensification of regulation and to the embedding of intervention as the standard normative position within systems of regulation globally. The pre-crisis position, which privileged market discipline over intervention, is unlikely to return, not least given the extent to which financial stability and the governance arrangements which support it are monitored internationally, including by the FSB and the IMF.[94] Domestic regulatory systems are now increasingly shaped by the standards set by the ISSBs and so are buttressed, at least to some extent, against local political forces. Compliance with these soft standards is the subject of peer review and monitoring, including by the Basel Committee, through its Regulatory Compliance Assessment Programs (RCAPs); the FSB, through its peer review exercises; and the IMF, through its regular Financial Sector Assessment Programs (FSAPs). In its 2016 FSAP of the UK, the IMF lauded the UK's financial governance system, noting that the increased resilience of the UK financial system 'reflects to a large extent a wave of regulatory reforms since the crisis, which are now near completion', and that the reforms were aligned with the global reform agenda in relation to which the UK had played a major role.[95] As a key player in international financial governance, and a major global centre for finance, the UK is unlikely to defect from international standards it has supported or to signal a related weakening of its commitment to financial stability which could, in an extreme scenario, have implications for its sovereign debt rating.

---

[93]   On the merits of higher capital requirements, see the influential analysis by A ADMATI and M HELLWIG, *The Bankers' New Clothes: What's Wrong with Banking and What to Do about It*, Princeton University Press, Princeton 2013.

[94]   Including through the regular IMF Global Financial Stability Reports.

[95]   IMF, *UK Financial Sector Assessment Program. Financial System Stability Assessment IMF Country Report No 16/167* (2016) p 7.

Change will also be constrained by the EU rulebook. It remains to be seen how EU/UK access arrangements will be configured after Brexit. If the status quo governs the new relationship, the UK will have limited room to change its governance given the need to show 'equivalence' with EU financial governance: the EU's current rules governing third country access (to the extent they apply – the third country rules apply only in limited sectors) require that the third country financial governance regime is equivalent to that of the EU's, as assessed in accordance with identified benchmarks. While the equivalence assessment as currently constituted does not require a granular, line-by-line identity between EU and third country rules,[96] significant departures by the UK from the EU's approach to regulation can be expected to cause difficulties – whether for political/competitive reasons or because of EU concerns to protect the integrity of its financial governance arrangements and to manage the stability risks posed to the EU market from third country access in accordance with EU standards. Even if the current third country regime is not the basis of EU/UK market access after Brexit, any bespoke arrangement will almost certainly include some form of equivalence assessment (however labelled) given the EU's incentives to protect its approach to regulating the EU market, as well as to limit the risk which UK deregulation could pose to its competitive position globally. In reality, UK regulation is likely to shadow EU financial regulation closely – particularly as the main planks of EU regulatory governance are, for the most part, in place, and changes are more likely to be at the administrative level and directed to refinements.[97] Domestic market dynamics also come into play. As noted in Section 3 (above), UK firms have built their business models and operating systems around the EU rulebook and are unlikely to welcome major change – however strong the opposition to the original EU requirements.

This is not to suggest that changes to regulatory governance will not follow. The UK can be expected to remove those elements of the EU rulebook which have posed most difficulties in the past and where removal might be expected to deliver some competitive advantage, such as the cap on bankers' bonuses. UK regulators can also be expected to deploy regulation and supervision in a proportionate manner as part of their response to any Brexit-related change in the UK financial market. The need to operate in a proportionate manner is required of the FCA and PRA under the Financial Services and Markets Act[98] and, in practice, can be identified as an animating principle of FCA/PRA

---

[96]   On the current equivalence regime, see the assessments at n 5.

[97]   As is suggested by the Commission's November 2016 package of reforms: see above n 54.

[98]   The FCA and PRA must follow the principle that a burden or restriction which is imposed on a person, or on the carrying on of an activity, should be proportionate to the benefits, considered in general terms, which are expected to result from the imposition of that burden or restriction: Financial Services and Markets Act 2000 (section 3B).

activities.[99] In a post-Brexit environment the proportionality principle may lead to some thinning out of the current rulebooks, even if only at the margins. The UK regulators can also be expected to review and refresh the current rulebooks (as they have always done) with an eye to strengthening the competitiveness of the UK market. The ongoing and wide-ranging review of the rules which govern how capital is raised in the UK market,[100] for example, form part of a long series of reforms to the regime over time,[101] but have been associated with a Brexit-related concern to strengthen the market.[102]

## 5. CONCLUSION

UK financial governance will experience change after Brexit. Much of the change will likely be operational and directed to Brexit-related risk management and to ensuring the EU supervisory coordination and cooperation arrangements which support the UK regulators are replicated. Large-scale regulatory change is unlikely; regulatory governance can be expected to shadow EU financial regulation for some time. The UK has shaped much of EU financial regulation in its image; it has repeatedly engaged in experimentation and innovation, suggesting there is little pent-up demand for change; and there are several frictions obstructing major deregulation.

The great unknown relates to the competitive position of the UK financial market over the medium term. If there is a material deterioration in the UK's dominant position as a major global financial centre it is unlikely that the financial governance lever will not be used to restore the UK's position. But the shadow of the financial crisis is a long one and it is unlikely that large-scale deregulation will follow.

---

[99] The FCA's 2016/17 Business Plan, eg, notes that its 'overall priority is to ensure an effective and proportionate regulatory approach which tackles the problems of the past without inhibiting the developments of the future': FCA, *Business Plan 2016/17* (2016) p 8. Similarly, the PRA has stated its commitment to 'applying the principle of proportionality in our supervision of firms': PRA, *The Prudential Regulation Authority's Approach to Banking Supervision* (2014) p 1.

[100] FCA, Consultation Paper CP 17/5, *Reforming the Availability of Information in the UK Equity IPO Process* (2017); FCA, Consultation Paper CP 17/4, *Enhancements to the Listing Regime* (2017); FCA, Discussion Paper DP 17/2, *The UK Primary Markets Landscape* (2017).

[101] Including the major 2008 review of the listing (admission to stock exchange trading) regime which was concerned in particular with the international competitiveness of the UK market: FSA, Discussion Paper DP 08/1, *A Review of the Structure of the Listing Regime* (2008).

[102] C BINHAM, D MCCRUM and M HUNTER, 'IPO Shake-Up Plan to Keep Britain "Open for Business"', *Financial Times*, 2 March 2017.

# CHAPTER 8

# INTELLECTUAL PROPERTY LAW AND BREXIT: A RETREAT OR A REAFFIRMATION OF JURISDICTION?

Luke McDonagh and Marc Mimler*

---

\* City, University of London and Bournemouth University (respectively). Thanks go to Giancarlo Moretti, Dr Maria Ioannidou and Dr Dev Gangjee.

## 1.  INTRODUCTION

The effect of European Union law on intellectual property (IP) law in the United Kingdom has been profound. There is no area of IP law that does not feature EU legislation or CJEU case law. In fact, it may be the most 'Europeanised' area of private law.[1] For this reason, 'Brexit' will undoubtedly have a massive impact on the current IP framework in the UK. A clear picture of the post-Brexit IP landscape, however, can only be drawn once we know the outcome of the negotiations pursuant to the Article 50 TEU procedure. Our intention with this chapter is to give an overview of the current state of play in terms of EU law's impact on IP law, and to consider the most likely outcome of Brexit on IP law in the UK.

At the outset, we must emphasise that the United Kingdom's 'exiting' of the European Union will primarily affect IP laws, currently valid in the UK, that derive from EU measures. Long before the UK joined the then European Economic Community (EEC) in 1973 it had established its own national jurisdiction to grant, for example, trade marks and patents, and it will continue to possess this jurisdiction, post-Brexit. Moreover, the UK can claim an indigenous tradition of copyright legislation going back to the Statute of Anne in 1710. Finally, the UK is a signatory to several measures which have been negotiated and agreed outside of the European Union, and which need to be distinguished from EU measures. For instance, there is the UPOV Convention establishing a *sui generis* right for plant varieties, as well as the European Patent Convention (EPC) which provides for a centralised system for granting European patents (EPs). These measures operate outside the ambit of the European Union and Brexit will not directly affect the UK's involvement in these measures. With this chapter, we aim to explain what areas *will* be affected by Brexit, and which ones will not.

## 2.  THE INTEGRATION OF EUROPEAN IP LAW

The Europeanisation of intellectual property via EU law is a history of ever-growing integration. Yet, the Treaty of Rome did not bestow any relevant legislative competence to the European Economic Community (EEC). The Treaty rather stipulated that what would become EU law would not 'prejudice the system existing in Member States in respect of property' within its Article 222.[2] This meant that efforts to harmonise national IP laws in Europe took place at

---

[1]  J PILA, 'Intellectual Property as a Case Study in Europeanization: Methodological Themes and Context' in A OHLY and J PILA (eds), *The Europeanization of Intellectual Property Law*, Oxford University Press, Oxford 2013, p 3.

[2]  Additionally, Article 36 states that the protection of industrial and commercial property could be regarded as exceptions for the prohibition of restrictions to the freedom of movement of goods.

the international level through multilateral measures.[3] One such measure was the Community Patent Convention of 1975 which was devised as a special agreement between Member States of the then EEC.[4]

The European Court of Justice, however, perceived that national rules for IP protection and their discrepancies were capable of creating obstacles to fundamental principles of the EEC Treaties, like freedom of movement of goods or competition.[5] Thereafter the scope for scrutiny under rules of the Treaty was enabled by distinguishing between the existence of IP rights which were governed by national law and their exercise, thus delineating the future relationship between EU law and national IP rights.[6] In due course, the exercise of IP rights would fall under the shared scrutiny of the Union and Member States.[7] Initially, it was perceived that national rules on intellectual property would conflict with the competition rules in the Treaty,[8] as early cases indicated.[9] The focus, however, soon shifted to the adverse effects of intellectual property rights on the free movement of goods which led to the development of the rules on exhaustion of IP rights by the CJEU.[10]

Additionally, the discrepancies between Treaty principles and national IP rights led the European Commission to harmonise national IP laws via Directives based on Article 114(1) TFEU and its predecessor,[11] which provided that the Union may provide legislation for the establishment and functioning of the internal market.[12] Directives have been used to harmonise national IP laws on trade marks, copyright (and related rights), registered designs and, in the patent area, with regards to biotechnology inventions.[13]

---

[3]    G Tritton, *Tritton on Intellectual Property in Europe*, 4th edn, Sweet & Maxwell, London 2014, para 1-039.

[4]    While the Convention never came into force, its provisions were used as templates for national patent laws (see eg UK Patents Act 1977, section 130(7)); 'Resolution on the Adjustment of National Patent Law Records of the Luxembourg Conference on the Community patent 1975' in *Records of the Luxembourg Conference on the Community Patent 1975* (Office for Official Publications of the European Communities, 1982) p 332.

[5]    Case 24/67, *Parke, Davis and Co v Probel, Reese, Beintema-Interpharm and Centrafarm*, ECLI:EU:C:1968:11, 55, 71.

[6]    Tritton, above n 3, para 1-039.

[7]    Pila, above n 1, p 10.

[8]    P Groves, T Martinoi, C Mishkin and J Richards, *Intellectual Property and the Internal Market of the European Community*, Graham & Trotman, London 1993, p 5; Tritton, above n 3, para 1-039.

[9]    See eg Case 56 and 58/64, *Consten SaRL and Grundig Verkaufs GmbH v Comm*, ECLI:EU:C:1966:41; *Parke, Davis and Co v Probel, Reese, Beintema-Interpharm and Centrafarm*, above n 5.

[10]   Tritton, above n 3, para 1-039.

[11]   Article 100 EEC; Article 95 EC.

[12]   Case C-376/98, *Federal Republic of Germany v European Parliament and Council of the European Union*, ECLI:EU:C:2000:544, paras 83–84.

[13]   UK adoption of a Directive with regard to trade secrets was envisaged in 2017–18 but the UK may not bring it into force if Brexit occurs: <http://ec.europa.eu/growth/industry/intellectual-property/trade-secrets_en>.

These efforts to harmonise national IP laws have additionally been supplemented by unitary EU wide rights through regulations.[14] Such measures were initially based on Article 352 TFEU[15] which required a unanimous vote of the Council. The inception of the Lisbon Treaty introduced Article 118 TFEU which allows the introduction of EU-wide IP rights. Currently, there are EU Regulations with regards to EU trade mark rights, registered and unregistered Community design rights, protected geographical indications and protected designations of origin, Community plant variety rights and supplementary protection certificates (SPCs).

One final thing is worth noting: the impact of EU law on national IP rights varies from right to right. The effect on design and trade mark law has been profound since both areas have been harmonised via Directives and the creation of unitary rights. Copyright law has fared less harmoniously but the impact has still been considerable. Patents were, for many years, the least affected IP right, but over the past two decades there has been a dramatic increase in patent-related EU legislation, culminating in the Regulation on the European patent with unitary effect.

The future framework of intellectual property law in the UK will depend on the kind of Brexit that will occur. A so-called hard Brexit, which currently appears to be the UK government's line, would sever all links with the EU *acquis*. However, the February 2017 Government's White Paper on the Great Repeal Bill states that 'historic CJEU case law be given the same binding, or precedent, status in our courts as decisions of our own Supreme Court.'[16] The malleability of the common law system will enable UK courts to continue to apply EU-derived principles like 'intellectual creation' within UK copyright law until new UK legislation provides otherwise. However, any future CJEU case law would not have to be followed, though it can be anticipated that UK courts would find CJEU judgments persuasive, similar to the current practice with regards to the decisions of the EPO Board of Appeals.[17] 'Soft Brexit', ie where the UK stays within the European Economic Area (EEA), would mean that much of EU IP Law would remain valid.

## 2.1. TRADE MARKS

Of all IP rights, EU law has had the most profound impact on trade mark law. The activity by the Union in this field of IP can be explained by the Union's goal

---

[14]    T COOK, *EU Intellectual Property Law*, Oxford University Press, Oxford 2010, para 1.06.
[15]    Previously: Article 308 EC; Article 235 EEC.
[16]    Department for Exiting the European Union, *Legislating for the United Kingdom's withdrawal from the European Union* (Cm 9446, March 2017), para 2.16.
[17]    *Conor v Angiotech* [2008] UKHL 49; *Human Genome Sciences v Eli Lilly* [2011] UKSC 51. See further the contribution by T HORSLEY (Ch 4) in this edited collection.

to establish a single market.[18] Trade marks became a prime harmonising area in the context of marketing goods and services throughout the single market.[19] In 1989 the first Trade Marks Directive was brought forward with the aim of harmonising trade mark law within EU Member States.[20] The United Kingdom implemented the Directive with the UK Trade Marks Act 1994.

The EU, however, considered that the mere approximation of national laws would not eliminate the barriers of territoriality.[21] To ensure the free movement of branded goods the Community Trade Mark was initiated by the European Commission.[22] The Community Trade Mark Regulation created a unitary right – the Community Trade Mark – which would be valid in all EU Member States. Following the entry in force of the Lisbon Treaty in 2009, the Community Trade Mark Regulation was substituted with the EU Trade Mark Regulation and Community Trade Marks were relabelled as EU Trade Marks.

### 2.1.1. EU Trade Marks and CJEU Jurisprudence

EU Trade Marks are granted by the EU IP Office (formerly, the Office for the Harmonisation in the Internal Market, OHIM) in Alicante. The EU Trade Mark has unitary effect in all EU Member States and can only be assigned and licensed as a whole.[23] The enforcement of such EU Trade Marks is conducted by national courts as courts of the EU with the possibility of the General Court and the European Court of Justice being involved. Indeed, the majority of cases of the CJEU in the field of intellectual property law are trade mark cases.[24]

European courts are directly involved in the adjudication of EU Trade Marks stemming from appeals from the EUIPO. In addition, national courts frequently seek CJEU guidance on interpreting provision deriving from the TM Directive through preliminary rulings pursuant to Article 267 TFEU. The fact that the substantial provisions of both the Directive and Regulation correspond to one another makes case law based on the Directive relevant for the interpretation

---

[18]   Tritton, above n 3, para 3-035.
[19]   A von Mühlendahl, D Botis, S Maniatis and I Wiseman, *Trade Mark Law in Europe*, 3rd edn, Oxford University Press, Oxford 2016, para 2.07.
[20]   First Council Directive 89/104/EEC of 21 December 1988 to approximate the laws of the Member States relating to trade marks [1989] OJ L40.
[21]   Council Regulation (EC) No 207/2009 of 26 February 2009 on the Community trade mark [2009] OJ L78/1, Recital 4.
[22]   Memorandum on the Creation of an EEC Trade Mark, Bulletin of the European Communities, Supplement 8/76, para 34.
[23]   Article 1(2) Council Regulation (EC) No 207/2009 of 26 February 2009 on the Community trade mark [2009] OJ L78/1.
[24]   G Dinwoodie, 'The Europeanisation of Trade Mark Law' Law' in Ohly and Pila, above n 1, p 91.

of provisions of the Regulation and vice versa, thus increasing the harmonising effect.[25]

In practice, the decisions of the European courts on trade mark matters have not always been welcomed by national courts. Some UK IP practitioners and judges consider that the European Courts, as generalist courts, do not have the expertise to decide on a complex, specialist matter like trade mark law. UK judicial discontentment can be seen with the High Court decision, following a CJEU reference, in *Arsenal v Reed* (2002)[26] and similarly, at the Court of Appeal level in *L'Oréal v Bellure* (2009).[27] Central to the *L'Oréal* case was the question of whether Bellure was taking unfair advantage of the reputation or the distinctiveness of L'Oréal's marks. The CJEU held that this would occur when the alleged infringer was 'riding on the coattails' of the famous mark, noting that such use of the mark would be uncompensated. The CJEU's interpretation of the respective provisions left the UK courts with no other avenue but a finding of infringement, despite concerns about the wider impact of the decision. Indeed, the CJEU's de facto extension of trade mark protection to the wider 'brand' has received substantial academic criticism.[28]

### 2.1.2. The Impact of Brexit

Article 1(2) of the EU Trade Mark Regulation prescribes that the unitary character of the EU Trade Mark shall have equal effect within the Union. A hard Brexit will mean that EU trade marks granted by the EUIPO will have no effect within the United Kingdom. The impact of this will be significant. Currently, there are millions of EU Trade Marks registered at the EUIPO. Moreover, the United Kingdom had, along with Germany, the highest number of applications of EU Trade Marks in the year 2015 according to Eurostat.[29] The fate of these registrations remains unclear and would largely depend on any agreement between the UK and the remaining EU Member States. In August 2016, the Chartered Institute of Trade Mark Attorneys (CITMA) provided a list of seven options that could apply post-Brexit.[30]

---

25 R ARNOLD, 'An Overview of European Harmonziation Measures in Intellectual Property Law' in OHLY and PILA, above n 1, p 31.
26 Case C-206/01, *Arsenal Football Club plc v Matthew Reed*, ECLI:EU:C:2002:651.
27 Case C-486/07, *L'Oréal SA v Bellure NV*, ECLI:EU:C:2009:378.
28 See eg D GANGJEE and R BURELL, 'Because You're Worth It: L'Oréal and the Prohibition on Free Riding' (2010) 73 *Modern Law Review* 282–304; and L MCDONAGH, 'From Brand Performance to Consumer Performativity: Assessing European Trade Mark Law after the Rise of Anthropological Marketing' (2015) 42 *Journal of Law and Society* 611–636.
29 <http://ec.europa.eu/eurostat/statistics-explained/index.php/Intellectual_property_rights_statistics>.
30 <https://www.citma.org.uk/membership/eu_resources/eu_brexit/eu_registered_rights_-_trade_marks>.

The *Jersey option* provides that the UK would unilaterally declare EU Trade Marks to have effect within the territory of the United Kingdom through an accompanying piece of legislation. This effect would be acknowledged by both the UK Intellectual Property Office (UK IPO) and UK courts. The *UKplus option* foresees an amendment of Article 1(2) of the EU Trade Mark Regulation. Rather than extending to the territories of Union Member States the effect of such a trade mark would extend to the UK and potentially other non-EU European Countries. The *Montenegro option* envisages that all existing EU Trade Mark registrations would be entered automatically entered within the UK's trade mark register. The *Tuvalu model* follows basically the Montenegro model with the distinction that registration of the EU Trade mark in the UK registry would be dependent on the owner's positive decision to extend the protection to the UK. The *Veto model* resembles the Tuvalu option but provides the UK IPO with the option to refuse registration of the mark in question. The *Republic of Ireland option* provides EU Trade Mark owners with the option to create a corresponding UK trade mark registration when renewing the registration at the EUIPO or another cut-off date after Brexit. Finally, the *Conversion model* would replicate the currently used system that applies where current EU Trade Marks are converted into national trade mark registrations.[31] This is, for instance, done where an application for an EU Trade Mark is not possible because of an earlier right in just one EU Member State prohibiting registration with an EU Trade mark with unitary effect. With regard to applying this framework to the post-Brexit scenario, applications would undergo full examination but would be able to retain their initial priority date at the EUIPO.

'Hard Brexit' would mean that national trade mark law (statutory provisions) would not have to be amended. The proposed Great Repeal Bill would mean that the current statutory trade mark law would remain as it is but Parliament would be able to amend the law as it sees fit. Importantly, however, the link to the EU *acquis* and the adjudication of the CJEU would be severed. By contrast, 'Soft Brexit' and EEA membership would not change much with regard to UK trade mark law as the Trade Marks Directive would still apply. It is as yet unclear as to which option will be taken. The current UK White Paper on the Great Repeal Bill states that the case law of the CJEU prior to Brexit will have the same status as UK Supreme Court cases within the UK legal system,[32] but subsequent case law of the CJEU would no longer be binding on the UK.

---

[31] Articles 112–114 EU Council Regulation (EC) No 207/2009 of 26 February 2009 on the Community trade mark [2009] OJ L78/1.

[32] *Legislating for the United Kingdom's withdrawal from the European Union*, above n 16.

## 2.2.   DESIGNS

As with trade mark law, design law in the UK is heavily influenced by EU law. However, design protection is multi-layered: designs can be protected through registration at the EU or UK levels; but protection is also available through unregistered design rights, again at both the EU and UK levels. Unitary EU rights are available for registered and unregistered designs (ie Community registered designs and Community unregistered designs), with registrations occurring at the EUIPO.[33] National laws in EU Member States with regard to registered rights were harmonised through the Design Directive[34] which was implemented in the UK through an amendment of the Registered Designs Act 1949. The Directive, however, left the regime of national unregistered design rights untouched.[35] UK unregistered designs are legislated within Part III of the Copyright, Design and Patents Act 1988 (CDPA 1988). This somewhat complex framework of design protection[36] means that only the law of registered designs is fully Europeanised, and the rules for EU and national unregistered designs can vary.

The parallel to the situation under trade mark law means that similar considerations and options for the post-Brexit scenario are relevant for the protection of Community registered designs. Hence, CITMA have put forward a similar scenario to the one outlined above for trade marks with regards to registered EU designs.[37] The situation is, however, different for unregistered Community designs, where the right subsists automatically when it is first made available in the EU.[38] Post-Brexit, an EU unregistered design right could in theory be accepted as a UK unregistered design right. There are difficulties with this, however, due to differences between the regimes of protection of unregistered designs in the EU and the UK. For instance, the UK right lasts significantly longer (15 years in comparison to three years), and contrary to the unregistered Community design, its UK counterpart does not protect surface decoration.[39] Therefore, further considerations will be required in this field to develop adequate post-Brexit protection.

---

[33]   Council Regulation (EC) No 6/2002 of 12 December 2001 on Community designs [2002] OJ L3/1.
[34]   Directive 98/71/EC of the European Parliament and of the Council of 13 October 1998 on the legal protection of designs [1998] OJ L289.
[35]   Directive 98/71/EC of the European Parliament and of the Council of 13 October 1998 on the legal protection of designs [1998] OJ L289, Recital 7.
[36]   This complexity is raised by the fact that copyright protection may additionally be available: see M Howe (ed), *Russel-Clarke and Howe on Industrial Designs*, 9th edn, Sweet & Maxwell, London 2016, para 1-001.
[37]   <https://www.citma.org.uk/membership/eu_resources/eu_brexit/eu_registered_rights_-_designs>.
[38]   Council Regulation (EC) No 6/2002 of 12 December 2001 on Community designs [2002] OJ L3/1. Article 11(1).
[39]   Copyright, Designs and Patents Act 1988, section 213(3)(c).

## 2.3.  GEOGRAPHICAL INDICATIONS

A related field to IP is the protection provided to geographical indications and designations of origin. These two fields aim to protect agricultural products and foodstuffs manufactured within a certain locality which possess certain characteristics. Both of these measures are currently based on an EU Regulation.[40] The protection is granted, inter alia, against any false or misleading use of the indication.[41] Products such as Champagne, Roquefort cheese, Bavarian Beer and Parma ham are protected by these measures. The UK currently has several products registered under this framework such as Welsh Lamb, Stilton Blue and White Cheeses, Cornish Pasties and the Melton Mowbray Pork Pie.[42]

After Brexit, neither Protected Geographical Indications (PGI) nor Protected Designations of Origin (PDOs) would have effect in the United Kingdom (similar to the situation with EU Trade Marks). This has led to fears that British producers could be free to use previously protected names.[43] Already registered UK products, however, would ironically not lose their registration as PGIs or PDO in the EU. This is because the framework established by the Regulation is open for products from non-EU Member States.

A form of supplementary protection in this area could be provided by the law of passing off (an aspect of the law of torts). This would bring the UK back to the situation prior to the introduction of the Regulation on PGIs and PDOs, whereby an extended from of passing off allowed groups of producers to file an action against misrepresentation by other traders. For instance, the producers of Champagne, that were entitled to use the term under French law, were able to successfully take action in the UK against producers labelling their beverage Spanish Champagne.[44]

Nevertheless, passing off would not provide the same level of protection as the current system. GIs provide protection not just against confusingly similar designations but also where association is merely evoked. Conversely, a successful claim of passing off would need to demonstrate a misrepresentation, and that consumers would rely on such misrepresentation when purchasing the

---

[40]   Council Regulation (EC) No 510/2006 of 20 March 2006 on the protection of geographical indications and designations of origin for agricultural products and foodstuffs [2006] OJ L93/12.

[41]   Council Regulation (EC) No 510/2006 of 20 March 2006 on the protection of geographical indications and designations of origin for agricultural products and foodstuffs [2006] OJ L93/12, Article 13(1).

[42]   <https://www.gov.uk/government/collections/protected-food-name-scheme-uk-registered-products>.

[43]   <https://www.theguardian.com/business/2017/feb/15/eu-fears-influx-of-british-champagne-once-brexit-ends-food-naming-rules>.

[44]   *Bollinger v Costa Brava Wine Co Ltd* [1960] RPC 16.

goods of the defendant.[45] The prospect of divergent levels of protection post-Brexit means that a negotiated arrangement as to what happens with currently protected GIs is necessary.

Indeed, any post-Brexit deal between the UK and the EU would very likely deal with the issue of currently protected PGIs and PDOs. For one thing, the United Kingdom is required to provide some form of protection owing to its membership at the World Trade Organization. The WTO's Agreement on Trade related Aspects of Intellectual Property Rights (TRIPS), which mandates minimum standards of IP protection, provides in its Article 22 that legal means to protect interested parties against misleading uses must be provided by WTO member states. Aside from this, any future deal with the European Union will necessarily involve protections of PGIs and PDOs. The EU places great importance on their protection within their trade negotiations as recently observed during discussions over the CETA treaty between the EU and Canada.[46]

## 2.4. COPYRIGHT

Unlike trade mark law, there is no overarching single regulatory system for EU copyright. Nonetheless, major elements of copyright law have been harmonised in the EU via national implementation of the following 10 EU Directives:

- Directive on the harmonisation of certain aspects of copyright and related rights in the information society ('InfoSoc Directive').[47]
- Directive on rental right and lending right and on certain rights related to copyright in the field of intellectual property ('Rental and Lending Directive').[48]
- Directive on the resale right for the benefit of the author of an original work of art ('Resale Right Directive').[49]
- Directive on the coordination of certain rules concerning copyright and rights related to copyright applicable to satellite broadcasting and cable retransmission ('Satellite and Cable Directive').[50]

---

[45] C WADLOW, *The Law of Passing-Off*, 5th edn, Sweet and Maxwell, London 2016, para 7-178.

[46] Comprehensive Economic and Trade Agreement (CETA), Chapter 20, Subsection C. See <http://ec.europa.eu/trade/policy/in-focus/ceta/ceta-chapter-by-chapter>.

[47] Directive 2001/29/EC of the European Parliament and of the Council of 22 May 2001 on the harmonisation of certain aspects of copyright and related rights in the information society [2001] OJ L167/10.

[48] Directive 2006/115/EC of the European Parliament and of the Council of 12 December 2006 on rental right and lending right and on certain rights related to copyright in the field of intellectual property (codified version) [2006] OJ L376/28.

[49] Directive 2001/84/EC of the European Parliament and of the Council of 27 September 2001 on the resale right for the benefit of the author of an original work of art [2001] OJ L272/32.

[50] Council Directive 93/83/EEC of 27 September 1993 on the coordination of certain rules concerning copyright and rights related to copyright applicable to satellite broadcasting and cable retransmission [1993] OJ L248/15.

- Directive on the legal protection of computer programs ('Software Directive').[51]
- Directive on the enforcement of intellectual property rights ('IPRED').[52]
- Directive on the legal protection of databases ('Database Directive').[53]
- Directive on the term of protection of copyright and certain related rights amending the previous 2006 Directive ('Term Directive').[54]
- Directive on certain permitted uses of orphan works ('Orphan Works Directive').[55]
- Directive on collective management of copyright and related rights and multi-territorial licensing of rights in musical works for online use in the internal market ('CRM Directive').

There is insufficient space here to consider all of these legal areas. In the context of Brexit the EU-specific rights are of particular interest. One is the *sui generis* right for databases.[56] In a hard Brexit scenario, this EU right would no longer be binding in the UK. Post-Brexit, the UK could legislate on a national basis to establish a UK *sui generis* right; or alternatively, the courts may fall back on, or expand upon, the UK's traditional form of protection of databases as literary works under copyright.[57] Another example of an EU-specific right is the artist's resale right.[58] This right entitles authors of original works of art to a royalty each time one of their works is resold through an art market professional. This too would cease to be binding, post-Brexit, and the UK would need to legislate to bring in a UK equivalent right (if the UK Government wanted this form of protection to continue).

Yet another interesting point concerns the relevance of the case law of the CJEU.[59] This body of case law, post-Brexit, will in principle cease to be binding

---

[51] Directive 2009/24/EC of the European Parliament and of the Council of 23 April 2009 on the legal protection of computer programs (codified version) [2009] OJ L111/16.
[52] Directive 2004/48/EC of the European Parliament and of the Council of 29 April 2004 on the enforcement of intellectual property rights [2004] OJ L157/45, corrigendum [2004] OJ L195/16.
[53] Directive 96/9/EC of the European Parliament and of the Council of 11 March 1996 on the legal protection of databases [1996] OJ L77/20.
[54] Directive 2006/116/EC of the European Parliament and of the Council of 12 December 2006 on the term of protection of copyright and certain related rights (codified version) [2006] OJ L372/12 (as amended by Directive 2011/77/EU of the European Parliament and of the Council of 27 September 2011 amending Directive 2006/116/EC on the term of protection of copyright and certain related rights [2011] OJ L265/1).
[55] Directive 2012/28/EU of the European Parliament and of the Council of 25 October 2012 on certain permitted uses of orphan works [2012] OJ L299/2.
[56] Directive 96/9/EC of the European Parliament and of the Council of 11 March 1996 on the legal protection of databases [1996] OJ L77/20.
[57] See eg *Blair v Alan S Tomkins & Anor* (1971) 21 QB 78 and *R Griggs Group Ltd v Evans* (2003) EWHC 291.
[58] Resale Right Directive, above n 49.
[59] See further the contribution by T HORSLEY (Ch 4) in this edited collection.

on the UK (unless there is a transitional or longer-term agreement between the UK and the EU that provides for the compulsory jurisdiction of the CJEU on copyright). Of particular significance is the EU originality threshold of 'author's own intellectual creation' – as put forward by the CJEU in *Infopaq* as the standard for all copyright works.[60] Since that 2009 case, this test has displaced the traditional UK standard of 'skill, labour and judgment' (though the impact of this in practice has not been dramatic).[61] It is unknown at this stage whether the UK courts will revert to the old understanding of the originality test. Similarly, regarding the CJEU's definition of parody for the purpose of exceptions and limitations, as expressed in the *Deckmyn* case, this will no longer be binding on the UK, post-Brexit.[62] The UK courts could therefore develop their own understanding of parody in the context of the fair dealing exception. However, the malleability of the common law means that the UK courts will be free to continue to apply the EU-derived tests of originality and parody, post-Brexit, even if they are no longer bound by CJEU rulings on copyright matters. Indeed, they may begin to develop these tests in ways that differ from the CJEU's approach.

## 2.5. PATENTS

Historically, patent law has not been harmonised within the EU. The European Patent Convention (EPC) – agreed in 1973 – exists outside the Union and has a wider membership, including Turkey, Iceland and Switzerland as well as several other non-EU territories. Under the EPC, European patents (EPs) are filed, prosecuted and administered at the European Patent Office (EPO) in Munich.

Even though the primary governing law – the EPC – exists outside of the EU's authority, the EU has, in fact, legislated in several areas relating to patents. The following pieces of EU legislation have a direct impact on patents:

– Directive 98/44/EC (biotechnological inventions);[63]
– Regulation 2100/94 (plant variety rights);[64]

---

[60] Case C-5/08, *Infopaq International A/S v Danske Dagblades Forening*, ECLI:EU:C:2009:465.
[61] See discussion by Proudman J in *The Newspaper Licensing Agency Limited and others v Meltwater Holding BV and others* [2010] EWHC 3099 (Ch) and Arnold J in *SAS Institute Inc v World Programming Ltd* [2010] EWHC 1829 (Ch) at [319].
[62] Case C-201/13, *Johan Deckmyn and Vrijheidsfonds VZW v Helena Vandersteen and Others*, ECLI:EU:C:2014:2132.
[63] Directive 98/44/EC of the European Parliament and of the Council of 6 July 1998 on the legal protection of biotechnological inventions [1998] OJ L213/13.
[64] Council Regulation (EC) No 2100/94 of 27 July 1994 on Community plant variety rights [1994] OJ L227. See also Council Regulation (EC) No. 873/2004 of 29 April 2004 amending Regulation (EC) No 2100/94 on Community plant variety rights [2004] OJ L162.

- Enforcement Directive 2004/48/EC;[65]
- Regulation 469/2009/EC (SPCs for medicinal products);[66]
- Directive 2001/82/EC (veterinary medicinal products);[67]
- Directive 2001/83/EC (medical products for human use);[68]
- Directive 2009/24/EC (computer programs);[69]
- Regulation 1257/2012 (UP Regulation).[70]

For present purposes, it is important to concentrate on two elements of the current system: (1) the jurisprudence of the CJEU in the above areas, most notably in the areas of biotechnology, supplementary protection certificates (SPCs) and enforcement; and (2) the Unified Patent Court and Unitary Patent – a new reformed patent enforcement system for participating EU Member States.

### 2.5.1. CJEU Jurisprudence on Patent-Related Matters

Given the limited nature of the above Regulations and Directives, the jurisprudence of the CJEU in patent matters is surprisingly wide-ranging. It is not the intention of this part of the chapter to give an authoritative overview of CJEU patent case law – instead, three important cases in three different areas of EU law are highlighted here to show the breadth of the CJEU's jurisdiction.

### 2.5.1.1. The Biotechnology Directive (98/44/EC)

The Biotech Directive establishes the rules for the patenting of biotechnological inventions. It rules out patentability for inventions that involve 'uses of human embryos for industrial or commercial purposes'. However, the legislators did not give an answer to the politically loaded question – exactly what constitutes a 'human embryo'? Thus, in the *Brüstle* case the CJEU had to answer a series of questions on the meaning of human embryo in the context of patenting.[71]

---

[65]   Directive 2004/48/EC of the European Parliament and of the Council of 29 April 2004 on the enforcement of intellectual property rights [2004] OJ L195.
[66]   Regulation (EC) no 469/2009 of the European Parliament and of the Council of 6 May 2009 concerning the supplementary protection certificate for medicinal products [2009] OJ L152.
[67]   Directive 2001/82/EC of the European Parliament and of the Council of 6 November 2001 on the Community code relating to veterinary medicinal products [2001] OJ L118.
[68]   Directive 2001/83/EC of the European Parliament and of the Council of 6 November 2001 on the Community code relating to medicinal products for human use [2001] OJ L311.
[69]   Directive 2009/24/EC of the European Parliament and of the Council of 23 April 2009 on the legal protection of computer programs [2009] O J L111.
[70]   Council Regulation (EU) No 1260/2012 of 17 December 2012 implementing enhanced cooperation in the area of the creation of unitary patent protection with regard to the applicable translation arrangements [2012] OJ L361.
[71]   Case C-34/10, *Brüstle v Greenpeace*, ECLI:EU:C:2011:669.

The CJEU ruled in 2011 that Article 6(2)(c) of the Biotech Directive must be interpreted as meaning that:

'The use of human embryos for scientific research purposes is not patentable. A 'human embryo' within the meaning of Union law is any human ovum after fertilisation or any human ovum not fertilised but which, through the effect of the technique used to obtain it, is capable of commencing the process of development of a human being.'

It is for the referring court to ascertain, in the light of scientific developments, whether a stem cell obtained from a human embryo at the blastocyst stage constitutes a 'human embryo' within the meaning of Article 6(2)(c) of the Biotech Directive.

2.5.1.2.    Regulation 469/2009/EC (SPCs for Medicinal Products)

This Regulation covers the granting of SPCs – effectively, extending the life of the patent – where there was a delay in granting the marketing authorisation for a patented medicine. In the case of *Arne Forsgren*,[72] the limits of SPC protection were examined by the CJEU. In the case, Protein D was present in a vaccine for paediatric use – Synflorix – where it was a carrier protein, conjugated by covalent bonds. However, the SPC application was for Protein D per se, not in the conjugated form found in Synflorix. The application for the SPC was therefore rejected by the Austrian national authority on the basis that Protein D is not present in Synflorix other than as a conjugate of other active ingredients as well as the fact that in Synflorix it is an excipient. The CJEU had to consider:

(1) whether an SPC could be obtained in respect to a product per se in 'separate' form when the marketing authorisation was for a medicine in which the product is covalently bonded to other ingredients; and

(2) whether the SPC could rely on a marketing authorisation which only described the product as a 'carrier protein' and did not provide any information about an independent therapeutic effect

The CJEU found in 2015 that the 'covalent bonding' issue should not prevent the granting of an SPC. On the issue of whether the marketing authorisation was adequate to support the grant of the SPC, the Court stated that for Protein D to be an 'active ingredient' as required by the Regulation it must produce 'a pharmacological, immunological or metabolic action of its own which is covered by the therapeutic indications of the marketing authorisation'. It left that determination – whether to grant the SPC – to the referring court.

---

[72]    Case C 631/13, *Arne Forsgren v Österreichisches Patentamt*, ECLI:EU:C:2015:13.

### 2.5.1.3.   The Enforcement Directive (2004/48/EC)

The Enforcement Directive governs the rules for enforcing intellectual property in the courts of the EU Member States. In the *OTK* case the operative question was as follows: does the Enforcement Directive prevent Member States from providing in their legislation the possibility to award punitive damages in IP cases?[73] The Polish Supreme Court sought guidance from the CJEU. The CJEU in 2017 ruled that the fact that Directive 2004/48 does not entail an obligation on the Member States to provide for 'punitive' damages cannot be interpreted as a prohibition on introducing such a measure.

### 2.5.2.   *The Unified Patent Court (UPC)*

Although the grant of patents takes place at a centralised level – at the EPO – European patent litigation involving European patents (EPs) is actually undertaken on a largely national basis.[74] The reason is that EPs must be validated – and subsequently, litigated – within national jurisdictions.[75] National courts, therefore, have the ability to issue binding rulings concerning patent infringement within their national territories, and they also may consider questions of patent validity – although the EPO retains the final say on validity via its patent opposition service.[76] Nonetheless, it is not uncommon for national patent litigation to take place at the same time as parallel EPO opposition proceedings; and the lengthy backlog at the EPO means that national courts sometimes rule on questions of validity and infringement before the EPO Board of Appeals has reached a final decision regarding validity.[77] This has led in some cases to fragmentation of outcomes on validity and infringement across

---

[73]   Case C-367/15, *OTK v SFP*, ECLI:EU:C:2017:36.
[74]   Text of the European Patent Convention, of 5 October 1973, as revised by the Act revising Article 63 EPC of 17 December 1991, and the Act revising the EPC of 29 November 2000, available at <http://documents.epo.org/projects/babylon/eponet.nsf/0/00E0CD7FD461C0D5C1257C060050C376/$File/EPC_15th_edition_2013.pdf>. Also accessible at <http://www.epo.org/law-practice/legal-texts/html/epc/2010/d/index.html>.
[75]   Even though at present a patentee can apply to the EPO for an EP with a single application in 1 of the 3 official EPO languages, once granted a patent must be filed and translated into the other 2 official EPO languages. See also The Agreement on the application of Article 65 of the Convention on the Grant of European Patents agreed on 17 October 2000 (see OJ EPO 549 (2001)) (hereafter known as the London Agreement) – available at <http://documents.epo.org/projects/babylon/eponet.nsf/0/7FD20618D28E9FBFC125743900678657/$File/London_Agreement.pdf>.
[76]   See generally EPO, *Patent Litigation in Europe – An overview of national law and practice in the EPC contracting states* (2013), <https://www.epo.org/learning-events/materials/litigation.html>.
[77]   K Cremers, M Ernicke, D Harhoff, C Helmers, G Licht, L McDonagh, I Rudyk, P Schliessler, C Schneider and N Van Zeebroek, 'Patent Litigation in Europe' (2013) *ZEW Discussion Paper* No 13–07, pp 1–3.

EU jurisdictions, something that impacts upon the single market and raises competition issues.[78]

To try to resolve these issues, on 19 February 2013 the UK and 24 other countries signed an intergovernmental agreement (the UPC Agreement) to create a Unified Patent Court (UPC), which will be a new specialist patents court common to participating states.[79] Overall, the package of measures is designed to establish and enforce unitary patent protection within the European Union,[80] with the ultimate ambition of unifying the European patent system as much as possible.[81]

In addition to the UPC Agreement, the new reform measures also include two EU Regulations which establish the European Patent with Unitary effect – also known as the Unitary Patent (UP) – and the associated translation arrangements.[82] The application and grant process for the UP will be the same as for the regular European patents (EPs); the option for unitary protection across participating EU Member States comes post-grant.[83] Importantly, the UPC will not only hear disputes regarding the validity and infringement of the new UPs but also existing and prospective EPs (subject to the transition period).[84]

---

[78]   Ibid, pp 1–5.

[79]   Agreement on a Unified Patent Court (The UPC Agreement) [2013] OJ C175/1, accessible at <http://eur-lex.europa.eu/LexUriServ/LexUriServ.do?uri=OJ:C:2013:175:0001:0040:EN:PDF>.

[80]   J PILA, 'The European Patent: An Old and Vexing Problem' (2013) 62 *International & Comparative Law Quarterly* 917, 917–921. See also B VAN POTTESBERGHE, *Lost Property: The European Patent System and why it Doesn't Work* (Bruegel Blueprint Series, 2009) available at <http://bruegel.org/wp-content/uploads/imported/publications/patents_BP_050609.pdf>.

[81]   Regulation (EU) No 1257/2012 of the European Parliament and of the Council of 17 December 2012 implementing enhanced cooperation in the area of the creation of unitary patent protection (UP Regulation), [2012] OJ L361/1 and Council Regulation (EU) No 1260/2012 of 17 December 2012 implementing enhanced cooperation in the area of the creation of unitary patent protection with regard to the applicable translation arrangements (Translation Regulation) [2012] OJ L361/89. For a further explanation of the changes, see the EPO website: <http://www.epo.org/law-practice/unitary.html>. See also R ROMANDINI and A KLICZNIK, 'The Territoriality Principle and Transnational Use of Patented Inventions – the Wider Reach of a Unitary Patent and the Role of the CJEU' (2013) 44 *International Review of Intellectual Property and Competition Law* 524–540; and M BRANDI-DOHRN, 'Some Critical Observations on Competence and Procedure of the Unified Patent Court' (2012) 43 *International Review of Intellectual Property and Competition Law* 372–389.

[82]   Regulation (EU) No 1257/2012 of the European Parliament and of the Council of 17 December 2012 implementing enhanced cooperation in the area of the creation of unitary patent protection (UP Regulation), [2012] OJ L361/1 and Council Regulation (EU) No 1260/2012 of 17 December 2012 implementing enhanced cooperation in the area of the creation of unitary patent protection with regard to the applicable translation arrangements (Translation Regulation) [2012] OJ L361/89.

[83]   R HILTY, 'The Unitary Patent Package: Twelve Reasons for Concern' (2012) 41 *CIPA Journal* 553–555.

[84]   T COOK, 'The Progress to Date on the Unitary European Patent and the Unified Patent Court for Europe' (2013) 18 *Journal of Intellectual Property Rights* 584, 586.

### 2.5.3. *The Legal Sources of the Unified Patent Court and the UPC*

Legally, the existence of the Unitary Patent is enabled by a longstanding option under the EPC allowing the validation of patents on a supranational basis.[85] The EU Regulations were passed into law via the system of enhanced cooperation as reformed by the Lisbon Treaty.[86]

The EU Regulations are technically already in force.[87] However, they will apply only once the UPC Agreement is ratified by the requisite 3 + 10 countries, ie Germany, France and the UK plus 10 more signatory states. As of March 2017, this ratification has yet to take place. Until the Brexit referendum, the UK seemed to be well on the way to full ratification of the UPC. Indeed, for the past four years the UK Government has been making plans to host one of the new Court's central divisions in Aldgate, east London, where a building has already been leased in preparation for the new Court's establishment and mock trials have taken place.[88]

What is crucial in the Brexit context is that even though the UPC will have its own jurisdiction to rule with respect to most patent issues – like the infringement of patented drugs – it must defer to the CJEU in a small number of areas of EU law, arising under the areas considered earlier, such as biotechnology, enforcement or matters relating to Supplementary Protection Certificates. Under Article 21 of the UPC Agreement a referral can be made by the UPC to the CJEU in much the same way as an EU Member State national court would make such a referral.[89] In line with this, the CJEU in Opinion 1/09 held that only states that accept the supremacy of EU law and the jurisdiction of the CJEU may sign up.[90] Thus, the CJEU will undoubtedly have some judicial input within the UPC system, though every effort has seemingly been made by the planners to keep this role to a minimum with regard to substantive patent matters.[91] The experience of the

---

[85] Articles 2 and 142 EPC.

[86] Treaty of Lisbon amending the Treaty on European Union and the Treaty establishing the European Community, signed at Lisbon, 13 December 2007, entered into force on 1 December 2009 [2007] OJ C306.

[87] Article 18(2) UP Regulation and Article 7(2) Translation Regulation.

[88] L MCDONAGH, *European Patent Litigation in the Shadow of the Unified Patent Court*, Edward Elgar, Cheltenham, 2016, pp 1–16. See also L MCDONAGH, 'Exploring Perspectives of the Unified Patent Court and the Unitary Patent within the Business and Legal Communities' *A Report Commissioned by the UK Intellectual Property Office* (July 2014), available at <https://www.gov.uk/government/publications/exploring-perspectives-of-the-up-and-upc>.

[89] See also Article 1(2) UPC Agreement and Article 267 Consolidated version of the Treaty on the Functioning of the European Union [2012] OJ C326/01.

[90] Opinion 1/09 [2011] OJ C211/28.

[91] R ROMANDINI and A KLICZNIK, 'The Territoriality Principle and Transnational Use of Patented Inventions – the Wider Reach of a Unitary Patent and the Role of the CJEU' (2013) 44 *International Review of Intellectual Property and Competition Law* 524, 524–529.

CJEU's expansive interventions in the areas of trade mark law and copyright law within the EU may have had an influence in this respect.[92]

It is here that UK Prime Minister Theresa May's recent speech on Brexit – she reiterated her vow that the UK would, post-Brexit, escape the jurisdiction of the Court of Justice of the European Union (CJEU) – becomes important. Furthermore, the same claim is made in the Government's Brexit White Paper.[93]

If the UK is indeed intent on a hard Brexit it is difficult to see how the UK could participate in the UPC, which requires accepting that the decisions of the Court of Justice – in patent law, at least – will be binding with respect to UPC decisions enforceable in the UK. Yet in November 2016, several months after the EU referendum result, the UK Government announced that the UK would ratify the UPC Agreement after all. Furthermore, in January 2017, a mere few days prior to May's speech, the new UK Minister for Intellectual Property, Jo Johnson, stated that the UK still intends to participate in the UPC, emphasising that the UPC is an international court rather than an EU one.[94] The UPC is now expected to be up and running by December 2017 or thereafter in 2018.

Though the decision to go for the twin strategy of a hard Brexit while maintaining UPC ratification at first appears to make little sense, on further contemplation there may actually be some method behind it. In its Brexit White Paper, the Government suggests that the creation of new dispute resolution panels or tribunals will be necessary to determine questions arising out of whatever agreement the UK and EU reach upon Brexit. The point made by Jo Johnson about the UPC being an international court, not an EU one, may not be mere rhetoric – it may indicate that the UK is willing to accept the jurisdiction of international courts or tribunals, like the UPC, to determine specific legal questions – for example, patent matters – that are common to the UK and its 'new partnership with the European Union' (as referred to in the Brexit White Paper).

In this respect, the UK Government may consider that although the UPC is bound by rulings of the CJEU on a number of EU-related patent matters – and UPC decisions on patent injunctions and revocations will be binding within the UK – this is a very different situation from that that currently exists under the sweeping jurisdiction of the CJEU, whose decisions can have the effect of immediately changing UK domestic law in a wide range of different areas.

---

[92]    See J GRIFFITHS, 'Constitutionalising or Harmonising – the Court of Justice, the Right to Property and European Copyright Law' (2013) 38 *European Law Review* 65; and L MCDONAGH, 'From Brand Performance to Consumer Performativity: Assessing European Trade Mark Law after the Rise of Anthropological Marketing' (2015) 42 *Journal of Law and Society* 611–636.

[93]    <https://www.gov.uk/government/uploads/system/uploads/attachment_data/file/588948/The_United_Kingdoms_exit_from_and_partnership_with_the_EU_Web.pdf>.

[94]    <https://www.twobirds.com/en/news/articles/2017/uk/uk-government-appoints-new-ip-minister>.

If this is the UK Government's view, then UK UPC ratification makes a lot more sense. Indeed, the UK may even see the UPC as a model for the kind of specialist commercial court – maintaining a direct but limited link with the CJEU and the wider EU economy – that it would be willing to tolerate in its purported new 'partnership' with the EU. Of course, we do not know whether the EU would be willing to accept these kinds of bespoke arrangements, but the UK's own intentions may be becoming a bit clearer.

One final point: the fate of the UK's continued participation in the unitary patent scheme remains less certain. The UP, unlike the UPC, is created by an EU Regulation, and there is no way to consider it a purely 'international right' (although the existing EP granted by the EPO would fit this definition). Accepting the UP would require a more extensive assessment of EU law and as yet the UK Government has not given any clues as to its intentions. It remains possible that the UK – post-Brexit – will stay within the UPC but not the UP. A UK exit from the UP while UPC membership is maintained would mean that UP protection would not apply in the UK, but EPs valid in the UK could be litigated at the UPC.

## 2.6. THE INTERFACE OF INTELLECTUAL PROPERTY AND COMPETITION LAW

The ramifications of Brexit on IP law actually go beyond pure issues of intellectual property. The reason is that the interface between competition law and intellectual property is of practical importance with regards to the exercise and enforcement of IP rights (which by their nature are exclusive rights that can be used against competitors). EU law is of utmost relevance here since the EU has competence to legislate in the area of competition law, as deemed necessary for the functioning of the internal market pursuant to Article 3(1)(b) TFEU. In addition, the substantive provisions within the UK Competition Act 1998 are based on the competition law provisions within the TFEU.[95]

The two main provisions with regards to competition law, Articles 101 and 102 TFEU, have been applied to sanction certain anti-competitive behaviours of IP right holders. Article 101, for instance, prohibits restrictive agreements that could prevent, restrict or distort competition within the internal market. In order not to sanction beneficial agreements with regards to technology transfer, the EU Commission provides technology transfer block exemption regulations which specify which agreements would not fall foul of Article 101 TFEU.[96]

---

[95]   M Mimler, 'United Kingdom' in P Chrocziel, M Lorenz and W Prinz zu Waldeck und Pyrmont (eds), *Intellectual Property and Competition Law*, Kluwer Law International, The Netherlands 2016, p 129.

[96]   Article 2(1) Commission Regulation (EU) No 316/2014 of 21 March 2014 on the application of Article 101(3) of the Treaty on the Functioning of the European Union to categories of technology transfer agreements [2014] OJ L93/17.

Article 102 TFEU prohibits the abuse of a dominant position in the market. This can, for instance occur, where an undertaking that has a dominant position on the market refuses to license an IP right to a competitor.[97]

Brexit would mean that the links to the EU *acquis* would be severed subject to any transitional arrangements. Therefore, the impact of Brexit on this utterly 'European' field of law and its impact on the interface of intellectual property and competition law in the UK remains to be seen. A key question that arises with regards to IP practice is the future of so-called Euro-Defences. Such defences could be applied by a defendant in an IP infringement case arguing that a positive finding of infringement could be a violation of the principles enshrined within Article 101 or 102 TFEU.[98] Such defences are often brought forward in cases surrounding standard essential patents (patents essential to a technological standard).[99] Brexit would undermine the rationale of such defences as stemming from the TFEU. Owing to the similarity of the Chapter I and II prohibitions within the Competition Act 1998[100] with Articles 101 and 102 TFEU a similar application in future could be applied. Therefore, it can be expected that UK competition law practice would closely follow developments within EU practice.

## 2.7. EXHAUSTION

Finally, Brexit would place the doctrine of exhaustion under new scrutiny. As mentioned, IP rights have the potential to impede freedom movement of goods under Article 34 TFEU. In order to prevent IP rights from impairing this fundamental principle, it was held that once a product has been placed on the market with the IP right holder's consent, he or she is prevented from restricting any further circulation, ie the rights are exhausted.[101] Importantly, this principle also applies to all states within the EEA pursuant to Protocol 28 of the EEA Agreement. Therefore, the current framework presents itself as a system of regional exhaustion where IP rights are no longer enforceable once they have been put onto the market in the EEA by the right holder, subject to certain exceptions.

This current system has been criticised since it prevents EU Member States from applying a different system of exhaustion.[102] Soft Brexit, hence

---

[97] Joined Cases C-241/91P and C-242/91P, *Radio Telefis Eireann v Commission (Magill)*, ECLI:EU:C:1995:98.
[98] MIMLER, above n 95, 129.
[99] eg *IPCom v Nokia* [2012] EWHC 1446 (Ch).
[100] Competition Act 1998, sections 2–16 and sections 18–24.
[101] Case 16-74, *Centrafarm BV et Adriaan de Peijper v Winthrop BV*, ECLI:EU:C:1974:115.
[102] With regards to trade marks: Case C-355/96, *Silhouette International Schmied GmbH & Co KG v Hartlauer Handelsgesellschaft mbH*, ECLI:EU:C:1998:374.

EEA membership, would not alter the application of the current EU doctrine of exhaustion in the UK. In the case of a hard Brexit, however, the UK could prevent the importation of goods that were put onto the market within the EEA; alternatively, the UK could apply principles of international exhaustion, which would permit the importation of goods that have been placed onto the market anywhere in the world. The specific framework, however, will depend on the outcome of the Brexit negotiations.

## 3.  CONCLUSION

There are myriad challenges in untangling the UK from EU intellectual property law. The most pressing concern for UK IP holders will be the loss of the EU Intellectual Property Office at Alicante, which registers EU trade marks and registered designs. To ensure continuity in the protection of trade marks and designs, a new regime to convert existing EU rights into UK rights will likely be required, which could stretch the resources of the UK Intellectual Property Office. For the other major rights – copyright and patents – the crucial issues are only of slightly less consequence. Copyright lawyers will be watching in earnest to see if the UK legislates to mirror EU-rights such as the artist's resale right and the *sui generis* database right, and will be keenly observing how UK judges interpret EU-derived tests for concepts such as originality and parody in a post-Brexit environment. In the patent context, all eyes are on the Unified Patent Court and the Unitary Patent, as the UK intends, as of March 2017, to continue to play a major part in Europe's new reformed patent litigation system. Yet, even if the UK is willing, it cannot be taken for granted that the EU will allow the UK, soon to be a non-Member State, to participate in a system specifically tailored with the EU single market in mind. There is no doubt that Brexit will be a headache for IP owners and legislators, but it also promises to be a fascinating process.

# CHAPTER 9

# MAY WE STAY? ASSESSING THE SECURITY OF RESIDENCE FOR EU CITIZENS LIVING IN THE UK

Stephanie REYNOLDS*

## 1. INTRODUCTION

The seismic effects of the British electorate's decision to leave the European Union will be felt in almost every corner of the UK's political and legal landscape over the short, medium and longer term. On the day of the referendum result, however, one question arose immediately: would currently resident non-national EU citizens – most of whom did not themselves have a say in the

---

\* Liverpool Law School, University of Liverpool. I am grateful to Eleanor Drywood for comments on previous drafts and in particular her insights on UK nationals as Ruiz Zambrano carers. Any errors remain my own.

outcome of the referendum[1] – be able to remain in the UK? Despite assurances from the UK Government that it wanted to secure residence rights for such EU citizens[2] when it formally notified the European Council of UK withdrawal, concrete commitments were yet to be made. Consequently, EU citizens were left, somewhat blindly, seeking means of pre-emptively securing their residence in the UK in the absence of any indication from Government as to the correct path to follow. The UK Prime Minister consistently asserted that the Government's hands were tied, arguing that it needed to ensure reciprocal protection for UK citizens living in the remaining Member States and claiming that 'one or two' EU leaders refused to reach early agreement on the issue, ahead of the commencement of formal negotiations.[3]

The Government's delay in responding to the question of EU citizens' residence rights and its preoccupation with reciprocity has already led to 'a great deal of anxiety and uncertainty' amongst the UK's resident EU population about their security of residence.[4] The Government's stance has also increased the urgency of the residence question, with both substantive and procedural consequences for any agreement reached. First, a deal is now likely to focus on the immediate question of whether and how currently resident EU citizens can stay in the UK, with reduced time and space to consider equally pertinent longer-term residence issues. Second, the emphasis on reciprocity further limits the opportunity for a legally binding outcome, while any political agreement will still need to be translated into legal reality.

By analysing the potential benefits and pitfalls of options for safeguarding residence rights, this chapter offers an opportunity to reflect both on the challenges currently facing EU citizens living in the UK, but also on the obstacles that will have to be overcome further down the line, not only by Union citizens who wish to remain in Britain, but also by the legal and political actors tasked with realising Brexit. To that end, Section 2 will outline the residence rights currently enjoyed by EU citizens in the UK as a matter of Union law. Section 3 will explain, in more detail, the UK Government's approach to the question of EU citizens' residence security and assess the alternatives presented by other actors, primarily parliamentary committees. Section 4 will then situate this analysis against the broader need to secure meaningful residence rights for EU

---

[1]   Those eligible to vote in national parliamentary elections were entitled to vote in the referendum, including British, Irish, Cypriot and Maltese nationals: European Union Referendum Act 2015, section 2.

[2]   HM Government, *The United Kingdom's exit from and new partnership with the European Union* (Cm 9417, February 2017) section 6.

[3]   Lancaster House Speech, 17 January 2017 <https://www.gov.uk/government/speeches/the-governments-negotiating-objectives-for-exiting-the-eu-pm-speech>.

[4]   House of Commons Exiting the EU Committee, *The Government's Negotiating Objectives: the Rights of UK and EU Citizens* (HC 2016–17, 1071) para 16.

citizens in the UK and critique the Government's emphasis on a reciprocal deal in this context.

## 2. UNION CITIZENS' CURRENT RESIDENCE RIGHTS IN THE UK UNDER EU LAW

Pursuant to Article 21 TFEU, EU citizens enjoy the right to move and reside freely throughout the Union. The practicalities of this right are, however, broadly realised through secondary Union legislation, largely via the Citizens' Rights Directive (the CRD/the Directive).[5] Under the Directive, EU citizens have a right to enter the UK, as an EU Member State, and reside there for up to three months with minimal formalities.[6] If EU citizens wish to remain in the UK for longer, Article 7 CRD subjects their residency to additional requirements. The Union citizen must be a worker or self-employed, or, if she/he is non-economically active, she/he must have sufficient resources and comprehensive sickness insurance for herself/himself and any accompanying family members so as not to become a burden on the social assistance system of their host state.[7] These latter conditions are however subject to proportionality assessment as a result of Court of Justice case law (CJEU/the Court).[8] The Directive also offers a right of permanent residence, via Article 16, for those who have resided legally in the UK for a continuous period of five years.

Nevertheless, some individuals derive EU residence rights outwith the CRD framework. For example, the primary caregiver of the school-age child of a Union worker may draw residence entitlements from the Free Movement of Workers Regulation,[9] by virtue of the CJEU's *Teixeira* and *Ibrahim* judgments,[10] irrespective of whether the primary caregiver is self-sufficient or the EU worker continues to be employed in the UK. Third country nationals may be able to reside in the UK as a result of the citizenship rights that the EU Treaties bestow

---

5    Directive 2004/38 of the European Parliament and of the Council of 29 April 2004 on the rights of citizens of the Union and their family members to move and reside freely within the territory of the Member States [2004] OJ L158/77.

6    Article 6 CRD: passport/ID card upon entry; Article 14(1) CRD: requirement not to become an 'unreasonable burden' on the host state's social assistance system.

7    Article 7 CRD.

8    Case C-184/99, *Grzelczyk*, ECLI:EU:C:2001:458; Case C-413/99, *Baumbast*, ECLI:EU:C:2002:493. Though see the more textual judicial approach in Case C-333/13, *Dano*, ECLI:EU:C:2014:2358; Case C-67/14, *Alimanovic*, ECLI:EU:C:2015:597.

9    Specifically, Article 10 Regulation 492/2011 of the European Parliament and of the Council of 5 April 2011 on freedom of movement for workers within the Union [2011] OJ L141/1.

10   Case C-480/08, *Teixeira*, ECLI:EU:C:2010:83; Case C-310/08 *Ibrahim and SSHD*, ECLI: EU:C:2010:80.

on their Union citizen family members. In *Chen*,[11] the third country national primary caregiver of an EU citizen minor had a right to reside in the UK, in order that the child could exercise her Article 21 TFEU right to move and reside freely around the Union, subject to sufficient resources and comprehensive sickness cover. In *Ruiz Zambrano*, a third country national primary caregiver derived a right to reside and to work in their child's Member State of nationality because to refuse this would seemingly have required the child to leave the Union territory and thus have 'deprive[d] them of the genuine enjoyment of the substance of their rights conferred by' their Union citizenship.[12]

All of these EU-law derived residence entitlements are transposed into UK law via the Immigration (European Economic Area) Regulations 2016 (the EEA Regulations).[13] However, the clear concern for the UK's EU population is whether these rights will continue after the UK leaves the Union, particularly given the many obstacles to the potential routes to residence security.

## 3. MAY WE STAY? SPECULATING ON THE RETENTION OF RESIDENCE RIGHTS IN THE ABSENCE OF GOVERNMENT GUIDANCE

Despite these concerns, when the Government published its White Paper on 'the UK's exit from and new partnership with the European Union' (the White Paper), it offered little in the way of firm assurances. The White Paper simply reaffirmed that while the UK remains an EU Member State, residence rights are unchanged,[14] while conveying the Government's wish to secure the status of EU citizens living in the UK, and British nationals in other Member States 'as early as we can … in forthcoming negotiations'.[15] However, the White Paper stopped far short of providing immediate clarification, omitting to offer a unilateral declaration as to EU citizens' residence entitlements in the UK. Instead, the White Paper retained the Government's position on the need for a reciprocal deal, which would see the UK and the remaining Member States mutually commit to protecting the residence rights of EU citizens and UK nationals living in their respective territories.[16]

---

[11]    Case C-200/02, *Zhu and Chen*, ECLI:EU:C:2004:639.
[12]    Case C-34/09, *Ruiz Zambrano*, ECLI:EU:C:2011:124, para 41.
[13]    Immigration (European Economic Area) Regulations 2016, SI 2016/1952. Article 6 CRD through Regulation 13; Article 7 CRD via Regulation 14; Article 16 by Regulation 15; the *Teixeira, Ibrahim, Chen* and *Ruiz Zambrano* judgments via Regulation 16.
[14]    *The United Kingdom's exit from and new partnership with the European Union*, above n 2, p 30.
[15]    Ibid, pp 29–30.
[16]    Ibid, p 30.

Against this vacuum in Government guidance as regards how EU citizens might secure their residence rights, other actors, such as parliamentary committees, have sought to outline the potential options available. These include UK membership of the European Economic Area; ongoing status for EU citizens in the UK as a consequence of the doctrine of 'acquired rights'; security of residence for those EU citizens qualifying for permanent residence status under Article 16 CRD; reliance on human rights protection conferred by the separate framework of the European Convention on Human Rights (ECHR/the Convention); or unilateral conferral by the UK Government either of the rights currently enjoyed by EU citizens or through 'light-touch' permanent residence.

## 3.1. EEA MEMBERSHIP AND THE DOCTRINE OF ACQUIRED RIGHTS: ROADS TO NOWHERE

Membership of the European Economic Area, which would have meant the preservation, generally speaking, of existing EU rules on free movement of people,[17] was explicitly ruled out as an option for the UK's future partnership with the EU in the White Paper.[18] Consequently this route to securing residence for EU citizens in the UK is necessarily closed off.

The House of Lords EU Committee (Lords EU Committee) accurately concluded that despite 'much speculation before the referendum that EU law rights would somehow be protected as "acquired rights", meaning that they would continue irrespective of the UK's withdrawal from the EU ... [this] is highly unlikely to provide meaningful protection against the loss of EU rights upon Brexit'.[19] Article 70 of the Vienna Convention stipulates that termination of an international treaty 'does not affect any right, obligation or legal situation of the parties created through the execution of the treaty prior to its termination'.[20] However, the Committee correctly noted that the provision was not 'in any way concerned with the question of the vested interests of individuals', rather Article 70 covers state parties.[21] Similarly, the scope of the customary

---

[17]   Article 28 and Annexes V and VIII, Agreement on the European Economic Area [1994] OJ L1/3. The Decision of the EEA Joint Committee No 158/2007 [2007] OJ L124/20 incorporates the CRD into EEA law legal framework but an accompanying joint declaration expressly states that 'the concept of Union citizenship ... has no equivalent in the EEA Agreement'.

[18]   *The United Kingdom's exit from and new partnership with the European Union*, above n 2, pp 25 and 35.

[19]   House of Lords European Union Committee, *Brexit: Acquired Rights* (HL 2016–17, 82) p 3.

[20]   United Nations, Vienna Convention on the Law of Treaties, 23 May 1969, Treaty Series, Vol 1155, p 331. For reliance on this approach, see 'Debate must be about future immigration policy', Letter to the Financial Times, signed by both Leave and Remain campaigners, 11 April 16, <https://www.ft.com/content/c5d52fe8-fd80-11e5-b5f5-070dca6d0a0d>.

[21]   *Acquired Rights*, above n 19, para 58, citing written evidence from S Douglas Scott.

international law doctrine of acquired rights is 'limited to certain contractual and property rights which, even if they were to coincide with EU rights, are highly unlikely to be enforceable'.[22]

## 3.2. PERMANENT RESIDENCE: A BUMPY (YET EXCLUSIVE) ROAD

By contrast, the option of securing rights for EU citizens who enjoy permanent residence – either via continued domestic recognition of that status[23] or through the automatic eligibility of permanent EU residents for the broad domestic equivalent of indefinite leave to remain – continues to attract attention.[24] The White Paper explicitly references the availability of Article 16 CRD to EU citizens, though without indicating its pertinence to post-Brexit residence rights.[25] Moreover, parliamentary committees have explored the potential of permanent residence as a means of retaining residence rights.[26] Crucially, applications by EU citizens to the UK Home Office for permanent residence certificates soared by 264 per cent between the first and fourth quarter of 2016 – from 12,117 to 44,112 – in other words, over the periods before and after the referendum.[27] This indicates that, regardless of the Government's refusal to shine a light upon the correct path to follow, resident Union citizens are understandably – given that many would consider the UK their home – searching in the dark, nevertheless, for a possible route to residence security.

And indeed, there are advantages to the use of permanent residence as a means of safeguarding residence in the UK, even if these are ultimately outweighed by the disadvantages. First, permanent residence status brings access to equal treatment – for instance, in terms of social support, healthcare and student maintenance – without the need for an EU citizen to meet the conditions attached to residence under Article 7 CRD.[28] Second, continued domestic recognition of permanent residence acknowledges that many EU citizens, having lived in the UK under that framework, cannot be slotted into

---

[22]  Ibid, paras 61–62, citing written evidence from V Lowe.

[23]  Regulation 15, EEA Regulations.

[24]  See eg British Future, *Report of the Inquiry into Securing the Status of EEA+ Nationals in the UK*, 1 December 2016, <http://www.britishfuture.org/wp-content/uploads/2016/12/EUNationalsReport.Final_.12.12.16.pdf>, p 26.

[25]  *The United Kingdom's exit from and new partnership with the European* Union, above n 2, p 30.

[26]  *Acquired Rights*, above n 19, paras 19–23; Joint Committee on Human Rights, *The Human Rights Implications of Brexit*, (2016–17, HL 88 and HC 695) paras 29–34.

[27]  Home Office Immigration Statistics, eea-q4-2016-tables, published 23 February 2017, available at <https://www.gov.uk/government/publications/immigration-statistics-october-to-december-2016/list-of-tables>.

[28]  Article 16(1) CRD; Article 24 CRD.

the more restrictive national immigration categories, currently applicable to non-EU immigrants. In particular, they may not qualify for the domestic broad equivalent of indefinite leave to remain.[29] While permanent residence generally requires five years' continuous legal residence under the CRD, indefinite leave to remain carries different requirements dependent on the many tiers of visa category applicable to non-EU nationals living in the UK, not all of which qualify for such settlement in any case. Generally speaking, however, between five and ten years' continuous, lawful residence is needed.[30] The majority of routes to settlement require applicants to demonstrate sufficient knowledge of the English language and of life in the UK. Applications may be rejected on character grounds, and on the basis of unspent convictions, and indefinite leave to remain is subject to the sizeable fee of £2,297 per applicant.[31] Moreover, the summary provided here does not do justice to the 'degree of complexity' behind the system that 'even the Byzantine emperors would have envied'.[32]

Nevertheless, whether as a consequence of EU law, UK implementation of Union rules, or a combination of the two, permanent residence is, in practice, far from a catch-all solution. Some individuals, currently resident under EU law, are automatically excluded from the status. Others might fail to meet eligibility requirements in practice. In any case, providing evidence that those conditions have been met can be a challenging task.

First, under the UK's EEA Regulations,[33] accurately implementing CJEU case law,[34] those residing in the UK under a 'derivative right of residence', specifically the *Teixeira, Chen* and *Ruiz Zambrano* carers outlined in Section 2 (above), are not eligible for permanent residence since they do not reside under the CRD's own residence categories. Accordingly, their residence entitlements would not be protected if this model were used to safeguard residence rights post-Brexit. Conversely, UK nationals residing in other Member States, with primary caregiving responsibilities for citizens of those countries, may well seek to rely on *Ruiz Zambrano*, should any gaps in a UK/EU deal affect their residence. This will make for potentially interesting twists in this line of jurisprudence, particularly since the principle developed in that judgment has generally been pushed to the peripheries of Union citizenship in subsequent CJEU case law.[35] Specifically,

---

[29]  *Human Rights*, above n 26, paras 35–45.
[30]  As summarised in *Acquired Rights*, above n 19, p 13.
[31]  Home Office Immigration and Nationality Charges 2017, available at <https://www.gov.uk/government/uploads/system/uploads/attachment_data/file/606076/Visa_Fees_table_Apr2017.pdf>.
[32]  Jackson LJ, *Pokhriyal v SSHD* [2013] EWCA Civ 1568, para 4, cited in *Acquired Rights*, above n 19, [27].
[33]  Regulation 15(2), EEA Regulations.
[34]  Case C-424/10, *Ziolkowski*, ECLI:EU:C:2011:866.
[35]  See eg Case C-434/09, *McCarthy*, ECLI:EU:C:2011:277; Case C-256/11, *Dereci*, ECLI:EU:C:2011:734. I am grateful to Eleanor Drywood for highlighting the particular issue of UK *Ruiz Zambrano* carers to me.

should EU citizen children have to leave the Union territory to return to the UK with their parents, a reversal of judicial reluctance to ensure the 'genuine enjoyment of the substance of the rights' conferred by Union citizenship may be irresistible, given that such children would fall squarely within the parameters of *Ruiz Zambrano*, even if that decision was clearly not delivered in knowledge of the wholesale exit of a Member State.

The second obstacle that emerges from reliance on permanent residence relates to meeting eligibility requirements. Even those who appear to reside under the Directive might struggle to accumulate the five years' *continuous, legal* residence required by Article 16 CRD. A common barrier arises from the need for non-economically active Union citizens to have comprehensive sickness insurance (CSI). Consider the position of a French national who has been living continuously in the UK for five years. For the past two years he has worked as a nurse and so resides in accordance with the Directive. However, for his first three years in the UK, he was a student and not economically active. He had sufficient resources to support himself but did not realise he needed CSI. He never really relied on national health services during this time, though he was able to register with his university GP.[36] Regardless, since he did not have insurance, he will not, technically, have been living in the UK in accordance with the Directive and may not qualify for permanent residence status. Similarly, an EU citizen who has not worked continuously for five years, nor retained worker status when unemployed,[37] is unlikely to have been aware that she/he changed residence categories – from worker to non-economically active – during periods of economic inactivity, with the consequent need to obtain insurance.

Though little known prior to the referendum, the CSI requirement has become one of the most prominently reported potential barriers to residence security,[38] resulting, positively, in increased parliamentary scrutiny of the issue. The Commons Committee on Exiting the EU (Exiting the EU Committee) has explicitly called on the UK Government to 'state that access to the NHS is considered sufficient to fulfil the requirements for CSI, and that it will introduce legislation to that effect'.[39] The Home Office response has been limited to a media statement indicating that 'EU citizens will not be removed from the UK

---

[36] A number of EU citizens informed the Exiting the EU Committee that they had been able to access NHS services and register with universities or jobcentres without ever being told about the need for CSI: above n 4, para 70.

[37] In certain circumstances, EU citizens may retain their worker status during periods of unemployment. See Article 7(3) CRD and Case C-507/12, *Saint Prix*, ECLI:EU:C:2014:2007.

[38] eg R HAWKINS, 'EU citizens 'denied residency documents', *BBC News*, 18 February 2017 <http://www.bbc.co.uk/news/uk-39014191>; L O'CARROLL, 'Dutch woman resident in the UK for 30 years may have to leave after Brexit', *The Guardian*, 14 January 2017 <https://www.theguardian.com/politics/2017/jan/14/dutchwoman-resident-in-uk-for-30-years-may-have-to-leave-after-brexit>.

[39] *Negotiating Objectives*, above n 4, para 73.

or refused entry solely because they do not have this insurance'.[40] However, since its emphasis was on removal, the statement offers little guidance to those applying for permanent residence certificates as a means of safeguarding their UK residence into the future.[41] Indeed, in the permanent residence context, refusal to recognise national health services as meeting the CSI requirement was Home Office policy long before the referendum and has even been confirmed as lawful by domestic courts.[42]

The EEA Regulations also impose more onerous requirements on the issuing of permanent residence documents than those operating under the Directive. Specifically, a refusal to issue such documentation can be justified 'on grounds of public policy, public security or public health or on grounds of misuse of rights'.[43] CJEU case law dictates that residence documentation reflects but does not confer residence status, while the CRD stipulates that permanent residents may only be removed for 'serious reasons of public policy or public security'.[44] The compliance of UK rules with Union law is therefore open to serious question.

The third hurdle confronting permanent residence applicants relates to evidence. The combination of EU law's clear stipulation that residence documents do not, of themselves, bestow residence rights on EU citizens – since these entitlements are intrinsic to one's status as a Union citizen[45] – with the fact that the UK does not operate a registration or ID card system means that, for many EU citizens in the UK, their post-referendum application for a permanent residence certificate might be their first application for residence documentation. Accordingly, the sudden need for evidence to support applications might only be met by historical records not easily to hand. This evidential burden will be particularly difficult for individuals who have moved between the CRD's residence categories and those who have not been in long-term, more secure, employment in the UK.

This problem is exacerbated by the now mandatory[46] completion of an 85-page application form for permanent residence documents.[47] Arguably, the form's complexity stems from its attempts to cover the various routes to permanent residence offered by the CRD.[48] Nevertheless, a more streamlined

---

[40]  Home Office in the Media Blog, 'Current residency rights of EU citizens', 1 March 2017 <https://homeofficemedia.blog.gov.uk/2017/03/01/home-office-in-the-media-1-march-2017/>.

[41]  Ibid.

[42]  *FK (Kenya) v SSHD* [2010] EWCA Civ 1302; *Ahmad v SSHD* [2014] EWCA Civ 988.

[43]  Regulation 24(1), EEA Regulations.

[44]  Case C-325/09, *Dias*, ECLI:EU:C:2011:498; Article 25(1) CRD.

[45]  Ibid.

[46]  Since March 2016, Regulation 21, EEA Regulations.

[47]  Available at <https://www.gov.uk/government/uploads/system/uploads/attachment_data/file/505032/EEA_PR__03-16.pdf>.

[48]  eg Article 17 CRD confers permanent residence status before 5 years' residence in set circumstances.

process has been designed by outside actors, which relies principally on existing Government data on applicants rather than placing the administrative burden on the EU citizen.[49] Crucially, the inaccessibility of the current document might be one of the reasons behind the increasing number of applications declared 'invalid' by the Home Office. This occurs, for instance, where the form is incorrectly completed or evidence is missing. Applicants may resubmit their application, subject to the second payment of a £65 processing charge; a fee not permitted by the CRD.[50] Between the first and third quarter of 2016 – ie before and after the referendum – the number of invalid applications nearly doubled, from 6.7 per cent to 11.8 per cent, though this steadied back to 6.8 per cent by the year end.[51] More broadly, commentators recognise that the logistical challenge facing the Home Office – should permanent residence prove to be the route to residence security for EU citizens and current methods be maintained – is simply too great to be achieved in the two years between the triggering of Article 50 TEU and UK departure.[52]

Crucially, the Government is still to confirm the pertinence of permanent residence status to residence security. Nonetheless, against the void in Government guidance, the high percentage of refusals to issue permanent residence documents – on average 22 per cent over 2014–16[53] – is a source of anxiety for EU citizens who consider that a rejection indicates they might not be able to remain in the UK post-exit. Further, in some instances, rejection letters have also contained the conclusion that the applicant is not residing legally and an accompanying instruction 'to prepare to leave the UK'.[54] This has led some EU citizens to express concern about being caught between the need to secure their residence into the future – albeit through an unconfirmed means of achieving this – and the desire to avoid alerting the Home Office to what it might view as unlawful residence, by placing a permanent residence application.[55] Given the anxiety that can arise not only about future but also current residence rights in the UK as a result of a rejected permanent residence application, the Exiting the EU Committee has also been openly critical both of the 'prepare to leave' statement and of the lack of clarity offered by Government 'on whether it intends the permanent residence system to be the basis for EU nationals to demonstrate their eligibility to reside in the UK'.[56]

---

[49]  *EEA+ Nationals*, above n 24, paras 27–28.
[50]  Article 25(2) CRD.
[51]  Above n 27.
[52]  Evidence to the Exiting the EU Committee, above n 4, para 77.
[53]  Above n 27.
[54]  *Negotiating Objectives*, above n 4, para 72.
[55]  Questions to the panel, 'Arrangements for EU Nationals', Cambridge Stays Meeting, 11 January 2017.
[56]  *Negotiating Objectives*, above n 4, para 80.

In light of the abundant problems with the permanent residence framework, its presentation as a comprehensive answer to the question of residence security has been accurately described as a myth.[57] Crucially, permanent residence would offer nothing for EU citizens who fall short of five years' residence in the UK, whether in compliance with the Directive or otherwise. Yet medium-term EU citizens in particular might still have forged family and social ties in the UK. If the UK fails to cater for such individuals, and/or maintains its strict approach to permanent residence eligibility, it leaves itself open to potential human rights litigation. This invites the question of whether the ECHR might offer an alternative means of ensuring currently resident EU citizens can remain in the UK.

## 3.3. THE ECHR BASELINE: NOT ALL ROADS LEAD TO THE SAME LEVEL OF PROTECTION

In the absence of a UK/EU agreement on residence rights, or the focus within any agreement only on certain categories of resident, the ECHR might indeed offer some opportunity for protection from removal, since, regardless of its exit from the EU, the UK must still meet its separate obligations under the Convention. In particular, pursuant to Article 8 ECHR, the UK will be required to respect the right to the family and private lives that resident EU citizens have established in the UK and confer residence rights where necessary.[58] The European Court of Human Rights (the ECtHR) considers a 'lawful and genuine marriage' to amount to a 'family life', while a parent-child relationship, apart from in exceptional circumstances, will automatically qualify.[59] Moreover, Article 8 does not merely encompass family life in a strict sense but also 'private life', including the 'totality of social ties between settled migrants and the community in which they are living'.[60] Once a private or family life is established, a prima facie breach of Article 8 ECHR will almost always be triggered by removal,[61] though, of course, under Union law no such links are needed at all, at least for those residing as EU citizens.[62] Union citizens currently enjoy independent rights in the UK simply by virtue of their EU citizenship.

Moreover, prima facie interferences with the right to private and family life may be justified under Article 8(2) ECHR. Restrictions must be in accordance

---

[57]   *Human Rights*, above n 26, para 31; *Acquired Rights*, above n 19, paras 21–23.
[58]   Other human rights issues may also arise, eg under Article 1, Protocol 1 ECHR (right to property).
[59]   *ZH (Tanzania) v SSHD* [2011] UKSC 4.
[60]   *Üner v Netherlands* [2006] ECHR 873.
[61]   *DM (Zambia) v SSHD* [2009] EWCA Civ 474.
[62]   Article 2(2) CRD outlines those 'family members' who may accompany or join their EU citizen family members in the host state.

with the law and necessary in a democratic society. They must be in the interests of national security, public safety, the economic well-being of the country, for the prevention of crime and disorder, or the protection of health, morals or the rights and freedoms of others. Thus, the reasons justifying removal of an individual from the UK under the Convention are far broader than those available to a host state under the CRD, which permits removals only for reasons of public health, public security or public policy.[63] For permanent residents serious grounds of public policy or public security are needed, while those resident in the UK for 10 years may only be deported for imperative grounds of public security.[64] Both legal frameworks, however, require decisions to be taken at the individual level, subject to the requirements of proportionality, which takes various factors, such as length of residence in the UK, the strength of family ties, the language skills of the family, access to employment and social needs, into account.[65] Therefore, though the proportionality assessment under the CRD might be harder for public authorities to overcome,[66] the ECHR does offer a clear baseline of protection. Where the applicant is married to a British national '[i]t cannot be permissible to give less than detailed and anxious consideration to the situation of a British citizen who has lived here all his life before it is held reasonable and proportionate to expect him to emigrate to a foreign country in order to keep his marriage intact'.[67] Similarly, it will rarely be proportionate if the effect of the order is to sever a genuine and subsisting relationship between parent and child.[68] Ultimately, however, Article 8 ECHR does not impose any obligation on a state to respect the choices of a married couple.[69] The question largely hinges on whether family life can reasonably be expected to be enjoyed elsewhere, by reference to the material but not decisive consideration of whether there are any 'insurmountable obstacles' to this,[70] and the need to achieve a balance between the interests of society and the individual.[71]

Crucially, then, while Article 8 ECHR will be useful in preventing the adoption, by the UK Government, of a bright line rule that foresees the removal of EU citizens who arrived in the UK after an arbitrarily set date,[72] it cannot

---

[63]   Article 27 CRD.
[64]   Article 28 CRD. Though this is broader than 'national security' (Case C-348/09, *PI*, ECLI:EU:C:2012:300).
[65]   *EB (Kosovo)* [2008] UKHL 41; Article 27(2) CRD.
[66]   Since beyond proportionality questions related, inter alia, to health, family life and social integration, pursuant to Article 28(1) CRD, Article 27(2) CRD also requires a genuine, present and sufficiently serious threat to a fundamental interest of society, posed by the personal conduct of the individual concerned.
[67]   *AB (Jamaica)* [2007] EWCA Civ 1302.
[68]   *EB (Kosovo)*, above n 65.
[69]   *DM (Zambia)*, above n 61.
[70]   *R (on the application of Agyarko) v SSHD* [2015] EWCA Civ 440.
[71]   *Huang and Kashmiri* [2007] UKHL 11.
[72]   The Government asserts that it does not foresee Article 8 ECHR litigation since a 'speedy agreement' is anticipated: *Human Rights*, above n 26, para 41.

offer an all-encompassing solution to the issue of residence security. On the question of the right simply to be in the UK, it would depend on family or social ties between the Union citizen and individuals with firmer residence in the UK. Moreover, critically, it does not necessarily provide access to equal treatment in the UK once residence has been secured, as is generally the case for EU citizens residing legally under the Directive.[73] This is instead dependent on which domestic immigration categories individuals are subsequently placed.

The various pitfalls to the options considered thus far have led an increasing number of political actors to call for a unilateral conferral upon EU citizens resident in the UK, either of the rights they currently enjoy under Union law, or of the rights arising from permanent residence status, though with a light-touch approach to its eligibility criteria.

## 3.4. UNILATERAL CONFERRAL OF CURRENT RESIDENCE RIGHTS OR A 'LIGHT-TOUCH' PERMANENT RESIDENCE

Having conducted inquiries into the viability of different means of safeguarding the residence rights of the UK's EU population, various parliamentary committees, across both Houses of Parliament, have 'urge[d] the Government to change its stance and to give a unilateral guarantee now'.[74] The pertinence of the issue is also reflected in the fact that the rights of EU citizens in the UK were the focus of attempted parliamentary amendments to the Notification of Withdrawal Act.[75] Several proposed Commons amendments sought to ensure that it preserved the same citizenship rights enjoyed by EU nationals who were lawfully resident in the UK at certain points in time.[76] Others pursued the inclusion of a 'fast-track' to permanent resident status, for instance for those who had been resident in the UK on the referendum date and at least since 23 December 2015.[77] However, the amendment selected – focused on continuation of residence rights for those lawfully resident in the UK on 23 June – was ultimately defeated in the Commons, 332 to 290.[78] While amendment on the issue was passed by the House of Lords, the upper chamber later accepted the Commons' rejection of that amendment.

---

[73] Article 18 TFEU and Article 24(1) CRD. Article 24(2) CRD allows for certain derogations. See also recent CJEU case law that allows for restrictions to equal treatment for non-economically active Union citizens: above n 8.

[74] *Acquired Rights*, above n 19, para 147. See also *Human Rights*, above n 26, para 45; and *Negotiating Objectives*, above n 4, para 45.

[75] House of Commons, Committee of the Whole House, Tables Amendments to the European Union (Notification of Withdrawal) Bill, 8 March 2017, <https://www.publications.parliament.uk/pa/bills/cbill/2016-2017/0132/amend/european_daily_cwh_0207.pdf>.

[76] Ibid, NC6, NC27, NC146, NC57, NC135.

[77] Ibid, C17.

[78] *Hansard* HC Deb Vol 621, cols 556–560 (8 March 2017).

Unilateral conferral either of current residence entitlements or of permanent residence via less restrictive eligibility criteria has a number of advantages. A light-touch approach to permanent residence status would avoid the bright light distinction created by the five-year cut-off under Article 16 CRD. In fact, it would offer some EU citizens, who would not yet qualify for permanent residence, more extensive residence security than they would have enjoyed had the UK opted to remain in the EU. Meanwhile, focus on the retention of current entitlements would protect, for instance, *Ruiz Zambrano* carers. However, the retained emphasis on *legal* residence in the tabled amendments, particularly in relation to historical points in time, still raises substantive issues, for instance around the question of CSI, as well as administrative and evidential challenges, even if these are lower if the time period to qualify for permanent residence is shorter.

Crucially, while it is commendable that political actors seek to protect EU citizens living in the UK, the complexity of retaining the plethora of rights arising from EU citizenship status, within what will become a former Member State, requires rather more consideration of how this would work in practice than was arguably reflected in the broad-brush proposed amendments to the Notification of Withdrawal Act.[79] Nevertheless, the Government's insistence on waiting to secure a quick reciprocal deal with the wider EU is no indication of the Government's understanding of the intricacies involved, since a reciprocal deal in fact invites further complexity.

## 4.   CAN WE STAY? ENSURING MEANINGFUL RESIDENCE AND THE RECIPROCITY DISTRACTION

What is reassuring about parliamentary support for the retention of all of the rights arising from EU citizenship that are currently conferred on Union citizens living in the UK is its implicit understanding that a simple right to *be* in the UK is insufficient. As the House of Lords EU Committee neatly summarised:

> 'EU citizenship rights are indivisible. Taken as a whole, they make it possible for an EU citizen to live, work, study and have a family in another Member State. Remove one, and the operation of others is affected. It is our strong recommendation, therefore, that the full scope of EU citizenship rights be fully safeguarded in the withdrawal agreement.'[80]

Indeed, for many EU citizens, the ability to remain in the UK will depend on whether they continue to enjoy those rights that make the exercise of their

---

[79]   For analysis of Parliament's role in the Notification of Withdrawal Act, see the contribution by M GORDON (Ch 1) in this edited collection.

[80]   *Acquired Rights*, above n 19, para 121.

residence entitlements possible in practice. For example, EU citizens residing legally in their host state have the right to equal access to employment and remuneration,[81] and, generally speaking, social assistance, education and healthcare, on the same basis as nationals.[82] Certain family members are also able to accompany or join the EU citizen in the UK, and enjoy equal treatment there.[83] As discussed above, Union citizens who were able to move to the UK as a result of EU free movement rules might struggle to remain there under the more restrictive conditions of its national immigration law, such as the minimum earnings threshold of £35,000 for settlement under the Tier 2 (general) visa.[84] By contrast, Union citizens qualify as a worker, a route to legal residence under the CRD, so long as their work is 'genuine and effective' and not 'marginal and ancillary'.[85] British citizens who have not exercised free movement rights, and settled third country nationals must generally also satisfy a minimum income threshold if they wish to bring family members with them to the UK.[86] Residence permits are commonly granted 'without recourse to public funds'[87] and are normally subject to a surcharge to access national health services.[88]

Indeed, this appears to be the crux of the matter. It seems unlikely that the UK will systematically remove EU citizens from its territory – whether a UK/EU agreement on residence is reached or not – if only because this would be administratively extremely burdensome, as well as exposing the UK to potentially lengthy and expensive litigation.[89] What requires more vigilance is whether Union citizens, if denied the equal treatment rights that they currently enjoy under Union law, will face the choice of leaving or living in destitution. The UK's decision to treat non-economically active Union citizens as 'lawfully present' in the UK but lacking a 'right to reside' for the purposes of access to social support, is potentially portentous here.[90]

And yet, parliamentary calls for the Government to safeguard all of the rights arising from Union citizenship arguably overlook the complexity of the issue,

---

[81]   Article 45(2) TFEU.
[82]   Article 24 CRD. Ongoing tensions exist in CJEU case law as to whether those residing as 'self-sufficient' under the Directive are then able to access social assistance: see above n 8.
[83]   Articles 2 and 3 CRD.
[84]   UKVI, 'Tier 2 of the Points-Based System', Version 11/16, 65. Subject to certain exemptions for labour shortages.
[85]   Case 139/85, *Kempf*, ECLI:EU:C:1986:223.
[86]   Statement of Changes in Immigration Rules, HC 194, 13 June 2012, 4.
[87]   UKVI, Guidance on Public Funds, <https://www.gov.uk/government/publications/public-funds--2/public-funds>.
[88]   <https://www.gov.uk/healthcare-immigration-application>.
[89]   *Human Rights*, above n 26, para 42.
[90]   eg The Social Security (Persons from Abroad) Amendment Regulations, SI 2006/1026; see C O'Brien, 'The Pillory, the Precipice and the Slippery Slope: the Profound Effects of the UK's Legal Reform Programme Targeting EU Migrants' (2015) 37(1) *Journal of Social Welfare and Family Law* 111–136.

particularly those made via the proposed amendments to the Notification of Withdrawal Act. While the EEA Regulations could be maintained short-term and therefore preserve some of the central rights of Union citizenship, such as residence and equal treatment, others will simply be lost by virtue of the fact that the UK will no longer be an EU Member State. For example, Union citizens will no longer be able to vote for or stand as an MEP in their constituency of residence. The retention of other rights is likely to be politically controversial and it seems probable that they will be reassessed, as part of what seems an inevitable wider review of the national immigration framework.[91] For instance, as outlined above, non-national EU citizens presently enjoy more generous family reunification rights in the UK than British nationals, who have not exercised their free movement rights, do. The maintenance of this for family members already residing in the UK with EU citizens seems only fair. However, it would be interesting to see how the retention of those rights for family members not yet in the UK would play out politically, particularly since, as part of its pre-referendum negotiations with the EU, the Government already sought to tighten up on the ability of British nationals to circumvent national immigration rules through the exercise of their free movement rights.[92]

Perhaps the clearest example of the complexity of the task ahead is the EU Social Security Regulation.[93] This instrument coordinates social security provision across the Member States – and therefore facilitates free movement – in a number of ways, one of which is to permit the aggregation of periods of residence and/or social security contributions made by individual Union citizens in different Member States. This ensures that the exercise of free movement rights does not place EU citizens at a disadvantage by causing them to lose contributions made in one Member State when moving to another.[94] For instance, should Germany require 35 years' contributions to qualify for a state pension there, a French national who has worked for 10 years in France, 15 years in the UK and 10 years in Germany, who then decides to retire in the latter Member State, is able to satisfy the German rules since she can combine contributions made across different Member States. Crucially, an implementing Regulation provides specific formulae for calculating her entitlements and a set

---

[91] The White Paper indicates that primary legislation on immigration will follow exit: see above n 2, para 10. However, the Government has also stated that it judges the UK's non-EEA immigration system to be 'very effective' such that 'it may be that some aspects of those non-EEA systems could be applicable to [arriving] EU citizens': House of Lords EU Committee, *Brexit: UK-EU Movement of People* (HL 2016–17, 121) para 133.

[92] Possible following Case C-370/90, *Surinder Singh*, ECLI:EU:C:1992:296; Conclusions of the European Council, 18–19 February 2016, EUCO 1/16, 35.

[93] Regulation 883/2004 of the European Parliament and of the Council of 29 April 2004 on the coordination of social security systems [2004] OJ L166/1.

[94] Article 6.

of procedures and deadlines for Member States to follow in order to claim back money from one another.[95]

Critically, when the UK leaves the EU, it will drop out of this complex system. This will leave Union citizens and British nationals in the UK, who have been employed elsewhere in the Union for parts of their working lives, at risk of losing contributions and therefore of lesser pension entitlement in the UK if agreement is not reached. Likewise, EU citizens and British nationals who have worked for periods of time in the UK but also in other Member States, and wish to retire outside the UK might lose sizeable portions of their state pension entitlement.

Yet, the Government's steadfast refusal to confer existing rights unilaterally upon the UK's resident EU population is no indication of its understanding of the intricacies involved in safeguarding a set of rights borne from, and embedded in, EU law. This is demonstrated by its consistent emphasis on the need for a reciprocal deal, which simultaneously overcomplicates and oversimplifies the Union legal framework.

First, the UK can already look to existing Union legislation on third country nationals as an indicator of the rights that the EU might be able to offer UK nationals living in other Member States. Arguably, there are question marks over whether the Union will change its existing one-size-fits-all legislation to offer a custom fit for the UK. For instance, secondary EU legislation already offers third country nationals the capacity to acquire long-term resident status, following five years' continuous, legal residence in a Member State.[96] This provides rights comparable, but in no way identical, to permanent residence for EU citizens. For example, the status is not available to students or seasonal workers.[97] Applicants are required to show that they have the stable and regular resources required to support themselves without recourse to the Member State's social assistance and appropriate sickness insurance.[98] Integration requirements may be imposed[99] and equal access to social assistance may be limited to core benefits.[100] As regards social security, Regulation 1231/2010 extends the Social Security Regulation to third country nationals in a cross-border situation.[101]

---

[95]   Articles 60–66, Regulation 987/2009 of the European Parliament and of the Council of 16 September 2009 laying down the procedure for implementing Regulation 883/2004 [2009] OJ L284/1.

[96]   Council Directive 2003/109/EC of 25 November 2003 concerning the status of third country nationals who are long-term residents, [2003] OJ L16/44.

[97]   Ibid, Article 3(2).

[98]   Ibid, Article 5.

[99]   Ibid, Article 5(2).

[100]   Ibid, Article 11(4), though this term must be interpreted in light of the EU Charter of Fundamental Rights: see Case C-571/10, *Kamberaj*, ECLI:EU:C:2012:233.

[101]   Regulation 1231/10 of the European Parliament and of the Council of 24 November 2010 extending Regulation 882/2004 and Regulation 987/2009 to nationals of third countries [2010] OJ L344/1.

However, though an increasingly present feature of association agreements,[102] where intra-EU movement is not present, social security coordination generally remains within the domain of bilateral agreements between individual EU Member States and third countries. Nevertheless, Member States willing to reach such an arrangement with the UK will still consider the effects of applicable Union principles, such as those arising from the CJEU's *Gottardo* judgment.[103] Following this decision, an agreement under which, for example, Ireland recognises contributions made in the UK when individuals make a claim to its social security system, would have to be extended not just to Irish and British nationals but also to any EU citizens who have worked in the UK and come to Ireland, with potential financial and administrative difficulties for Ireland as a result.[104]

Second, the EU remains reliant on the powers conferred upon it by its Member States to act. Consequently, although some secondary Union legislation also exists for those who do not meet the eligibility requirements for long-term residence, relating, for instance, to a single application procedure for residence and work permits and a minimum level of rights for third country nationals,[105] the creation of something more far-reaching for UK nationals will need to overcome significant legal hurdles. At the very least, it makes agreement on a reciprocal deal by EU leaders prior to the UK's formal exit negotiations and even early agreement during them more legally complicated than the White Paper was willing to admit. Specifically, UK nationals' residence and equal treatment rights within the other Member States currently arise from their Union citizenship. After exit, British nationals will no longer be EU citizens and therefore will cease to derive these rights from the Treaties. Given that securing residence, and the equal treatment rights that make such residence meaningful, will largely fall within areas of shared or Member State competence,[106] the inclusion of this issue within the withdrawal agreement could make it mixed in nature. If so, the agreement may not be able to be processed via the procedure foreseen by Article 50 TEU; ie with the approval of a qualified majority of the Council of Ministers and the consent of the European Parliament. Instead, it could also

---

[102]    eg Article 39, Additional Protocol and Financial Protocol, 23 November 1970, annexed to the Agreement establishing the Association between the EEC and Turkey [1972] OJ L293/3; Decision 3/80 of the Association Council of 19 September 1980 on the application of social security schemes of the Member States of the European Communities to Turkish workers. Neither of these covers contributions made in Turkey.

[103]    Case C-55/00, *Gottardo*, ECLI:EU:C:2022:16.

[104]    For further discussion, see the contribution by M Dougan (Ch 3) in this edited collection.

[105]    eg Directive 2011/98/EU of the European Parliament and of the Council of 13 December 2011 on a single application procedure for a single permit for third-country nationals to reside and work in the territory of a Member State and on a common set of rights for third country workers legally residing in a Member State [2011] OJ L343/1.

[106]    Article 4 TFEU.

require the ratification of the 27 remaining Member States, in accordance with their domestic constitutional requirements.

That said, the Commission's negotiating recommendations identified a somewhat novel 'exceptional [Union] horizontal competence … for all matters necessary to arrange the withdrawal', derived from Article 50 itself.[107] This would appear, under these very specific circumstances, to give the Union competence over substantive areas in which the EU would ordinarily share power with the Member States or where competence might even remain with them. On the one hand, this could be beneficial as it would bypass the need for a mixed agreement and therefore perhaps avoid some of the delays that might arise from the requirement of Member State agreement in accordance with national constitutional arrangements, since these can include, for example, national referendums, or the approval of regional parliaments.[108] On the other hand, inclusion in the withdrawal agreement of fields in which the EU's power is usually more limited is likely to make the negotiations themselves lengthier, particularly given the Union's consistent attitude towards EU/UK withdrawal: that nothing is agreed until everything is agreed. In short, the UK Government's accusations against 'one or two EU leaders' who refused to come to the pre-negotiating table therefore overlooks the legal complexity of the matter, treating the EU as a single entity when, in this context, it is a body of 27 independent states, each with their own experiences of UK free movement on their territories.

Given that a legal agreement outside the formal withdrawal agreement would face identical challenges, what seems more probable is a *political* commitment. The UK would agree to adopt legislation to protect the rights of its resident EU population and the Union would similarly pledge to adopt secondary Union legislation to offer specific rights to UK citizens in the remaining 27, though with less time and space, at least at the moment, to consider very technical medium- and longer-term issues, such as the future framework for social security coordination. However, the translation of a political agreement into a legal reality would still be subject to the requirements of the Union's legislative procedures, though the Commission's recent negotiating recommendations introduce some ambiguity in the specific context of UK withdrawal. Specifically, while those recommendations identify special horizontal competence for the Union in the context of 'the Agreement', it is unclear whether this extends to any future implementation, since they also state that '[t]he exercise by the Union of this specific competence in the Agreement will not affect in any way

---

[107] Opinion 1/94, ECLI:EU:C:1994:384; Annex to the Recommendation for a Council Decision authorising the opening of negotiations for an agreement with the United Kingdom of Great Britain and Northern Ireland setting out arrangements for its withdrawal from the European Union, COM(2017) 218 final, para 5.

[108] eg Belgium's signature of the EU/Canada trade agreement was delayed by disagreement amongst regional parliaments.

the distribution of competences between the Union and the Member States as regards the adoption of any future instrument in the areas concerned'.[109] In any case, it is highly likely that secondary instruments would need to be jointly adopted by the Council of Ministers and the European Parliament, with no legal comeback for the UK should this fail. Moreover, it is also probable that since UK citizens would, by that stage, be third country nationals, the instrument would fall within the Area of Freedom, Security and Justice and therefore require the positive opt-in of Denmark[110] and Ireland.[111]

Clearly, the question of converting a political commitment into a legal reality is equally pertinent for EU citizens in the UK, if not more so, since the UK will implement the agreement outside the Union's legal structures. While the EEA Regulations could maintain the status quo in the shorter term, in the longer term, the Government envisages immigration reform via separate primary legislation. Thus far, it has been clear that 'the Free Movement Directive will no longer apply' and that it seeks to 'control the numbers of people who come here' to address 'public concern about pressure on public services'.[112] Effective scrutiny of these measures as regards future EU movement is clearly pivotal. However, any proposals must also be examined to ensure that those already resident in the UK prior to Brexit continue to benefit from any EU/UK deal reached, particularly in relation to equal treatment, rather than also falling within the UK's new immigration framework. While a clear delineation might be apparent in legislative instruments, it will be important to ensure that lines do not become blurred in practice. Even as an EU Member State, the UK's decision to process EU citizens through its national 'permissions-based' administrative and adjudicative immigration structures, means that concepts developed in the context of domestic immigration law can seep into, and restrict, the 'rights-based' model that operates under EU citizenship.[113]

Effective mechanisms by which Union citizens can enforce their maintained rights before the courts will be needed and, relatedly, an approach to interpreting any agreement that seeks to avoid divergence between UK and EU law, particularly if some level of reciprocity is achieved. The Lords EU Committee has reported on a number of enforcement options, albeit in the context of the formal withdrawal

---

[109]   Articles 77(2) and 79(2) TFEU; above n 107.

[110]   Protocol No 22 on the position of Denmark [2012] OJ C326/299.

[111]   Protocol No 21 on the position of the United Kingdom and Ireland in respect of the Area of Freedom, Security and Justice [2016] OJ C202/295.

[112]   *The United Kingdom's exit from and new partnership with the European Union*, above n 2, p 25. Research has consistently found that EU migrants rely less on public services than resident populations: Eurofound Report (EF1546), *Social Dimension of intra-EU Mobility: Impact on Public Services*, 10 December 2015.

[113]   See J SHAW and N MILLER, 'When Worlds Collide: An Exploration of What Happens When EU Free Movement Law Meets UK Immigration Law' (2013) 38 *European Law Review* 137–166.

agreement.[114] The first is the freezing of safeguarded rights, including current interpretations, at the point of exit, through the Great Repeal Bill, with the opportunity for repeal and reform in subsequent legislation. This raises a number of questions. For instance, as a matter of EU law, though a non-economically active Union citizen must ordinarily be self-sufficient in order for their residence to be legal, revocation of any right to reside as the result of financial hardship must be subject to a proportionality assessment.[115] The concept of proportionality is an increasingly common feature of UK case law as a result of its 'Europeanisation' – not just by EU law but also by the ECHR – but its maintenance as the British legal system enters a period of 'de-Europeanisation' is open to question.[116] And yet, proportionality is a central feature of those rights the UK's resident EU population wish to retain and will continue to form part of CJEU development of residence rights post-exit. Conversely, the UK could, second, opt to permit safeguarded rights to continue to evolve in line with Union law. However, this seems unlikely given the clear hostility towards the CJEU visible in the White Paper.[117] The third option considered fell between these two extremes, and followed the Swiss approach of 'taking account of developments in EU law' and incorporating it into domestic jurisprudence. However, as expert witnesses to the Committee pointed out, this mechanism has become difficult in practice with the Swiss Supreme Court opting to assume the incorporation of Union case law unless there is good reason not to do so.[118] Finally, the House of Lords speculated on the possible introduction of a mutual case law transmission system, which allowed for the two-way influence of UK and EU case law through intergovernmental meetings. Nevertheless, despite the House of Lords' assertion that clear precedent for such a system exists in the agreement between the EU, Norway and Iceland on extradition procedures, it seems unlikely that a third country would be able to exert such influence over the development of Union citizenship, particularly given that the UK will not even be a participant in the single market.

## 5. CONCLUSION

Despite its assertion that providing certainty to EU citizens living in the UK is 'the right and fair thing to do',[119] when the UK Government triggered exit

---

[114]  *Acquired Rights*, above n 19, paras 123–137.

[115]  Case C-184/99, *Grzelczyk*, above n 8.

[116]  For further discussion of the impact of exit on the courts, see the contribution by T Horsley (Ch 4) in this edited collection.

[117]  *The United Kingdom's exit from and new partnership with the European Union*, above n 2, p 13.

[118]  *Acquired Rights*, above n 19, para 129, citing evidence by C Barnard.

[119]  *The United Kingdom's exit from and new partnership with the European Union*, above n 2, p 30.

negotiations on 29 March 2017 it was still to offer concrete assurances to the UK's resident EU population. This was due to its insistence on the need for a reciprocal deal, which would protect both EU citizens in the UK, and British nationals resident in the remaining Member States. The Government's preoccupation with reciprocity, however, is ultimately something of a distraction. On the one hand, it overcomplicates the issue, since existing Union legislation, for instance on the long-term residence status of third country nationals, already provides some insight into what the Union is able to offer non-EU citizens. On the other hand, it oversimplifies the matter, treating the EU as a single entity, rather than an organisation reliant on the powers conferred upon it by its Member States, each with their own experiences of welcoming British nationals into their territories.

Consequently, a *political* settlement is the likely outcome of EU/UK negotiations on this question. As with the majority of Brexit issues, which will require legal solutions to realise political deals, scrutiny of the mechanisms used to translate any political agreement into a legal reality will be essential to ensure that commitments made come to fruition. On the EU side, secondary Union legislation that seeks to implement any residence agreement will be subject to the EU's legislative procedures and will likely require the opt-ins of Denmark and Ireland. From the UK side, it will be particularly important that rights secured for the UK's resident EU population are enforceable under the domestic framework and are not subsequently lost when the UK enacts primary legislation on *future* EU migration. Crucially, a quick, reciprocal deal early in negotiations simply cannot cater for technically complex and longer-term issues, such as ongoing social security coordination, and must be accompanied by rigorous legal legwork.

While attempts by actors outwith the UK executive to outline the options available for resident EU citizens represent a significant failure by the Government to offer the certainty to Union citizens it claims to wish to offer, they nonetheless provide useful insights into the benefits and pitfalls of legal routes to realising future political commitments. In particular, the focus on permanent residence status, whether subject to the current eligibility criteria or more light-touch conditions, highlights the problem of reliance on legal residence under the CRD, which will give rise to substantive and administrative hurdles for both Union citizens and the Home Office, as well as exposing the Government to potential human rights litigation. Conversely, emphasis on such status reflects an encouraging consensus across the UK's broader political institutions of the need to secure the package of rights, beyond simply the right to *be* in the UK, which make residence possible in practice. This political pressure must continue into and past formal negotiations on the issue to ensure that *meaningful* residence rights are available to the UK's resident EU population.

# CHAPTER 10

# CROSS-BORDER CRIMINAL COOPERATION AFTER BREXIT

Valsamis Mɪᴛsɪʟᴇɢᴀs*

## 1. INTRODUCTION

The exit of the United Kingdom from the European Union poses a series of questions regarding the future relationship of the UK with the EU and its Member States in the field of cross-border criminal cooperation, and the place of the UK in Europe's internal security architecture more broadly. This chapter will attempt to cast light on the legal position of the UK in this context after Brexit. In order to do so, it is necessary to place any future arrangements within the constitutional and structural context underpinning the evolution of Europe's area of criminal justice and the place of the United Kingdom within this area. The impact of Brexit to the UK's position in cross-border criminal justice cooperation will then be assessed, focusing on the impact of potential

---

\*      Queen Mary University of London.

withdrawal from key EU cooperative mechanisms including on surrender (the European Arrest Warrant Framework Decision), on mutual legal assistance (the European Investigation Order Directive) and on policing (inter alia the Prüm instruments). The chapter will then go on to assess potential legal avenues of future UK association with the EU *acquis* and mechanisms of EU criminal justice cooperation. The chapter will demonstrate that any form of meaningful association or cooperation post-Brexit must entail compliance by the UK with the EU *acquis*, including with rulings of the Court of Justice of the European Union. Ironically, post-Brexit cooperation in the field of criminal justice may entail a higher level of compliance by the UK with EU law in comparison to its current position as an EU Member State: post-Brexit, the UK will have to comply with the EU *acquis* viewed in a holistic manner, rather than under the current UK's piecemeal, 'pick-and-choose' approach to EU criminal justice which has emerged as a consequence of the legal possibilities for UK 'opt-outs' from EU criminal law.

## 2. CRIMINAL JUSTICE COOPERATION IN EUROPE'S AREA OF FREEDOM, SECURITY AND JUSTICE

In order to understand the challenges underpinning the position of the UK vis-à-vis the European Union and its Member States after Brexit in the field of judicial cooperation in criminal matters, it is essential to clarify the main constitutional and legislative architecture of the current intra-EU criminal justice cooperation framework within Europe's Area of Freedom, Security and Justice. There are three main features of this framework which it is important to highlight in this context: cooperation, interdependence and constitutionalisation.

In terms of cooperation, it is important to note that European integration in criminal matters has evolved thus far primarily on the basis of a model of cooperative integration, rather than on the basis of a model of integration based upon the unification of criminal law (via, for example, the codification of substantive and procedural criminal law at EU level), or even based upon a high level of harmonisation of substantive and procedural criminal law. Rather, EU criminal law has favoured the establishment of strong horizontal and vertical channels of cooperation. Horizontal cooperation consists of the interaction and cooperation between national authorities in the field of criminal justice. The prime example in this context has been the application of the principle of mutual recognition in criminal matters, with key instruments including the pre-Lisbon Framework Decision on the European Arrest Warrant in the field of extradition and the post-Lisbon Directive on the European Investigation Order in the field of mutual legal assistance. Vertical cooperation on the other hand consists of the establishment of channels of communication and cooperation between

EU criminal justice agencies – including Europol and Eurojust – and national criminal justice agencies. The input by national agencies into EU-wide databases (such as the Europol Information System and the second generation Schengen Information System – the SIS II) and the receipt of subsequent information and intelligence analysis outputs by Member States are key in this context.[1] It is in these cooperative arrangements that the United Kingdom will primarily seek to participate after Brexit, and in this context the willingness of the UK to comply with the EU rules underpinning these arrangements will be central in securing a continuation of a degree of inter-connectedness and cooperation with EU mechanisms and partners after Brexit.

The second feature of EU criminal justice cooperation is increasingly interdependence. The hesitant, piecemeal adoption of EU criminal law measures in the first years of the third pillar has gradually being replaced by a more dynamic process of European integration in criminal matters which has resulted in the proliferation of measures under the criminal justice *acquis* and increasingly, and especially post-Lisbon, in the interdependence of these measures. The operation of the emblematic and arguably most successful EU criminal justice cooperation instrument, the Framework Decision on the European Arrest Warrant, is linked with the input by Member States of alerts in the SIS II. After the entry into force of the Treaty of Lisbon, the operation of the European Arrest Warrant is also linked inextricably with the effective operation of a series of measures on defence rights, adopted under Article 83(2) TFEU which has granted the EU for the first time express competence to adopt minimum standards in the field of criminal procedure if these standards are necessary to ensure the effectiveness of the operation of the principle of mutual recognition in criminal matters.[2] The effective operation of the European Arrest Warrant is thus inextricably linked with the effective operation and meaningful granting of defence rights across the EU, and these measures must be implemented and viewed in a holistic, systemic manner. Similar considerations arise in the field of police cooperation, where the emergence of EU secondary law on exchange of personal data must be viewed in conjunction with the adoption of detailed secondary data protection law either within the sectoral enforcement instruments or under the major EU data protection Regulation and Directive.[3] The interdependence of these measures

---

[1]    For an overview, see V MITSILEGAS, *EU Criminal Law*, Hart Publishing, Oxford 2009; *EU Criminal Law after Lisbon*, Hart Publishing, Oxford 2016.

[2]    MITSILEGAS, *EU Criminal Law after Lisbon*, ibid, Ch 3.

[3]    Regulation (EU) 2016/679 of the European Parliament and of the Council of 27 April 2016 on the protection of natural persons with regard to the processing of personal data and on the free movement of such data, and repealing Directive 95/46/EC (General Data Protection Regulation) [2016] OJ L119/1. Directive 2016/680/EU on the protection of individuals with regard to the processing of personal data by competent authorities for the purposes of prevention, investigation, detection or prosecution of criminal offences or the execution of criminal penalties, and the free movement of such data [2016] OJ L119/89.

means that the United Kingdom must be prepared to adopt the EU *acquis* as a whole should it wish to remain part of or close to current EU cooperation mechanisms after Brexit. As will be analysed in detail below, this position is a far cry from the United Kingdom's current almost unfettered 'pick-and-choose' approach, whereby Protocols agreed upon the entry into force of the Lisbon Treaty and their application have enabled the UK to remain party to a series of major EU enforcement measures (such as the European Arrest Warrant and the European Investigation Order) without being obliged to participate in parallel measures securing a level playing field in the areas of procedural law, in particular on the rights of the defendant. The constitutional and protection inconsistencies of this 'pick-and-choose' approach have been documented in greater detail elsewhere.[4]

The third feature of EU criminal justice cooperation involves its constitutionalisation, notably after the entry into force of the Lisbon Treaty.[5] With few exceptions, the latter has brought about the normalisation of EU criminal law as a field of supranational law, with fundamental principles of EU law now being unquestionably applicable in the field of criminal justice cooperation. Central to this process of constitutionalisation has been the EU Charter of Fundamental Rights, which forms a major constitutional benchmark for the interpretation of EU criminal law. As will be seen below, the application of the Charter has already had a considerable impact in the interpretation of EU criminal justice cooperation instruments such as the Framework Decision on the European Arrest Warrant and the Court of Justice has confirmed the broad applicability of the Charter, even beyond areas where Member States implement specific provisions of EU secondary law. The Charter has thus had and will continue to have a transformative effect on the interpretation of the EU *acquis* in the field of criminal justice, which the UK will have to respect if it wishes to maintain close cooperative links with the EU and its Member States after Brexit. Compliance with the EU *acquis* as interpreted in conformity with the Charter is an essential requirement for the European Union and its Member States in the development of their external relations with third countries, a status which the United Kingdom will acquire in one form or another after Brexit. The Union must not only respect, but also promote its own internal values – which include the protection of fundamental rights and the rule of law – after Lisbon.[6]

---

4   For further details, see V MITSILEGAS, 'The Uneasy Relationship between the United Kingdom and European Criminal Law. From Opt-outs to Brexit?' (2016) 8 *Criminal Law Review* 517.
5   MITSILEGAS, *EU Criminal Law after Lisbon*, above n 1, Ch 2.
6   V MITSILEGAS, 'Transatlantic Counter-Terrorism Cooperation after Lisbon' (2010) 3 *EUCRIM – The European Criminal Law Associations' Forum, Max Planck Institute for Foreign and International Law* 111.

# 3. THE IMPACT OF BREXIT ON DOMESTIC CRIMINAL JUSTICE AND SECURITY

If the current legal landscape regarding the United Kingdom's participation in EU criminal law leaves much to be desired in terms of effectiveness, coherence and legal certainty, the situation will become even more challenging following Brexit. The aim of this section is to highlight key areas of EU criminal law currently in force from which the United Kingdom will be excluded post-Brexit in the fields of judicial cooperation in criminal matters, of police cooperation and surveillance, and of the operation of EU criminal justice bodies and agencies. The next section will flesh out potential legal avenues of cooperation between the United Kingdom and the EU and its Member States and demonstrate the limits of such avenues to provide a level of cooperation in criminal matters which is equivalent to that of a state enjoying full EU membership.[7]

## 3.1. JUDICIAL COOPERATION IN CRIMINAL MATTERS – MUTUAL RECOGNITION

Judicial cooperation has been the motor of European integration in criminal matters, most notably by the application of the principle of mutual recognition in the field.[8] This subsection will focus on three key measures in the field of judicial cooperation: the pre-Lisbon Framework Decision on the European Arrest Warrant and the post-Lisbon Directive on the European Investigation Order, applying the principle of mutual recognition in the fields of surrender and evidence respectively; and measures establishing EU-wide cooperation in terms of exchange of criminal record information. The tangible benefits of these measures for intra-EU cooperation will be demonstrated, and the improvements in the EU legal framework – in particular regarding the protection of fundamental rights – will be highlighted.

### 3.1.1. The European Arrest Warrant

The Framework Decision on the European Arrest Warrant[9] is the most emblematic and most widely implemented EU criminal law instrument.

---

7       The following sections build upon MITSILEGAS, 'The Uneasy Relationship between the United Kingdom and European Criminal Law. From Opt-outs to Brexit?' above n 4 and MITSILEGAS, 'European Criminal Law after Brexit' (2017) *Criminal Law Forum* forthcoming.

8       On the application of the principle of mutual recognition in criminal matters, see MITSILEGAS, *EU Criminal Law*, above n 1, Ch 3.

9       Framework Decision 2002/584/JHA of 13 June 2002 on the European Arrest Warrant [2002] OJ L190/1.

It aims to compensate for the freedom of movement enabled by the abolition of internal borders by ensuring that Member States' justice systems can reach extraterritorially in order to bring individuals who have taken advantage of the abolition of borders to flee the jurisdiction to face justice. The Framework Decision applies the principle of mutual recognition in the field of criminal law and has established a system which requires the recognition of EAWs and the surrender of individuals wanted for prosecution or to serve a custodial sentence with a minimum of formality, automaticity and speed.[10] A key innovation introduced is the (in principle) abolition of the non-extradition of own nationals. Mutual recognition is based on mutual trust, premised on the presumption that EU Member States are in principle human rights compliant. This presumption of trust has been recently highlighted by the Court of Justice in its Opinion 2/13 on the accession of the European Union to the ECHR, where the Court elevated mutual trust into a principle of fundamental importance in EU law.[11] Yet critics of the European Arrest Warrant system and the automaticity it has introduced have rightly pointed out that the presumption of trust is not always justified, with human rights violations being ascertained across EU Member States by the Strasbourg Court on a regular basis. A key question related to the legitimacy of the European Arrest Warrant system is whether the system can operate on the basis of blind trust, or whether national authorities have leeway to examine the consequences of executing Warrants for the human rights of the requested persons.

European Union law has dealt with the human rights concerns arising from the operation of the EAW system in three main ways: by allowing national authorities to consider refusing to execute warrants if there are concerns that execution would result in human rights breaches; by introducing a test of proportionality in the operation of the EAW system; and by legislating for human rights, namely adopting legally binding instruments harmonising defence rights legislation and aiming to facilitate the operation of mutual recognition.[12] In terms of taking into account of human rights by the executing authorities, it is noteworthy that – with the exception of a general human rights clause[13] – the operative provisions of the Framework Decision do not include a ground of refusal to execute an EAW on human rights grounds. However, a number of EU Member States, including the United Kingdom in the Extradition Act 2003, have 'goldplated' transposition by expressly including human rights grounds

---

[10] V Mitsilegas, 'The Constitutional Implications of Mutual Recognition in Criminal Matters in the EU' (2006) 43 *Common Market Law Review* 1277.

[11] Opinion 2/13, ECLI:EU:C:2014:2454, para 191.

[12] V Mitsilegas, 'Mutual Recognition, Mutual Trust and Fundamental Rights After Lisbon' in V Mitsilegas, M Bergström and T Konstadinides (eds), *Research Handbook on EU Criminal Law*, Edward Elgar, Cheltenham 2016, pp 148–168.

[13] Framework Decision, Article 1(3).

for refusal in national implementing law. Significantly, the Court of Justice has recently confirmed that execution may be refused on human rights grounds. In Joined Cases *Aranyosi and Căldăraru*,[14] the Court found that

'where there is objective, reliable, specific and properly updated evidence with respect to detention conditions in the issuing Member State that demonstrates that there are deficiencies, which may be systemic or generalised, or which may affect certain groups of people, or which may affect certain places of detention, the executing judicial authority must determine, specifically and precisely, whether there are substantial grounds to believe that the individual concerned by a European arrest warrant, issued for the purposes of conducting a criminal prosecution or executing a custodial sentence, will be exposed, because of the conditions for his detention in the issuing Member State, to a real risk of inhuman or degrading treatment, within the meaning of Article 4 of the Charter, in the event of his surrender to that Member State. To that end, the executing judicial authority must request that supplementary information be provided by the issuing judicial authority, which, after seeking, if necessary, the assistance of the central authority or one of the central authorities of the issuing Member State, under Article 7 of the Framework Decision, must send that information within the time limit specified in the request. The executing judicial authority must postpone its decision on the surrender of the individual concerned until it obtains the supplementary information that allows it to discount the existence of such a risk. *If the existence of that risk cannot be discounted within a reasonable time, the executing judicial authority must decide whether the surrender procedure should be brought to an end.*'[15]

The Court's ruling is significant not only in affirming for the first time that execution of a Warrant may be refused in certain circumstances, but also in negating a system of mutual recognition based on automaticity and blind trust: human rights compliance must be queried and ascertained on the ground, and on the basis of concrete evidence. In addition to these safeguards, the EAW system must operate in compliance with the principle of proportionality. The need to address these proportionality concerns was acknowledged by the European Commission in its latest Report on the implementation of the Framework Decision.[16] The prevailing view has thus far been for proportionality to be dealt with in the issuing and not in the executing Member State. This is the interpretative guidance given in the revised version of the European Handbook on how to issue a European Arrest Warrant.[17] A step further with regard to the

---

[14]     Joined Cases C-404/15 and C-659/15 PPU, *Pál Aranyosi and Robert Căldăraru v Generalstaatsanwaltschaft Bremen*, Judgment of 5 April 2016.

[15]     Ibid, para, 104 (emphasis added).

[16]     Commission, 'Report from the Commission to the European Parliament and the Council on the implementation since 2007 of the Council Framework Decision of 13 June 2002 on the European Arrest Warrant and the surrender procedures between Member States' COM(2011) 175 Final, p 8.

[17]     Council Document 17195/1/10 REV 1, Brussels, 17 December 2010.

treatment of proportionality as a limit to mutual recognition has been taken in the United Kingdom, which in its latest version of the European Arrest Warrant implementing legislation (the Extradition Act 2003) has treated non-compliance with proportionality as a ground of refusal to execute a Warrant (and not merely as a requirement to be checked in the issuing state).[18] The amended provisions provide for an exhaustive list of matters to be taken into account by the judge when ruling on proportionality[19] and thus far English judges have interpreted these matters restrictively.[20] Brexit will have the consequence that the United Kingdom – which has been pioneering in introducing human rights safeguards in the European Arrest Warrant – will leave the system at the very time when EU institutions appear to have begun to take these very human rights considerations seriously.

### 3.1.2. The European Investigation Order

The Directive on the European Investigation Order[21] regulates the exchange of evidence between EU Member States in the field of criminal justice. The Directive applies the principle of mutual recognition in the field of evidence, and is the first major instrument on mutual recognition adopted after the entry into force of the Lisbon Treaty. The Directive is of major importance with regard to its applicability, as it will replace, as of 22 May 2017, the corresponding provisions applicable between Member States bound by it of the Council of Europe Mutual Legal Assistance and its protocols, the Convention implementing the Schengen Agreement and the EU Mutual Legal Assistance Convention and its Protocol.[22] The Directive will also replace the Framework Decision on the European Evidence Warrant[23] and the relevant provisions of the Framework Decision on the mutual recognition of freezing orders.[24] In this manner, the Directive on the

---

[18]   Section 157 of the Anti-Social Behaviour, Crime and Policing Act 2014 has amended section 21A of the Extradition Act 2003 to treat lack of proportionality as a ground for refusal (section 21A(1)(b)).

[19]   Ibid, section 21A(2). These matters are: the seriousness of the conduct alleged to constitute the extradition offence; the likely penalty that would be imposed if the individual was found guilty of the extradition offence; and the possibility of the relevant foreign authorities taking measures that would be less coercive than the extradition sought (section 21(A)(3)).

[20]   See *Miraszewski v Poland* [2014] EWCH 4261 (Admin); *Celinski v Poland* [2015] EWHC 1274 (Admin).

[21]   Directive 2014/41/EU of the European Parliament and of the Council of 3 April 2014 regarding the European Investigation Order in criminal matters [2014] OJ L130/1.

[22]   Ibid, Article 34(1).

[23]   Council Framework Decision 2008/978/JHA of 18 December 2008 on the European evidence warrant for the purpose of obtaining objects, documents and data for use in proceedings in criminal matters [2008] OJ L350/72.

[24]   Council Framework Decision 2003/577/JHA of 22 July 2003 on the execution in the European union of orders freezing property or evidence [2003] OJ L196/45, Article 34(2).

European Investigation Order will become the sole legal instrument regulating the exchange of evidence and mutual legal assistance between EU Member States. 22 May 2017 is also the transposition deadline for Member States.[25] This will mean in practice that judicial cooperation in the key field of evidence for Member States parties to the European Investigation Order will take place speedily and as a matter of priority in relation to requests by third countries.

Following on from ongoing concerns regarding the potential adverse human rights implications of automatic mutual recognition, the Directive on the European Investigation Order has introduced a number of provisions aiming to protect human rights and avoid arbitrary and unlawful use of the system. The Directive expressly includes non-compliance with fundamental rights as a ground for refusal to recognise and execute an EIO,[26] with the Preamble also stating that the presumption of compliance of Member States with human rights is rebuttable.[27] The Directive has also introduced a proportionality check in the issuing state stating that the issuing authority may only issue an EIO where the issuing of the latter is necessary and proportionate and where the investigative measures indicated in the EIO could have been ordered under the same conditions in a similar domestic case.[28] Moreover, the Directive contains provisions aiming to curb arbitrary or unlawful action by the issuing and the executing authorities. The executing authority may refuse to recognise and execute an EIO when the latter has been issued in proceedings brought by administrative or judicial authorities referred to in Article 4(b) and (c) of the Directive and the investigative measure would not be authorised under the law of the executing state in a similar domestic case.[29] On the other hand, the issuing authority may only issue an EIO where the investigative measures indicated therein could have been ordered under the same conditions in a similar domestic case.[30] This provision has been included to avoid instances where Member States use the EIO to 'fish' for evidence and obtain evidence abroad which they are not able to obtain under their own domestic legal and constitutional procedures. Brexit would mean that the United Kingdom would be excluded from a system of cooperation underpinned by both efficiency and a high level of human rights protection and from an instrument participation in which has been strongly advocated by UK practitioners.

---

[25]   European Investigation Order Directive, Article 36(1).
[26]   Ibid, Article 11 on optional grounds for non-recognition or non-execution; Article 11(1)(f): where there are substantial grounds to believe that the execution of the investigative measure indicated in the EIO would be incompatible with the executing state's obligations in accordance with Article 6 TEU and the Charter.
[27]   Ibid, Preamble, Recital 19.
[28]   Ibid, Articles 6(1)(a) and (b) respectively.
[29]   Ibid, Article 11(1)(c).
[30]   Ibid, Article 6(1)(b).

## 3.2. INFORMATION SYSTEMS – FROM SIS II TO ECRIS

An adverse security consequence of Brexit would be the withdrawal of the United Kingdom from a series of EU information systems and databases which contribute to the EU criminal justice architecture. A key plank of this system is participation in the police aspects of the second generation Schengen Information System (SIS II), in which the United Kingdom has heavily invested and which is closely linked with the effective operation of the European Arrest Warrant via the insertion of SIS alerts.[31] However, Brexit may mean the UK's exclusion from another significant mechanism of cooperation on the basis of the establishment of communication avenues at EU level, namely in the field of exchange of criminal records. EU law has developed an extensive mechanism of exchange of information on criminal records of EU citizens, which should enable national authorities to have a full picture of the criminal record status of EU citizens who enter their territory. There are two main elements of the EU-wide system of exchange of criminal records. Framework Decision 2009/315/JHA on the organisation and content of the exchange of information extracted from the criminal record between Member States[32] calls for the establishment of a central authority for managing criminal records in each Member State[33] and places the central authority of the convicting Member State under the obligation to inform as soon as possible the central authorities of other Member States of any convictions handed down within its territory against the nationals of such other Member States, as entered in the criminal record.[34] Information provided includes information on the nature of the criminal conviction, the offence giving rise to the conviction and the contents of the conviction.[35] A parallel Decision on the establishment of the European Criminal Records Information System (ECRIS)[36] establishes ECRIS as a decentralised information technology system based on the criminal records databases in each Member State composed of an interconnection software enabling the exchange of information between Member States' criminal records databases and a common communication infrastructure that provides an encrypted network.[37] These legislative instruments have

---

[31]   On the importance of the SIS II in this context, see House of Lords European Union Committee, *Schengen Information System II (SIS II)* (HL 2006–07, 49) para 89.

[32]   Council Framework Decision 2009/315/JHA of 26 February 2009 on the organisation and content of the exchange of information extracted from the criminal record between Member States [2009] OJ L93/23.

[33]   Ibid, Article 3.

[34]   Ibid, Article 4(2).

[35]   Ibid, Article 11 (1).

[36]   Council Decision 2009/316/JHA of 6 April 2009 on the establishment of the European Criminal Records Information System (ECRIS) in application of Article 11 of Framework Decision 2009/315/JHA [2009] OJ L93/13.

[37]   Ibid, Article 3(2).

provided a solid EU-wide mechanism of exchange of criminal records, which according to the Commission has led to significant progress in improving the exchange of criminal records information within the Union.[38] This view is shared by the UK Government, which has noted that the EU system

> 'has allowed the police to build a fuller picture of offending by UK nationals and allowed the courts to be aware of the previous offending of EU nationals being prosecuted. The previous conviction information can be used for bail, bad character and sentencing, as well as by the prison and probation service when dealing with the offender once sentenced'.[39]

After the Paris attacks, the Commission has proposed legislation extending the exchange of criminal records to third country nationals,[40] a move which the UK Government seems to support in principle.[41] Brexit would mean that the United Kingdom would not be at the forefront of developments in this field, which may provide crucial information for the protection of public safety in the country. Withdrawal from these systems would entail a significant security and financial cost for the UK, while maintaining an ongoing connection with systems established under EU law will entail, as will be mentioned in the subsections below, compliance by the UK with EU privacy and data protection law requirements.

## 3.3. SURVEILLANCE AND POLICE COOPERATION

Another consequence of Brexit would be to exclude the United Kingdom from the development of sophisticated – and far-reaching – legal frameworks enabling the collection and exchange of a wide range of personal data for law enforcement purposes. The Prüm measures constitute key examples of innovation (or, arguably, widening and deepening the web of surveillance) by facilitating the collection and exchange of DNA data. Another form of police and judicial cooperation from which the United Kingdom may be excluded post-Brexit is the establishment of joint investigation teams,[42] to which UK officers currently

---

[38]  Commission, *Implementation report on Framework Decision 2009/315*, COM(2016) 6 Final.

[39]  Command Paper (8671) cited in House of Commons European Scrutiny Committee, *Exchanging Information on Criminal Convictions*, 2 March 2016, para 10.11, <http://www. publications.parliament.uk/pa/cm201516/cmselect/cmeuleg/342-xxiii/34213.htm>.

[40]  Proposal for a Directive amending Council Framework Decision 2009/315/JHA as regards the exchange of information on third country nationals and as regards the European Criminal Records Information System (ECRIS), and replacing Council Decision 2009/316/JHA, COM(2016) 7 Final.

[41]  House of Commons European Scrutiny Committee, above n 39.

[42]  For the principal legal framework, see Council Framework Decision 2002/465/JHA of 13 June 2002 on joint investigation teams [2002] OJ L162/1.

participate extensively.[43] The capacity to act at a multilateral, transnational level has been highlighted as a key advantage of joint investigation teams.[44] In addition to this 'public' form of surveillance, the EU has innovated by promoting public/private partnerships in the field of policing and surveillance. After the Paris attacks, the focus in this context has been on the surveillance of mobility, with EU institutions having recently agreed upon a Directive establishing an EU Passenger Name Records (PNR) transfer system.[45] It introduces an EU PNR system for flights flying into the EU, with Member States being given the option to apply it also to intra-EU flights. The Directive has been welcomed by UK security professionals as a significant step towards the security of the EU and the UK.[46] A further aspect of public/private partnership in the field of the collection and exchange of personal data involves financial data surveillance. The recently adopted Fourth EU Money Laundering Directive calls for the intensification of information exchange and collaboration between national financial intelligence units (FIUs).[47] The Directive requires Member States to ensure that FIUs cooperate with each other 'to the greatest extent possible' irrespective of the model they have chosen for their organisation,[48] while FIUs are empowered to exchange, spontaneously or upon request, any information that may be relevant for the processing or analysis of information by the FIU related to money laundering or terrorist financing, 'even if the type of predicate offence that may be at stake is not identified at the time of the exchange'.[49]

The impact of Brexit on police cooperation and surveillance capacity may be considerable. In this context, the entry into force of the Lisbon Treaty has made

---

[43] According to the Director of Public Prosecutions Alison Saunders, 'we get a lot out of joint investigation teams because they help us to make sure that we collect the right evidence. It is much quicker than doing individual letters of request because you collect it all together and it is there; it helps with issues around jurisdiction. It helps with disclosure issues'. – evidence to House of Lords EU Committee, Q 54.

[44] Ibid, paras 74 and 75.

[45] Directive (EU) 2016/681 of the European Parliament and of the Council of 27 April 2016 on the use of passenger name record (PNR) data for the prevention, detection, investigation and prosecution of terrorist offences and serious crime [2016] OJ L119/132.

[46] J EVANS and J SAWERS (former heads of MI5 and MI6 respectively), 'The EU Can't Dictate to Us on Security but Staying in It Can Keep Us Safer', *The Sunday Times*, 8 May 2016 <http://www.strongerin.co.uk/the_eu_can_t_dictate_to_us_on_security_but_staying_in_it_can_keep_us_safer#kvMJ2k7Tq3dD0GPu.97>.

[47] Directive (EU) 2015/849 of the European Parliament and of the Council of 20 May 2015 on the prevention of the use of the financial system for the purposes of money laundering or terrorist financing, amending Regulation (EU) No 648/2012 of the European Parliament and of the Council, and repealing Directive 2005/60/EC of the European Parliament and of the Council and Commission Directive 2006/70/EC [2015] OJ L141/73.

[48] Ibid, Article 52.

[49] Ibid, Article 53(1). For an analysis, see V MITSILEGAS and N VAVOULA, 'The Evolving European Union Anti-Money Laundering Regime: Challenges for Fundamental Rights and the Rule of Law' (2016) 23(2) *Maastricht Journal of European and Comparative Law* 261.

it clearer that EU action on policing and surveillance must be compatible with the EU Charter of Fundamental Rights, the ECHR and secondary EU law on data protection. Already both the Strasbourg and Luxembourg Courts have sent strong signals limiting state power in the field. In the case of *S and Marper*,[50] the Strasbourg Court placed considerable limits on the power of the state to retain sensitive personal data without charge, while in the cases of *Digital Rights Ireland*[51] and *Schrems*[52] the Luxembourg Court placed clear limits on mass surveillance in cases involving personal data generated by the private sector. In this light, Brexit may for some be a welcome development in 'liberating' the UK executive from the requirement to comply with the EU Charter of Fundamental Rights. Indeed, the UK can introduce domestic law mirroring – and going beyond – EU developments in the field. However, Brexit will have the concrete consequence of the UK being excluded from the EU cooperative mechanisms on policing and surveillance (whether these are speedy DNA exchanges under Prüm or suspicious transaction reports from FIU to FIU), in particular if the United Kingdom does not comply with EU human rights benchmarks.[53]

## 3.4. PARTICIPATION IN EU CRIMINAL JUSTICE BODIES AND AGENCIES

While even within the framework of its current membership of the European Union the United Kingdom has stated that it will not participate in the Regulation establishing a European Public Prosecutor's Office, the question of the impact of Brexit on the UK's cooperation with the two other key EU bodies in the field of criminal justice, Europol and Eurojust, remains open. The establishment of both Europol and Eurojust has been innovative, with the powers, tasks and mandate of these bodies being in constant evolution.[54] Europol has developed into an important source of criminal intelligence for Member States, whereas the value of Eurojust lies primarily with its coordination functions.[55] Brexit would come

---

[50]   *S and Marper v the United Kingdom*, Nos 30562/04 and 30566/04 1581.
[51]   Joined Cases C-293/12 and C-594/12, *Digital Rights Ireland Ltd and Seitlinger*, ECLI:EU:C:2014:238.
[52]   Case C-362/14, *Schrems*, ECLI:EU:C:2015:650.
[53]   See Section 3.4 below.
[54]   For the legal framework currently in force, see Regulation (EU) 2016/794 of the European Parliament and of the Council of 11 May 2016 on the European Union Agency for Law Enforcement Cooperation (Europol) and replacing and repealing Council Decisions 2009/371/JHA, 2009/934/JHA, 2009/935/JHA, 2009/936/JHA and 2009/968/JHA [2016] OJ L135/53; and Council Decision 2002/187/JHA of 28 February 2002 setting up Eurojust with a view to reinforcing the fight against serious crime [2002] OJ L63/1, as amended by Council Decision 2009/426/JHA [2009] OJ L138/14.
[55]   On the key issues in negotiations on the future of Eurojust see MITSILEGAS, *EU Criminal Law after Lisbon*, above n 1, Ch 4.

as a shock here as the United Kingdom has been instrumental in shaping the evolution and role of these bodies: two out of four of the Presidents of Eurojust thus far have come from the UK (Aled Williams and Eurojust's inaugural President, Mike Kennedy), while the current Director of Europol, Rob Wainwright, is also British. The United Kingdom has been instrumental in exporting parts of its model of intelligence-led policing into Europol and its absence as a full member from the organisation will be felt not only within Europol, but also in terms of the UK security landscape.[56] As will be seen below, the United Kingdom is one of the highest contributors to EU security cooperation as regards contributions to Europol and its databases.[57] In terms of participation in Eurojust activities, UK authorities organised 28 and participated in 69 Eurojust coordination meetings in 2015, and organised one and participated in seven of Eurojust's coordination centres, which facilitate the exchange of information among judicial authorities in real time and enable direct support towards the coordinated, simultaneous execution of, inter alia, arrest warrants, searches and seizures in different countries.[58] Brexit will not only take away the UK's strategic leadership in the development of these EU criminal justice agencies, but will also pose a challenge vis-à-vis maintaining cooperation channels between UK authorities and the agencies. Future cooperation will again depend on the extent to which the United Kingdom will be deemed to comply with key EU law standards, including – in particular in cases involving the exchange of personal data – an assessment by EU institutions that the UK provides an adequate level of data protection.[59]

## 4. THE LEGAL POSITION OF THE UK AFTER BREXIT

As seen above, the UK Government has put forward the benefits of EU criminal justice initiatives when called to justify opting back into a list of 35 third pillar measures (including the European Arrest Warrant and Decisions forming the legal bases for the operation of the key EU criminal justice agencies Eurojust and Europol) after the expiry of the deadline prescribed in the Lisbon Transitional

---

[56]  See in this context the warnings by Rob Wainwright on the adverse security consequences of Brexit for the UK: 'Brexit would bring serious security consequences – Europol head' at <http://uk.reuters.com/article/uk-britain-eu-europol-idUKKCN0XG16B>, 19 April 2016.

[57]  The National Crime Agency pointed out that the UK was 'the second-largest contributor in Europe' to the Europol Information System, and that it led on "four or five" of the 13 EMPACT [European Multidisciplinary Platform Against Criminal Threats] projects, which coordinate actions by Member States and EU organisations against threats identified by Europol in its Serious and Organised Crime Threat Assessment': see evidence to House of Lords European Union Committee, *Brexit: Future UK-EU Security Cooperation*, Q 19.

[58]  Eurojust, *Annual Report 2015*, pp 15–17.

[59]  See Article 25 of the Europol Regulation (above n 54) regarding transfer of personal data to third countries and international organisations.

Provisions Protocol. The willingness of the UK Government to continue participating in such cooperative arrangements in the post-Brexit era has been expressed in a variety of ways by Secretary of State for Exiting the European Union David Davis,[60] by Prime Minister Theresa May,[61] and enshrined in the Government's White Paper on Brexit.[62] While the political will may be present, the legal reality of the post-Brexit relationship between the UK and the EU in the criminal justice field is complex. There are three possible legal scenarios concerning the UK's relationship with the EU in the field of criminal justice after Brexit: the conclusion of EU-UK agreements on various aspects of criminal justice cooperation; the conclusion of bilateral agreements between the UK and individual EU Member States; and, in the absence of such agreements with the EU or Member States, falling back to existing Council of Europe mechanisms of cooperation.

The first scenario (EU-UK agreements) appears the most desirable in terms of ensuring legal certainty, the establishment of an EU-wide level playing field for the UK, and operational efficiency to the extent that they have the potential to maintain the UK's position as close as possible to its current position as an EU Member State. There are precedents of conclusion of agreements between the EU and third countries in the field of judicial cooperation in criminal matters (see the EU agreements on surrender with Norway and Iceland);[63] of conclusion of agreements on police cooperation (see the agreements with Norway and Iceland on Prüm);[64] of conclusion of agreements between EU agencies such as Europol

---

[60]   According to David Davis, 'maintaining strong security co-operation we have with the EU' as one of the Government's top four overarching objectives in negotiations and future relationship with the EU': *Hansard*, HC Deb Vol 615, col 328 (12 October 2016).

[61]   'I therefore want our future relationship with the European Union to include practical arrangements on matters of law enforcement and the sharing of intelligence material with our EU allies': PM Speech, 'The Government's Negotiating Objectives for Exiting the EU', 17 January 2017 <https://www.gov.uk/government/speeches/the-governments-negotiating-objectives-for-exiting-the-eu-pm-speech>.

[62]   'As we exit, we will therefore look to negotiate the best deal we can with the EU to cooperate in the fight against crime and terrorism. We will seek a strong and close future relationship with the EU, with a focus on operational and practical cross-border cooperation': *The United Kingdom's exit from and new partnership with the European Union* (Cm 9417, February 2017).

[63]   Council Decision of 27 June 2006 on the signing of the Agreement between the EU and the Republic of Iceland and the Kingdom of Norway on the surrender procedure between the Member States of the European Union and Iceland and Norway [2006] OJ L292/1.

[64]   Council Decision of 21 September 2009 on the signing, on behalf of the European Union, and on the provisional application of certain provisions of the Agreement between the European Union and Iceland and Norway on the application of certain provisions of Council Decision 2008/615/JHA on the stepping up of crossborder cooperation, particularly in combating terrorism and cross-border crime and Council Decision 2008/616/JHA on the implementation of Decision 2008/615/JHA on the stepping up of cross-border cooperation, particularly in combating terrorism and cross-border crime, and the Annex thereto (2009/1023/JHA) [2009] OJ L353/1.

and Eurojust with third countries;[65] and of participation of third countries in EU databases such as the Schengen Information System.[66] However, it should be noted that in the cases of both judicial cooperation in criminal matters and access to EU databases, close cooperation has been confined to third countries which are also full Schengen members.[67] It will be more challenging for a third country maintaining its own border controls such as the UK to follow this precedent and achieve a level of cooperation which comes close to intra-EU cooperation arrangements. While cooperation arrangements in the case of EU agencies are more common, existing precedents demonstrate that there are significant limitations to the position of third countries in comparison to EU Member States, most notably relating to the lack of direct access to EU databases and to non-participation in the core functions of the management bodies of these agencies, with limited say or powers to shape the future direction of these agencies.

The conclusion of bilateral agreements between the UK and individual EU Member States may serve to prioritise cooperation with key countries in areas of common interest (an example could be a simplified extradition agreement between the UK and Poland given the volume of European Arrest Warrants currently being processed between authorities of these two EU Member States). However, the conclusion of bilateral agreements will not grant the UK facilitated cooperation arrangements across the EU and from an operational perspective will not guarantee, even in cases where bilateral agreements are actually concluded, that UK requests for cooperation will be treated by EU partners with an equal priority status in comparison to requests of EU Member States under EU law mechanisms such as the European Arrest Warrant and the European Investigation Order. Last, but not least, a fall-back to bilateral agreements may mean that existing innovations in judicial cooperation under EU law (such as the judicialisation of and speed in judicial cooperation and innovations in the field of extradition such as the effective abolition of the political offence exception, the abolition of the requirement to verify dual criminality for a wide range of criminal conduct and the abolition of the power of EU Member States not to extradite their own nationals) may cease to apply, rendering judicial cooperation slower and more cumbersome.

---

[65] For lists of third state agreements concluded by Eurojust and Europol, see <http://eurojust.europa.eu/about/Partners/Pages/third-states.aspx>, and <https://www.europol.europa.eu/partners-agreements>.

[66] See eg the agreement between the European Union and Switzerland on the development of the Schengen *acquis*.

[67] See evidence of Security Commissioner Julian King to the House of Commons Home Affairs Committee, 28 February 2017, according to which outside of non-EU Schengen countries there are no precedents for third countries locking into those information-sharing platforms (Q92).

The same considerations apply to the third scenario, of the UK falling back to existing Council of Europe agreements such as the agreements on Extradition and Mutual Legal Assistance in its relations with EU Member States. These agreements have been superseded in terms of innovation and in terms of their intra-EU applicability by EU criminal law instruments and they cover limited areas of EU criminal justice cooperation.

Whichever of these broad scenarios materialises after Brexit, it is clear that the United Kingdom must comply with EU law if it wishes to pursue meaningful cooperation in the field of criminal justice and security with the EU and its Member States. This is obviously the case in the first scenario, namely the conclusion of agreements with the European Union. EU external action must be consistent with EU internal action, with the TEU affirming that the Union must not only respect, but also promote its internal values in its external action.[68] The same applies however also in the cases of UK bilateral cooperation with EU Member States either under specific bilateral agreements or by falling back into existing Council of Europe instruments, as EU Member States are under the duty to comply with EU law in their external relations with third states, especially in cases where the EU has acted internally (this is the case in particular with major cooperation instruments such as the European Arrest Warrant and the European Investigation Order). The role of the Court of Justice is key in this context. In the current models of cooperation with third states, third countries are not subject directly to the Court's jurisdiction[69] and dispute resolution mechanisms have been devised.[70] However, the Court of Justice remains competent to monitor the legality of such agreements under EU law and its case law must be taken into account in defining and complying with the EU *acquis* which forms the benchmark for EU external relations and cooperation between EU and third countries.

The need to respect requirements of the EU internal *acquis* in EU external action in the field of criminal justice has been confirmed recently by the CJEU in

---

[68]   For an analysis, see MITSILEGAS, 'Transatlantic Counter-Terrorism Cooperation after Lisbon', above n 6.

[69]   According to Article 37 of the Agreement on surrender with Norway and Iceland, 'The Contracting Parties, in order to achieve the objective of arriving at as uniform an application and interpretation as possible of the provisions of this Agreement, shall keep under constant review the development of the case law of the Court of Justice of the EC, as well as the development of the case law of the competent courts of Iceland and Norway relating to these provisions and to those of similar surrender instruments. To this end a mechanism shall be set up to ensure regular mutual transmission of such case law.'

[70]   According to Article 36 of the Agreement, 'Any dispute between either Iceland or Norway and a Member State of the European Union regarding the interpretation or the application of this Agreement may be referred by a party to the dispute to a meeting of representatives of the governments of the Member States of the European Union and of Iceland and Norway, with a view to its settlement within six months.'

an extradition case where the Court found that extradition to a third state must be consistent with fundamental rights standards established by the Court in relation to the internal EU *acquis* on the European Arrest Warrant.[71] The requirement to comply with EU law has been even more visible in the field of exchange of personal data and data protection. Cooperation of third countries with the EU must be based on the adoption of an EU adequacy decision confirming that the UK offers an adequate level of data protection in the eyes of the EU.[72] In the case of *Schrems*, which concerned the EU-US safe harbour agreement, the Court of Justice confirmed that adequacy in this context means that the system of the third country must be 'essentially equivalent' to the EU system and that any finding of adequacy must be subject to regular reassessment and monitoring.[73] In a consistent line of case law, the Court of Justice has affirmed that the bulk collection of personal data on an indiscriminate basis is contrary to EU law.[74] The current approach of the UK Government regarding the extensive collection, sharing and transfer of personal data for security purposes sits ill at ease with EU law as interpreted by the Court of Justice. This has been confirmed by the Court of Justice in the recent case of *Watson*, where UK law on data retention was found to fall foul of EU law.[75]

It becomes thus obvious that, if the UK wishes to continue cooperating with the EU and its Member States, it will have to reassure its partners that its legal and human rights system offers a level of protection which is acceptable under EU law. While the UK may not be directly subject to the jurisdiction of the Luxembourg Court, the case law of the latter will play a key part in determining what the EU requirements will be in this context. Meeting EU law requirements by the UK will be subject to ongoing monitoring by EU institutions including the European Commission in order to ensure that equivalence remains, and

---

[71]  Case C-182/15, *Aleksei Petruhhin v Latvijas Republikas Ģenerālprokuratūra*, ECLI:EU:C:2016:630.

[72]  See Articles 35 and 36 of Directive (EU) 2016/680 of the European Parliament and of the Council of 27 April 2016 on the protection of natural persons with regard to the processing of personal data by competent authorities for the purposes of the prevention, investigation, detection or prosecution of criminal offences or the execution of criminal penalties, and on the free movement of such data, and repealing Council Framework Decision 2008/977/JHA [2016] OJ L119/ 89.

[73]  In the case of *Schrems* (C-362/14, above n 52), the CJEU found in para 73 that the term 'adequate level of protection' must be understood as requiring the third country in fact to ensure, by reason of its domestic law or its international commitments, a level of protection of fundamental rights and freedoms that is essentially equivalent to that guaranteed within the European Union.

[74]  See *Digital Rights Ireland and Seitlinger*, above n 51; *Schrems*, above n 52; Joined Cases C-203/15 and C-698/15, *Tele2 Sverige AB v Post- och telestyrelsen and Secretary of State for the Home Department v Tom Watson and Others*, ECLI:EU:C:2016:970.

[75]  *Tele2 Sverige*, ibid.

the UK will have to adjust its internal legislation to follow developments in EU law in order to maintain any ensuing cooperation arrangements. Importantly, the UK must accept the EU *acquis* as a whole, emanating from an increasingly interdependent EU area of criminal justice. To take an example, the EU *acquis* on the European Arrest Warrant will take also into account EU legislation and case law on the rights of the defence in criminal proceedings, an area from which the UK has currently partially opted out. Brexit will thus bring with it the paradox that the UK will no longer be able to maintain, outside the EU, the 'pick-and-choose approach' to EU criminal law it is currently enjoying. It will be take-it or leave-it in terms of accepting the EU *acquis* if the UK wishes to maintain meaningful cooperation with the EU and its Member States post-Brexit.

## 5. CONCLUSION

The ongoing relationship between the United Kingdom and the European Union in the field of criminal law and its reconfiguration as we are heading towards the post-Brexit era is characterised by a high level of constitutional complexity and is underpinned by a double paradox. In the first place, the United Kingdom's current position as an EU Member State is marked by the tension between maintaining (or being seen as able to maintain) national sovereignty in the field of criminal law while at the same time seeking maximum cooperation with EU Member States and EU agencies in the field of security. The collateral damage in this tension lies in the limited protection of fundamental rights, easily sacrificed in the various UK opt-outs from post-Lisbon European criminal law. The dynamic evolution of EU law in the field however leads to a second paradox in the post-Brexit era: the United Kingdom's willingness to continue to reap the security benefits of EU cooperation after Brexit can be accommodated only if the UK complies fully with the EU *acquis*, including the *acquis* on the protection of fundamental rights, part of which it currently is at liberty to disregard under its 'opt-outs' as an EU Member State. Brexit will thus bring the United Kingdom in the paradoxical position of having to accept *more* EU law than it currently does as an EU Member State. Whichever legal scenario for the day after Brexit is adopted in terms of cross-border cooperation in criminal matters, it is clear that the United Kingdom will have to comply with an increasingly interdependent and constitutionalised EU *acquis* if it is to secure meaningful cooperative arrangements with the EU and its Member States.

# PART III
# EXTERNAL RELATIONS

# CHAPTER 11

# MEMBERSHIP OF THE WORLD TRADE ORGANIZATION

Gregory MESSENGER[*]

## 1. INTRODUCTION

On withdrawal from the European Union, the United Kingdom's trading relations with the overwhelming majority of its trading partners will be regulated by the

---

[*] Liverpool Law School, University of Liverpool.

law of the World Trade Organization (WTO). While the UK has been a member of the WTO since its entry into force in 1995, it has not had to consider the impact of WTO law on the UK legal system in a meaningful manner as this has been managed and filtered through the EU.[1]

The WTO is an international organisation with a membership of 164 countries and customs unions, and which covers over 95 per cent of world trade.[2] It is home to an institutional framework for trade negotiations, resolving disputes and manging trade relations, as well as a set of comparatively detailed rules to regulate the involvement of governments or public power in the market.[3] While trade law once primarily concerned itself with the regulation of tariff barriers and core principles of non-discrimination, WTO law now extends into a wide range of areas of governmental activity, from the application of taxes and labelling regulation to intellectual property and services.

Given its scope and effect, it is clear that WTO law will play a critical role in the future of the UK's trade relations as well as the direction it takes in national policies. As the UK's default trade law, determining both the ability of the UK to conclude agreements with others, as well as the range of permissible and impermissible acts of the government in matters covered by the WTO, the UK will have to become familiar with its legal and institutional peculiarities. The UK's withdrawal from the EU will mean having to ensure (1) effective representation and engagement at the WTO and (2) compliance with WTO law within the UK legal system.

This chapter examines these two aspects of the UK's membership of the WTO.[4] It is not a comprehensive account of all areas of WTO law which would extend well beyond a single chapter, or indeed, single book, but instead aims to highlight a selection of key issues. Section 2 identifies the key elements involved in the UK's involvement at the WTO including its existing obligations, where it will likely need to conclude new agreements, and the institutional dimensions of UK involvement at the WTO. Section 3 turns to the effect of WTO law on UK

---

[1] See eg Council Regulation (EU) 2015/478 of 11 March 2015 on common rules for imports (codification) [2015] OJ L83/16, which incorporates WTO rules on the imposition of safeguard measures found in the Agreement on Safeguards, 15 April 1994, 1869 UNTS 154 ('Agreement on Safeguards').

[2] For a general guide on the WTO and its law, see M MATSUSHITA ET AL, *The World Trade Organization*, 3rd edn, Oxford University Press, Oxford 2016; P VAN DEN BOSSCHE and W ZDOUC, *The Law and Policy of the World Trade Organization*, 4th edn, Cambridge University Press, Cambridge 2017; MJ TREBILCOCK, *Advanced Introduction to International Trade Law*, 2nd edn, Edward Elgar, Cheltenham 2015.

[3] The point of comparison is to other branches of public international law, not EU law which is considerably more developed than anything found in the international legal order.

[4] Note: this chapter does not examine the future relationship of the UK with the EU or third countries through the conclusion of a possible free trade agreement. See further the contributions of M CREMONA (Ch 12) and P CRAIG (Ch 15) in this edited collection.

law and policy. Specifically, it identifies three areas of government policy which will have to engage with WTO law in a meaningful and comprehensive fashion: tax policy; industrial policy; and health and environmental policy. Section 4 concludes, reflecting on the possible impact of WTO law on the UK, and the UK's possible influence on the direction of WTO law.

## 2. UK MEMBERSHIP AT THE WTO

The UK is an original member of the WTO, as well as a founding contracting party of the WTO's predecessor, the General Agreement on Tariffs and Trade 1947.[5] Though the UK is a WTO member, it has not conducted its own independent trade policy at the WTO as the EU has enjoyed that exclusive competence as part of the common commercial policy.[6] As a consequence, the UK has been represented by the EU which acts on behalf of all Member States at the WTO. While the EU has spoken for the UK and other Member States at the WTO, this does not mean that the UK does not already have existing rights and obligations at the WTO.[7]

This section sets out the existing rights and obligations of the UK at the WTO (Section 2.1), the areas in which the UK will likely have to make new commitments (Section 2.2), and the nature of institutional arrangements at the WTO in which the UK will have to take part (Section 2.3).

### 2.1. EXISTING UK RIGHTS AND OBLIGATIONS

Rights and obligations under WTO law can be divided, broadly speaking, into two categories: general obligations and specific commitments. General obligations apply to all members equally. For example, members are (as a general rule) prohibited from discriminating between domestic and imported goods.[8]

---

5   General Agreement on Tariffs and Trade, 30 October 1947, 55 UNTS 194. The GATT 1947 was applied provisionally as the wider institution it was to be part of (the International Trade Organization) never came into force. See DA IRWIN, PC MAVROIDIS and AO SYKES, *The Genesis of the GATT*, Cambridge University Press, Cambridge 2008. The ITO was to be part of the new set of institutions agreed upon at the Bretton Woods Conference, including the International Monetary Fund and the International Bank for Reconstruction and Development (the World Bank). See B STEIL, *The Battle of Bretton Woods*, Princeton University Press, Princeton 2013. The GATT 1947 was subsequently incorporated into the GATT 1994 (1867 UNTS 187). For the avoidance of doubt, GATT references refer to the GATT 1947 articles as incorporated into the GATT 1994.

6   Articles 3(1)(e), 206 and 207 Consolidated Version of the Treaty on the Functioning of European Union [2012] OJ C326/49.

7   The most detailed account of this process: L BARTELS, 'The UK's Status in the WTO after Brexit' (23 September 2016) pp 3–7, available at <https://ssrn.com/abstract=2841747>.

8   Principally (though not exclusively) reflected in Article III GATT.

Specific obligations differ, however. For example, one member may commit not to raise tariffs on a certain good above a certain level. This obligation does not apply to all members – each decides at what level they wish to cap tariffs, and they are each bound by such a commitment.[9] This section sets out the UK's existing commitments (both general and specific) and the potential means of clarification where unclear.

### 2.1.1. General Obligations

Members of the WTO are bound by a number of legal obligations of general application. These are found within the 'covered agreements' – a set of treaties which form the backbone of WTO law. Membership of the WTO requires compliance with the covered agreements that include rules on trade in goods, trade in services, intellectual property, technical regulations and the use of measures designed to protect human, animal and plant life or health, as well as subsidies, responding to import surges, or trade in agriculture, amongst others. Importantly an agreement also includes rules on how to resolve trade disputes, providing for negotiations and subsequently a judicialised form of dispute settlement by an ad hoc panel of experts, with potential for appeal to a standing tribunal (the Appellate Body), as well as providing detail on appropriate retaliation in cases of non-compliance.[10]

As a contracting party of the GATT 1947 at the time of the entry into force of the WTO's founding treaty, the UK became an original member of the WTO.[11] As a result the UK became a party to the covered agreements in its own right, along with (but separate from) the EU. The impact of some of these general obligations is examined below in Section 3.

A complication exists in relation to the specific commitments made by the EU on behalf of, or jointly with, the UK (Section 2.1.2) and the changes that will be necessary when dividing the appropriate shares of existing quotas and permissible levels of agricultural subsidies (Section 2.1.3).

### 2.1.2. Schedules of Concessions and Commitments

Members of the WTO 'bind' their tariffs through the creation of Schedules of Concessions – documents which set out the maximum tariff applicable to a good or class of goods. These run to hundreds of pages, as goods are divided into categories (customarily with a numerical code) that begin at a general level and

---

[9]     Article II GATT.
[10]    Understanding on Rules and Procedures Governing the Settlement of Disputes, 15 April 1994, 1869 UNTS 401 ('DSU').
[11]    Article XI:1 Marrakesh Agreement Establishing the World Trade Organization, 15 April 1994, 1867 UNTS 154 ('WTO Agreement'). See BARTELS, above n 7, p 3.

then become more detailed. For example, 'textiles' (these run from 50 to 63) are then subsequently sub-divided into more specific categories such as 'cotton yarn; (not sewing thread), containing 85 per cent or more by weight of cotton, put up for retail sale' (with a specific digit code of 520710).[12] The Schedules constitute an integral part of the GATT, and thus are treaty obligations.[13] Members can apply a lower rate than that committed to (referred to as the applied tariff), though any reduction must necessarily be applied to all like goods from other WTO members.[14]

A comparable system exists for the Schedules of Commitments for the liberalisation of services under the GATS. Unlike the GATT, which applies to all goods, whether a tariff is bound or not, under the GATS commitments are more limited. Market access under the GATS is provided through a process of 'positive listing', that is, only where specific commitments have been made are members required to allow access to their services market.[15] For example, a member may limit access of foreign service suppliers to specific industries, or within industries to specific modes of service provision such as presence through branches or cross-border.[16] Aside from sector-specific limitations, members may also schedule 'horizontal' limitations which apply across all sectors.

The question for tariff bindings and services commitments arises as the UK's Schedule of Concessions (setting out commitments in goods) is shared with the EU. On withdrawal, the UK would have to have its own Schedule, not that of the EU's. In practice, however, on the matter of tariff bindings, the rates would be the same (that is, the UK would just copy the existing EU Schedule) leaving trading partners in no different position, thus negating the requirement to compensate members negatively affected.[17]

A similar situation exists with regard to the UK's Schedule of Commitments for trade in services. Where the UK ensures that it maintains the same commitments it currently holds under the shared GATS Schedule with the

---

[12]  This system of classification of goods is based on the Harmonised System which encourages uniformity amongst members' Schedules. This system is periodically updated to reflect new types of goods traded: International Convention on the Harmonized Commodity Description and Coding System (20 July 1987) L198, 3.

[13]  Article II.7 GATT.

[14]  Under 'Most Favoured Nation' (MFN) treatment, Article I GATT. Exceptions to the application of MFN exist, most notably under Article XXIV GATT and Article V GATS which provide for the conclusion of free trade agreements, customs unions and regional agreements to liberalise services.

[15]  Article XVI General Agreement on Trade in Services, 15 April 1994, 1869 UNTS 183 ('GATS').

[16]  The 'four modes' of service provision are provided for under Article I.2 GATS.

[17]  The system for modified Schedules under the GATT is provided for under Article XXVIII where the modifying member must negotiate with members 'primarily concerned', including the provision of temporary compensation where they are negatively affected.

EU, members would be in no different a position to before,[18] and thus even if they were to raise a claim, the quantum for calculating remedies would be non-existent. In effect, there would be no meaningful change.[19]

This is not the case, however, for the division of tariff-rate quotas between the EU and the UK that currently exist in the Schedule, or to a lesser extent agricultural subsidies.

### 2.1.3.    Commitments Relating to Agricultural Goods

Tariff-rate quotas (TRQs), as their name suggests, constitute a blend of tariff and quota. For example, where the bound rate for a good is 25 per cent, they may grant 5 per cent on the first 500 tonnes. TRQs became popular as a compromise during negotiations over the liberalisation of trade in agricultural goods. Under the Agreement on Agriculture, members are required to turn non-tariff barriers and other forms of protection into tariffs.[20] This has the advantage of being more visible, and facilitating progressive reduction of tariffs in agricultural goods which were historically high. To counteract instances where the process of 'tariffication' would be so great as to introduce a tariff which precluded any possible competition, TRQs were seen as a second-best solution.[21] Who has access to TRQs depends from member to member – some use a first-come-first-served basis, while others base them on historical bilateral agreements, and some (such as the EU) use a combination of these systems.

TRQs under the EU's Schedule will have to be divided between it and the UK. While complex, the technical exercise of calculating appropriate division of TRQs is possible.[22] Yet the difficulty in this instance arises from potential complaints from third members who could find themselves with reduced access as a result of the division.[23] There appears to be no easy answer to this challenge

---

[18]    Article XXI GATS sets out the process for compensating affected members.

[19]    There is a technical question as to whether or not this will entail a 'modification' or 'change' of the schedules which would potentially require the agreement of other members. See BARTELS, above n 7, pp 13–18. Cf the views of González García: House of Lords European Union Committee, *Brexit: The Options for Future Trade* (HL 2016–17, 72) p 55. In practice, the Government's intention is for simple certification which would place the membership on notice, and it would be for an individual member negatively affected to raise the issue with the UK. Where the UK maintains the same bindings as the EU, on this matter, it is hard to imagine a scenario where this would be the case (tariff rate quotas present a different matter).

[20]    Article 4.2 Agreement on Agriculture, 15 April 1994, 1867 UNTS 410.

[21]    Detail on existing TRQs is available in members' specific Schedules (for those that use them). An overview was prepared in a background note by the WTO Secretariat: 'Tariff and Other Quotas' (21 March 2002) TN/AG/S/5. See also Written Evidence from Peter Ungphakorn to House of Lords, European Union Committee (ETG005); *Brexit: The Options for Future Trade*, above n 19, p 53.

[22]    BARTELS, above n 7, suggests some options at pp 9–11.

[23]    The subject of a recent dispute at the WTO between China and the EU: *European Union – Measures Affecting Tariff Concessions on Certain Poultry Meat Products* (DS492).

aside from negotiating and offering compensation to those affected. This is an area where ensuring the goodwill of trading partners at the WTO will be essential, as well as a willingness to offer greater access than might otherwise be expected.

Just as TRQs principally apply in agriculture, so does the special regime for the management of agricultural subsidies. Such subsidies can support local communities and encourage food security; however, they distort prices and restrict the ability of agricultural exporters (often from the developing world) from competing. The WTO restricts the use of agricultural subsidies in a number of ways, including the setting of limits on the value of subsidies which can distort trade (aggregate measurement of support, 'AMS'). As with TRQs, the EU's AMS will have to be divided between the UK and EU. In practice, this does not constitute a particular problem as the EU does not provide subsidies to the value of its AMS.[24]

## 2.2. NEW UK COMMITMENTS

There are some areas where the UK will likely have to make explicit new commitments. This is the case with existing agreements which were concluded only by the EU, as well as others which are currently under negotiation.

Unlike the GATT or GATS which were concluded by both the EU and its Member States, some agreements have been concluded exclusively by the EU.[25] This is the case with the Revised Government Procurement Agreement (GPA),[26] a treaty that sets out rules for the purchase by governments and national agencies of goods and services.[27] While not all members of the WTO are parties to the GPA, it is particularly popular with large developed economies, and is an area in which the UK has particular interests, both for UK companies to sell goods and services but also to increase competition within the procurement market within the UK. An equivalent issue arises with the Trade Facilitation Agreement, a WTO agreement designed to reduce red tape and increase the ease and efficiency of customs procedures. The EU is a party to the agreement, not the UK,[28] and as

---

[24] *Brexit: The Options for Future Trade*, above n 19, p 55; BARTELS, above n 7, p 11.
[25] The Uruguay Round agreements that include the covered agreements and created the WTO were concluded as a set of mixed agreements (that is, by both EU and Member States) in light of Opinion of the Court of Justice, Opinion 1/94, ECLI:EU:C:1994:384.
[26] Revised Agreement on Government Procurement, (entry into force, 6 April 2014), available at <https://www.wto.org/english/docs_e/legal_e/rev-gpr-94_01_e.pdf>.
[27] The WTO suggests that the GPA covers activities worth an estimated $1.7 trillion annually: <https://www.wto.org/english/tratop_e/gproc_e/gp_gpa_e.htm>.
[28] It is possible to interpret the Instrument of Acceptance (16 October 2015) WLI/100 of the EU as including the UK, as reference is made to the EU's acceptance 'in respect of its Member States' in a footnote.

such one would expect the UK to accede to both on withdrawal from the EU. It is possible that the UK argue that it acts as a successor to the EU with regard to its obligations under the GPA on withdrawal.[29] Though contentious, such practice is not without precedent,[30] and would offer many advantages.[31] As with other matters at the WTO, it will depend to a large degree on the goodwill (or at least an absence of ill-will) on the part of trading partners.

In the case of new agreements currently being negotiated (the Environmental Goods Agreement, for example, which seeks to provide tariff-free treatment for goods that are marked as 'green' or environmentally supportive), the UK will need to engage with the substance of them sooner to maximise the projection of its interests in these fields.

## 2.3. INSTITUTIONAL INVOLVEMENT

The WTO is unusual within the international legal order in that it contains a comparatively detailed set of legal instruments (the covered agreements) that together constitute the majority of WTO law. It is not only the law of the WTO that makes it an important priority for the UK but also its institutions. The WTO is home to a network of councils, committees and working groups that together monitor developments in a range of trade-related areas, and provide fora for the development of rules and the raising of concerns.[32] Beyond the committee system, the WTO also contains what is widely considered a highly effective system for the settlement of trade disputes, considered the most successful form of inter-state international dispute resolution today.[33] Awareness and engagement with these institutions will be essential for the UK to ensure that it can pursue its interests in trade policy and shield itself from criticism or claims by other members.

### 2.3.1. The WTO Committee Structure

The WTO is a 'member-driven' organisation, which is to say it has a relatively small Secretariat, and no body able to act in the interests of the institution in any meaningful manner, unlike for example, the Commission within the EU.

---

[29]   This argument is made by BARTELS, above n 7, at pp 18–21.

[30]   NB the Rhodesian situation during the GATT years, described in BARTELS, above n 7, at pp 19–20.

[31]   If accepted, a similar argument could also be made for the UK to maintain its membership of EU free trade agreements to which it is currently a party only through the EU.

[32]   See G MESSENGER, The Development of World Trade Organization Law, Oxford University Press, Oxford 2016, Ch 3.

[33]   J CRAWFORD, 'Continuity and Discontinuity in International Dispute Settlement: An Inaugural Lecture' (2010) 1(1) Journal of International Dispute Settlement 4, p 4.

The member-driven nature of the organisation means that all members are entitled to sit on all committees, and each committee hears concerns raised over specific trade issues.[34] For example, the Committee on Technical Barriers to Trade acts as a testing ground for members who must notify regulatory instruments they plan to introduce.[35] Where such a regulation may raise concerns from other members (such as the recent example of food labelling in the case of unhealthy foods), discussions over the appropriate extent of application of such a measure and its compliance with the law and policy of the WTO ensues.[36]

Further, some committees act as rule-elaborators – not creating new rules per se but rather developing the existing rules through the creation of Decisions.[37] As the 'legislative' branch of the WTO has been deadlocked for so long,[38] other branches of the institution are required to step into the gap.[39]

Aside from specifically WTO committees, WTO law also grants special recognition to international standards that come from three other international organisations: the World Organisation for Animal Health; the International Plant Protection Convention; and the Codex Alimentarius Commission.[40] These bodies act as international regulatory standard-setting bodies, producing standards that relate to a wide range of issues, from the definition of marmalade to the potential harmful effects of growth hormones in beef.[41] Though these standards are not binding in and of themselves, where WTO members' measures conform to the international standard, they are presumed to comply with elements of WTO law.[42] Compliance with WTO law can be assured or undone before litigation even arises, determined in part at these institutions. The UK will have to engage not only with the variety of representative bodies at the WTO

---

[34]   The term 'committee' is used here to include Councils, working groups, the Dispute Settlement Body, the Trade Policy Review Mechanism and the Ministerial Council. The WTO Agreement sets out the institutional framework of the WTO.

[35]   In particular, Articles 2.9.2 and 2.10.1 Agreement on Technical Barriers to Trade, 15 April 1994, 1868 UNTS 120.

[36]   The number of notifications under the TBT Information Management System is considerable: currently 21,473 regular notifications. Data is available at <http://tbtims.wto.org/>.

[37]   eg Decision of the Committee on Sanitary and Phytosanitary Measures, 'Implementation of Article 4 of the Agreement on the Application of Sanitary and Phytosanitary Measures' (23 July 2004) G/SPS/19/rev. 2.

[38]   The current negotiating round, the 'Doha Round' was started in 2001. Advances made since then have been piecemeal and modest. See Bali Ministerial Declaration (11 December 2013) WT/MIN(13)/DEC; Nairobi Ministerial Declaration (19 December 2015) WT/MIN(15)/DEC.

[39]   See A LANG and J SCOTT, 'The Hidden World of WTO Governance' (2009) 20 *European Journal of International Law* 57.

[40]   Annex A.3 Agreement on the Application of Sanitary and Phytosanitary Measures, 15 April 1994, 1867 UNTS 493 ('SPS Agreement').

[41]   See M BURKARD, 'The Ractopamine Dispute in the Codex Alimentarius Commission' (2012) 4 *European Journal of Risk Regulation* 610.

[42]   Article 3.2 SPS Agreement.

but also re-energise its involvement at bodies such as Codex, where though a current member, the Commission nonetheless represents the UK on all matters of exclusive and mixed competence.

### 2.3.2. Dispute Settlement

If the UK wishes to challenge the trade measures of other WTO members it will need to resort to the dispute settlement system at the WTO. Equally, should the UK introduce a measure which another WTO member considers violates their rights under the covered agreements, the UK will have to respond to any legal claim.[43]

Dispute settlement is the jewel in the crown of the WTO.[44] It is widely considered to be an effective method of resolving disputes and provides a comparatively successful compliance mechanism. Whereas in most areas of international law, the jurisdiction of tribunals is subject to the consent of the parties, at the WTO, membership of the organisation necessarily entails consent to dispute settlement.[45] As such, unlike other systems of international law, the potential to challenge the compliance of other WTO members' policies is a real opportunity and danger.

Under the WTO, any dispute is subject to a period of negotiations (60 days) before moving to an ad hoc panel which hears the dispute and produces a report, customarily within six months of hearing the case.[46] Appeal is possible on points of law to a standing tribunal, the Appellate Body. The timeframes are comparatively quick: from the notification of a dispute to the final Appellate Body report (assuming appeal), a member can expect to have a final report within a year and half.[47] This may not be fast in domestic law terms but within international law this is considerably faster than many other tribunals.[48]

Where a member does not comply with a panel or Appellate Body report,[49] remedies most often take the form of 'suspension of concessions', most commonly an increase in tariffs. Retaliation is limited to the value of nullification or impairment suffered by the member,[50] and are, in nearly all instances,

---

[43] The UK will wish to intervene in any dispute that is of relevance for its interests as a third party also.
[44] See above n 32 and corresponding text.
[45] Article 1.1 DSU.
[46] Articles 4.7 and 12.8 DSU.
[47] Article 17.5 DSU. Though it is worth noting that increasing delays are now taking place.
[48] It should be noted that factually complex cases such as those related to scientific evidence or trade defence instruments may well take longer.
[49] Formally, the report is of the Dispute Settlement Body, a plenary body that adopts reports of panels or the Appellate Body thus giving it its legal effect. However, adoption is (as contrasted with the prior GATT system) now de facto automatic working under a system of negative consensus: Articles 16 and 17.14 DSU.
[50] Article 22.4 DSU.

prospective.[51] From the UK perspective, two elements of WTO retaliation are of particular note.

First, the impact of such retaliation is dependent on the relative economic power of the parties involved.[52] Small members seeking compliance from large trade partners may find themselves in a worse position by suspending concessions, while the prospective nature of remedies, and lack of effective injunctive relief, can give the impression that larger, more powerful members can pay their way out of their obligations.[53] Should the UK face increased tariffs from the US, for example, it is in a less secure position than the EU were it to wish to withstand retaliation.

Second, the targeting involved in retaliation at the WTO is unusual. The suspension of concessions are first to affect the sector subject to the dispute.[54] Failing this, members may seek to suspend concessions for other sectors under the same agreement, and where this is not 'practicable or effective', may seek to suspend obligations under another agreement.[55] Consequently, traders or producers in an industry entirely unrelated to the dispute in question can be harmed by the imposition of trade barriers on their goods.

The combination of compulsory jurisdiction for WTO disputes and the nature of countermeasures under WTO law make the dispute settlement system a subject of great interest for the UK. It will offer opportunities for the UK to ensure that its trade partners do not discriminate against UK products or services, but will present considerable challenges. In a climate where the UK Government insists that escaping the jurisdiction of the Court of Justice is a key priority, acknowledging that tribunals at the WTO will also rule on a number of matters of UK policy, and that there are meaningful economic consequences for non-compliance, will require considerable political effort if Geneva is not to replace Brussels in the popular imagination.

This also makes the UK's compliance with WTO law a priority, as relative market size to China, the US, or indeed the EU, will shift considerably. The following section examines some of the key policy areas which will have to consider WTO law during their formulation and application, or potentially face challenges from trade partners at the WTO.

---

[51] Cf Article 21.5 Panel Report, *Australia – Automotive Leather II*, WT/DS126/RW (21 January 2000). See G VIDIGAL, 'Re-Assessing WTO Remedies: The Prospective and the Retrospective' (2013) 16(3) *Journal of International Economic Law* 505.

[52] On the general challenges faced by WTO dispute settlement, see P SUTHERLAND ET AL, *The Future of the WTO*, WTO, Geneva 2005.

[53] Note the hormones, GMOs and zeroing disputes which all centred on EU or US non-compliance (DS26, DS291 and DS294 respectively).

[54] Article 22.3(a) DSU.

[55] Article 22.3(b) and (c) DSU.

# 3. MEMBERSHIP OF THE WTO WITHIN THE UK

The effect of WTO law is wide: it regulates the use of fiscal measures, subsidies, technical regulations, trade in services, import and export licensing procedures, rules of origin, intellectual property and far more besides. The previous section identified a number of legal and institutional developments that the UK will need to take into account with regard to the WTO. Many of these can be resolved through greater resourcing. It is compliance with WTO law *within* the UK legal system, however, which will present a greater challenge. This section outlines three policy areas of particular concern for the UK which will require close attention to ensure that WTO obligations are not violated unintentionally. In each case, the UK will need to ensure a holistic awareness of WTO law across ministries and departments, not only in the Department of International Trade and/or Foreign and Commonwealth Office.

## 3.1. TAXATION

Taxation constitutes the principal source of revenue for government expenditure in most developed economies; it forms a central part of government policies relating to business, family, environment, health and education, and its misuse (whether perceived or real) has led to civil disobedience, riots and rebellion.

WTO law regulates the powers of state to levy and collect taxes in a number of different ways. For the purposes of this section, two are of most importance: the acknowledgement that a tax break may constitute a subsidy for the purposes of WTO law, and the impact of using tax policy to privilege domestic producers or traders over foreign competitors. The challenge that arises, and WTO law seeks to manage, is that there are often very good reasons to want to introduce such measures. The key issue, therefore, is to avoid unintended violations of WTO law when pursuing otherwise potentially legitimate objectives.

### 3.1.1. *Tax Breaks*

Government is often expected (or seeks) to encourage the private sector. As direct state management of enterprises is no longer commonplace,[56] government instead focuses on providing advantageous conditions to draw new investment to a region, encourage businesses to expand where already in situ, or to support the creation of new local industries. A principal tool for such policies is through tax breaks – reducing tax that is otherwise due. Under EU law this practice is regulated by the law of state aid, and while it is likely that a future

---

[56] Though China, and to a lesser degree India, challenge this trend.

EU-UK agreement will include provisions on state aid limitations,[57] the UK will nonetheless be limited by WTO law, and specifically the Agreement on Subsidies and Countervailing Measures.[58]

To take a specific example, the UK Government recently made clear that it was going to support Nissan to ensure that the North East remained an attractive location for investment and the presence of automotive manufacturing.[59] The danger is that any benefit granted to a specific industry or enterprise or region, and that confers a benefit, may constitute a subsidy for the purposes of WTO law.[60] A tax break, from the perspective of WTO law, is no different from a direct transfer of funds: in both cases the net result is the same, an industry finds itself in a better position than it would have were it not for the tax break.[61] Depending on the circumstances of the tax break, trading partners can either investigate the nature and value of the subsidy and introduce tariffs to the value of the subsidy (thus counteracting its effect in their market),[62] or alternatively raise a claim at the WTO.[63]

A particularly contentious form of tax break is for companies to encourage exports (so-called export subsidies). These are considered especially harmful and have now been prohibited for both agricultural and non-agricultural goods.[64] The UK will need to fight the temptation to use existing bodies, such as UK Export Finance (now within the Department of International Trade) to support enterprises to export in a manner that could trigger a complaint at the WTO or the introduction of countervailing duties.[65]

### 3.1.2. Health Taxes

An area which requires attention is the increasing use of tax policy to pursue objectives considered to be of societal benefit: for example, the introduction of higher sales taxes on tobacco, products high in fat, or high in sugar. While WTO law does not stop members from introducing such measures, it does condition

---

[57]  See Draft European Council Guidelines following the United Kingdom's notification under Article 50 TEU (31 March 2017) para 19.

[58]  Agreement on Subsidies and Countervailing Measures, 15 April 1994, 1869 UNTS 14 ('SCM Agreement').

[59]  'UK told Nissan it wants tariff-free trading for motor industry, Clark says', *BBC News*, 30 October 2016, <http://www.bbc.co.uk/news/uk-politics-37815864>.

[60]  Articles 1.1 and 2 SCM Agreement.

[61]  Article 1.1(a)(1) SCM Agreement.

[62]  On countervailing duties, see Section 3.2.1 below.

[63]  Article 5 SCM Agreement.

[64]  Article 3.1(a) SCM Agreement, Ministerial Conference, *Export Competition*, Ministerial Decision of 19 December 2015, WT/MIN(15)/45 WT/L/980 (2015).

[65]  The issue of export banks arose in *Korea – Measures Affecting Trade in Commercial Vessels*, Panel Report (7 March 2005) WT/DS273/R.

their application to ensure that they do not discriminate (whether intentionally or not) against imported goods.

For example, the UK Government has, for some years now, discussed the use of a 'sugar tax' in an effort to combat rising rates of obesity in both adult and child populations.[66] When introducing such a measure, there is a risk that certain exclusions (for fresh fruit juice, for example, which is high in sugar) might trigger a claim by a member whose exporters compete with such products.[67] The structure of the tax, the exceptions applicable, and its effect are all important factors in determining whether or not the measure is WTO compliant. Intention alone is not a central factor, stressing the importance of ensuring that government is aware of its WTO obligations.[68] There are exceptions available on the basis of measures that protect human health, for example, yet to be 'on the back foot' and relying on a defence is not a politically desirable position.[69]

## 3.2.    INDUSTRIAL POLICY

As mentioned above, governments take a keen interest in the success or otherwise of domestic industry.[70] However, success in encouraging business is a difficult task for a number of reasons, not least the complex multifaceted factors involved including (among many others) protection from international competition and appropriate available infrastructure. These two examples serve as useful illustrations to examine the WTO dimensions the UK Government will have to keep in mind as it pursues a 'modern industrial strategy'.[71]

### 3.2.1.   Trade Defence Instruments

While the general presumption of the WTO is that benefits accrue from trade liberalisation,[72] there are times when members can act to protect domestic

---

[66]    See HMRC, 'Policy Paper: Soft Drinks Industry Levy' (5 December 2016) available at <https://www.gov.uk/government/publications/soft-drinks-industry-levy/soft-drinks-industry-levy>.

[67]    WTO law prohibits discrimination between 'like products' but also between 'directly competitive or substitutable products' (Article III.2 GATT). For an illustrative example, see Appellate Body Report, *Japan – Alcoholic Beverages II*, WT/DS8,10,11/AB/R (4 October 1996).

[68]    Appellate Body Report, *Chile – Alcoholic Beverages*, WT/DS87,110/AB/R (13 December 1999) paras 71–72. See also D REGAN, 'Regulatory Purpose and "Like Products" in Article III:4 of the GATT (With Additional Remarks on Article III:2)' (2002) 36 *Journal of World Trade* 443.

[69]    There is a closed list of exceptions available under Article XX GATT.

[70]    Section 3.1.1 above.

[71]    Department for Business, Energy and Industrial Strategy, *Green Paper: Building our Industrial Strategy* (23 January 2017).

[72]    See Preamble to the WTO Agreement, first Recital.

industries through the use of trade defence instruments (TDIs). These are the principal tools available to governments to protect national industries from unfair trade practices or unforeseen developments in the global economy. Each TDI responds to a different set of circumstances: countervailing duties; anti-dumping duties; and safeguard measures.

Countervailing duties are used to respond to subsidies. A UK manufacturer may, for example, find it more difficult to export to a market where the local government subsidises domestic industries making their products cheaper and more competitive than they otherwise would be. Similarly, the UK producer may have difficulties selling within the UK itself where the foreign subsidised good (artificially more competitive) is imported into the UK market. Where subsidised goods enter the UK market, the principal tool is the introduction of countervailing duties, an increase in tariffs designed to increase the imported good's price and offset the effect of the subsidy. A number of industries are affected by the use of subsidies, from aircraft manufacturers to renewable energy.[73]

Anti-dumping duties are used to respond to goods being exported below their actual value ('dumping'). Dumping is considered a form of predatory pricing, where an industry exports goods at an artificially low price to drive competitors out of business. Dumping can also result from cases of overcapacity, with industries trying to export as much of their stock as possible, though it may injure foreign manufacturers. To respond to dumping, anti-dumping duties can be introduced, calculated at the difference between the normal value of the good and its export price (thus countering the effect of the price reduction).[74] Debates over the appropriate response to (allegedly) dumped steel from China and its relation to the closing of steel mills in the UK is emblematic of the contentious nature of anti-dumping policy.[75]

Safeguard measures are used to respond to an increase in imports resulting from unforeseen developments in the global economy. Unlike the other two TDIs, they do not respond to 'unfair' trade practices but to a change in the economic climate. They are temporary in nature, designed to allow local industry time to adapt or to protect it until the sudden change in conditions passes. Compensation is granted to affected trade partners in the form of reduced tariffs, and the measures are time-limited.[76] Nonetheless, safeguard measures

---

[73]   See the illustrative disputes in *EC and certain member States – Large Civil Aircraft* (DS316) and *Canada – Feed-In Tariff Program* (DS426).

[74]   Article 9.3 Agreement on Implementation of Article VI of the General Agreement on Tariffs and Trade 1994, 15 April 1994, 1868 UNTS 201 ('AD Agreement').

[75]   'Port Talbot matters more than China', *The Guardian*, 1 April 2016, <https://www.theguardian.com/commentisfree/2016/apr/01/the-guardian-view-on-the-steel-crisis-port-talbot-matters-more-than-china>.

[76]   Not more than 8 years in duration, and even then only in extraordinary circumstances. There is an obligation to review and progressively reduce the measures, where in place for 3 years or longer. See Article 7 Agreement on Safeguards.

can provide temporary protection for an efficient industry that would otherwise be irreparably harmed.[77]

Currently TDIs are investigated by the Commission but once the investigation and introduction of TDIs falls to the UK, it will need to introduce a system for this purpose. The process is customarily as follows: industry petitions government for support and requests protection (whether in the form of countervailing duties, anti-dumping duties, or safeguard measures). A governmental investigating authority then examines the claim and provides an account of whether a case of subsidisation/dumping/import surge exists and what the appropriate response should be. This process is highly technical, and the tests involved both economic and legal. Any error in this process and the member against whose goods the measure is introduced will raise a claim challenging the (from their perspective) unjustified increase in trade barriers.[78]

Used correctly, TDIs can encourage fair trading practices and provide useful protection to industries that find themselves under unexpected pressure. In practice, however, there is considerable scope for misuse, as one country's belief that there is a case of dumping or an import surge might be viewed by another as barely concealed protectionism and spark retaliatory TDIs,[79] or a legal claim at the WTO. This is exacerbated by the fact that WTO rules setting out the requirements for the use of each instrument are detailed but not comprehensive.[80]

The UK will need to develop the appropriate framework to respond to demands from national industries (such as steel mills, for example) to offer protection, without sliding into protectionism and violating WTO obligations. This will entail the creation of a new legislative framework setting out the requirements for petitioning and the introduction of TDIs and the creation of a new government agency.[81]

### 3.2.2.   Infrastructure Investment

Another method for supporting business, often raised by policy-makers, is the improvement of infrastructure. Infrastructure projects raise WTO concerns in two areas: government procurement and the possible claim of a subsidy. In the first instance, rules on government procurement (should the UK accede to the

---

[77]   The economic evidence for the effectiveness of safeguard measures is not especially strong; see, however, CP Bown and R McCulloch, 'Trade Adjustment in the WTO System: Are More Safeguards the Answer?' (2007) 23(3) *Oxford Review of Economic Policy* 415, p 416.

[78]   Disputes of this kind have accounted for over half of disputes filed at the WTO.

[79]   This was the case for the US steel industry in the early 2000s.

[80]   On the failings, eg, of the Agreement on Safeguards, see A Sykes, 'The "Safeguards Mess" Revisited – A Reply to Professor Jones' (2004) 3(1) *World Trade Review* 93; A Sykes, 'The Fundamental Deficiencies of the Agreement on Safeguards: A Reply to Professor Lee' (2006) 40(5) *Journal of World Trade* 979.

[81]   See the acknowledgement of the Government on this point: House of Commons International Trade Committee, *UK Trade Options beyond 2019* (HC 2016–17, 817) para 29.

Revised GPA, which it is expected to do), the process for deciding to whom a contract is given for the infrastructure spend must be conducted in a transparent and non-discriminatory fashion.[82]

The second objective is to ensure that the infrastructure project is one of general use, and not only for the benefit of a specific industry. For example, in a dispute over support given to the large civil aircraft manufacturer, Airbus, the extension of the main runway at Bremen airport in Germany near a plant was considered a 'financial contribution' as it was not part of general infrastructure (only Airbus was able to use the extended part of the runway), no matter that the general population benefited from increased commercial opportunities and jobs.[83]

## 3.3. HEALTH AND ENVIRONMENTAL POLICY

Unlike EU law which sets agreed-upon standards of social protection among the Member States, the WTO does not impose any such requirements. At the WTO, the concern relates to the introduction of measures which may otherwise violate the protected rights of trade partners. For example, measures designed to protect local species from invasive pests might also unnecessarily restrict goods from other countries.[84] More broadly, measures to protect, for example, the marine environment or air quality may also trigger violations of WTO law. It is to these areas of health and environmental policy that this section now turns.

### 3.3.1. Agriculture and Food Safety

The increase of international trade, especially in agricultural goods, increases the potential risks to human, animal and plant life or health through the potential spread of pests, disease or otherwise harmful foodstuffs. Combined with greater demands by the public for health protection and improved detection and management techniques, and the relationship between trade and health becomes contentious. The WTO attempts to balance the legitimate objectives of members as they protect the health of humans, plants and animals with concerns over unjustifiable restrictions on trade such as overtly burdensome regulation or import bans.[85]

---

[82] In particular, the non-discrimination obligations in Article IV Revised GPA.
[83] Panel Report, *EC and Certain Member States – Large Civil Aircraft*, WT/DS316/R (30 June 2010) paras 71113–1121.
[84] See the illustrative disputes: *Japan – Apples* (DS245) and *Australia – Salmon* (DS18).
[85] Acknowledged by the Appellate Body as the 'shared, but sometimes competing, interests of promoting international trade and of protecting the life and health of human beings'. Report of the Appellate Body, *European Communities – Measures Concerning Meat and Meat Products*, (16 January 1998) WT/DS26/AB/R and WT/DS48/AB/R ('EC – Hormones Appellate Body'), para 177.

To manage this challenge, WTO law requires that members base their measures on international standards (of the kind discussed above in Section 2.3.1) or failing that, on the basis of sound scientific evidence.[86] The difficulty arises in areas where the evidence for the potential risks is not clear, or does not support the widely held public view. For example, restrictions placed on genetically modified organisms have already been subject to litigation at the WTO, as has the EU's ban on a number of growth hormones used to increase cattle size.[87]

The dispute over beef hormones is a useful case to consider as it raises several questions for the UK's management of the same issue. There is considerable opposition within the EU to the use of beef hormones in cattle rearing, with most attention focused on whether the consumption of such hormone-treated beef may cause cancer. The US and Canada raised parallel claims at the WTO arguing (inter alia) that the EU ban on certain growth hormones constituted a violation of WTO obligations as it was not based on sufficient scientific evidence. In short, a set of EU regulatory measures closed off the beef market to many exporters in the US and Canada where the use of growth hormones is common.[88] The EU was found not to have based its measure 'on an assessment, as appropriate to the circumstances, of the risks to human, animal or plant life or health, taking into account risk assessment techniques developed by the relevant international organizations'.[89]

Given the contentious nature of food safety, however, the EU did not come into compliance, raising the prospect of considerable retaliation until the point at which a negotiated settlement was reached with Canada and the US. The EU–Canada free trade agreement (CETA) in part solidifies this commitment: no change on hormone-treated beef but an increase in beef quotas available to Canada to allow it greater access to the EU market.[90] Since the US' withdrawal from the negotiations on a bilateral agreement with the EU, the prospect of a return to retaliation has raised its head.[91]

From a UK perspective, this dispute raises two key points. The first is the importance of ensuring that the UK's considerable capacity in scientific

---

[86]   Article 5 SPS Agreement.

[87]   *EC – Approval and Marketing of Biotech Products* (DS291) and *EC – Hormones* (DS26, DS48, DS320, DS321).

[88]   The range of measures in question are identified in Panel Report, *EC – Hormones*, WT/DS26/R/US (18 August 1997) para 2.1.

[89]   Article 5.1 SPS Agreement; Appellate Body Report, *EC – Hormones*, WT/DS26,48/AB/R (16 January 1998) para 255.

[90]   Comprehensive Economic and Trade Agreement between Canada, of the one part, and the European Union and its Member States, of the other part. Text is available at <http://data.consilium.europa.eu/doc/document/ST-10973-2016-INIT/en/pdf>.

[91]   'US Weighs Tariffs Against Vespas, Cheeses in Trade Beef With EU', *Wall Street Journal*, 30 March 2017. This is a clear example of the impact of WTO retaliation on other industries discussed in Section 2.3.2 above.

investigation and research is effectively targeted and appropriate procedures are put into place so that any measure that the UK introduces can be defended as based on sound science and appropriate risk assessment techniques. Second, where there is considerable domestic pressure to restrict the entry into the UK of a good for which there is little to no evidence that it is harmful, should the UK lose, it will have to decide whether to accept retaliation or come into compliance. This raises the concern referred to above, that retaliation at the WTO is heavily dependent on relative market size, and the ability to sustain increased trade barriers by a large trading partner may have a damaging impact on the UK economy.[92] This is not a hypothetical concern: beef hormones, genetically modified organisms and chlorine-washed chicken are all the subject of ongoing disputes at the WTO with the EU restricting their import or marketing in many different ways. The UK will need to decide if it wishes to inherit this approach or change course.

*3.3.2. Environmental Policy*

The relationship between trade law and the environment has long been contentious. The principal concern is this: the WTO contains a comparatively detailed set of rules, a relatively effective dispute settlement mechanism and strong economic backing from influential interest groups within states, while international environmental law has none of these things. Thus, where a government has to choose between pursuing environmental obligations or erring on the side of caution to ensure it complies with its trade obligations, it is likely to choose trade. This is a caricature but the potential overlap between trade obligations and environmental protection is a real one: as with all areas of international law, states are bound by their commitments and are therefore not free to act without consideration of these obligations, no matter how worthy the objective.

For the UK, there are several areas where this may raise WTO-related issues. The first is in maritime conservation. Prohibiting, for example, the sale of fish caught in a certain manner (such as through pair trawling which risks catching large cetaceans), though well intentioned, can trigger a WTO claim if not carefully managed. This was the case for the US which prohibited the sale of shrimp caught with nets that did not exclude turtles.[93] While the WTO Appellate Body acknowledged that the US was entitled to introduce measures to protect the environment,[94] it could not do so 'in a manner which would constitute a means of arbitrary or unjustifiable discrimination … or a disguised

---

[92]  Section 2.3.2 above.
[93]  See Appellate Body Report, *US – Shrimp*, WT/DS58/AB/R (12 October 1998).
[94]  Formally, 'exhaustible natural resources' as provided for by Article XX(g) GATT.

restriction on international trade',[95] something that failing to negotiate with all affected trade partners in that case indicated.[96] Where a member attempts to use labelling to counter similar problems (such as 'dolphin-friendly' tuna labels) it must also ensure that these policies do not violate their WTO obligations, in this instance under the Agreement on Technical Barriers to Trade.[97]

Another area is increased regulation to combat air pollution, a pressing concern in UK cities, most notably London.[98] As with other measures discussed, difficulty arises in the manner the objective is pursued. There is nothing under WTO law from stopping the UK acting to improve air quality; where WTO law concerns itself is where such measures constitute a form of discrimination. Prohibiting diesel cars, for example, may raise questions from producers of such vehicles why equivalent measures are not in place for similarly polluting vehicles,[99] or whether alternatives which would manage the problem without a prohibition might be available.[100] It will be important for the UK to integrate an awareness of these questions which arise from the text and accompanying jurisprudence of WTO law into regulatory decision-making at each stage.

## 4.   CONCLUSIONS

The nature and function of WTO and EU law are dramatically different and the UK will have to adapt to the new legal framework in which it finds itself. Most notably, while EU law provides clear instruction and oversight, WTO law provides only general rules against which each member must assess its practice to determine the likelihood of another raising a claim. The lack of a dense regulatory framework and common rules will require the UK to be sensitive to the potential WTO-related consequences of its policies, not only in trade but also in myriad domestic spheres. Unlike EU law which spreads compliance mechanisms through the EU legal order, including domestic courts, at the WTO a dispute is a

---

[95]   Chapeau, Article XX GATT. See the discussion in Appellate Body Report, *US – Shrimp*, WT/DS58/AB/R (12 October 1998) paras 157–159.

[96]   Appellate Body Report, *US – Shrimp*, WT/DS58/AB/R (12 October 1998) para 172.

[97]   See eg Appellate Body Report, *US – Tuna II*, WT/DS381/AB/R (16 May 2012).

[98]   'London's air pollution worse than Beijing's as smog chokes capital', *The Independent*, 25 January 2017.

[99]   A common thread in questions of discrimination with regard to regulatory measures under Article III.4 GATT is whether the 2 products in question are 'like' (in this hypothetical, eg, diesel and petrol cars). Ultimately this is a determination based on a number of factors including the competitive relationship between the products: Appellate Body Report, *EC – Asbestos*, WT/DS135/AB/R (12 March 2001) para 103. A similar question arises under Article 2.1 Agreement on Technical Barriers to Trade. See: Appellate Body Report, *US – Clove Cigarettes*, WT/DS406/AB/R (4 April 2012) para 111.

[100]  Air quality has arisen in two important disputes at the WTO: *US – Gasoline* (DS2) and *Brazil – Tyres* (DS332).

contentious affair only ever between opposing members, and with the retaliation on offer for instances of non-compliance blunt yet relatively effective.[101]

Once the UK has the relevant institutional framework in place, and capacity on trade law has grown sufficiently, what can we expect to see for the UK legal system? One area of growth is in administrative trade law: the area of law that will determine the grounds upon which companies may challenge decisions of an investigating authority in determining the existence of subsidies, dumping, or import surges. Membership of the WTO managed exclusively by the UK will also require a more effective method of oversight for the executive in trade matters and its conduct at the WTO, as well as an appropriate legal framework for the incorporation of WTO obligations into the UK legal system. The UK's constitutional law will thus also have to catch up to the distinct nature of trade regulation and negotiations at the WTO. Most importantly, the UK will have to increase awareness of WTO law across ministries and departments in short order to avoid unnecessary conflicts with trade partners. This process is not unheard of; indeed, China has increased its capacity in WTO law dramatically from entry to the organisation to taking a leading role in litigation. As is often the case, this will be a decision based on resourcing, and for the UK to decide where it wishes to invest.

The influence of the UK's withdrawal from the EU need not be only in one direction. The UK too will be able to influence developments at the WTO. It is likely that the UK will want to be seen as a team player in Geneva and garner goodwill amongst trading partners. As such, there are a number of sensitive issues where, should the UK be willing, it could show leadership not least of all in matters relating to food security, subsidies that contribute to illegal, unregulated and unreported fishing, reform of trade defence instruments or liberalisation of trade in 'green' goods. How the UK chooses to engage with these contentious issues and others at the WTO will be a test. The UK alone will not be able to set the agenda or determine outcomes. It will have to form alliances which ultimately may produce no meaningful outcomes in the deadlock-prone WTO system. Nonetheless, should the UK learn how to play the game, it will be an opportunity to identify new alliances and shape trade law in a manner coincident with its, and the international community's, interests.

---

[101]    When compared to the generality of public international law, not EU law.

# CHAPTER 12

# UK TRADE POLICY

Marise Cremona[*]

## 1. SETTING THE SCENE: WHAT IS TRADE POLICY?

Although there is still a great deal of uncertainty over the UK's future relationship with the EU, the most likely post-Brexit options involve the UK leaving the EU's customs union and consequently no longer being bound by its common commercial (trade) policy. This chapter will proceed on the basis of that assumption, and therefore that the UK will need to determine its own trade policy and negotiate a whole range of new trade relationships.

The future UK-EU relationship will have an impact on UK trade policy in another way. Were the UK to remain a member of the EU's single market, continuing as a result to apply the EU's regulatory systems for goods and services, then goods and services coming from third countries into the UK market would

---

\*    European University Institute.

find it easier to access the EU market; as a consequence a trade agreement with the UK would be more attractive (not as attractive as it would be if the UK were still a Member State, but more attractive than if the UK were outside the single market). The Government has indicated that it does not envisage continued membership of the single market, and this chapter will assume that this policy will not change.[1]

These assumptions are based on the Government's White Paper on exiting the EU, published on 2 February 2017, which states:

> 'We will not be seeking membership of the Single Market, but will pursue instead a new strategic partnership with the EU, including an ambitious and comprehensive Free Trade Agreement and a new customs agreement.[2]
>
> After we have left the EU, we want to ensure that we can take advantage of the opportunity to negotiate our own preferential trade agreements around the world. We will not be bound by the EU's Common External Tariff or participate in the Common Commercial Policy.'[3]

In such circumstances, external trade policy will become critically important for the UK. A recent study estimates that if the UK withdraws from membership of the single market, replacing this with a Free Trade Agreement (FTA) with the EU, over the long term (5–10 years) it will lose 35 per cent of its trade in goods and 61 per cent of its trade in services with the EU.[4] Trade with non-EU partners will therefore be even more important, although it should be said that the same study indicates that even the conclusion of large numbers of FTAs will come nowhere near to replacing the lost trade with the EU.[5] Despite new technologies, geography is still very important to trade flows: as expressed by Angus Armstrong, 'the Iron-Law of Trade Models: trade between two countries approximately halves as the distance between them doubles'.[6]

---

[1]   On the future UK-EU relationship, see the contribution by P CRAIG (Ch 15) in this edited collection.

[2]   *The United Kingdom's exit from and new partnership with the European Union* (Cm 9417, February 2017) para 8.

[3]   Ibid, para 8.43.

[4]   M EBELL, Will New Trade Deals Soften the Blow of Hard Brexit? National Institute of Economic and Social Research, 27 January 2017. Available at <http://www.niesr.ac.uk/blog/will-new-trade-deals-soften-blow-hard-brexit#.WJuMADsrI2y>.

[5]   Ibid. The Ebell study estimates that the conclusion of FTAs with all the BRIICS (Brazil, Russia, India, Indonesia, China, South Africa) will lead to a long-term increase in goods and services trade of 3.2% and the conclusion of FTAs with all the Anglo-American countries (USA, Canada, New Zealand, Australia) will lead to a long-term increase of 3%. These figures are based, not on an estimate of how good a trade deal the UK is likely to achieve, but on the benefits of 'average' FTAs.

[6]   A ARMSTRONG, National Institute of Economic and Social Research, NIESR Press Note, 2 February 2017, <http://www.niesr.ac.uk/sites/default/files/NIESR%20Press%20Note%20-%20NIESR%27s%20Director%20of%20Macroeconomics%20comments%20on%20the%20Brexit%20White%20Paper%20-%20FOR%20IMMEDIATE%20RELEASE_0.pdf>.

The precise meaning of the phrase 'a new customs agreement' with the EU in the above passage from the White Paper is not immediately clear; however, it is clear that the new customs agreement would not involve membership of the EU customs union.[7] According to the White Paper the purpose of the agreement would be 'to support our aim of trade with the EU that is as frictionless as possible',[8] and thus it is likely that what is intended is a strong form of customs cooperation agreement. Such an agreement would not impact the UK's trade policy with non-EU countries and will therefore not be considered here. Although the UK's trade relations with the EU will in fact be part of its new trade policy, their complexity and importance deserves a separate chapter.[9]

Given that other chapters cover the UK's position in the WTO and international investment policy, this chapter will focus on other aspects of trade policy towards non-EU states (third countries), including preferential trade agreements and autonomous trade measures, bearing in mind that these will operate within the legal framework of WTO rules.

The common commercial policy (trade policy) is one of the Union's longest-standing exclusive competences. It has been exclusive since the establishment of the customs union in the late 1960s,[10] and its status is now defined by the Lisbon Treaty (Article 3(1) TFEU). This means that as an EU Member State the UK has not had (and could not have had as a matter of EU law) a national trade policy. In this, trade policy is very different from (for example) environment, development or social policies. This, and the fact that trade policy is necessarily concerned with relations with third countries, also means that a temporary continuation of the existing EU trade policy *acquis* after withdrawal via the Great Repeal Bill[11] will not generally be possible: since the EU has been the international actor responsible for trade policy, it is the bearer of the international rights and obligations and they cannot be transferred to the UK simply by a unilateral internal UK decision. The possibility of engineering some continuity via agreements with the EU's trade partners is considered below.

That said, and although the scope of EU trade policy has expanded over the years, there are still a number of aspects of modern trade agreements which fall outside EU exclusive competence; in addition, trade may be embedded

---

7    A customs union agreement (of which the EU itself is an example) establishes a single customs territory for WTO purposes, and thus a single external tariff, precluding its members from negotiating separate tariff agreements with non-members.

8    *The United Kingdom's exit from and new partnership with the European Union*, above n 2, para 8.1.

9    See further the contribution by P CRAIG (Ch 15) in this edited collection.

10   Opinion 1/75, ECLI:EU:C:1975:145; Case C-41/76 *Suzanne Criel, née Donckerwolcke and Henri Schou v Procureur de la République*, ECLI:EU:C:1976:182.

11   *The United Kingdom's exit from and new partnership with the European Union*, above n 2, para 1.1.

in broader agreements. For both these reasons, a number of important trade agreements (or broader agreements with trade chapters) have been concluded as 'mixed agreements' – ie jointly by the EU and its Member States, and we need to consider the implications of this for future UK trade policy.

Both these points remind us that although the UK will have some important choices to make regarding its post-Brexit trade policy, it will also be dependent on the interests and position of third countries.

We should first outline what the concept of trade policy normally includes. An initial distinction needs to be made between, on the one hand, trade policy *strictu sensu*, encompassing the legal conditions under which trade takes place, including tariffs, rules of origin, regulatory controls and trade defence instruments (the subject of this chapter) and, on the other hand, trade promotion. Trade promotion – which is often loosely referred to as trade policy – covers a country's efforts to expand its export markets or to attract inward investment by selling itself overseas via the activities of its chambers of commerce and/or high-profile political visits and deal-making. This form of trade promotion on behalf of the UK is not precluded by the EU's exclusive competence over trade policy and has always been open to the UK. Arguably it will become more important after Brexit, since the UK will presumably no longer have its membership of the single market as a selling point.[12] But Brexit will not open up any new opportunities on this front that were not already possible from within the EU.

What is covered by the term trade policy? We would include as a minimum:

- WTO/GATT schedules on goods (Most Favoured Nation (MFN) bound and applied tariffs) and WTO/GATS schedules for services.[13]
- Mutual Recognition Agreements and regulatory cooperation arrangements.
- Trade defence instruments.
- Export and import controls.
- Autonomous trade preferences for developing countries (Generalised System of Preferences, or GSP).
- Plurilateral agreements such as the Agreement on Government Procurement and the agreement on trade in services (TiSA) currently under negotiation.
- Bilateral and regional preferential trade agreements (PTAs), normally Free Trade Agreements (FTAs) although customs union agreements are also possible in theory. The scope of these has a basic content established by the WTO but beyond elimination of tariffs may vary considerably; the possibilities are discussed below.

---

[12]  A selling point in the sense that (1) third countries know that UK exports comply with EU standards – the CE mark is an important asset; and (2) inward investment into the UK will no longer carry the automatic right to sell into the rest of the EU.

[13]  This aspect is discussed by G MESSENGER (in Ch 11 of this edited collection) and will not be discussed here, except incidentally.

## 2. EXISTING EU TRADE AGREEMENTS – A POSSIBLE CONTINUITY STRATEGY

The EU has PTAs with a large number of countries, approximately 74.[14] Some of these are longstanding 'first generation' FTAs dating from the 1970s and covering free trade in goods, while some represent the new generation of 'deep and comprehensive trade agreements', covering services, investment, regulatory cooperation, sustainable development and trade-related disciplines such as intellectual property rights (IPR), procurement and anti-trust. In some cases the trade provisions are embedded in broader Association Agreements. These agreements are important for the future of UK trade policy, in the first place because they will in principle be lost on withdrawal from the EU, but in the second place and somewhat paradoxically because they could represent a significant step in building a post-Brexit trade policy.

The EU's PTAs fall into two types. Some are concluded by the EU alone and are binding on the Member States by virtue of Article 216(2) TFEU; in other words, by virtue of EU law not international law. For this category of agreement, the contracting party in international law is the EU, the territory to which the agreement applies is defined in terms of the territory of the EU, and once the UK ceases to be a member the agreement will simply cease to cover the UK.[15]

The other group of PTAs (the majority) have been concluded as 'mixed agreements' and the UK participates alongside the EU itself and the other Member States. Here the result of the UK withdrawing from the EU is more complex. On the one hand the UK is a party to these agreements and that does not change after withdrawal from the EU. On the other, it is a party as a member of the EU and all its rights and obligations under the agreement have been established on that basis. In the more recent of these agreements, this is made clear in the initial setting out of the parties in the Preamble, with the EU Member States listed together with the EU as 'of the one part' and the other state party/ies as 'of the other part'. It may also be clear from the description in

---

[14]   It is perhaps surprising that the exact number is not easy to come by, since it depends on how the agreements with groups of countries (such as Cariforum or SADC) are to be counted, and whether to include agreements signed but not yet in force, and agreements which are being provisionally applied. The above figure includes the 15 Cariforum states, the 6 members of SADC and the 6 countries of Central America, but does not include agreements with Singapore, Vietnam, the 5 countries of the East African Community and the 16 countries of ECOWAS (Western Africa), which are not yet in force nor provisionally applied. Once these agreements come into force, the number will rise to 97. Agreements are also under negotiation with several other states or regional groups, including the USA, Japan, India, China and Mercosur.

[15]   eg the FTA between the European Economic Community and the Swiss Confederation [1972] OJ L300/189 (references to the EEC are to be read as referring to the EU).

the agreement of the territories to which the agreement applies,[16] and in cases where the agreement establishes institutions, there will be representation for the EU and its Member States collectively rather than individually. All this points to the fact that these mixed agreements will require an amending protocol to adjust the agreement on UK withdrawal, just as they are amended via a protocol to accommodate the accession of a new EU Member State.

All this seems more relevant to the process of disengagement from the EU than the UK's future trade policy. But it points to a choice facing the UK, an opportunity. It could seek to negotiate a protocol that instead of managing UK withdrawal from the mixed PTA, would instead establish the UK's continued participation as a non-EU party. Thus, for example, the EU-Korea FTA (which is a mixed agreement) could become an EU-Korea-UK FTA; or the EU-Canada Comprehensive Economic and Trade Agreement (CETA, also a mixed agreement) might become an EU-Canada-UK agreement. This strategy would of course require agreement from both the EU and the other contracting party/ies, and it would require negotiation of the detail, but it does offer considerable advantages for the UK in lessening the shock of suddenly abandoning FTA-status with around 100 third countries.[17] The third country may also welcome the continuity and continued FTA access to the UK market. Three points may be noted in particular.

First, this strategy could also be used with non-mixed EU FTAs, if both parties were willing. In this case the UK would become a new party to the agreement under international law.

Second, agreements with a more complex institutional structure would be trickier to handle (though it would not be impossible). For example, would Canada accept the idea that the UK has equal representation on the relevant committee structures alongside the EU and Canada? The EEA is even more complex since it requires its parties to be a member of either EFTA or the EU (so the UK would need to seek EFTA membership), and relies on an EFTA Surveillance Authority (an enforcement body) and an EFTA Court, which the UK would need to participate in (and agree to their authority).

Third, attention would need to be paid to the fit between the EU-third country FTA on the one hand, and the FTA that is eventually negotiated between the EU

---

[16]    eg the Agreement on the European Economic Area [1994] OJ L1/3, Article 126(1) of which provides: 'The Agreement shall apply to the territories to which the Treaty establishing the European Economic Community is applied and under the conditions laid down in that Treaty, and to the territories of Iceland, the Principality of Liechtenstein and the Kingdom of Norway.'

[17]    The Government may be thinking along these lines: the White Paper has a rather vague reference to 'seeking to achieve continuity in our trade and investment relationships with third countries, including those covered by existing EU free trade agreements or EU preferential arrangements': see *The United Kingdom's exit from and new partnership with the European Union*, above n 2, para 9.11.

and the UK on the other. It is perhaps not very likely, but it might theoretically be the case that the EU-third country FTA offers more in terms of market access in a specific sector than the EU-UK deal, or (perhaps more likely) different types of arrangement for regulatory cooperation. For this reason, the protocol to the third country agreement might need to include a clause ensuring that EU-UK relations are covered by their bilateral agreement rather than by the EU-third country FTA. Partly for this reason it is likely that all parties (and especially the third country) would want to know the details of the EU-UK deal before agreeing on the details of such a solution.

A possible alternative to retaining UK participation in existing EU-third country FTAs would be to seek to negotiate a new, separate FTA with the third country partner that would reflect the EU-third country FTA. Thus, to use South Korea as an example, instead of seeking agreement on an EU-Korea-UK FTA, the UK would seek a UK-Korea FTA that would be closely aligned – but not identical – to the existing EU-Korea FTA. This would appear to have the advantage of giving the UK greater freedom to negotiate a deal that favours specifically UK interests. But that freedom carries considerable risk and costs. First, since the UK is a much less powerful negotiating partner than the EU, the third country is unlikely to offer similar levels of reciprocal market access to the UK alone; the liberalisation of services in the EU-Korea FTA, for example, is similar to the US-Korea FTA.[18] Second, under the EU-Korea FTA origin is cumulative (it is possible to include components or value from anywhere in the EU and/or Korea so as to meet the relevant threshold). Under a bilateral agreement, the UK alone will find it difficult to satisfy normal rules of origin percentages for key exports (such as cars). In contrast, were the UK to (re-)join the EU-Korea FTA, as suggested above, it is likely that such cumulation of origin could be maintained.

## 3. PREFERENTIAL TRADE AGREEMENTS

Even were the above 'continuity strategy' to be pursued, the UK will certainly want to conclude some new FTAs, for example with India, Australia or the USA. Here the main questions will be the degree of depth and scope of the FTA. Of course the deeper and more comprehensive the FTA the longer and more complicated they are to negotiate. More recent EU FTAs have taken considerable time to negotiate, partly for this reason and partly because in the last decade the EU has sought new FTAs with highly developed economies,

---

[18]   S HIX and H-W JUN, 'Can Global Britain forge a better trade deal with South Korea? This is why it's unlikely', LSE Brexit Blog, 7 February 2017: <http://blogs.lse.ac.uk/brexit/2017/02/07/can-global-britain-forge-a-better-trade-deal-with-south-korea-this-is-why-its-unlikely/>.

such as Korea, Canada, Japan and the USA, where the stakes are high and the bargaining tough. If the UK does not manage (or choose) to adopt the 'continuity strategy' outlined above, then it will be a high priority to conclude some quick FTAs, and therefore to go for agreements which are relatively simple in terms of coverage (goods and perhaps some services). If it does inherit many of the EU's existing agreements, then it will be better able to take its time to negotiate ambitious deals with new partners. Here are some of the choices.

## 3.1. FTA OR CUSTOMS UNION?

Both FTAs and customs unions are possible under Article XXIV GATT; however, FTAs are far more common and the EU is unlikely to want to establish a customs union with any third country. A customs union ties the parties to maintain the same common external tariff towards third countries, and so tends to operate regionally.[19] One of its main advantages is that Rules of Origin (RoOs) do not have to be applied in trade between customs union members, thus facilitating complex value chains. The UK will be leaving the largest customs union in the world and if it has made that choice it is unlikely to want to replace it with another, especially as this would tie its hands in negotiating FTAs with other countries. Its nearest European neighbours have opted for FTAs (for example, EFTA and the EEA), with the exception of the EU-Turkey customs union.[20] In what follows, we are assuming the choice for FTAs.

## 3.2. COVERAGE

The WTO/GATT's MFN clause imposes constraints on its members with respect to tariff barriers. Essentially, a tariff reduction below the bound rate has to take place either to everyone (MFN), to developing countries as part of a GSP scheme (see below) or down to zero with one or more parties as part of a WTO-compliant FTA.[21] We are considering the latter here. For an FTA to be WTO-compliant, Article XXIV GATT requires that 'the duties and other

---

[19]   The EU has customs union agreements with Turkey (originally seen as a precursor to accession), San Marino and Andorra.

[20]   For a convincing account of the unsatisfactory operation of the EU-Turkey customs union from the point of view of Turkey, see the written evidence of P ARTIRAN (ETG0012) to the House of Lords EU Committee, *Brexit: the options for trade* (HL 2016– 17, 72) available at: <http://data.parliament.uk/writtenevidence/committeeevidence.svc/evidencedocument/eu-external-affairs-subcommittee/brexit-future-trade-between-the-uk-and-the-eu/written/42106.html>.

[21]   Note that under MFN each WTO member sets its tariff schedules which are 'bound', meaning it cannot go above them. It can, however, go below them voluntarily and most states set their bound rates at a level which allows them some room for manoeuvre (developing countries in general have a greater gap than industrial economies, partly because the smaller the

restrictive regulations of commerce [with some allowable exceptions such as under Article XX GATT] are eliminated on substantially all the trade between the constituent territories in products originating in such territories'. Thus two parameters are pretty clear, as far as goods are concerned: the FTA must cover 'substantially all trade' and it must eliminate tariffs. The timetable for elimination should not normally be longer than 10 years, although some asymmetry in timing is allowable, especially when the deal is with a developing country. Some exceptions for sensitive products are allowed but not the exclusion of a whole sector (such as agriculture). So the variations between FTAs as far as customs duties are concerned should not be very significant (there may be differences in products excluded, or in the timetable for abolition, or in defining originating status). Note that Article XXIV GATT does not mention quotas because quotas are prohibited in any case between WTO parties.[22]

The reduction of tariffs to zero under a FTA is of course a preference, but how significant an offer it represents depends on the applied MFN starting point. On the assumption that the UK will adopt the EU's WTO bound and applied tariffs,[23] MFN rates are generally low at an average of 4 per cent, although with some peaks (such as for cars), so the significance of a reduction to zero is limited. In practice the real leverage will come from preferential tariff quotas on agricultural products and from services. Agricultural preferential tariff quotas are likely to be an important part of negotiations with many of the UK's likely FTA partners (Australia, New Zealand, Brazil, USA, Canada); they will also be contentious as far as domestic industry is concerned (already under pressure with the loss of the EU's Common Agricultural Policy subsidies) and will need to take place against an agreed (domestic) agricultural policy, which implies substantial interaction with the devolved administrations of Northern Ireland, Scotland and Wales.

For services, GATS Article V requires substantial sectoral coverage 'in terms of number of sectors, volume of trade affected and modes of supply. In order to meet this condition, agreements should not provide for the *a priori* exclusion of any mode of supply'.[24] Article V also requires the 'absence or elimination of

---

difference between bound and applied tariffs the more predictable trade is, and business likes predictability). But MFN applies to duties actually applied ('applied MFN') and that means that a party cannot decide unilaterally to reduce its tariff below the bound rate for some partners only, unless the reduction falls within the provision for developing country preferences (GSP) or operates within an Article XXIV-compliant FTA.

22  Agricultural goods may be subject to tariff quotas, ie imports of a limited quantity of the product are allowed at a reduced tariff; above that amount, the tariff rate increases.

23  See the contribution by G MESSENGER (Ch 11) in this edited collection.

24  Article V GATS. There are 4 modes of supply under GATS: (1) direct cross-border supply; (2) supply to a consumer present in the supplier's territory; (3) commercial presence; (4) supply through presence of natural persons. It will thus be seen that 'services' under GATS includes what in EU law is termed establishment.

substantially all discrimination' (ie national treatment) in the covered sectors. Reflecting GATS itself, parties may decide on which modes of supply to liberalise for each sector covered (ie how much market access to grant), although Article V does not allow the complete exclusion of a mode of supply.

So there is some room to differentiate between services agreements as regards coverage of sectors and modes of supply. As a result, two main models have emerged, the positive list and the negative list systems. In brief, the positive list system (used in GATS itself) requires the listing of all covered sectors and modes of supply; any not listed are not covered. The negative list system, used by the EU in some more recent agreements such as EU-Vietnam and CETA, provides that all modes and sectors are covered unless they are listed as excluded. The latter of course entails a very careful attention to drafting exceptions and runs the risk that new forms of service provision will be covered automatically (because not excluded). Some services will be sensitive, eg public services, transport (including air services – often the subject of stand-alone agreements), cultural services and financial services. For the UK negotiators, the movement of persons associated with liberalising Mode 3 services may also prove to be a sensitive issue. As with trade in goods, the Government will need to set priorities based on the balance of export interests and the concerns of domestic industry.

These are the baselines for WTO compatibility. It is of course not required to include both goods and services, although given the UK's interests it is very likely to want to include services in any FTA.

## 3.3.  REGULATION BEHIND THE BORDER

Modern PTAs will attempt to reduce barriers to trade in goods that result from regulation (product and labelling standards, such as food safety, vehicle safety standards, electronic products, cosmetics and pharmaceuticals) as well as regulatory and 'behind the border' barriers to services liberalisation. Advanced agreements may include some provision for mutual recognition of standards and/or conformity assessment and this will be done sector by sector. Stand-alone mutual recognition agreements – MRAs – are also possible and are considered below. Institutional arrangements for regulatory cooperation may be included, ranging from information and consultation to ongoing negotiation and cooperation designed to extend mutual recognition. As we have seen in relation to CETA and TTIP, these provisions on regulatory cooperation, whether relating to goods or services, may prove politically contentious and are premised on the existence of domestic regulatory institutions with the capacity for such international negotiation. As far as services are concerned (and recalling that 'services' in this context includes establishment in the EU law sense), some aspects of regulation (investor protection) fall within the scope of investment liberalisation.[25]

Reducing these regulatory barriers is less about bargaining and reciprocal 'offers' than about establishing relationships of trust between regulators, something which is hard to achieve at speed. The UK has such relationships, of course, with the EU as a result of its single market membership. Reducing regulatory standards in order to be able to offer third countries more liberalisation than the EU (should the UK want to consider this) would carry the high risk of losing access to the EU market.

## 3.4.    TRADE-RELATED ISSUES

Trade-related issues include domestic policies with a direct link to trade, such as competition policy (anti-trust), procurement policy and IPR. FTAs may sometimes include specific substantive commitments on competition (such as core anti-trust commitments on cartels) but more often would include procedural provisions on cooperation, information-sharing and comity between agencies. Provisions on IPR will generally reference existing international conventions as far as defining rights is concerned and may contain additional commitments on enforcement.

Public procurement is a slightly special case, since the GATT generally excludes government procurement from its provisions; the EU and its Member States (counted as one party) are among 19 parties to a plurilateral agreement on government procurement and the UK will presumably continue that membership alongside its other WTO commitments. A factor to take into account will be the extent to which the UK decides to retain in its domestic law rules similar to (or the same as) its existing EU-based procurement legislation. Since EU Member States have already opened up their government procurement markets within the EU, the barrier to further opening is (relatively-speaking) low, and since government procurement is potentially important in financial terms the EU has regularly sought to include commitments to opening procurement in goods and services through specific sectoral commitments in its modern FTAs. The UK's position may thus be influenced by its trade agreement with the EU; if this includes substantial commitments on government procurement (carrying the implication that current domestic laws will be retained) then the barrier to opening further to other third countries will be lower given the potentially significant gains in terms of reciprocal market access.

---

[25]    See the contribution by M Sattorova (Ch 13) in this edited collection.

## 3.5. NON-TRADE CONCERNS

EU trade policy is well known for introducing 'linkage' between trade and non-trade issues and the UK will need to consider to what extent it wishes to continue that practice. This has tended to take two forms.

First, conditionality clauses, linking the FTA to commitments on human rights and the rule of law; these are discussed below.

Second, trade and sustainable development chapters, committing the parties to environmental and labour standards, usually linked to specific international agreements (such as core ILO conventions, sustainable forestry standards, or the protection of endangered species), corporate social responsibility (CSR) and facilitating trade in sustainably produced goods. These chapters are useful in demonstrating the parties' commitment to certain non-trade values, including human rights and core labour standards, and also help to support and promote standards established in multilateral environmental conventions. But at present they are largely rhetorical, lacking enforcement provisions.[26] They may become more important insofar as trade agreements start to contain substantive commitments on foreign direct investment in helping to mitigate a deregulatory bias that such commitments may entail.[27]

## 3.6. DISPUTE SETTLEMENT AND DIRECT EFFECT

Dispute settlement provisions in FTAs normally include provision for a joint committee to discuss problems that arise in implementation, and for arbitration in case of a dispute which cannot be resolved informally; these procedures tend to be modelled on WTO dispute settlement. Inclusion of investment chapters has given rise to the insertion of provision for investor-state arbitration, which has been highly contentious.[28]

In general, trade agreements do not expressly envisage the possibility of private parties directly invoking its provisions in domestic courts (referred to as 'direct effect'). The domestic effect of international agreements generally depends on domestic constitutional law. EU agreements, or provisions of those agreements, may or may not be directly effective in the EU (and before the national courts of its Member States) depending on their wording and the

---

[26] That said, there do exist examples of effective procedural mechanisms, such as the Forest Law Enforcement, Governance and Trade (FLEGT) system; see further GM DURÁN and E MORGERA, *Environmental Integration in the EU's External Relations: Beyond Multilateral Dimensions*, Modern Studies in European Law, Hart Publishing, Oxford 2012.
[27] See the contribution by M SATTOROVA (Ch 13) in this edited collection.
[28] Ibid.

interpretation of the agreement by the CJEU.[29] The current tendency is for the EU to expressly exclude the direct effect of trade agreements.

As far as new FTAs concluded by the UK are concerned, the dualist nature of the UK's constitutional system will preclude direct effect, and the agreements (like any other international treaty in the UK) will need to be implemented via legislation. Should the UK decide to maintain existing EU trade agreements, as suggested above, then provision would need to be made for maintaining their effects within the UK.

# 4.  MUTUAL RECOGNITION AGREEMENTS

Agreements on the mutual recognition of standards and conformity assessment procedures (MRAs) attract much less attention than FTAs but are immensely important for oiling the wheels of trade, especially with third countries where no FTA (yet) exists (as already mentioned, mutual recognition is also frequently included in trade agreements).[30] The EU, for example, has MRAs on conformity assessment with many third countries with which it does not yet have a FTA in force, including the USA, Canada, Japan, Australia and New Zealand.[31]

Mutual recognition relates both to conformity assessment and to product standards and technical regulations. Mutual recognition of standards and technical regulations are often linked to international standards and procedures for regulatory cooperation. Mutual recognition of conformity assessment means that each party agrees to 'accept attestations of conformity including test reports, certificates, authorisations and marks of conformity' issued by the designated bodies of the other party.[32] This does not in itself imply any recognition of the other party's standards or technical regulations, or of their equivalence. A national assessment body will therefore need to assess conformity with both sets of standards (for the home and the third state market). MRAs on conformity assessment will establish general principles and then will normally contain sectoral annexes with details as to the procedures for assessing standards in (for example) pharmaceutical good manufacturing practices, telecommunications equipment, electro-magnetic compatibility and medical devices. Industry

---

[29]  The CJEU ruling will then apply to the EU, not to the third country party. The direct effect of mixed agreements can be complex, depending on the degree to which the different provisions of the agreement are covered by EU law.

[30]  K NICOLAIDIS and G SHAFFER, 'Transnational Mutual Recognition Regimes: Governance without Global Government' (2005) 68 *Law and Contemporary Problems* 263.

[31]  MRAs on conformity assessment are encouraged by WTO agreements, including the Agreement on Technical Barriers to Trade (TBT) Article 6, and GATS Article VII.

[32]  The quotation is taken from the EU-Australia MRA on conformity assessment [1998] OJ L229/3, Article 2.

representatives as well as national regulatory bodies will be involved and in the UK case both will have experience in such negotiations at EU level as well as involvement with EU international MRA negotiations.

Insofar as the Government plans, at least initially, to translate EU regulation into domestic law, the negotiation of MRAs with existing EU MRA partner countries may be relatively straightforward, especially as UK agencies and procedures will have been included within these EU MRAs. Nevertheless in terms of impact on trade these agreements should have a high priority.

## 5. AUTONOMOUS TRADE MEASURES

Autonomous, or unilateral, measures form an important part of trade policy. Before we look briefly at the different types of measure there are some general considerations. In each case, WTO rules supply a backdrop.

EU trade policy measures are adopted in the form of Regulations, so that they can be applied directly by the national authorities in each Member State. Decisions will need to be taken as to how to translate these EU Regulations (or their equivalent) into national law, and in most cases framework legislation will need to be combined with the establishment of procedures for taking decisions in individual cases – decisions which have until now been taken at EU level (in other words, a combination of primary and secondary legislation). EU trade legislation (for example, on anti-dumping) has procedures in place to balance the different interests involved, including exporters, importers and the 'Union interest'; in addition, provision is made for the participation of those with legitimate interests in the decision-making process, and for judicial review. Consideration will need to be given as to how to reflect these sometimes diverging interests in a domestic decision-making process, and what type of review process to introduce.

Trade defence includes safeguard measures (limited, temporary measures applicable to specific products from all countries) and anti-dumping measures (applicable to specific products from specific countries, alleged to be exporting below normal cost). FTAs commonly contain provisions on trade defence, not normally to exclude such measures but to impose institutional requirements such as prior consultation.

The UK will also need to consider the need and desirability of imposing import or export controls on certain products, such as controls on the export of dual-use goods; authorisation requirements for types of armaments sale; controls over the export of cultural goods (art works); controls on imports of endangered species; controls on imports of 'conflict minerals'; authorisation systems for specific products under international conventions (environmentally dangerous chemicals, chemicals that may be used to manufacture weapons of mass destruction (WMD)).

WTO rules allow members to establish unilateral non-reciprocal tariff preferences for developing countries. There is room for selection as to product categories covered. The EU has had a generalised system of preferences (GSP) scheme since the 1970s,[33] and the UK will need to decide whether to adopt such a scheme and if so how far to mirror the characteristics of the EU scheme. The EU has a tripartite system: the standard preference scheme, covering about 60 countries and applied to about two-thirds of all product lines; the 'Everything But Arms' (EBA) scheme which applies zero duties to imports of all products (except arms) from the Least Developed Countries (LDCs), covering about 40 countries; and GSP+, by which countries may receive an additional preference of zero-tariffs if they commit to ratify and effectively implement 27 core international human and labour rights, environment and good governance conventions and which currently has eight beneficiaries.[34]

The WTO requires the GSP preferences to be non-discriminatory as between developing countries, so these different schemes have to be based on objective criteria and open to all countries that meet the criteria (so for example a Commonwealth-based preference would not be permissible). Clearly the choice of GSP scheme will need to be considered as part of a broader UK trade and development policy. In the case of the EU, GSP complements PTAs concluded with developing countries within the framework of the Cotonou Convention; essentially it is intended for countries which do not have an FTA with the EU.

## 6. THE MULTILATERAL TRADING SYSTEM AND GLOBAL TRADE ENVIRONMENT

The UK will need to find its place within the WTO-based multilateral framework for trade policy, and to decide how supportive it wishes to be of multilateral trade governance. The WTO has been struggling for some time to achieve agreement across its very diverse membership so as to achieve progress on services liberalisation, or agreement on trade-related issues such as anti-trust, and some would argue that the main challenge in the next few years will be to avoid roll-back of existing trade disciplines. The EU still voices strong support for the WTO (while also pursuing other avenues) and the White Paper indicates that the UK is likely to follow the same approach:

'We have long been a strong supporter of global trade liberalisation and of the rules based system for trade. An international rules based system is crucial for underpinning free trade and to ward off protectionism.[35]

---

[33]   Regulation 978/2012 [2012] OJ L303/1.
[34]   Note that LDCs benefit from EBA and so there is no incentive to sign up to GSP+.
[35]   *The United Kingdom's exit from and new partnership with the European Union*, above n 2, para 9.1.

The UK will also pursue our long-held pro-trade and pro-development stance in the relevant international institutions and organisations, such as the G7 and G20, the UN and the OECD, with enhanced vigour.'[36]

The challenge with this approach for the UK is first, that it is much easier for very large economies such as the EU, USA or China to benefit from global free trade; and second, that the UK will not wield much power within multilateral negotiations. In practice, these will be driven by the established groups (EU, USA, the Cairns group of agricultural exporting countries and the G-90 developing countries group) and it is difficult to see how the UK might fit into these (except as an EU fellow-traveller).

The lack of progress in the multilateral agenda has led to greater importance being placed on bilateral and regional PTAs which offer more extensive liberalisation in areas covered by the WTO and rules on issues currently outside WTO disciplines. There has also been an attempt to move forward services liberalisation for a group of the 'willing and able', in a plurilateral agreement which would be open to any WTO member to join; this agreement (TiSA) is under negotiation and the White Paper indicates that the UK would wish to continue to play a role in its negotiation:

'The EU is a party to negotiations on the Trade in Services Agreement (TiSA) with more than twenty other countries. The UK continues to be committed to an ambitious TiSA and will play a positive role throughout the negotiations.'[37]

Participation in a plurilateral agreement such as TiSA will carry implications for possible future bilateral PTAs, by setting a new baseline for the services dimension of the bilateral. In negotiating a future agreement with another TiSA party the parties would be likely to seek to go beyond TiSA; a PTA with a non-TiSA party might use TiSA level commitments as a reference point.

## 7. TRADE AND POLITICS

Trade and politics have of course always been, and will continue to be, connected. Although sometimes presented as such, trade has never been a purely technocratic policy issue left entirely to trade diplomats behind closed doors. In the last few years the politics of trade has intensified and trade policy has become much more politicised (witness TTIP and CETA, as well as the successful campaign against the Anti-Counterfeiting Trade Agreement). This is for a number of reasons.

---

[36]  Ibid, para 9.19.
[37]  Ibid, para 8.20.

First, trade agreements now concern themselves more with domestic regulation (behind the border restrictions), including of services, which is seen as more intrusive and threatening domestic policy choices. Second, partly because of the stagnation of multilateral negotiations within the WTO, advanced economies such as the USA and the EU have started negotiating bilateral and regional PTAs with other advanced economies and these agreements are also seen as potentially more threatening to domestic markets and regulatory preferences. Third, since 2010 the European Parliament has had a much greater say in trade policy, including a veto right over trade agreements.

In the UK public opinion is very divided even among 'Leave' supporters, some being ardent free-traders claiming that the EU was holding back the UK from being more open to global markets, and others seeing membership of the EU as threatening domestic regulation via agreements such as TTIP. Clearly UK trade policy post-Brexit will engage with these divisions. However there are two more specific ways in which trade and politics are intertwined and which should be briefly considered here.

First is the fact that the UK will continue to participate in UNSC-mandated economic sanctions against third countries and its trade policy will reflect this. The UK already implements these sanctions, mediated via the EU, and after withdrawal it will do so directly. In addition, the UK may wish to consider adopting sanctions regimes that go beyond a UNSC regime, or imposing unilateral sanctions which have not been mandated by the UNSC. Currently, since trade policy is exclusive, such sanctions are decided at EU level, but after withdrawal the UK will need to decide itself, including possibly the decision to align itself to the EU sanctions regimes, as several other European states routinely do (an example would be the current EU sanctions against Russia).

Second is the possibility of attaching political conditionality to trade agreements. The EU does this through its so-called 'essential elements' clauses, which make the agreement conditional upon compliance with fundamental principles of human rights, democracy and the rule of law. The agreement normally contains a commitment to these concerns, together with provision for consultation and the possibility of 'appropriate measures', including suspension of the agreement, in case of serious breach. In practice enforcement is very uneven. The practice emerged in part because trade policy is one of the EU's most powerful foreign policy instruments and so can be used as leverage in persuading third countries to align themselves with broader EU foreign policy concerns, and in part as a result of the EU's specific external mission to 'uphold and promote' its values as well as its interests.[38] Although the UK, like other countries, will no doubt informally link trade policy and broader political concerns, such as a common commitment to implementing international standards on combatting

---

[38]    Article 3(5) TEU.

terrorism, money laundering or WMD, it seems unlikely that it will choose to include specific commitments of this kind in its trade agreements.

## 8.   TIMING AND SEQUENCING

A number of sequencing and timing issues arise. First is the sequencing of different trade deals. An initial priority will be to establish the UK's autonomous position in the WTO.[39] The WTO provides the baseline for preferential trade deals (they are preferential because they offer more than the MFN baseline) so a third country will need to know what the UK's MFN rates are (bound and actual) before it can judge the benefit and overall balance of a FTA.

Third countries will also want to have a pretty good idea of the UK's trade relationship with the EU before negotiating an FTA, since the value of the deal will depend on the degree to which the UK shadows EU regulation, or to what extent the UK will have market access for services, such as financial services. A highly specific tailor-made EU-UK deal on cars or aerospace, for example, would be highly significant for third countries who supply those industries.

Second is the timing of UK trade negotiations with third countries against the timetable of the withdrawal process. The UK is up against the constraints of – as well as continuing to benefit from – EU membership. Before the Article 50 notification has been given the UK is still under full Member State obligations and is not empowered to negotiate on trade matters; it could even be in breach of its obligation of sincere cooperation by engaging in informal talks about possible future negotiations, especially where this takes place in the context of ongoing EU negotiations with that trade partner.[40]

The period between Article 50 notification and withdrawal is more complex. Certainly the UK is still a Member State, and thus in principle the position is the same as that just outlined. But it can be argued that after an Article 50 notification a change of status takes place. The procedure for withdrawal has been set in motion and a withdrawal agreement is under negotiation. Part of this agreement will presumably be designed to ensure a smooth legal transition for those international agreements currently binding the UK by virtue of EU participation, as well as the future of 'mixed' agreements. It is in the interest of both the EU and the UK to ensure clarity in discussions with third country

---

[39]   See the contribution by G Messenger (Ch 11) in this edited collection.
[40]   Article 4(3) TEU. Once the Council has authorised the Commission to start negotiations with a third country the Member States are, if not under a duty of abstention, at least under a duty of close cooperation with the EU institutions 'to ensure the coherence and consistency of the action and its international representation': Case C-433/03, *Commission v Germany*, ECLI:EU:C:2005:462, para 66.

partners. This implies both that the future withdrawal of the UK should not be ignored in the EU's own trade relations and that the UK will need to discuss future relations and the management of the transition with existing EU (and future UK) trade partners; such discussions could include the 'continuity strategy' referred to above. The emphasis here is on working together, something which may pose a challenge against the background of withdrawal negotiations, but which is manifestly in the interests of all parties. Such an approach would be legally defensible (a practical expression of the duty of cooperation working in a post-notification transitional context) and politically astute, since it brings the economic weight of the EU to the table alongside the UK.

# CHAPTER 13

# UK FOREIGN INVESTMENT PROTECTION POLICY POST-BREXIT

Mavluda Sattorova*

## 1. INTRODUCTION

The debate about the future of UK foreign economic relations post-Brexit has so far been dominated by issues of global trade. However, despite having so far attracted relatively limited attention in political and legal discourse, the development of UK foreign investment policy remains a tremendously important issue, not least because of the scale of the UK's existing investment treaty commitments. Prior to the transfer of competence over foreign investment to the EU in 2010, the UK concluded at least 106 bilateral investment treaties and 75 treaties with investment provisions (most of the latter signed by the EC and subsequently the EU). There is also a strong likelihood of investment promotion and protection rules being included in future UK trade agreements both with the EU and with third states, including the eagerly anticipated free trade deals with the United States, Australia and India. Furthermore, the UK Government's economic priorities, as articulated in its recent policy documents, suggest that inward foreign investment is expected to play a key part in governmental efforts to foster economic growth after the country withdraws

---

\*    Liverpool Law School, University of Liverpool.

from the EU.[1] 'UK plc' is open for business, but what does that mean from the point of view of international investment law?

This chapter will focus on three key areas which are not only of fundamental importance to the UK as both a recipient and exporter of investment, but are also likely to pose challenges to policy-makers in formulating the country's future priorities in the field of foreign investment promotion and protection. These key areas include (1) the content of commitments to be incorporated in UK investment agreements with the EU and other countries around the globe; (2) the telos, or object and purpose, of future UK investment agreements; and (3) the process of drafting, negotiating and concluding UK investment agreements. This chapter does not aim to provide a comprehensive analysis of UK investment treaty policy but rather seeks to highlight some of the most contentious overarching issues and challenges that policy-makers would need to address after reclaiming competence over investment issues from Brussels.

## 2. LEGAL SIGNIFICANCE OF UK INTERNATIONAL INVESTMENT AGREEMENTS

What are international investment agreements and why do they matter for the UK after Brexit? Historically, the UK was at the forefront of the movement to create what we know as the contemporary investment treaty regime – a network of bilateral, regional and sectoral agreements containing investment promotion and protection rules. An historic impetus for such agreements came with the end of World War II, when the newly independent developing countries asserted their 'right to throw off the yoke of economic colonialism and rules of international law fashioned before their admission to the family of nations'.[2] Prior to that, during the colonial period, assets of British investors overseas in British territories were protected through a combination of customary international law, bilateral agreements, concession contracts and, most importantly, political and military pressure.[3] Following the demise of the imperial order, Britain – alongside other Western capital-exporting countries – faced a significant difficulty to

---

[1]  For references to deepening investment relations with the wider world and maximising wealth creation through supporting Foreign Direct Investment and Outward Direct Investment, see HM Government, *The United Kingdom's exit from and new partnership with the European Union* (Cm 9417, February 2017) pp 54–55.

[2]  E DENZA and S BROOKS, 'Investment Protection Treaties: United Kingdom Experience' (1987) 36 *International & Comparative Law Quarterly* 908, p 909.

[3]  See LN SKOVGAARD POULSEN, *Bounded Rationality and Economic Diplomacy: The Politics of Investment Treaties in Developing Countries*, Cambridge University Press, Cambridge 2015, p 48. Also S SUBEDI, *International Investment Law Reconciling Policy and Principle*, 3rd edn, Hart Publishing, Oxford 2016, Ch 4.

persuade the newly-independent developing countries to endorse the customary international norms on investment protection.[4] The primary bone of contention was the requirement that any expropriation or nationalisation of foreign-owned investments must be accompanied by a prompt, adequate and effective compensation. Since asserting economic independence from their former colonial masters inevitably entailed nationalisation of hitherto foreign-owned assets, an overwhelming majority of developing states opposed customary international rules arguing that the latter no longer suited the new economic and political reality.[5]

As customary international law on the protection of foreign property became vigorously contested, the UK – alongside its European counterparts such as Germany and Switzerland – resorted to bilateral investment protection and promotion agreements with developing states. These agreements were designed to ensure that British investments overseas would at all times be protected against expropriation and nationalisation as well as other forms of host government interference.[6] Many of the contemporary investment treaties owe their origins to the so-called Abs-Shawcross agreement, named after a German banker Herman Abs and a British lawyer and diplomat, Lord Shawcross.[7] The Abs-Shawcross Draft Convention on Investments Abroad was conceived and drawn up in 1959 as a unified 'system of joint measures' designed 'to resuscitate, on a reciprocal basis, the principle of *inviolability of private property and other private rights*' (emphasis added).[8] The idea was subsequently taken up by the OECD.[9] Despite having not been formally adopted, the draft convention became a blueprint for a rapidly growing number of investment treaties between developed and developing countries.

Many of the UK bilateral investment agreements currently in force follow this blueprint, but would it be appropriate in the new economic and political realities? First, the major issue with relying on the existing drafting patterns is that, historically, investment treaty protection was designed to safeguard

---

4   eg Latin American states refused to include the international minimum standard into multilateral agreements during the inter-war years. See also A NEWCOMBE and L PARADELL, *Law and Practice of Investment Treaties: Standards of Treatment*, Kluwer Law International, Alphen aan den Rijn 2009, Ch 1. Also S MONTT, *State Liability in Investment Treaty Arbitration: Global Constitutional and Administrative Law in the BIT Generation*, Hart Publishing, Oxford 2009.

5   See K MILES, *The Origins of International Investment Law: Empire, Environment and the Safeguarding of Capital*, Cambridge University Press, Cambridge 2013, pp 97–100.

6   H SHAWCROSS, 'The Problems of Foreign Investment in International Law' (1961) 102 *Recueil des Cours* 335. See also generally AF LOWENFELD, 'Investment Agreements and International Law, (2003) 42 *Columbia Journal of Transnational Law* 123.

7   See G SCHWARZENBERGER, 'The Abs-Shawcross Draft Convention on Investments Abroad: A Critical Commentary' (1960) 9 *Journal of Public Law* 147.

8   SHAWCROSS, above n 6.

9   OECD Draft Convention on the Protection of Foreign Property (1968) 7 *ILM* 117.

primarily UK investments in developing countries. If we examine the early generation of UK investment treaties as well as the most recent drafting patterns that emerged just before the transfer of competence to Brussels, the UK investment treaties have unequivocally prioritised investment protection over any other competing policy considerations. The forefathers of investment treaties saw investment protection as an overriding and principal goal of investment treaties. To ensure that investors from traditional capital-exporting states, including the UK, are shielded from political and other vicissitudes when investing in capital-importing states (ie developing countries) investment treaties offer substantive and procedural guarantees that are largely unparalleled in other areas of international law. These guarantees can be grouped into three key pillars of investment protection. First, under traditional investment treaties investors can enjoy broad and far-reaching substantive rights vis-à-vis host governments, such as the guarantee of fair and equitable treatment, compensation for expropriation, and sanctity of contract. These guarantees go beyond what investors would enjoy under the national laws of developed economies.[10] Second, in a manner unseen in other areas of international law, such as WTO law and international human rights, investment treaties enable investors to claim monetary remedies, ie damages, in cases where the host state fails to abide by investment treaty standards.[11] Third, investment treaties allow investors to bypass the national judicial system and bring their claims against the host government directly before an international tribunal comprised of party-appointed arbitrators.[12] Arbitral awards rendered in investor-state arbitration cases are readily enforceable in most jurisdictions and can be executed even against the will of a respondent state.[13]

The question that inexorably arises at this point is whether Brexit changes anything, given that the UK has been signing investment treaties since the 1970s. Why the need to reformulate UK investment treaty priorities? First and foremost, the need to identify and formulate new investment policy priorities stems from the fact that the UK has long led a 'double life'. It signed bilateral investment treaties with third states across the globe, including some EU Member States in Central and Eastern Europe, yet by and large investment relations between the UK and European partners were and still are regulated by EU law, in particular the disciplines on free movement of goods, services and capital and the freedom

---

[10] See MONTT, above n 4, p 76.
[11] For an overview, see A VAN AAKEN, 'Primary and Secondary Remedies in International Investment Law and National State Liability: A Functional and Comparative View' in SW SCHILL (ed), *International Investment Law and Comparative Public Law*, Oxford University Press, Oxford 2010, p 721.
[12] See Article 26 ICSID. See also C SCHREUER ET AL, *The ICSID Convention: A Commentary*, 2nd edn, Cambridge University Press, Cambridge 2009, pp 403–04; and the Report of the Executive Directors on the ICSID Convention (1993) 1 *ICSID Reports* 28, para 32.
[13] See eg *Republic of Argentina v NML Capital* 134 SCt 2250 (2014).

of establishment. As outlined below, there are fundamental differences between protections afforded to foreign investors under the bilateral investment treaty regime and EU law respectively. The question is: would the future UK investment protection policy be modelled on its investment treaties with third states or inspired by rules and practices of the EU?

One crucial difference is that under EU law investor rights come with much more 'policy space' than the existing international investment treaties.[14] Consider, for example, the key investment treaty guarantee against uncompensated expropriation. The characteristic feature of the protection against expropriation under EU law is that proprietary rights generally do not constitute an unfettered prerogative and their scope depends on the social function of the right or freedom. As the CJEU stressed in one of its judgments, the rules governing property protection,

> '... form part of the general principles of Community law. However, those principles are not absolute but must be viewed in relation to their social function. Consequently, the exercise of the right to property and the freedom to pursue a trade or profession may be restricted, provided that any restrictions do not constitute a disproportionate and intolerable interference ...'[15]

By contrast, the considerations of the margins of appreciation and proportionality are not widely endorsed by investment tribunals. As one recent tribunal suggested, investment treaty protections *should not be diluted* by precisely the same notions of 'margins of appreciation' (emphasis added).[16] Investment arbitration practice has attracted considerable criticism because expropriation provisions in investment treaties have been given a very broad interpretation. The well-known definition of expropriation was provided by an investment tribunal in *Metalclad v Mexico* which held that the finding of expropriation was justified even in cases not involving the outright taking of a foreign investor's assets. Rather, expropriation could be found whenever the state interference with the use of investment 'has the effect of depriving the owner, in whole or in significant part, of the use or reasonably-to-be-expected

---

14    J KLEINHEISTERKAMP, 'Investment Protection and EU law: The Intra- and Extra-EU Dimension of the Energy Charter Treaty' (2012) 15(1) *Journal of International Economic Law* 85, p 97. See also S HINDELANG, 'Member State BITs – There's Still (Some) Life in the Old Dog Yet: Incompatibility of Existing Member State BITs with EU Law and Possible Remedies' in KP SAUVANT (ed), *Yearbook on International Investment Law and Policy 2010–2011*, Oxford University Press, Oxford 2012, p 227.

15    CJEU, Case C-200/96, *Metronome Musik GmbH v Music Point Hokamp GmbH*, ECLI:EU:C:1998:172, para 21.

16    *Renta 4 SVSA, Ahorro Corporación Emergentes FI, Ahorro Corporación Eurofondo FI, Rovime Inversiones SICAV SA, Quasar de Valors SICAV SA, Orgor de Valores SICAV SA, GBI 9000 SICAV SA v The Russian Federation*, SCC No 24/2007, Award (20 July 2012) paras 21–23.

economic benefit of property'.[17] According to some tribunals, the fact that the allegedly expropriatory governmental measures were undertaken in pursuit of certain public policy objectives was irrelevant: 'where property is expropriated, even for environmental purposes – whether domestic or international – the state's obligation to pay compensation remains'.[18]

The first wave of arbitration cases concerning alleged expropriation by host states of foreign investments prompted concerns that a broad interpretation of the already exacting expropriation standard would fetter sovereign regulatory powers and limit states' capacity to pursue competing policies in such areas as public health and safety, environmental protection, labour standards and human rights.[19] In some countries, the debate over the scope of expropriation provisions has spilled over into domestic political discourse and forced policy-makers to clarify and scale back the relevant clauses in the new and revised investment treaties.[20] For instance, the recent Canadian investment treaties have been modified to incorporate a provision excluding certain categories of governmental action from the scope of the otherwise absolute obligation to compensate:

> 'Except in rare circumstances, such as when a measure or series of measures are so severe in the light of their purpose that they cannot be reasonably viewed as having been adopted and applied in good faith, non-discriminatory measures of a Contracting Party that are designed and applied to protect legitimate public welfare objectives, such as health, safety and the environment, do not constitute indirect expropriation.'[21]

Another highly contentious investment treaty provision is the guarantee of fair and equitable treatment. Originally it was conceived as the politically more palatable semantic alternative to the customary international minimum standard. The aim was to overcome the resistance and suspicion on the part of developing states towards the language of 'international minimum'

---

[17] *Metalclad Corporation v Mexico*, Award, 25 August 2000 (ICSID Case No ARB (AF)/97/1) (2001) 40 *ILM* 36, para 103.

[18] *Compañía del Desarrollo de Santa Elena SA v Costa Rica*, Final Award, 17 February 2000 (ICSID Case No ARB/96/1) (2000) 439 ILM 1317, para 171.

[19] See eg S Subedi, 'The Challenge of Reconciling the Competing Principles within the Law of Foreign Investment with Special Reference to the Recent Trend in the Interpretation of the term "Expropriation"' (2006) 40 *International Lawyer* 121; V Been and J Beauvais, 'The Global Fifth Amendment? The NAFTA's Investment Protections and the Misguided Quest for an International "Regulatory Takings" Doctrine' (2003) 78 *NYU Law Review* 30.

[20] See eg J McIlroy, 'Canada's New Foreign Investment Protection and Promotion Agreement: Two Steps Forward, One Step Back?' (2004) 5 *Journal of World Investment and Trade* 621. Also JE Mendenhall, 'The Evolving US Position on International Investment Protection and its Impact on the U.S. Position in the Trans-Pacific Partnership Negotiations' in NJ Calamita and M Sattorova (eds), *The Regionalization of International Investment Treaty Arrangements*, BIICL, London 2015, p 255.

[21] Annex A to Article VI of the 2009 Canada – Czech Republic BIT.

standard.[22] Over time, however, the fair and equitable treatment standard outgrew the original intentions of its protagonists and came to encompass much more than customary international law guarantees. Today, the guarantee of fair and equitable treatment is not confined to protection against denial of justice, arbitrariness and discrimination. Investment tribunals have construed the standard to require protecting investors from governmental misconduct that displays 'a relatively lower degree of inappropriateness' in comparison with the higher threshold required in establishing a violation of customary international law.[23] For instance, a lack of transparency, predictability or consistency in governmental action may be found to constitute a breach of the fair and equitable treatment standard. As one critic has put it, the fair and equitable treatment is not a standard but rather is 'a description of a perfect public regulation in a perfect public world, to which all States should aspire, but very few (if any) will ever attain'.[24] As far as its material scope is concerned, the fair and equitable treatment can be invoked to challenge actions of the executive, judiciary and legislative bodies. The 'good governance' ideals which the fair and equitable treatment has been construed to embody go beyond the classical core of administrative law practised in the UK and other Western democracies.[25]

Does EU law provide a standard of protection that would match the fair and equitable treatment standard contained in bilateral investment agreements? In the investment arbitration case of *Eastern Sugar v Slovak Republic*, the respondent state argued that a similar protection is afforded by the guarantee of equal treatment contained in Article 18 TFEU. The tribunal, however, refused to accept such an argument, instead pointing to the absence of 'any principle of EU law that specifically forbids treatment that is not fair and equitable'. The tribunal held that a protection similar to that offered under the fair and equitable treatment standard is not yet established in EU law.[26] Indeed, it is the flexibility and uniquely broad protective reach of the fair and equitable treatment standard enabling investors to obtain a remedy in a wide range of circumstances that elevates the standard well above other investment protection standards available to investors under EU law.[27]

---

[22]  JC Thomas, 'Reflections on Article 1105 of NAFTA: History, State Practice and the Influence of Commentators' (2001) 17 *ICSID Review – FILJ* 21.

[23]  *Saluka Investments BV v Czech Republic*, Partial Award, 17 March 2006 (PCA – UNCITRAL Arbitration Rules) para 293.

[24]  Z Douglas, 'Nothing if Not Critical for Investment Treaty Arbitration: *Occidental, Eureko*, and *Methanex*' (2006) 22 *Arbitration International* 28.

[25]  C Harlow, 'Global Administrative Law: The Quest for Principles and Values' (2006) 17 *European Journal of International Law* 187, p 193.

[26]  *Eureko v Slovak Republic*, PCA Case No. 2008–13, Award on Jurisdiction (26 October 2010) para 250.

[27]  See M Sattorova, 'Investment Treaty Breach as Internationally Proscribed Conduct: Shifting Scope, Evolving Objectives, Recalibrated Remedies?' (2012) 4(2) *Trade Law and Development* 315.

Last but not the least, another potentially highly problematic provision frequently featuring in investment treaties is the so-called umbrella clause – also known as the observance of undertakings, sanctity of contract, or *pacta sunt servanda* standard.[28] While the wording of the standard may vary significantly, a typical umbrella clause requires that each contracting party observes any obligation it may have entered into with regard to an investment of an investor of another contracting party. For instance, Article 2(2) of the 1994 UK–Estonia BIT provides that '[e]ach Contracting Party shall observe any obligation it may have entered into with regard to investments of nationals or companies of the other Contracting Party'.[29] In its original design, the primary objective of the umbrella clause was to protect against the interference by a host state with investors' contractual rights and to ensure that the same remedy as in the case of expropriation – full compensation – was available to investors in the event the host government reneged on or otherwise breached its contractual promises to an investor.

The umbrella or sanctity of contract clause is likely to present a challenge to the drafters of future UK investment treaties. While many of the existing UK investment treaties contain the umbrella clause, some of its key future treaty partners are emphatically against it. To name some notable examples, it is by now an established practice of the US and Canada not to include umbrella protection in their ever-growing network of investment treaties with countries around the globe. In fact, the inclusion of the umbrella clause in the un-adopted OECD Draft Convention in the 1960s was met with opposition from the US, with the Department of State seeing it as 'an undesirable attempt through international law to fetter the US Government's sovereign right of eminent domain and to bargain away its police powers'.[30] The degree of sacrosanctity which the umbrella clause affords to an investor's contract is largely unprecedented. It goes beyond the advantages of international commercial arbitration and domestic adjudication in most sophisticated national legal systems. Opposition to the idea of sanctity of state contracts has long been a feature of English law. The traditional position has been that 'where a contract is concluded by the UK Government and governed by English law, such a contract is always subject to future legislation the operation of which cannot be precluded by acts of the local authority or the central government'.[31]

---

[28] See SW SCHILL, 'Enabling Private Ordering: Function, Scope and Effect of Umbrella Clauses in International Investment Treaties' (2009) 18 *Minnesota Journal of International Law* 1.
[29] The full text is available at <http://investmentpolicyhub.unctad.org/IIA>.
[30] AC SINCLAIR, 'The Origins of the Umbrella Clause in the International Law of Investment Protection' (2004) 20 *Arbitration International* 411, p 431.
[31] DW BOWETT, 'State Contracts with Aliens: Contemporary Developments on Compensation for Termination or Breach' (1988) 59 *British Yearbook of International Law* 49, p 58.

Neither does EU law offer an equivalent standard whereby an individual or corporation would enjoy a direct standing against the host state merely on the basis of a contractual breach. Of course, although a breach of contract per se is insufficient to give rise to state liability in EU law, it is possible to envisage a scenario where a claim could be brought against an EU Member State based on a breach of contract if the state action leading to such a breach constitutes an impediment to one of the economic freedoms, such as the free movement of goods or services. However, unlike umbrella clauses in investment treaties which grant protection to investor claims arising from *any* breach of contract, the ability of an economic actor to claim redress for a contractual breach under EU law would necessitate showing something more.[32]

Likewise, investors in the EU could also rely on the Charter of Fundamental Rights, in particular Article 17 (property rights) and Article 16 (freedom to conduct business). Yet even a cursory overview of EU jurisprudence in this area suggests that neither of these fundamental rights offers the same level of protection as umbrella clauses under investment treaties. The CJEU recently had the opportunity to interpret Article 17 in *Sky Austria*.[33] It held that a contractual right – even if qualifying as an asset having economic value – should not be seen as an absolute right the interference with which would entitle the right holder to monetary redress in cases it clashes with other fundamental freedoms.[34] The more restrictive stance of EU law is in stark contrast with investment treaty law where treaties containing an umbrella clause enable investors to benefit from undiluted protection of their contractually acquired entitlements.

Not only are the investment treaty standards described above unparalleled in EU law or, for that matter, UK law and that of developed national legal systems, but international investment treaties also grant investors the right to claim damages in cases where a host government's action falls short of those standards.[35] As the recent OECD study observes,[36] the prevalence of damages in

---

[32] In this regard, the position of EU law is similar to that favoured in public international law as summarised in the *Ambatielos* case: 'It is generally accepted that, so long as it affords remedies in its Courts, a State is only directly responsible, on the international plane, for acts involving breaches of contract, where the breach is not a simple breach ... but involves an obviously arbitrary or tortuous element, e.g. a confiscatory breach of contract – where the true basis of the international claim is the confiscation, rather than the breach *per se*' (G FITZMAURICE, 'Hersch Lauterpacht – The Scholar as Judge – Part I' (1961) 37 *British Yearbook of International Law* 64–65). See also GH HACKWORTH, *Digest of International Law*, US Government Printing Office, Washington 1943, Vol 5, p 611.

[33] CJEU, Case C-283/11, *Sky Österreich GmbH v Österreichischer Rundfunk*, ECLI:EU:C:2013:28.

[34] Ibid, para 34.

[35] See SATTOROVA, above, n 27.

[36] Investor-State Dispute Settlement: Summary Reports by Experts at 16th Freedom of Information Roundtable, Organisation for Economic Cooperation and Development, Investment Division, 20 March 2012) available at <http://www.oecd.org/daf/inv/investment-policy/50241347.pdf>.

investment treaty law is almost mystifying: monetary redress is rarely available to claimants challenging governmental conduct in either national legal systems or general international law (both traditionally favour non-pecuniary forms of relief). National legal systems have traditionally restricted the use monetary damages as a remedy for governmental action and even so for governmental omissions. The longstanding maxim of 'the King can do no wrong'[37] continues to underpin legal regulation of state liability even in the UK.[38] As Lord Browne-Wilkinson cautioned,

> 'it is not really in the interests of society as a whole if you spend your time concentrating on rights of individuals to damages – because that is what we are talking about, financial compensation – against public authorities who are charged with looking after society as a whole and doing their best to perform a social welfare function; the creation of ever more duties giving rise to financial compensation is actually counterproductive in a society.'[39]

The recent rise in the number of investor-state arbitration cases has led to profound concerns about the large sums awarded to claimant investors, the high cost of the arbitration process and the budgetary implications of these losses for host states, in particular developing countries.[40] To comply with the arbitral awards, respondent states could be forced to divert the already limited funds from important socio-economic objectives, such as investment in infrastructure, education and health. Even in cases where the final award is in favour of the respondent state, the latter would have to bear significant amounts in legal expenses and the costs of the arbitral proceedings.[41] For instance, it has been reported that the successful defence against the investment arbitration claim by Philip Morris cost Australia US$35 million.[42]

---

[37] In English law, eg, although the Crown remains subject to the law, procedural requirements effectively delimited opportunities for redress in practice. See D FAIRGRIEVE, *State Liability in Tort. A Comparative Law Study*, Oxford University Press, Oxford 2003, p 8.

[38] For an overview, see I MARBOE, 'State Responsibility and Comparative State Liability for Administrative and Legislative Harm to Economic Interests' in SCHILL, above n 11, pp 382–99.

[39] FAIRGRIEVE, above n 37, p 133.

[40] OECD, above n 36.

[41] UNCTAD, *Best Practices in Investment for Development. How to prevent and manage investor-State disputes: Lessons from Peru*, Investment Advisory Series, Series B, number 10 (United Nations 2011) p 8.

[42] See 'Philip Morris fails in PCA arbitration against Australia over plain packaging laws', 29 February 2016, <https://www.iisd.org/itn/2016/02/29/philip-morris-fails-in-pca-arbitration-against-australia-over-plain-packaging-laws/>.

## 3.   TELOS: WHY SIGN INVESTMENT TREATIES?

Why should the UK sign international investment agreements that might hurt it?[43] Why afford foreign investors protection that is higher than that they would enjoy under EU law and most developed national legal systems? As the above comparative overview of the key investment protection standards under investment treaties and EU law shows, investment treaties were designed to protect investors, not to safeguard regulatory space for host governments. When examined closely, even the most recent reformed treaty models – featuring hortatory provisions such as a state's right to regulate – continue to prioritise investment protection.[44]

While one of the key premises behind the UK's withdrawal from the EU was to 'take back control', policy-makers should be mindful that new and much touted investment deals are likely to entail considerable restraints upon UK sovereignty. Political discourse after the 2016 EU referendum exposed a profound tension in how international economic agreements, including investment treaties, are portrayed in the UK. While some view global deals as a crucial, if not primary, vehicle for achieving economic prosperity post-Brexit, others express deep anxieties over the impact of such agreements on the future of public health, labour rights and the UK's regulatory sovereignty in general. One widespread (and well-founded) charge often levelled by critics against the investment treaty regime is that by subjecting states to far-reaching investment protection commitments and allowing foreign corporations to challenge regulatory acts of the host state, investment treaties and their investor-state arbitration mechanism represent an 'inherent assault on democracy' and effectively mean 'unelected transnational corporations can dictate the policies of democratically elected governments'.[45] The risks associated with corporations deploying investment treaties to challenge governmental measures may dissuade legislative decision-making in such areas as environmental protection, public health and labour rights. Concerns have been voiced that the existence of investment treaties might discourage government agencies from exercising their executive powers against

---

[43]   This question was historically raised to examine the reasons why developing countries sign investment treaties that limit their sovereignty and hurt them financially. See AT Guzman, 'Why LDCs Sign Treaties that Hurt Them: Explaining the Popularity of Bilateral Investment Treaties' (1998) *Virginia Journal of International Law* 639.

[44]   See eg M Sattorova, 'Between Regional Harmonization and Global Fragmentation? The Variable Geometry and Geography of Investment Treaty Law through the Prism of Regulatory Flexibility Provisions' in NJ Calamita and M Sattorova (eds), *Investment Treaty Law Current Issues Volume V: The Regionalization of International Investment Treaty Arrangements*, BIICL, London 2015, pp 277–305.

[45]   L Williams, 'What Is TTIP? And Six Reasons Why the Answer Should Scare You', *The Independent*, 6 October 2015, <http://www.independent.co.uk/voices/comment/what-is-ttip-and-six-reasons-why-the-answer-should-scare-you-9779688.html>.

foreign investors whose activities fall short of national regulatory standards.[46] Examples of such 'chilling' effect of investment treaties on the exercise of regulatory powers by host states include the New Zealand Government which chose to delay the introduction of a new policy on tobacco plain packaging in light of the then ongoing investment arbitration dispute whereby Philip Morris challenged the plain tobacco packaging laws of Australia.[47]

Prior to the EU referendum, the risks of exposure to corporate claims under investment treaties was somewhat limited, first, because EU law – as discussed above – regulated investor-state relations within the EU in a manner that safeguarded policy space and did not elevate investor rights into absolute guarantees. Furthermore, most of the UK investment treaties outside the EU were signed with developing countries and this, one might argue, entailed a limited likelihood of an investor from a developing state making a tangible investment in the UK and subsequently bringing claims against the UK Government. Also, the recent large-scale trade and investment agreements with developed states, such as CETA and TTIP, have been concluded or are being negotiated by the EU on behalf of its Member States. After Brexit, UK investment treaties with EU Member States (there are a few with countries in Eastern and Central Europe) are likely to become a primary legal instrument to regulate investor-state relations in Europe, thus increasing the risk of the UK Government becoming at some point subjected to investment arbitration claims – something which it had escaped owing to the primacy of EU law.[48]

Another fundamental shift in investment treaty practice globally is a rise in the deployment of investment treaties against developed countries. Highly publicised and politically sensitive investment cases, such as that brought by Philip Morris against Australia because of its anti-tobacco laws, by Lone Pine against Canada because of moratoria on fracking, and by Vattenfall against Germany because of its phase-out of nuclear energy after Fukushima, have heralded the end of an era when investment treaty law and arbitration were primarily used by investors from developed states against the governments of developing countries.[49] These cases, and a string of arbitration disputes

---

[46]    See eg K TIENHAARA, 'Regulatory Chill and the Threat of Arbitration : A View From Political Science' in C BROWN and L MILES (eds), *Evolution in Investment Treaty Law and Arbitration*, Cambridge University Press, Cambridge 2011, pp 606–628.

[47]    L POULSEN, J BONNITCHA and J YACKEE, *Transatlantic Investment Treaty Protection*, Paper No 3 in the CEPS-CTR Project on *TTIP in the Balance* and CEPS Special Report No 102 (March 2015) p 28: available <https://www.ceps.eu/system/files/SR102_ISDS.pdf>.

[48]    The Commission consistently sought to eliminate any possibilities of the investment treaties that still remain in force being deployed in lieu of EU law.

[49]    See J KLEINHEISTERKAMP, 'Investment Treaty Law and the Fear for Sovereignty: Transnational Challenges and Solutions' (2015) 78(5) *Modern Law Review* 793. Also N BERNASCONI-OSTERWALDER and M D BRAUCH, 'The State of Play in Vattenfall v Germany II: Leaving the German public in the dark', <http://www.iisd.org/sites/default/files/publications/state-of-play-vattenfall-vs-germany-II-leaving-german-public-dark-en.pdf>.

brought against the US and Canada under the investment chapter of the North American Free Trade Agreement (NAFTA), have intensified concerns over the constraining effect of investment treaties on national regulatory sovereignty.[50] Since in the aftermath of Brexit the UK is aiming to conclude international trade and investment agreements with developed economies such as Australia, Canada and the US, there is a stronger likelihood than before that the UK will face investor claims challenging various governmental measures and claiming compensation. In the energy sector, European investors too will be able to rely on investment protection rules, in particular those enshrined in the Energy Charter Treaty, in leveraging their relations with the UK Government.[51]

So the question is: does the UK need investment treaties, and do the benefits such treaties entail justify sacrificing state sovereignty, especially in the new economic and political realities the UK is facing? Now that the UK is poised to act as a host and recipient of foreign investments from developed and emerging economies, would the Government wish to face claims from foreign investors – the current estimate is that there is £1 trillion in foreign direct investment (FDI) in the UK – challenging a broad array of governmental decisions, enjoying the right to claim damages where such decisions undermine profitability of their investments, and doing so by sidestepping UK courts?

The forefathers of the first generation investment treaties reasoned that developing countries would accept the limitations upon their sovereignty if the end result meant more inward FDI flows and fostering economic development in host states. What the makers of future UK investment treaties should bear in mind is the recently uncovered evidence showing that, at the time the UK embarked on signing its bilateral investment treaties with developing countries in the 1980s, UK negotiators were fully conscious that, while the treaty regime were 'very much in our interests, it might not serve the interests of developing countries equally well'.[52] Investment treaties were pushed in the knowledge that while they provide protections to UK investors overseas, economic development and growth in host countries would not necessarily follow.[53] The primary (yet publicly unspoken) objective of the treaties was to safeguard the interests of British investors in developing countries, not of the foreign investors in the UK.[54] It is with this objective in mind that the Confederation of British Industry

---

50     See eg B CHOUDHURY, 'Recapturing Public Power: Is Investment Arbitration's Engagement of the Public Interest Contributing to the Democratic Deficit?' (2008) 41 *Vanderbilt Journal of Transnational Law* 775. Also G SAMPLINER, 'Arbitration of Expropriation cases Under U.S. Investment Treaties – A Threat to Democracy or the Dog that Didn't Bark?' (2003) 18 *ICSID Rev-FILJ* 1.

51     See esp Article 13(1)(c) of the Energy Charter Treaty (signed 17 December 1994, entered into force 16 April 1998) 2080 UNTS 100.

52     POULSEN, above n 3, p 68.

53     Ibid.

54     See eg SHAWCROSS, above n 6.

contributed to the process of shaping the UK investment treaty programme in the 1980s by pressing for very high standards of investment protection, including protection against indirect and regulatory expropriation.[55] Owing to historical realities at the time the UK bilateral investment treaty programme was being formulated, the treaty drafters were unable to envisage a scenario where the UK would rely on inward foreign investment and where the UK Government could be exposed to the risk of being sued before an investor-state arbitration panel.[56]

The fact that investment treaties were seen as instruments for advancing the interests of British investors overseas has been amply illustrated when the UK Government was made aware of the reciprocal applicability of investment treaties and the prospect of foreign investors in the nationalised Northern Rock and Bradford & Bingley bringing claims against the UK. The debate in the House of Lords revealed both surprise and resentment over the fact that investment treaties could be invoked against the UK. In the words of the then Government Deputy Chief Whip, Lord Davies, '[n]othing could be more offensive ... than the idea that someone based abroad would be able to take advantage of bilateral treaties that were designed to – and this has been accurately reflected in discussion today – safeguard, on the whole, British taxpayers regarding regimes that can act on occasion in an extremely arbitrary and unfair manner.'[57]

Not only were the UK negotiators aware that investment treaties served the interests of investors, not of host states, and might not quite lead to an increased FDI and more economic prosperity in the countries on the receiving end, but this link between treaties, foreign investment and economic growth has been disproved in a number of recent econometric studies.[58] Some obvious examples casting doubt on the importance of investment treaties for attracting FDI and fostering development include Brazil which has enjoyed a large influx of foreign investment despite having historically refrained from ratifying any bilateral investment treaties.[59] Conversely, the signing and ratification of numerous investment treaties between African states and developed economies has not entailed a tangible increase in investment flows and economic growth.[60]

[55]  DENZA and BROOKS, above n 2, p 911.
[56]  Even though investment treaties were formally reciprocal, the rationale behind their creation was to protect investors from developed states investing in developing economies.
[57]  *Hansard*, HL Deb Vol 699, cols 1481–1482 (11 March 2008), cited in NJ CALAMITA, 'The British Bank Nationalizations: An International Law Perspective' (2009) 58 *International & Comparative Law Quarterly* 119, p 230.
[58]  See eg KP SAUVANT and LE SACHS (eds), *The Effect of Treaties on Foreign Direct Investment: Bilateral Investment Treaties, Double Taxation Treaties, and Investment Flows*, Oxford University Press, Oxford 2009. See also J YACKEE, 'Do Bilateral Investment Treaties Promote Foreign Direct Investment? Some Hints from Alternative Evidence' (2010–11) 51 *Virginia Journal of International Law* 397.
[59]  K TIENHAARA, *The Expropriation of Environmental Governance: Protecting Foreign Investors at the Expense of Public Policy*, Cambridge University Press, Cambridge 2009, p 59.
[60]  Ibid.

Furthermore, even if it could be proven that investment treaties lead to more foreign investment leading to higher growth, '[i]t does not mean that societal welfare will increase, especially once resource depletion and environmental degradation are taken into account'.[61]

Now that the UK is finding itself at a receiving end, poised as a recipient of foreign investment from other developed as well as emerging economies, would future UK investment treaties be re-designed to genuinely foster development both in partner states and in the UK, in particular its regions? If sovereignty is to be sacrificed for more foreign investment in the name of economic development, the question arises as to how the commitment to development would manifest itself in future UK investment treaties. Will future treaties feature a more development-friendly definition of investment, and will there be clearly articulated and effectively enforceable provisions on investor responsibilities, including corporate social responsibility and sustainable development commitments? How will the future treaties balance the protection and promotion of investment with the need to retain regulatory freedom and to make treaties work for all, for example, by fostering development in local communities?

The existing investment treaties of the UK (which the Government is likely to use as a springboard for its future agreements) remain strongly focused on investment protection and therefore cannot accommodate the inherently clashing concerns between investment protection and national regulatory sovereignty. Furthermore, as shown above, UK investment treaties have not been designed to foster economic development (even if they often claimed the development to be their primary objective). If they were to be re-crafted into economic instruments that work for all, including in the UK and its regions, it is tremendously important that relevant provisions are included in treaty texts and that such provisions are not merely hortatory in their nature. The truism that is becoming increasingly relevant for UK society is that 'the gains of economic liberalisation should not be lost to its beneficiaries'.[62] The challenge for those in charge of the new UK foreign investment policy is to design treaties that would facilitate socio-economic growth and prosperity while ensuring that the UK retains its sovereign right to regulate and legislate in pursuit of important public policy objectives. For post-Brexit investment protection policies to be compatible with the Government's promise to transform Britain into 'a country

---

[61]   JE STIGLITZ, 'Regulating Multinational Corporations: Towards Principles of Cross-Border Legal Frameworks in a Globalized World Balancing Rights with Responsibilities' (2008) 23 *American University International Law Review* 451, p 455.

[62]   C TAN, 'The New Disciplinary Framework: Conditionality, New Aid Architecture and Global Economic Governance' in C TAN and J FAUNDEZ (eds), *International Economic Law, Globalization and Developing Countries*, Edward Elgar, Cheltenham 2010, p 122.

that works not for a privileged few, but for every one of us',[63] a bold and radical overhaul of the existing model treaties is needed.

## 4. PROCESS: THE IMPORTANCE OF TRANSPARENT, INCLUSIVE AND PARTICIPATORY INVESTMENT TREATY-MAKING

Finally, another important question the UK policy-makers will need to address in designing post-Brexit investment protection policy is how to ensure democratic legitimacy of the investment treaty regime. Long before the UK referendum on the EU membership, the processes underpinning the formation and operation of international economic agreements had been criticised for their failure to secure the democratic character of the resulting decision-making structures and outputs. In the words of Harlow, 'in global space, power is diffused to networks of private and public actors, escaping the painfully established controls of democratic government and public law'.[64] Investment protection treaties form part of the global economic governance framework which is still seen as not only 'inherently less-permeable to democratically-grounded values and conceptions of the public interest or collective good, but also less capable of generating the public policy outcomes people want'.[65]

The concrete challenges UK policy-makers will face here relate to democratic input in the process of drafting and negotiating investment treaties. Historically, treaty negotiations were a largely technocratic affair and there was limited, if any, direct and representative democratic input. Both the processes giving rise to investment policy and investor-state arbitration are vociferously criticised for their inaccessibility, lack of transparency and democratic deficit.[66] Recent political developments, both in the UK in the aftermath of the EU membership referendum and in other developed economies, have not only highlighted the importance of democratically supported trade and investment policies but also exposed the consequences of failure to engage with public concerns in formulating the state's trade and investment policy priorities.

Do constitutional arrangements in the UK enable effective public input into the making and change of investment treaties? In the EU, the European

---

[63]    Statement from the new Prime Minister Theresa May, 13 July 2016, available at <https://www.gov.uk/government/speeches/statement-from-the-new-prime-minister-theresa-may>.

[64]    C Harlow, 'Global Administrative Law: The Quest for Principles and Values' (2006) 17 *European Journal of International Law* 187, p 193.

[65]    P Cerny, 'Globalization and the End of Democracy' (1999) 36 *European Journal of Political Research* 1, p 6.

[66]    See generally D Schneiderman, *Constitutionalizing Economic Globalization: Investment Rules and Democracy's Promise*, Cambridge University Press, Cambridge 2008.

Parliament has recently been seen asserting greater control over the negotiation of investment treaties, including through seeking greater transparency with regard to the Commission's negotiating objectives and providing its opinion on the most contentious aspects of EU investment treaties. The changes introduced by the Lisbon Treaty enabled the European Parliament, in its capacity as a co-legislator on the EU's trade agreements, to assume the responsibility of ensuring that the talks on EU investment agreements are transparent and that the final outcome 'respects European values stimulates sustainable growth and contributes to the well-being of all citizens'.[67] The European Parliament's involvement in the making of TTIP (Transatlantic Trade and Investment Partnership between the EU and the US) and CETA (EU-Canada Comprehensive Economic and Trade Agreement) has signalled a shift towards a more transparent and inclusive process of international trade and investment treaty negotiations. The European Parliament has offered a platform for relevant political factions to debate and contest various aspects of the EU investment agreements and by doing so it created opportunities for a more inclusive dialogue.

The Lisbon Treaty also introduced the so-called European Citizens Initiative instrument which allows citizens to bring new issues to the political agenda through collecting a certain number of signatures in support of a policy proposal.[68] This instrument was deployed by the EU citizens seeking to halt the negotiation of the much-debated TTIP. The STOP TTIP initiative was formally submitted on 15 July 2014 and requested the Commission to halt the process of negotiating TTIP and CETA owing to these agreements giving rise to 'several critical issues such as investor-state dispute settlement and rules on regulatory cooperation that pose a threat to democracy and the rule of law'.[69] Despite the initiative having been unsuccessful owing to the Commission's refusal to register it,[70] the European Citizens Initiative framework has played a significant role by enabling civil society concerns over investment treaties and their effects to be voiced, and the issues of investment treaty protection and investor-state arbitration to be brought to the forefront of political and legal discourse.

The pressure from civil society, alongside a more assertive exercise by the European Parliament of its powers of oversight, has prompted the Commission to depart from the traditional drafting patterns and to propose some quite far-reaching reforms in the area of investment protection and investor-state arbitration provisions. One example of such reform is the incorporation of 'a set

---

[67]  See Article 11(4) TEU.

[68]  For an overview, see A WARLEIGH, 'On the Path to Legitimacy? The EU Citizens Initiative Right from a Critical Deliberativist Perspective' in C RUZZA and V DELLA SALA (eds), *Governance and Civil Society in the European Union*, Manchester University Press, Manchester 2007, p 55; M DOUGAN, 'What are we to Make of the Citizens' Initiative?' (2011) 48 *Common Market Law Review* 1807.

[69]  <http://ec.europa.eu/citizens-initiative/public/initiatives/non-registered/details/2041>.

[70]  <http://ec.europa.eu/citizens-initiative/public/documents/2552>.

of modern provisions which rebalance the rights of the state and the investor in favour of the state, and its right to regulate in the public interest' in EU-Canada CETA.[71] Other proposed changes include measures to increase transparency of arbitral proceedings,[72] creating a code of conduct for arbitrators, access to an appeal system and, a medium-term goal, working towards the establishment of a permanent multilateral investment court.[73]

Although both the Commission and the European Parliament could be criticised for not going far enough to address citizens and other stakeholder concerns over investment treaties, EU law has set a commendable example by taking its first (and tentative) steps towards facilitating greater participative democratic input in international treaty-making.[74] One potential (and highly troublesome) consequence of Brexit is that, outside the EU, and in the absence of the equivalent legal and constitutional arrangements allowing for strong parliamentary oversight of, and direct civic participation in, the making of international investment treaties, the UK Government may return to its practice of negotiating these treaties in the absence of any political debate, with the general public and other stakeholders missing the opportunity to influence their content.

Excluding the public and civil society from having a say in the process of drafting and negotiating investment treaties may be dangerous. To name one example, the history of the failed Multilateral Agreement on Investment (MAI) – the first attempt at concluding a multilateral treaty framework on investment protection and promotion – amply showed that the secrecy surrounding the negotiation process would inevitably give rise to a feeling that the public and interested civil society and stakeholder organisations were being excluded from the process.[75] The downfall of MAI was attributed to, among other things, lack of attention to public opinion and to the views of civil society, which subsequently created an air of hostility around the project and made it politically hard to justify.[76] More recently, growing criticisms of, and backlash against, international trade and investment agreements – on the both sides of the Atlantic and globally – has

---

[71] See eg the statement by the Commissioner Cecilia Malmstrom, available at <http://ec.europa.eu/commission/2014-2019/malmstrom/blog/investments-ttip-and-beyond-towards-international-investment-court_en>.
[72] See eg 'European Commission pushes for full transparency for ISDS in current investment treaties', available at <http://europa.eu/rapid/press-release_IP-15-3881_en.htm>.
[73] See MALMSTRÖM, above n 71.
[74] To the extent that US NGOs called for similar opportunities to be created for public engagement with investment and trade negotiations in the US. See eg a letter to Ambassador Froman <https://www.etuc.org/sites/www.etuc.org/files/press-release/files/letter_to_amb._froman_requesting_public_consultation_on_investment_2014.pdf>.
[75] See PT MUCHLINSKI, 'The Rise and Fall of the Multilateral Agreement on Investment: Where Now?' (2000) 34 The International Lawyer 1033.
[76] Ibid, p 1040.

been underpinned by a broader concern over the 'denationalization of clusters of political, economic, and social activities that undermine the ability of the sovereign state to control activities on its territory'.[77]

As Cotterrel argued long before the EU referendum, the legitimacy of the international economic order 'needs strengthening in the face of political opposition to globalisation, perceptions of the remoteness of international regulatory processes and suspicion about their character'.[78] The introduction of a more participatory and inclusive treaty-making process will arguably not only counter the perceptions of remoteness of international investment agreements but also crucially would facilitate a 'bottom-up' formulation of investment policy priorities whereby the interests of UK society at large, will be protected alongside investment protection through the regulation by the state of social issues such as protection of the environment, observance of minimum labour and human rights standards, and local development. These issues have long been regarded as concerns for developing countries – as something from which developed countries had to insulate their investors. The reality that UK treaty-makers will face after Brexit is that economic development, environmental protection and labour rights will need to be safeguarded for the UK and its society. Yet without sufficient input from a diverse range of stakeholders and civil society groups, the UK Government alone might not be able to represent and safeguard various competing environmental, public health and socio-economic development imperatives in drawing up its new and revised investment treaty instruments.[79]

## 5. CONCLUSION

The overarching aim of this chapter was to highlight some of the key challenges UK policy-makers would need to address when drafting and negotiating UK investment treaty instruments after Brexit. These challenges stem from a combination of factors, including (1) the significant role that future investment and trade deals are expected to play in the Government's plans to foster economic growth and prosperity in the UK after Brexit; (2) the change in the direction of investment flows and the shift from investment treaties being

---

[77]   K NOWROT, 'Legal Consequences of Globalization: The Status of Non-Governmental Organizations Under International Law' (1999) 6 *Indiana Law Journal* 579, p 586. See also CHOUDHURY, above n 50.

[78]   R COTTERREL, 'Transnational Networks of Community and International Economic Law' in A PERRY-KESSARIS (ed), *Socio-legal Approaches to International Economic Law: Text, Context, Subtext*, Routledge, Abingdon 2013, p 148.

[79]   M GEHRING and D EULER, 'Public Interest in Investment Arbitration' in D EULER, M GEHRING and M SCHERER (eds), *Transparency in International Investment Arbitration: A Guide to the UNCITRAL Rules on Transparency in Treaty-Based Investor-State Arbitration*, Cambridge University Press, Cambridge 2015.

deployed primarily by British investors against overseas governments to foreign investors, including European investors, being able to deploy investment treaties vis-à-vis the British Government; and (3) the growing backlash against and contestation of investment and trade agreements both in the UK and globally. These factors, among a vast array of other policy concerns and rapidly changing political and socio-economic realities, necessitate revisiting the blueprints the UK Government relied upon in its treaty-making prior to the transfer of competence over investment to the EU. The existing investment treaty models were drawn up at the time when the UK was primarily interested in advancing the interests of British investors overseas. Now that Britain is increasingly acting as a host country to foreign investment – from the EU, China, Japan and major developed economies – there is an urgent need to fundamentally rethink and reform UK investment treaties.

Who stands to gain from international agreements that grant foreign investors greater privileges than those afforded to corporations and individuals under UK law? Since the existing UK investment treaties prioritise investor rights in a manner unseen in EU law and the UK legal system, such treaties are incompatible with the Government's intention to use Brexit as an opportunity to transform the country that works for all, not just the privileged few. Can investment treaties be re-designed into instruments that tangibly contribute to sustainable economic development in host states, including regional and local development, and will there be sufficient political will in the UK to push for such a radical overhaul of investment treaties post-Brexit? After Brexit, the UK policy-makers will need to face the question of whether there is enough *quid pro quo* to justify maintaining the treaty regime that is premised on over-protection of foreign investors. In deciding how to proceed and which models to use in drafting future investment protection policies, policy-makers will face the choice which is, put crudely, either to continue with the established but outdated and arguably dangerous investment treaty models that prioritise investment protection, or to create new models, perhaps using as the benchmarks the UK legal system and the protections it offers to its own investors, and balancing investor rights with concrete and enforceable investor responsibilities. If Brexit is truly about 'taking back control', investment treaties should go beyond offering merely a hortatory acknowledgement of the state's power to regulate in pursuit of public policy objectives. If post-Brexit Britain is to be transformed into a country that would work for all, treaty drafting and negotiation should become more transparent and inclusive, and the contribution of foreign investment to sustainable economic development – as well as the role of investment treaties in advancing this goal – need to be among the key negotiating objectives guiding those in charge of shaping future UK investment treaties.

# CHAPTER 14

# BREXIT AND INTERNATIONAL PEACE AND SECURITY: A CRISIS FOR CRISIS MANAGEMENT?

Christian HENDERSON*

## 1. INTRODUCTION

Both before and following the referendum of 23 June 2016, news coverage and discussion predominantly focused upon the economic and immigration consequences of the United Kingdom's exit from the European Union.[1] In the lead-up to the referendum, and since, there has been a more limited focus upon the impact of Brexit upon issues affecting international peace and security.[2] However, discussions that focus purely on issues of the economy and immigration

---

\*   Professor of International Law, University of Sussex.
1   L PETER, 'Brexit: Five challenges for the UK when leaving the EU', *BBC News*, 24 June 2016, <http://www.bbc.co.uk/news/uk-politics-eu-referendum-36575186>.
2   See eg P WINTOUR, 'Defence cooperation talks with EU could delay Brexit process', *The Guardian*, 18 November 2016, <https://www.theguardian.com/politics/2016/nov/18/defence-cooperation-talks-with-eu-could-delay-brexit-process>.

tend to forget both the fact that the initial overriding purpose of economic integration between European states was to preserve peace and security amongst them and that that ability to manage refugee flows is inextricably linked to the ability to deal with international conflict and crises. While issues of peace and security will undoubtedly play a role in the forthcoming negotiations,[3] the full implications of the UK's divorce from the EU on these issues may not be known for some time. Nonetheless, the potential implications deserve reflecting upon.

The purpose of this chapter is to thus offer some reflections upon how the UK's withdrawal from the EU might affect the system of international peace and security and, in particular, the three key organisations – the United Nations ('UN'), the North Atlantic Treaty Organisation ('NATO') and the European Union ('EU') itself, in particular its Common Security and Defence Policy ('CSDP') – that exist with a crisis management function. The term 'crisis management' is employed here as it provides a useful 'catch-all phrase' to describe the various civilian and military operations that these three organisations engage in 'to prevent conflict from bursting into crisis, assist in enforcing the peace, keep the peace or build the peace'.[4] The UK has been a prominent member of these three organisations, whether due to its permanent membership of the UN Security Council, a founding member and keen champion of NATO, or through its vital contribution in the development of the EU's CSDP. Questions thus arise as to how the UK's departure from the EU will impact upon each of these three organisations and their respective roles in crisis management, as well as upon the UK itself. In this respect, the chapter offers some thoughts towards ways in which the impact might be minimised and to how any positive opportunities might be maximised.

## 2. THE UNITED NATIONS

The UK is a founding member of the UN and played a central role, along with the United States and the Soviet Union, in the drafting of the UN Charter.[5] The UK's role in the Allied powers' defeat of the Axis powers at the end of the Second World War also provided it with particular privileges within the UN. Not only did it claim a permanent seat, alongside the United States, the Soviet Union, China and France,[6] within the Organisation's most powerful organ, the Security

---

[3]   Ibid.
[4]   S BLOCKMANS AND RA WESSEL, 'The European Union and Crisis Management: Will the Lisbon Treaty Make the EU More Effective?' (2009) 14 *Journal of Conflict and Security Law* 265, p 270.
[5]   ND WHITE, *Democracy Goes to War: British Military Deployments Under International Law*, Oxford University Press, Oxford 2010, pp 58–63.
[6]   Article 23(1) Charter of the United Nations (1945).

Council, but, with this, a veto power.[7] The UN Security Council is ordained with primary responsibility for the maintenance of international peace and security,[8] and, in line with this responsibility and its powers contained within Chapters VI and VII of the UN Charter, is involved in the peaceful settlement of disputes, peace enforcement actions and peacekeeping and peacebuilding operations. It is also the sole organ of the UN – or, indeed, any organisation – with the power to adopt legally binding decisions upon the international community of states.[9] While these may be adopted ad hoc in relation to particular situations, the Council has also demonstrated more recently the propensity to adopt resolutions of a more legislative nature, such as Resolution 1373 (2001), which was adopted following the terrorist attacks of 11 September 2001.[10]

The UK has been at the forefront on issues of international peace and security since the founding of the UN, and has made a constant contribution in directing the UN's policies in this area. It has continuously drafted and voted upon resolutions of the Security Council, as well as having played a vital practical role in military actions on the ground under the authorisation of the Council.[11] Given that the UK was thus provided with a powerful and permanent presence within an organ whose responsibility is at the heart of what the UN stands for,[12] the question under consideration here is whether the UK's triggering of Article 50 TEU, and its subsequent departure from the EU, will place the UK's privileged position within the UN in jeopardy, or will have any impact upon the UN and its efforts to effectively manage international crises.

The UK's exit from the EU does not mean that it will be leaving the UN, and neither will it have any immediate impact upon its membership. While many within the UK have been critical of the EU and its constraining influence, there is no sign of any real discontentment with the UN, either within political quarters or amongst the general public. Indeed, the UN is arguably seen as emboldening – if, perhaps, not accurately reflecting – the power and relevance of the UK within the international community, rather than restricting it. In the

---

7   Ibid, Article 27(3).

8   Ibid, Article 24(1).

9   Ibid, Article 25. While the binding power of its decisions is limited to members of the UN, given that today virtually all states are members of the UN this is a distinction without a difference.

10   This resolution contained a host of measures aimed at preventing and suppressing acts of terrorism. See in general PC Szasz, 'The Security Council Starts Legislating' (2002) 96 *American Journal of International Law* 901.

11   eg in one of the rare occasions during the Cold War era when agreement could be reached within the Security Council to issue an authorisation to a member state to use force, Britain was provided with authorisation by the Council in 1966 'to prevent by the use of force if necessary the arrival at Beira of vessels reasonably believed to be carrying oil destined for Rhodesia' (UN Security Council Resolution 221, 9 April 1966.)

12   The very first purpose of the UN, contained within Article 1(1) of the Charter of the United Nations, is '[t]o maintain international peace and security'.

short term, at least, Brexit is unlikely to have any real impact upon the UK's position and status within the Organisation. The UK will remain a veto-wielding permanent member of the UN Security Council, and an equal member of the UN General Assembly, an organ that also has a role in the maintenance of international peace and security.[13]

However, while the UK will retain, for the time being, its individual powers and general role within the UN, it will lose the additional voice that it possesses within the UN through its membership of the EU. Following the coming into force of the Treaty of Lisbon in 2009, and the formation of the EU External Action Service, the EU is now able to be a part of an international convention, or act in the capacity as an observer or, in exceptional cases, a member of an international organisation. In 2011, the UN General Assembly enhanced the EU's observer status within the UN to enable it to present common positions, make interventions, and present proposals and participate in the general debate that takes place within the General Assembly each September,[14] although this did not extend to voting rights.[15] Furthermore, twice a year EU Ambassadors in New York meet with the UN Secretary-General to discuss issues at the top of the UN's agenda and the UN Security Council holds regular meetings on UN-EU cooperation.[16] While continuing its seat within the UN as an individual member, the UK will no longer have a voice through the EU, thereby limiting its overall impact within the UN and upon matters affecting both organisations.

There are, however, a number of additional possible consequences stemming from the UK's departure from the EU with more profound implications for both the UN and the UK in the medium and longer terms. The UK's imminent departure has, for example, prominently raised the prospect of a further referendum on the independence of Scotland from the UK,[17] with murmurs of a similar referendum in the context of Northern Ireland.[18] While the UK's permanent membership of the UN Security Council survived the loss of its colonies, it is, for example, unclear whether England, Wales and Northern Ireland could retain the UK's seat on the Security Council upon the break-up of the UK.

The dissolution of the Union of Soviet Socialist Republics arguably provides a precedent for it doing so. Indeed, upon the break-up of the USSR in 1989,

---

[13]    See Articles 10–15 Charter of the United Nations (1945).
[14]    UN General Assembly Resolution A/65/276, 3 May 2011, para 1.
[15]    Ibid, para 3.
[16]    See <http://eu-un.europa.eu/about-the-eu-at-the-un/>.
[17]    S CARRELL, 'Scottish parliament votes for second independence referendum', *The Guardian*, 28 March 2017, <https://www.theguardian.com/politics/2017/mar/28/scottish-parliament-votes-for-second-independence-referendum-nicola-sturgeon>.
[18]    M MARDELL, 'Could Brexit mean a referendum in Northern Ireland?', *BBC News*, 20 March 2017, <http://www.bbc.co.uk/news/uk-northern-ireland-politics-39328073>. Note the contributions by J HUNT (Ch 2) and M DOUGAN (Ch 3) in this edited collection.

the Russian Federation assumed the seat within the Council, with the Russian Federation being declared by the UN Security Council as the successor to the Soviet Union.[19] Questions arise, nonetheless, as to whether it would be so simple this time around, particularly in light of the fact that reform of the Security Council has been on the agenda for some time,[20] although, as White notes, '[t]he reform debate has stalled over the issue of the size and composition of any executive body, and the inevitable disagreements about the value of the veto'.[21] While in light of contemporary geo-political realities arguable cases can be made for the continuation of US, Russian and Chinese permanent membership, legitimate questions may be asked as to whether a weakened UK (and, potentially, France) would be punching somewhat above its weight in continuing to retain such a privileged position within the pre-eminent organ of the UN. In this respect, the break-up of the UK may well reignite stalled talks on UN Security Council reform.

In reflecting upon the somewhat anachronistic composition of the UN Security Council, and as part of discussions regarding overall reform of the Council, plans have been proposed for an EU seat, either in addition to or in place of the positions held by the UK and France.[22] Alternatively, or in addition, India, Brazil, Germany or Japan might insist that they have more of a right to assume the seat. Should any of these options debunk the UK (and France) of its permanent seat, the UK would lose arguably its most important voice in the maintenance of international peace and security and crisis management, while the Council would lose a still highly relevant, if weakened, military power. Nonetheless, while such developments would not necessarily lead to a more effective Security Council, they would arguably result in a more democratic and legitimate organ. It could, in this sense, be perceived as a positive development for the UN. With a new UN Secretary-General in place, and one with a clear intent on reforming the peace and security architecture of the Organisation,[23] opportunities for reform may indeed be on the horizon post-Brexit.

Yet, this conclusion is accompanied by one major qualification, as while political pressure may be placed upon the UK (and France) to accept a downgrading of its status within the Council, and ultimately its role in international crisis management, '[t]he fact that the permanent members control

---

19     Although Article 23(1) of the UN Charter still talks of the 'Union of Soviet Socialist Republics' as opposed to the Russian Federation.

20     See in general Y BLUM, 'Proposals for UN Security Council Reform' (2005) 99 *American Journal of International Law* 632.

21     WHITE, above n 5, p 68.

22     See eg U ROOS, U FRANKE, G HELLMANN, 'Beyond the Deadlock: How Europe can contribute to UN reform (2008) 43 *The International Spectator* 43.

23     See UN News Centre, 'UN chief Guterres announces steps towards reforming Organization's peace and security architecture', 14 February 2017, available at <http://www.un.org/apps/news/story.asp?NewsID=56173#.WQW2cWWXVo4>.

the reform debate, and that any amendment to the Charter must be agreed to by all these members, makes any drastic changes to the veto, or to those states that hold it, very unlikely'.[24]

## 3.   THE NORTH ATLANTIC TREATY ORGANISATION

While the power of the veto formally provides the UK with an enhanced standing within the UN, it was the threat or use of this power by members of the Security Council, as part of the Cold War rivalry, that meant that the Council has spent the better part of its existence in a state of partial paralysis.[25] This reality became apparent a year after the UN Charter was adopted in 1945, by which time the Soviet Union had cast its veto seven times and France once.[26] As such, the formation of NATO just a few years later in 1949 'was a response to the demonstrated incapacity of the United Nations to deal with the fundamental cleavage of the post-war period, and that NATO rather than the United Nations had become the hub of British foreign policy'.[27]

Yet, NATO is not, and was never intended to be, a de facto substitute for the UN. Indeed, the UN Security Council's remit within the UN Charter is far broader than that of NATO's contained within the North Atlantic Treaty which, as made clear by Article 5, is to operate as a collective defence organisation so as to offer protection to its members against *external* aggression. This essentially means that when it is to take action it is in collective self-defence of one of its members under Article 51 of the UN Charter which provides for the right of individual and collective self-defence.[28] Primacy is, in this respect, both implicitly and expressly provided to the UN and the UN Charter and, as a consequence,

---

[24]   WHITE, above n 5, p 68. See Articles 108 and 109(2) of the Charter of the United Nations (1945).

[25]   ND WHITE, *Keeping the Peace: The United Nations and the Maintenance of International Peace and Security*, Manchester University Press, Manchester 1997, p 7.

[26]   By the end of the first 10 years the Soviet Union had used it on 42 occasions, France on 2, and China on 1.

[27]   GL GOODWIN, *Britain and the United Nations*, Clarendon Press, Oxford 1957, p 57.

[28]   Article 5 of the North Atlantic Treaty (1949) reads:

'The Parties agree that an armed attack against one or more of them in Europe or North America shall be considered an attack against them all and consequently they agree that, if such an armed attack occurs, each of them, in exercise of the right of individual or collective self-defence recognised by Article 51 of the Charter of the United Nations, will assist the Party or Parties so attacked by taking forthwith, individually and in concert with the other Parties, such action as it deems necessary, including the use of armed force, to restore and maintain the security of the North Atlantic area. Any such armed attack and all measures taken as a result thereof shall immediately be reported to the Security Council. Such measures shall be terminated when the Security Council has taken the measures necessary to restore and maintain international peace and security'.

NATO formally requires the authorisation of the UN Security Council for any type of enforcement action that falls outside of the scope of self-defence.[29]

At the founding of NATO, and for much its existence, external threats to Europe and the North Atlantic region were most prominent. Combined with the partial paralysis that the UN Security Council was suffering, it is unsurprising that NATO states, including Britain, placed their focus for defence and security upon NATO, often to the detriment of both resolving the deadlock within the UN Security Council and, as will be set out below, developing and implementing the EU's defence and security functions and capacities. Indeed, '[d]uring the Cold War, the British government concentrated on developing the deterrent effect of NATO, recognizing that coalitions of the willing under the UN authority such as that deployed in Korea in 1950 would be the exception rather than the rule'.[30] Further explanations for Britain placing most of its politico-military weight behind NATO can be found in the fact that NATO's transatlantic aspect arguably reflected the UK's strategic orientations more than the softer European security agenda of the EU's CSDP, as well as the fact that the UK's sovereignty in the military and security realm was not undermined by membership of NATO, whereas it was to a greater or lesser extent within both the UN and the EU. As such, NATO is a security organisation in which the UK has, since its inception, played an important role and, today, is not only one of the few states that meets the Alliance's 2 per cent spending goal on defence, but forms a vital link between North American and Continental European member states.

While, as discussed above, the UK's departure from the EU will unlikely impact upon its position and attitude towards the UN in the short term, it may have longer term negative consequences for its membership, position, prestige and influence within the Organisation, and in particular within the UN Security Council and its role in maintaining international peace security. In the context of NATO, however, the NATO Secretary General, Jens Stoltenberg, has claimed that following its departure from the EU 'the United Kingdom's position within NATO will remain unchanged', going on to predict that '[t]he UK will remain a strong and committed NATO Ally, and will continue to play its leading role in our Alliance'.[31] While this seemed to predict the maintenance of the status quo, it is perhaps arguable that the UK's divorce from the EU will in actual fact have a positive impact upon its relationship with NATO as well as the overall position and standing of the Alliance.

---

[29]   Article 53(1) Charter of the United Nations (1945). Although it is not a 'regional organisation' for the purposes of this provision, there is nothing precluding the Council from authorising NATO to carry out non-defensive enforcement missions.

[30]   WHITE, above n 5, p 113.

[31]   'NATO Secretary General's statement on the outcome of the British referendum on the EU', 24 June 2016, available at <http://www.nato.int/cps/en/natohq/news_132769.htm>.

As noted above, NATO is, in essence, a collective defence organisation. Yet, during the 1990s it sought to redefine itself, and its role and function, away from being an organisation solely concerned with defensive action. In 1991, after the fall of the Berlin Wall, and realising that it would need to adapt to the new geo-political realities, NATO adopted a new Strategic Concept.[32] This document, while maintaining the 'purely defensive' purpose of the Alliance[33] nonetheless understood that 'risks to Allied security'[34] were 'less likely to result from calculated aggression against the territory of the Allies' but rather that its members would more likely suffer adversely from the instabilities in Central and Eastern Europe.[35] As such, it framed 'its strategy within a broad approach to security'.[36] By the time of its 50th anniversary in 1999, however, things had changed. In its Strategic Concept of April 1999,[37] which was adopted during NATO's controversial, not to mention illegal, intervention in Kosovo in response to Serbian persecution of the Kosovo Albanians, there was a clear shift away from defence towards 'conflict prevention' and 'crisis management', including in taking 'non-Article 5 crisis response operations'.[38] Since this time, NATO has reasserted this broadening of its role in a further Strategic Concept adopted in 2010,[39] and has been involved in several operations that could be described as being of a 'non-Article 5 crisis response' nature, for example in Afghanistan in 2003 and Libya in 2011, albeit with the UN Security Council's authorisation.[40]

This broadening of NATO's functions from being solely concerned with collective defence to encompassing crisis management, while controversial in some quarters,[41] demonstrates that it is an organisation that is able and willing to adapt to changing geo-political realities and security conditions. In this respect, it raises the prospect of it evolving further. Indeed, NATO is still a very different organisation from the EU in terms of crisis management, with the focus of the EU more on softer threats and issues internal to the Union.[42] Yet, with NATO now being of greater relevance and importance to the UK, it remains to be seen

---

[32]   The Alliance's New Strategic Concept, 7 November 1991, available at <http://www.nato.int/cps/en/natohq/official_texts_23847.htm>.

[33]   Ibid, para 35.

[34]   Ibid, para 8.

[35]   Ibid, para 9.

[36]   Ibid, para 14.

[37]   The Alliance's Strategic Concept, 24 April 1999, available at <http://www.nato.int/cps/en/natohq/official_texts_27433.htm>.

[38]   Ibid, para 29.

[39]   Strategic Concept 2010, 19 November 2010, available at <http://www.nato.int/cps/en/natohq/official_texts_27433.htm>.

[40]   See respectively UN Security Council Resolutions 1386 (2001) and 1973 (2011).

[41]   See in general B SIMMA, '"NATO", the UN and the Use of Force: Legal Aspects' (1999) 10 *European Journal of International Law* 1.

[42]   Yet Article 42(7) TEU (as amended by the Treaty of Lisbon 2007) similarly provides a mutual defence clause.

how much further NATO might be adapted, both in meeting the security needs of the UK and in plugging the resource gap within the EU's CSDP in the absence of the UK.

Furthermore, the shifts that occurred in regards to NATO's 'crisis management' function have only increased the relevance of the Alliance more generally, which may well serve the longer-term interests of the UK. Not only is it now involved in military action under this new function, both with and in the absence of authorisation by the UN Security Council, but its relevance has been highlighted relatively recently in respect to Russia's actions in Ukraine and the feared future Russian manoeuvres in Eastern Europe and the Baltic states, many of which are NATO members. As Jens Stoltenberg noted, 'as we face more instability and uncertainty, NATO is more important than ever as a platform for cooperation among European Allies, and between Europe and North America'.[43] Indeed, it is NATO, not the UN or EU, that these states have turned to in respect of this crisis, and NATO has willingly responded, providing in the summer of 2016 four battalions of up to 4,000 troops into the Baltic states and eastern Poland on a rotating basis, as well as increasing sea and air patrols.[44] This threat has also meant that relatively neutral states, such as Sweden and Finland, have at least left open the possibility of NATO membership.[45] Ultimately, these developments, in turn, raise the question of the future significance of the EU's crisis management role and responsibility.

# 4. THE EUROPEAN UNION

## 4.1. THE (PARTIAL) DEVELOPMENT AND (PARTIAL) FUNCTIONING OF EU CRISIS MANAGEMENT

The project of economic integration is concerned to a large extent with European stability and security.[46] Yet, and with a dose of irony, while the process of integration has, on the whole, been remarkably successful, European states have demonstrated 'a marked reluctance to co-operate in defence and security matters, in contrast to the relative speed with which economic integration was achieved'.[47]

---

[43]  'NATO Secretary General's statement on the outcome of the British referendum on the EU', 24 June 2016, available at <http://www.nato.int/cps/en/natohq/news_132769.htm>.

[44]  Reuters, 'NATO agrees to reinforce eastern Poland, Baltic states against Russia', 8 July 2016, available at <http://www.reuters.com/article/us-nato-summit-idUSKCN0ZN2NL>.

[45]  'Chapter four: Europe' (2017) 117 The Military Balance 63, p 77.

[46]  WHITE, above n 5, p 117.

[47]  Ibid, p 113.

Military cooperation within Europe can be traced back to the Western European Union.[48] This defensive alliance, which was born in 1948, formed the basis for future European military and defence cooperation. Following the end of the Cold War, however, the EU began to develop its crisis management role and responsibilities. Since 1999, these can be found within the European Security and Defence Policy and, following the adoption of the Treaty of Lisbon in 2007, what has now come to be known as the EU's Common Security and Defence Policy.[49]

The CSDP is a prime example of British-French joint leadership in this area of EU policy, being an initiative first contained within the Saint Malo declaration signed by the two countries in 1998,[50] and later adopted at the 1999 European Council meeting in Cologne.[51] The CSDP was designed, in essence, to provide the institutional arrangements to enable EU Member States to combine and coordinate their security and defence efforts for crisis management operations should the need arise. The Treaty of Lisbon, which came into force in December 2009, was also a cornerstone in the development of the CSDP and Article 42 TEU states that the CSDP 'shall provide the Union with an operational capacity drawing on civilian and military assets. The Union may use them on missions outside the Union for peace-keeping, conflict prevention and strengthening international security in accordance with the principles of the United Nations Charter'.[52] Furthermore, and in elaborating upon the tasks contained within the Petersberg Declaration,[53] Article 43 TEU states that 'the Union may use civilian and military means, shall include joint disarmament operations, humanitarian and rescue tasks, military advice and assistance tasks, conflict prevention and peace-keeping tasks, tasks of combat forces in crisis management, including peace-making and post-conflict stabilisation'.

In line with its crisis management function contained within the CSDP, the EU has, since 2003, undertaken over 30 civilian and military missions, mostly in Africa and Europe, under the auspices of the CSDP.[54] The EU arguably began

---

[48]    See <http://www.weu.int/Treaty.htm>.

[49]    See in general P KOUTRAKOS, *The EU Common Security and Defence Policy*, Oxford University Press, Oxford 2013.

[50]    Joint Declaration Issued at the British-French Summit, Saint-Malo, France, 3–4 December 1998, available at <http://www.consilium.europa.eu/uedocs/cmsUpload/French-British%20 Summit%20Declaration,%20Saint-Malo,%201998%20-%20EN.pdf>.

[51]    Cologne European Council Declaration on Strengthening the Common European Policy on Security and Defence, 4 June 1999, available at <http://www.europarl.europa.eu/summits/ kol2_en.htm#an3>.

[52]    On the impact of the Lisbon Treaty on EU peace and security activities see in general BLOCKMANS AND WESSEL, above n 4.

[53]    See Petersberg Declaration, Western European Union Council of Ministers, Bonn, 19 June 1992, available at <http://www.weu.int/documents/920619peten.pdf>.

[54]    For a list of the missions see the EU's External Action Service website: <https://eeas.europa. eu/topics/military-and-civilian-missions-and-operations/430/military-and-civilian-missions-and-operations_en>.

to appear as a serious crisis management organisation upon its authorisation from the UN Security Council to take over security in Bosnia from NATO in December 2004.[55] Since then the EU has been authorised to use 'all necessary means' on further occasions – notably in the Democratic Republic of Congo in 2006[56] and in Chad, the Central African Republic, and the sub-region in 2007[57] and has currently, and arguably most prominently, had a role in combating piracy off the Horn of Africa,[58] and in efforts to prevent people trafficking in the Mediterranean.[59]

However, the CSDP has never fully realised its crisis management potential. Through the CSDP, the EU has expressed its clear desire to develop an independent military capacity for the purposes of crisis management. Indeed, the 1998 Saint Malo declaration stated that 'the Union must have the capacity for autonomous action, backed up by credible military forces, the means to decide to use them and a readiness to do so, in order to respond to international crises'.[60] Yet, the missions that have been deployed under the CSDP have largely been training, advisory or monitoring missions which have been deployed post-crisis and after the worst of any violence has ended.

While the CSDP could never have provided the EU with the power to act entirely autonomously, given that any crisis management mission with an enforcement element would require the prior authorisation of the UN Security Council,[61] it has struggled to develop any sort of credible military force. First, interaction between Member States on crisis management issues under the CSDP has generally remained at an intergovernmental as opposed to supranational level, with collective decisions being made unanimously within the European Council.[62] Yet, there has also always been a tension between the EU's ambition to develop the capabilities for autonomous action, on the one hand, while continuously either deferring to NATO or accepting at least the need for access to its assets and capabilities to carry out any meaningful action, on the other.

The 2003 Berlin Plus agreement referred to a comprehensive package of arrangements between the EU and the NATO that allowed the EU to make use of NATO assets for EU-led crisis management operations and emergency situations,[63] although the two organisations have never really implemented the

---

55    UN Security Council Resolution 1575 (2004).
56    UN Security Council Resolution 1671 (2006).
57    UN Security Council Resolution 1778 (2007).
58    For information about this operation see <http://eunavfor.eu>.
59    For information about this operation see <https://eeas.europa.eu/csdp-missions-operations/eunavfor-med/36/about-eunavfor-med-operation-sophia_en>.
60    1998 Saint-Malo Declaration, above n 50, para 3.
61    Article 53(1) Charter of the United Nations (1945).
62    Article 28 TEU.
63    See <http://www.consilium.europa.eu/uedocs/cmsUpload/78414%20-%20EU-NATO%20Consultation,%20Planning%20and%20Operations.pdf>.

agreement. As such, the NATO Warsaw Summit in 2016, at which NATO and the EU again signed a joint declaration pledging greater cooperation on defence and security issues, including greater cooperation on cyber security and defence, developing coherent, complementary and interoperable defence capabilities, and stepping up coordination on exercises,[64] almost felt like an attempt at reigniting the Berlin Plus agreement. Furthermore, on 28–29 June 2016, the European Council met (just after the UK's referendum on EU membership) to discuss the political and practical implications of Brexit.[65] In its Conclusions, while the Council welcomed the presentation of the Global Strategy for the European Union's Foreign and Security Policy by the High Representative, which it sought to take forward, in the fields of defence and security the Council, again, merely spoke in terms of cooperation between EU and NATO.[66] On the ground, then, when crises have arisen requiring a decisive and effective military response, as in Afghanistan in 2003 and Libya in 2011, NATO has been the organisation to respond. As things stand this pattern looks set to continue, particularly as moves towards the establishment of EU 'battle-groups', which were designed to be 'deployed in response to a UN request to stabilize a situation or otherwise meet a short-term need until peacekeepers from the United Nations, or regional organizations acting under a UN mandate, could arrive or be reinforced',[67] have never been deployed. Given that this was a British-French concept contained within the Saint Malo declaration of 2003, it would seem to be less likely to materialise in a post-Brexit era in the absence of the UK. There are, however, other reasons to believe that negative ramifications will flow for the CSDP following the UK's departure from the EU.

## 4.2. THE ROLE OF BRITAIN AND THE POTENTIAL IMPACT OF ITS DEPARTURE FROM THE EUROPEAN UNION

The EU's CSDP will soon lose one of its major shareholders. In addition to being one of the largest financial contributors to the EU, the UK also currently has the largest defence budget within the EU and the fifth largest in the world.[68] Indeed,

---

[64] NATO Warsaw Summit Communiqué, 9 July 2016, available at <http://www.nato.int/cps/en/natohq/official_texts_133169.htm>.
[65] European Council meeting, 28–29 June 2016, Conclusions, available at <http://www.consilium.europa.eu/en/press/press-releases/2016/06/28-euco-conclusions/>.
[66] Ibid.
[67] Franco-British Summit, Strengthening European Cooperation in Security and Defence, London, 24 November 2003, available at <http://ec.europa.eu/dorie/fileDownload.do;jsessionid=lBpNTk1G52mDpQslLFk2vY9Y79K2QKDZ8MrMj1GGjysBzzJ7cLbc!-750017855?docId=125359&cardId=125359>.
[68] 'Top 15 Defence Budgets 2016' (2017) 117 *The Military Balance* 63.

the UK makes up approximately 21 per cent of the EU's military spending[69] and, together, the UK and France make up more than 40 per cent of military investments in the Union.[70] The UK's military expenditure amounts to 2 per cent of GDP, making it one of the five EU Member States spending 2 per cent or more on public defence.[71]

In addition, as well as being one of only two nuclear – or 'full spectrum' – EU nations it also provides personnel, expertise and significant equipment for EU crisis management missions, most notably maritime support to combat piracy off the Horn of Africa and to prevent people smuggling in the Mediterranean.[72] These are the very capabilities the EU needs to be able to act independently of NATO or the US, meaning that the UK's exit will have a significant impact upon the EU's already limited military capability. Questions are therefore asked of the other EU members, notably the larger Member States, as to how to deal with an already under-resourced CSDP now that it is deprived of the UK's military assets. Not doing so risks the EU playing an ever-greater peripheral role in regional and global crisis management.

Given the UK's significant assets and capabilities, as well as its policy initiatives in the realms of EU crisis management, its departure from the EU also deprives the Union of one of its leaders, with the question arising as to which state might replace it. Germany is moving towards taking on greater responsibilities in international security and crisis management, including participation in military operations, as set out in the new White Paper on 'German Security Policy' released on 13 July 2016.[73] Indeed, the White Paper asserts Germany's commitment to accepting greater responsibility for international peace and security, leadership roles, and in playing a more active security role in both the EU and NATO. However, to be able to fill the void left in the absence of British economic and military power there needs to be a firmer commitment on the part of Germany and the demonstration of a stronger strategic partnership with France. As such, until another state emerges that contributes as much as Britain currently does to the EU's security and defence capabilities its departure is likely to, at least for the short term, place more of a burden upon the shoulders of NATO.

---

69  'Chapter four: Europe' (2017) 117 *The Military Balance* 63, p 72.

70  Ibid.

71  'Defence budget increases for the first time in six years', *GOV.UK*, 1 April 2016, <https://www.gov.uk/government/news/defence-budget-increases-for-the-first-time-in-six-years>.

72  Furthermore, the Ministry of Defence's Permanent Joint Headquarters are the operational headquarters for several EU operations.

73  Federal Government, 'White Paper 2016 on German Security Policy and the Future of the Bundeswehr', 13 July 2016.

## 4.3. POST-BREXIT OPPORTUNITIES FOR THE EU'S COMMON SECURITY AND DEFENCE POLICY

There will undoubtedly be a noticeable void within the strategic, personnel, financial and hardware capabilities of the EU's CSDP following the UK's departure from it. Nonetheless, there may well also, incidentally, be hidden opportunities for its future development. Indeed, while the UK has traditionally had an uneasy relationship with European integration in general,[74] this has, in particular, manifested itself in regard to defence and security matters. Although the development of the CSDP was a prime example of British-French leadership in European security and defence, this has also never really been accompanied by a consistently active commitment by the UK to it.

The UK has, for example, tended to have a negative disposition towards the possibility of deeper political and institutional integration in European security and defence, and has, instead, privileged pragmatic cooperation with other European military powers, notably France.[75] As a result, little progress has been made in areas such as force generation, capability development and defence industrial cooperation. The UK for a long time resisted increases to the European Defence Agency budget[76] and has vetoed the creation of a single permanent CSDP military headquarters in Brussels.[77] There has also been little progress made in the implementation of some innovative CSDP clauses introduced by the Treaty of Lisbon in 2009, for example the Permanent Structured Cooperation. Britain was even reluctant towards the institutionalisation of the external policy of the Union and, for example, vetoed the proposition to call the High Representative the 'European Union Minister of Foreign Affairs'.[78] This title arguably sounded too sovereign for Britain and perhaps was seen as signifying a certain loss of power for national foreign ministers of Member States.

Furthermore, despite the UK being one of the few EU Member States that fulfils the defence spending target of 2 per cent of GDP (although this is under threat), it has arguably underperformed in the missions of the CSDP relative to its actual capabilities. For example, despite its arguably pre-eminent military capabilities amongst EU Member States, it has been fifth in terms of troop

---

[74] WHITE, above n 5, p 113.

[75] eg the various agreements with France, including the 2004 proposal on EU Battle Groups, the 2010 Lancaster House Treaties and the 2014 Brize Norton Summit.

[76] R MAASS, 'EU approves budget increase for European Defence Agency', UPI, 16 November 2016, <http://www.upi.com/Defense-News/2016/11/16/EU-approves-budget-increase-for-European-Defence-Agency/1391479327856/>.

[77] B WATERFIELD, 'Britain blocks EU plans for "operational military headquarters"', The Telegraph, 18 July 2011, <http://www.telegraph.co.uk/news/worldnews/europe/eu/8645749/Britain-blocks-EU-plans-for-operational-military-headquarters.html>.

[78] S LEHNE, The Big Three in EU Foreign Policy, Carnegie Endowment for International Peace, Washington 2012, p 19.

deployments on CSDP military missions and seventh in civilian missions.[79] While the UK has contributed – and continues to contribute – to operations such as those off the coast of Somalia, an operation which arguably serves the UK's commercial and political interests,[80] the UK's contribution on the whole to CSDP missions is relatively poor.

In this respect, it might be argued that Brexit is an opportunity in disguise for the EU.[81] Indeed, the CSDP, even if deprived of certain funding and military hardware, would be free of the restraining effect of the UK. In the absence of a rather assertive, veto-wielding and often sceptical member, an opportunity arises for improved and greater crisis management functions and ambition among the remaining EU Member States. Without the constant British impediment, decision-making will be potentially easier and proponents of the CSDP will be able to begin building a truly European crisis management structure that is willing and able to intervene in crises and make peace. We might also possibly see the creation of a permanent EU military headquarters and the strengthening of the role of the European Defence Agency. Political commitment, however, continues to be the key to unlocking these dilemmas, and it is also possible that once the UK is gone, other Member States that were hiding behind the UK's veto will then emerge as potential brakes on the further development of the CSDP.

In any case, Brexit will not per se preclude the UK joining future EU military and civilian crisis management missions, although it would participate in such missions without a say with regard to the shape or the mandate of these missions.[82] Indeed, while non-EU states have previously participated in CSDP missions, the CSDP also operates more formal 'framework participation agreements' with a number of non-EU countries, including Norway, Iceland and the US, and in this respect it is significant that the UK Government has also not ruled out future voluntary cooperation on EU defence, security and crisis management.[83]

The idea of a 'European Army', while an unpopular concept from a British perspective, has been on the agenda for decades. Yet, plans have continuously stuttered, and there has, in recent times, been less of a drive amongst Member States towards the establishment of such an army. Indeed, recent conflicts, such as in Yugoslavia, Afghanistan and Libya, demonstrated that there was never a shared will among EU members to turn CSDP into a standing European Army,

---

[79] See <https://www.instituteforgovernment.org.uk/brexit-explained/uk-eu-defence-and-security-cooperation>.

[80] M BAUGH, 'Why a stable Somalia is in our interests', *Foreign and Commonwealth Office*, 21 February 2012, <https://blogs.fco.gov.uk/mattbaugh/2012/02/21/why-a-stable-somalia-is-in-our-interests/>.

[81] 'Chapter four: Europe' (2017) 117 *The Military Balance* 63, p 68.

[82] G FALEG, 'The Implications of Brexit for the EU's Common Security and Defence Policy', *CEPS*, 26 July 2016, <https://www.ceps.eu/publications/implications-brexit-eu's-common-security-and-defence-policy>.

[83] WINTOUR, above n 2.

but rather European countries preferred to rely heavily on existing NATO assets. Furthermore, European Security and Defence Policy forces, or EU 'battle groups', which could form the basis for any such future army, stemmed from a 2004 Franco-British proposal.[84] They were envisaged as operating under a UN mandate, helping to prepare the way for the involvement of UN peacekeeping forces, but have never been developed.

While there is reason to believe that post-Brexit plans for an EU army might be reintroduced,[85] the viability of such plans has to be questioned. On the one hand, of course, there would no longer be the constant British resistance to such a move.[86] Yet, since most EU members spend relatively little on defence and crisis management, questions arise as to where the financial resources for such an army would come from. Indeed, it is arguable that whatever might have been left of the earlier aspirations of developing a standing European army eroded with the Eurozone crisis. Countries such as Italy, Spain, Holland and even Germany may not be willing to divert attention away from dealing with the economic crisis to increasing military spending for such an army. Furthermore, when one considers that the combined military spending of the UK and France makes up nearly half of the overall EU spending on military and deterrence capabilities, the UK's exit from the EU represents a serious blow to the development of such plans. In this light, while a French-German Brigade exists ('Eurocorps'), the absence of Britain's financial and military contributions might mean that a serious EU army would appear to be less, not more, likely in light of Brexit.

## 5. CONCLUSION

It is unlikely that post-Brexit either the UN or NATO will suffer any direct loss in terms of their capabilities to deal with and manage crises. The UK's departure from the EU may, of course, lead to the break-up of the UK, and such a situation would potentially have implications for the composition of the UN Security Council. It cannot be ruled out that the permanent seat of the UK within the Council would be perceived as untenable in light of such events, leading to, on the one hand, a significant loss of influence for the UK in crisis management

---

[84] Franco-British Summit, Strengthening European Cooperation in Security and Defence, London, 24 November 2003, available at <http://ec.europa.eu/dorie/fileDownload.do;jsessi onid=lBpNTk1G52mDpQslLFk2vY9Y79K2QKDZ8MrMj1GGjysBzzJ7cLbc!-750017855?do cId=125359&cardId=125359>.

[85] B WATERFIELD, 'EU army plans kept secret from voters', The Times, 27 May 2016, <https://www.thetimes.co.uk/article/eu-army-plans-kept-secret-from-voters-3j3kg3zwj>.

[86] A SPARROW, 'Jean-Claude Juncker calls for EU army', The Guardian, 8 March 2015, <https://www.theguardian.com/world/2015/mar/08/jean-claude-juncker-calls-for-eu-army-european-commission-miltary>.

within the Council, while, on the other, arguably much needed and no doubt broadly welcomed reforms of this organ of the UN.

Furthermore, it may be that the UK's absence from the EU's CSDP will significantly weaken it, and its potential for crisis management operations in the future. The CSDP will certainly witness a considerable loss in terms of military spending, hardware, personnel and, it has to be said, leadership. But Brexit may actually prove to be a significant opportunity for the CSDP and a net gain in the longer term. The UK has been a leader in terms of developing the CSDP at a policy level. But while it has set the ambitions high, particularly in terms of developing an autonomous military capacity for high-end crisis management operations, it has then proved to be an impediment to realising them. The EU now has an opportunity to recalibrate both its aims and expectations with a realistic prospect of meeting them.

In terms of high-end crisis management operations, the EU will need to reassess its current ambitions for a fully autonomous capacity, and instead develop and implement the existing agreements it has with NATO in order to undertake such operations. Given that the operations it has thus far undertaken under the CSDP have mostly been civilian and low-end military operations, it perhaps needs to focus on developing its capacity in these realms. As history has shown, when a decisive military response is required to a crisis either within or outside the Euro-Atlantic region, NATO has the means and, since 1999, developed the strategy to respond. The EU does not need to duplicate NATO's role and function in this respect. In developing and focusing upon the civilian and low-end military operations side of its crisis management function, it will also not suffer a significant loss by the UK's departure from the EU, as the UK was never a main contributor to these operations.

For the UK, its loss of membership of the EU will mean that it will lose its influence over future crisis management operations undertaken under the auspices of the CSDP, a policy it has been so instrumental in shaping. Furthermore, the UK needs to realise that, while outside of the web of the EU, it is still in Europe as a European nation, and cannot isolate itself entirely from the CSDP, particularly given that the EU, through its CSDP, still provides the structures, legal regime and procedures of a common security framework against threats such as organised crime and international terrorism. While owing to the agreements between NATO and the EU the UK will still have a connection with the CSDP, it needs to also ensure that, through a standing agreement, it has an independent potential role and stake within the CSDP in the future, which will serve both the UK and EU's interests. Ultimately, opportunities present themselves for these three organisations and the UK in a post-Brexit future. But careful forethought is required to ensure that the framework for international and regional crisis management does not, itself, end up in crisis.

# CHAPTER 15

# BREXIT AND RELATIONS BETWEEN THE EU AND THE UK

Paul CRAIG[*]

This chapter considers relations between the UK and EU as a result of Brexit. The topic is far-reaching, since chapter-length studies could be undertaken on any of the particular issues analysed in this chapter, as well as many that could not be covered within the available space. Choices perforce have had to be made. The chapter therefore focuses on three major issues that will shape the nature of relations between the UK and the EU now and hereafter.

The discussion begins with examination of the topics that will be covered in the withdrawal agreement made pursuant to Article 50 TEU, highlighting the tensions between the negotiating positions of the respective parties. This is followed by analysis of trade relations between the UK and EU in a post-Brexit world. The analysis considers the relationship between negotiation of the

---

[*]   University of Oxford.

withdrawal agreement and the trade agreement; the bargaining parameters of
the two sides; political and legal difficulties concerning a possible transitional
agreement; and what it would mean to default to the trading rules of the World
Trade Organization. The final section of the chapter addresses relations between
the UK and the EU in relation to policing and security, and the difficult issues
that will have to be resolved to ensure that these are not jeopardised when the
UK leaves the EU.

## 1.   WITHDRAWAL

It is axiomatic that relations between the UK and the EU will be markedly
affected by the content of the withdrawal agreement, and the tenor of the
negotiations that lead to it. The topics that will be addressed in the withdrawal
agreement were specified in the European Council guidelines for negotiation,[1]
made pursuant to Article 50(2) TEU, and the Council negotiating directives.[2] .
The withdrawal agreement will cover the minimum for a divorce: people, money
and borders; the treatment of issues pending at the time of withdrawal; and
dispute settlement.

The resolution of the position of EU citizens living in the UK, and UK
citizens living in the EU, is regarded as central to the withdrawal agreement by
both sides.[3] It featured prominently in UK documentation,[4] exemplified by the
statement in the White Paper on Exit that 'securing the status of, and providing
certainty to, EU nationals already in the UK and to UK nationals in the EU
is one of this Government's early priorities for the forthcoming negotiations'.[5]
In similar vein President Tusk emphasised the need to think of people first,
and to settle 'their status and situations after the withdrawal with reciprocal,

---

[1]   European Council, Brussels, 29 April 2017, EUCO XT 20004/17, paras 8–21.
[2]   Council Decision EU/Euratom 2017/… authorising the opening of negotiations with
the United Kingdom of Great Britain and Northern Ireland for an agreement setting out
the arrangements for its withdrawal from the European Union, Annex, BXT 24, Brussels,
22 May 2017. The Council directives were based on Recommendation for a Council Decision
authorising the Commission to open negotiations with the UK setting out the arrangements
for its withdrawal from the EU, COM(2017) 218 Final.
[3]   See further the contribution by S REYNOLDS (Ch 9) in this edited collection.
[4]   Prime Minister Theresa May sets out the Plan for Britain, including the 12 priorities that
the UK Government will use to negotiate Brexit, 17 January 2017, p 5, <https://www.gov.
uk/government/speeches/the-governments-negotiating-objectives-for-exiting-the-eu-pm-
speech>; HM Government, *The United Kingdom's exit from and new partnership with the
European Union* (Cm 9417, February 2017), paras 6.1–6.4; Formal Notification of Withdrawal,
29 March 2017, <https://www.gov.uk/government/publications/prime-ministers-letter-to-
donald-tusk-triggering-article-50>, p 4.
[5]   *The United Kingdom's exit from and new partnership with the European Union*, above n 4,
para 6.3.

enforceable and non-discriminatory guarantees',[6] and the European Parliament was of like mind.[7] It is, however, often easier to agree on general propositions than their detailed working out. This is more especially so when there are prominent political pressures to contend with, as there are in the UK, given that control over immigration was the most significant factor driving the Leave vote. It remains to be seen, therefore, whether there is consensus on the more particular rights to be accorded to EU citizens in the UK and vice versa.

What is clear is that the EU believes that such people should be afforded a wide range of rights. This is readily apparent from the European Council guidelines, which stressed that guarantees for EU citizens in the UK 'must be effective, enforceable, non-discriminatory and comprehensive, including the right to acquire permanent residence after a continuous period of five years of legal residence'.[8] The list of rights is specified in greater detail in the Council negotiating directives.[9] The personal scope should be applicable to economic and non-economic migrants who have resided in the UK before the withdrawal date, and their family members who join them before or after withdrawal. The material scope is also broadly conceived. There is to be a right to reside, including the right to permanent residence after five years; the right to work, which is coupled with continuation of the existing rules on access to labour markets, housing and equality in social and tax advantages; the right to take up and pursue self-employment; rights to social welfare benefits; and the continued recognition post withdrawal of qualifications that were recognised as equivalent prior to exit.[10] The UK reaction to this package remains to be seen.

The resolution of financial commitments will feature prominently in the withdrawal negotiations. It is clear from the Council negotiating directives that the financial settlement will cover liabilities, including contingent liabilities, concerning the Union budget; the termination of the UK's membership in all EU institutions or bodies; the UK's participation in EU funds dealing with specific EU policies; and the cost of moving EU agencies currently located in the UK.[11] There will, moreover, be detailed supervision over payment of these liabilities,[12] the upper estimates being in the range of €60 billion or perhaps more. The ultimate bill will be determined as much by politics as by accountancy, since both sides will be playing to their respective political constituencies.

---

6    Remarks by President Donald Tusk on the next steps following the UK notification, <http://dsms.consilium.europa.eu/952/Actions/Newsletter.aspx?messageid=11790&customerid=16061&password=enc_3936444345424338_enc>.
7    Red Lines on Brexit Negotiations, <http://www.europarl.europa.eu/news/en/news-room/20170329IPR69054/red-lines-on-brexit-negotiations>.
8    European Council, above n 1, para 8.
9    Council Negotiating Directives, above n 2, Annex 1, para 21.
10   Ibid, paras 21–22.
11   Ibid, paras 24–26.
12   Ibid, para 30.

Borders constitute the third principal topic in the withdrawal agreement, with the focus on the need to avoid a hard border between Northern Ireland and Ireland.[13] This was a constant feature in communications from the UK.[14] It was echoed by President Tusk, who spoke of the need to 'seek flexible and creative solutions aiming at avoiding a hard border between Northern Ireland and Ireland'[15] and the European Parliament.[16] The Council negotiating directives affirmed the need for flexible solutions to the situation in Ireland, stating that 'negotiations should in particular aim to avoid the creation of a hard border on the island of Ireland, while respecting the integrity of the Union legal order'.[17]

There is, therefore, much to resolve concerning money, people and borders. There are, in addition, further issues, such as cases pending before the CJEU at the date of withdrawal, and administrative issues pending before the Commission. The Council negotiating directives are predicated on continuity for matters that are already in the system. Thus the CJEU should remain competent to adjudicate in cases lodged before the withdrawal date and its rulings must be binding on the UK; the same is true for administrative procedures that are ongoing at the date of withdrawal; and it should be possible to begin administrative and judicial proceedings after withdrawal for facts that occurred prior thereto.[18] The Prime Minister has made much about ending the authority of the CJEU,[19] and UK documentation shows a keen interest in exploring other dispute resolution mechanisms.[20] It will therefore be interesting to see how such proposals are treated by the UK negotiating team.

This is equally true of issues relating to resolution of disputes flowing from the withdrawal agreement. The European Council guidelines state that the choice of the relevant mechanism should be made 'bearing in mind the Union's interest to effectively protect its autonomy and its legal order, including the role of the Court of Justice of the European Union'.[21] This is reinforced by the Council negotiating directives, which state that the CJEU must have jurisdiction in relation to the terms of the withdrawal agreement that concern EU law, including citizens' rights and financial liabilities, and that an alternative

---

[13]   See further the contribution by M DOUGAN (Ch 3) in this edited collection.
[14]   *The United Kingdom's exit from and new partnership with the European Union*, above n 4, paras 4.1–4.10; Notification of Withdrawal, above n 4, p 5.
[15]   Remarks by President Donald Tusk, above n 6.
[16]   Red Lines on Brexit Negotiations, above n 7.
[17]   Council Negotiating Directives, above n 2, Annex 1, para 14.
[18]   Ibid, paras 34–38.
[19]   *The United Kingdom's exit from and new partnership with the European Union*, above n 4, para 2.3.
[20]   Ibid, paras 2.4–2.10.
[21]   European Council, above n 1, para 17.

adjudicative mechanism would only be acceptable for disputes on other matters if it offered equivalent guarantees of independence and impartiality.[22]


## 2.  TRADE

### 2.1.  TRADE RELATIONS: ARTICLE 50 TEU

The relations between the UK and the EU will be crucially dependent not only on the terms of the withdrawal agreement, but also on a future trade agreement between the two parties. Article 50(2) TEU provides for negotiation of a withdrawal agreement, 'taking account of the framework for its future relationship with the Union'. There has been significant disagreement as to whether discussion of withdrawal and future relations should proceed in parallel, or whether there should be a phased ordering, such that discussion about the latter only commenced when there had been sufficient progress on the former. The UK strongly favours parallel discussion, while the EU advocates phased ordering. The choice markedly affects the balance of power within the negotiations. Parallelism would enable the UK to engage in trade-offs between the terms of withdrawal and future trade relations; and it would reduce the dangers of falling off the cliff-edge after two years if no trade agreement has been concluded. The phased approach means that the EU can refuse to discuss trade relations until it has secured an acceptable withdrawal deal; and it is less troubled by the prospect that a comprehensive trade deal might not be forthcoming in the two-year period.

The UK's position was initially articulated in the Prime Minister's Lancaster House speech,[23] reinforced in the White Paper on Exit from the EU,[24] and reaffirmed in the Prime Minister's notification of withdrawal letter of 29 March 2017,[25] which stated that 'it is necessary to agree the terms of our future partnership alongside those of our withdrawal from the European Union',[26] a sentiment that was repeated on three further occasions in the letter.[27]

President Tusk rejected parallelism from the outset, stating that 'starting parallel talks on all issues at the same time, as suggested by some in the UK, will not happen'.[28] He reiterated this position before the European Council meeting

---

[22]  Council Negotiating Directives, above n 2, Annex 1, para 42.
[23]  Lancaster House speech, above n 4, p 10.
[24]  *The United Kingdom's exit from and new partnership with the European Union*, above n 4, para 12.2.
[25]  Notification of Withdrawal, above n 4.
[26]  Ibid, p 2.
[27]  Ibid, pp 4, 5 and 6.
[28]  Remarks by President Donald Tusk, above n 6.

in April 2017, when he stated that 'before discussing our future, we must first sort out our past'.[29] The German Chancellor, Angela Merkel, reaffirmed this position,[30] as did the European Parliament.[31]

The European Council formally endorsed the negotiation guidelines on 29 April 2017 and adopted the phased approach. The first phase is concerned with the withdrawal agreement, the 'disentanglement of the United Kingdom from the European Union'.[32] The second phase concerns future trade relations, which can only be finalised after the UK has left the EU; an overall understanding of the framework of this relationship may be agreed during the second phase, but 'preliminary and preparatory discussions to this end'[33] can only occur when the European Council decides that sufficient progress has been made towards 'reaching a satisfactory agreement on the arrangements for an orderly withdrawal'.[34] The Council negotiating directives are predicated on the phased approach, and specifically state that no details of negotiations on trade will be forthcoming until the European Council affirms that sufficient progress has been made on the withdrawal agreement.[35]

## 2.2. TRADE RELATIONS: BARGAINING PARAMETERS

It necessarily follows from the foregoing that there may be no trade agreement at the end of the two-year period. This would be so either if the talks on the withdrawal agreement break up in disarray, because of irreconcilable differences between the two sides, or because there is insufficient progress on the withdrawal agreement until very late in the day, such that the European Council is unwilling to signal that discussion can begin on trade before close to the end of the two-year period, and there is not the requisite unanimity to extend that timeframe. The trade relations that would pertain between the UK and the EU in this eventuality will be considered below. The discussion in this section is premised on the assumption that some such discourse does occur in the two-year period. It will perforce be shaped by the bargaining parameters that each side brings to the negotiating table, and we now know a considerable amount as to the respective preferences of the two sides.

---

[29] Invitation letter by President Donald Tusk to the members of the European Council: <http://www.consilium.europa.eu/en/press/press-releases/2017/04/28-tusk-invitation-letter-euco-art50/>.
[30] '"Brexit": Chancellor Merkel warns of UK "illusions" over talks with EU', BBC News, 27 April 2017, <http://www.bbc.co.uk/news/world-europe-39730326>.
[31] Red Lines, above n 7.
[32] European Council, above n 1, para 4.
[33] Ibid, para 5.
[34] Ibid, para 5.
[35] Council Negotiating Directives, above n 2, Annex 1, para 19.

From the UK's perspective, we know what the UK Government does not want. It does not seek membership of the entire single market, since this requires acceptance of free movement of people. It does not wish for a customs union deal, since this would unduly circumscribe the UK's ability to enter trading arrangements with other parties.[36] What the Government does seek is a far-reaching and comprehensive trade agreement, covering services, intellectual property and the like,[37] which embodies 'a deep and special partnership between the UK and the EU, taking in both economic and security cooperation'.[38] The economic reality for the UK is that a free trade agreement (FTA) in a post-Brexit world with the EU would have to include services, since if it did not then its significance would be greatly diminished. This is reflected in the withdrawal letter, which was framed in terms of a bold and ambitious FTA that would include financial services and network industries.[39]

From the EU's perspective, the European Council negotiation guidelines set the bargaining parameters. The EU's interest in a future trade deal is emphasised, but it is closely circumscribed: it cannot amount to participation in the single market; it precludes participation in the single market on a sector-by-sector approach; and it is predicated on the assumption that a 'non-member of the Union, that does not live up to the same obligations as a member, cannot have the same rights and enjoy the same benefits as a member'.[40] The guidelines also state that any trade deal must ensure 'a level playing field, notably in terms of competition and state aid, and in this regard encompass safeguards against unfair competitive advantages through, inter alia, tax, social, environmental and regulatory measures and practices',[41] thereby responding to the UK's suggestion that it might become a low-tax haven if it did not obtain a trade agreement from the EU.

The respective bargaining positions of the UK and the EU will not render it easy to complete a trade deal. The UK Government's oft-repeated desire is that the FTA should be concluded within the two-year period.[42] This is unlikely to occur, given the complexity of the negotiations required to secure such a far-reaching deal, even if discussion of the trade agreement takes place in parallel with the withdrawal agreement, which is improbable. It could take anywhere in the order of five to six years, before the terms of an ambitious FTA are secured.

This is in part because of the inherent complexity of the negotiations surrounding such agreements. Free trade deals do not come in only one size.

---

36    Lancaster House speech, above n 4, p 8.
37    Notification of Withdrawal, above n 4, p 5.
38    Ibid, p 5.
39    Ibid, p 5.
40    European Council, above n 1, paras 1 and 21.
41    Ibid, para 21.
42    *The United Kingdom's exit from and new partnership with the European Union*, above n 4, paras 12.2–12.3; Notification of Withdrawal, above n 4, p 6.

The core of a free trade agreement is the abolition of tariffs and quotas on goods. There will normally be provisions dealing with technical barriers to trade, phytosanitary matters, rules of origin, investment, safeguards, cross-border trade, the environment, customs administration and the like. More ambitious trade agreements aim for liberalisation in areas such as services and investment, cover intellectual property rights and competition, and include provisions on labour and environmental standards.[43] The US-Australia agreement is 264 pages long, which is about average. This is dwarfed by the EU-Canada Comprehensive Economic and Trade Agreement, CETA, which took seven years to negotiate. It is in excess of 1,500 pages, and this is so even though its coverage of services is limited.[44]

The length of time to secure a comprehensive trade agreement is also in part because such an agreement might be a mixed agreement,[45] since its subject matter might go beyond the EU's exclusive external competence.[46] It would therefore require ratification by the 27 Member States, plus the regions of some states, as well as the EU. Advocate General Sharpston conceded that a ratification process involving all the Member States alongside the European Union was likely to be both cumbersome and complex, and that it could involve the risk that the 'outcome of lengthy negotiations may be blocked by a few Member States or even by a single Member State',[47] but that the need for rapidity of EU external action could not affect the question of who had competence to conclude the agreement. To be balanced against this is the fact that, while the CJEU agreed that it was a mixed agreement, it took a broad view of the common commercial policy and the sphere of the EU's exclusive external competence, thereby reducing the range of agreements that would be regarded as mixed.[48]

## 2.3. TRADE RELATIONS: TRANSITION

The UK Government has in truth equivocated about the conclusion of a trade agreement. It has repeatedly contended that withdrawal and trade agreements can be concluded in two years.[49] It has, at the same time, acknowledged the

---

[43] <http://www.trade.gov/fta/; https://ustr.gov/trade-agreements/free-trade-agreements/australian-fta>.
[44] <http://ec.europa.eu/trade/policy/in-focus/ceta/>.
[45] P KOUTRAKOS and C HILLION, *Mixed Agreements Revisited: The EU and its Member States in the World*, Hart Publishing, Oxford 2010.
[46] See the Opinion of Advocate General Sharpston for the complexity of the issues that can arise: Opinion 2/15, *Conclusion of the Free Trade Agreement between the European Union and Singapore*, 21 December 2016.
[47] Ibid, para 565.
[48] Opinion 2/15, *Conclusion of the Free Trade Agreement between the European Union and Singapore*, 16 May 2017.
[49] Notification of Withdrawal, above n 4, p 6.

likely need for some transitional arrangement on the assumption that the new trade order to which the UK will move may not be fully determined by the end of the two-year period. This serves to explain statements of the following kind:

> 'In order to avoid any cliff-edge as we move from our current relationship to our future partnership, people and businesses in both the UK and the EU would benefit from implementation periods to adjust in a smooth and orderly way to new arrangements. It would help both sides to minimise unnecessary disruption if we agree this principle early in the process.'[50]

The European Council spoke of a transition agreement to the extent to which it was necessary and legally possible.[51] The legality of such an agreement is uncertain.[52] Much depends on its content and objective. It might assume three different forms.[53]

### 2.3.1. Transition and Change

A transitional agreement might be directed to the future, providing a bridge between the status quo and the future agreement, the details of which may not be concluded within two years. This is the assumption in the Council negotiating directives.[54] It might be conceived as part of the withdrawal agreement, or as independent thereof. There are, however, difficulties in both respects.

There are substantive issues as to how far transitional provisions concerning future trade could be appended to the withdrawal agreement. Article 50(2) TEU states that the withdrawal agreement can take account of the state's future relationship with the EU, which undoubtedly contains interpretive leeway, but if transitional provisions are to be of practical use, they will have to be detailed.

This leads to a procedural difficulty, which is that detailed transitional provisions smoothing future trade relations might not fall within the EU's exclusive competence. They would require ratification by all Member States, following the logic of mixed agreements, and hence could not readily be part of a withdrawal agreement, although this may be less likely now given the CJEU's broad interpretation of the EU's exclusive external competence in relation to the common commercial policy. If ratification in all Member States as well as

---

[50]   Ibid, p 6.
[51]   European Council, above n 1, para 6.
[52]   See also P ELEFTHERIADIS, '"Parallel Sources": How to Construct the Transitional Brexit Arrangement' available at <https://www.law.ox.ac.uk/business-law-blog/blog/2017/02/how-make-transitional-brexit-arrangement>.
[53]   The material in this section is taken from P CRAIG, 'Process: Brexit and the Anatomy of Article 50' in F FABBRINI (ed), *The Law and Politics of Brexit*, Oxford University Press, Oxford 2017, Ch 3.
[54]   Council Negotiating Directives, above n 2, Annex 1, para 19.

the EU were required, this could lead to considerable delay, hence undermining the rationale for transitional provisions. This problem would persist even if the transitional agreement were a separate agreement.

### 2.3.2.   Transition and Continuity

The concept of transition might alternatively connote continuation of some EU Treaty provisions, pending conclusion of a future agreement. If there is no meaningful discussion of future trade relations within the two-year period, the concept of transition could not connote a bridge between the old and the new, since by definition the content of the new order would not be known. The existing EU rules provide a framework that would obviate the dangers of the cliff-edge. There will be political challenges in securing acceptance of any deal in the UK and the EU. Such a transitional agreement might be part of the withdrawal agreement, or independent thereof, but there are legal difficulties.

There are substantive issues as to compatibility with the EU legal order. International agreements are regularly scrutinised in this regard.[55] It would therefore have to be decided whether continuation of some EU provisions was compatible with the EU Treaty, and its underlying principles, which would be determined by the CJEU. The CJEU would, moreover, have jurisdiction over the transitional provisions. Denial of its interpretive authority over Treaty provisions during a transitional period would be regarded as infringing the autonomy of the EU legal order.[56] As the European Council guidelines noted, prolongation of the EU *acquis* 'would require existing Union regulatory, budgetary, supervisory, judiciary and enforcement instruments and structures to apply'.[57]

There are, moreover, procedural problems if the transitional provisions are appended to the withdrawal agreement. Article 50(3) TEU provides that the Treaties cease to apply to the Member State from the date when the withdrawal agreement enters into force. This creates a Catch-22. The agreement must be legally in force for the transitional provisions to apply. However, when the agreement enters into force, Article 50 TEU stipulates that the Treaties cease to apply. There is no provision allowing some of the Treaty articles to continue pending completion of a trade agreement at an unspecified future date.

---

55   See eg Opinion 1/91, *Draft agreement between the Community, on the one hand, and the countries of the European Free Trade Association, on the other, relating to the creation of the European Economic Area*, EU:C:1991:490, paras 61–65; Opinion 1/92, *Draft agreement between the Community, on the one hand, and the countries of the European Free Trade Association, on the other, relating to the creation of the European Economic Area*, EU:C:1992:189, paras 32 and 41; Opinion 2/13, *Draft international agreement – Accession of the European Union to the European Convention for the Protection of Human Rights and Fundamental Freedoms*, EU:C:2014:2454, para 201.

56   Opinion 2/13, above n 55, para 205.

57   European Council, above n 1, para 6.

It is, moreover, questionable whether a withdrawal agreement could perpetuate some provisions of membership beyond two years, given that the voting rules for the withdrawal agreement only require a qualified majority, whereas unanimity is the criterion for extension of the time to secure a withdrawal agreement over and beyond two years. A withdrawal agreement concluded by qualified majority that did not terminate all the withdrawing state's rights and obligations on the date when the agreement took effect could be regarded as circumventing the unanimity requirement in Article 50(3) TEU for an extension beyond the two-year period.

### 2.3.3. *Transition, Change and Continuity*

The third possibility is that a transitional agreement is in part continuation of the past, in part a window to the future. This is likely, given that the first option is predicated on the assumption that the future trade relationship has been worked out to some degree. There may, however, be scant agreement on future trade relations within the two-year period, or the terms may be exiguous in the extreme, such that the transition would perforce be directed in part towards continuation with the EU status quo, and in part to smoothing the path towards whatever might have been concluded on trade relations. The legal concerns associated with transition and change, and those associated with transition and continuity, would both be relevant. It may well be that the best way to secure transition pending conclusion of an FTA with the EU would be for the UK to join EFTA and the EEA for a period of time.

## 2.4. TRADE RELATIONS: DEFAULT TO WTO RULES

If there is no agreement on trade within two years, and the negotiating time is not extended, then the Treaties cease to apply to the UK. The UK will then default to the World Trade Organization rules for the governance of its trade.[58] This raises complex issues that cannot be addressed within the limits of this chapter.[59] The principal contours of the WTO regime, and what it would mean for the UK, can nonetheless be conveyed.

The General Agreement on Tariffs and Trade, GATT, was signed in 1947 and entered into force in 1948. There were later rounds of negotiation, and the WTO emerged from the Uruguay round, which was signed in 1994, and entered into force in 1995. It created a new institutional framework based on the WTO;

---

[58]  World Trade Organization: <http://www.wto.org/>.
[59]  See eg L BARTELS, 'The UK's Status in the WTO after Brexit', 23 September 2016, <https://ssrn.com/abstract=2841747>. See further the contribution by G MESSENGER (Ch 11) in this edited collection.

introduced a more judicial dispute settlement mechanism; and extended the scope of world trade law through a number of new agreements.

The WTO regime embodies a series of different agreements relating to trade. The WTO Agreement distinguishes between multilateral trade agreements, and plurilateral trade agreements. The former agreements are regarded as binding on all WTO members; the latter are binding only on parties that have accepted them. The majority of agreements are characterised as multilateral, and they cover the most important areas of international trade: GATT; the Agreement on the Application of Sanitary and Phytosanitary Measures (the SPS Agreement); the Agreement on Technical Barriers to Trade (TBT Agreement); the Agreement on Trade-Related Investment Measures (TRIMS); the General Agreement on Trade in Services (GATS); the Agreement on Trade-Related Aspects of Intellectual Property Rights (TRIPS); the Dispute Settlement Understanding (DSU); and the Trade Policy Review Mechanism. There are Plurilateral Trade Agreements on Trade in Civil Aircraft and on Government Procurement.

### 2.4.1. Two Foundational Principles

The elimination of discrimination is central to the schema of world trade law. It finds expression in two complementary principles: the most favoured nation (MFN) treatment obligation[60] and the national treatment obligation.[61] Both principles are important in a post-Brexit world in which trade relations are governed by WTO rules. The relationship between the two principles is as follows:[62]

'While a national treatment obligation prohibits discriminatory treatment of lawfully "imported products vis-à-vis like domestic products" ("*inland parity*"), the MFN obligation restricts the rights of members to discriminate "between and among like products of different origins" ("*foreign parity*").'

The operation of the MFN principle can be exemplified in the context of customs duties. The core idea is that if a state imposes customs duties or charges on import or export then 'any advantage, favour, privilege or immunity granted by any contracting party to any product originating in or destined for any other country shall be accorded immediately and unconditionally to the like product originating in or destined for the territories of all other contracting parties.'[63] The way in which the MFN principle will circumscribe UK choices in a

---

[60]  GATT Article I; SPS Article 2.3; TBT Article 2.1; GATS Article II; TRIPS Article 4.
[61]  GATT Article III; GATS Article XVII; TRIPS Article 3.
[62]  M MATSUSHITA, T SCHOENBAUM, P MAVROIDIS and M HAHN, *The World Trade Organization: Law, Practice, and Policy*, 3rd edn, Oxford University Press, Oxford 2017, pp 155–156 (italics in original).
[63]  GATT Article I.1; MATSUSHITA ET AL, ibid, pp 158–173.

post-Brexit world where no trade deal has been reached with the EU is brought out forcefully by Damian Chalmers:

> 'If negotiations go south with the European Union, it [the UK] can punish the latter by imposing punitive tariffs on sensitive EU exports to the British market. However, if it does this, these tariffs will also have to be imposed on exports from Japan, Korea, the United States etc. And this would not be a promising start to the much vaunted trade negotiations with those States.'[64]

There are, however, exceptions to the MFN obligation, the most apposite of which is that it does not apply where there is a customs union (CU) or FTA.[65] Application of the most favoured nation principle would defeat the objective of such preferential trade arrangements between two or more states, since it would extend any concessions to all WTO members. The rationale for the exception is that the WTO contracting parties recognised the desirability of increasing freedom of trade by encouraging closer economic integration,[66] the assumption being that 'the overall benefits of these arrangements for world trade outweigh possible disadvantages'.[67] This assumption has been contested by economists, but the exception is legally embedded in the GATT. The rules are, however, structured to prevent abuse of the exception, which will only be applicable if the parties to the CU or FTA eliminate duties and other restrictive regulations of commerce 'on substantially all the trade' between them.[68] The salient point for present purposes is that if the UK concludes a FTA with the EU, or with other countries, then the MFN principle will no longer be applicable, such that differential trade rules could be applied to those outside the FTA. Pending the conclusion of such FTAs, the UK would continue to be bound by the MFN obligation and could not therefore accord privileged economic status to particular goods from one trading partner.

The national treatment obligation would also be applicable in a post-Brexit world in which the UK defaulted to WTO rules. The principle, embedded most notably in GATT Article III, provides that internal taxes and charges, and laws, regulations and the like affecting sale, purchase, transportation etc of goods, 'should not be applied to imported or domestic products so as to afford protection to domestic production'.[69] It affords broad protection against discriminatory treatment of domestic goods and foreign imports, covering actual and potential differential treatment, direct and indirect discrimination,

---

[64]     D Chalmers, *Trade after Brexit*, LSE Policy Brief No 23 (2017) p 2.
[65]     GATT Article XXIV.
[66]     GATT Article XXIV.4.
[67]     M Herdegen, *Principles of International Economic Law*, 2nd edn, Oxford University Press, Oxford 2016, p 215.
[68]     GATT Article XXIV.8; Matsushita et al, above n 62, pp 518–523.
[69]     GATT Article III.1.

and that which operates de facto as well as de jure. There are difficult issues concerning the scope of application of Article III, more especially in relation to the line between protectionist measures that are properly within its ambit, and regulatory measures that express national policy choices, but which can impact on foreign goods more than domestic ones, as exemplified by national measures designed to limit use of cars that are not environmentally friendly.[70]

### 2.4.2. Goods and Services

The WTO regime covers goods and services, but their respective treatment is very different, which is especially significant given the UK's economic reliance on services. Space precludes detailed treatment, but it is important to convey the essentials of the WTO approach to the respective areas.

The core rules concerning goods are contained in the GATT. The regime prohibits quantitative restrictions such as quotas, but does not prohibit tariffs. To the contrary, it establishes 'tariffs as the market access restriction of choice'.[71] GATT Article II does not prohibit tariffs, but 'provides the legal tools to render them more transparent and easy to negotiate by binding members vis-à-vis their fellow members to adhere to maximum tariff rates reflected in their respective schedules of concessions'.[72] Article II therefore provides certainty as to the maximum costs of gaining market access for goods to another state. It does not, however, require WTO members to establish tariffs. The strategy is rather to permit them to do so, and then stipulate that the tariffs thus chosen are the maximum rates for particular products.[73]

The exercise is completely voluntary: whereas the EU or the United States have bound tariffs for all product categories, some states have only bound their maximum tariffs for a very small number of products. However, once the mechanism of Article II has been activated by scheduling maximum tariff(s) for one or more product categories, binding obligations ensue (GATT Article II:1): the scheduled maximum tariff rates are a promise *erga omnes partes contractantes* and, pursuant to GATT Article II:7, an integral part of the GATT.

The *erga omnes* nature of the resulting obligation flows from GATT Article II:1(a), which provides that 'each contracting party shall accord to the commerce of the other contracting parties treatment no less favourable than that provided for in the appropriate Part of the appropriate Schedule annexed to this Agreement'. It is by parity of reasoning open to a state to impose a high tariff on a particular type of product, subject to the caveat that this must not exceed the

---

[70]    MATSUSHITA ET AL, above n 62, pp 185–192.
[71]    Ibid, p 216.
[72]    Ibid, p 216.
[73]    Ibid, p 218.

limit specified in the schedule of concessions. The upper tariff limit is known as the 'bound tariff', but a state may choose to apply a tariff below this level, hence the nomenclature of 'applied tariffs'. Each state party to the WTO has its own schedule, in which it sets out its chosen tariffs, subject to the qualification that a customs union such as the EU will have a schedule covering all EU Member States. These schedules will therefore have to be unpacked consequent upon the UK's exit from the EU.[74]

The WTO regime that pertains to services is less developed and is regulated through the General Agreement on Trade in Services (GATS). It is composed of 'General Obligations and Disciplines' in Part II and 'Specific Commitments' in Part III.

The General Obligations are, as the title indicates, prima facie applicable to all parties, including the most favoured nation obligation. The legal reality is more nuanced. Some of these 'general obligations' are 'tied to the liberalisation commitments, that is they become binding on WTO members only for the sectors where liberalisation commitments have been made, thereby adding to the complexity of the GATS'.[75] The peremptory force of the MFN obligation is further diminished by the fact that deviation is permitted provided that the relevant measure is listed in accord with conditions in the Annex on Article II GATS Exemptions. The reach of the MFN obligation is, moreover, limited where there is a preferential or free trade agreement that has substantial sectoral coverage,[76] the reasoning being analogous to that in the context of FTAs and goods.[77] The MFN obligation is also qualified by mutual recognition agreements.[78]

The Specific Commitments are contained in Part III and relate to market access, national treatment and additional commitments. They are only applicable when accepted by a particular state. It is therefore for each WTO member to signify in a schedule the specific commitments that it undertakes under Part III, making clear the sectors to which such commitments are undertaken, and specifying the terms, limitations and conditions on market access; the conditions and qualifications on national treatment; undertakings relating to additional commitments; where appropriate the timeframe for implementation of such commitments; and the date of their entry into force.[79] The contrast between goods and services is therefore significant. In the context of goods, GATT Article XI provides for market access, subject to any tariffs imposed, and the goods benefit from the obligation of national treatment when they have crossed the border (GATT Article III:1). By way of contrast, services only have

---

[74]   Bartels, above n 59.
[75]   Matsushita et al, above n 62, p 557.
[76]   GATS Article V.
[77]   GATT Article XXIV.
[78]   GATS Article VII.
[79]   GATS Article XX.

the benefit of market access[80] and national treatment[81] if the relevant service sector is included in the schedule of specific commitments accepted by that state.

## 2.5. TRADE RELATIONS: SIX CONCLUSIONS

There are numerous points that might be made by way of conclusion concerning trade relations between the UK and the EU in a post-Brexit world. Six such points will suffice for present purposes.

First, there is debate among trade scholars as to the impact that Brexit will have on the UK's rights and obligations under the WTO. Some contend that the UK would have to renegotiate core aspects of its WTO rights and obligations, its concessions under GATT Article II, and GATS Article XX, and that there would be difficult issues to resolve concerning the UK's rights to access tariff rate quotas that other WTO members have committed to allocate to the EU. Others contend that such concerns are misplaced.[82]

Secondly, there is a commonly voiced view to the effect that the EU constrains sovereignty, and that free trade in a post-Brexit world entails no such limitations on sovereign regulatory autonomy. This argument is fallacious. Many standards that regulate safety and the like are set at the global level, through transnational or international regulatory organisations. These standards are binding factually and legally in the UK and this will not change in a post-Brexit world. What will change is that the UK will have little or no voice in the framing of these rules. The principal players in this regard are the EU and the USA, and while we currently have influence through the former, this will cease if we leave the EU. There is, moreover, the fact that the WTO and FTAs contain a plethora of regulatory constraints in the different agreements that constitute the regime. The point is well made by Holger Hestermeyer and Federico Ortino:

> '[M]odern trade agreements go far beyond mere tariff arrangements. They encompass a wide variety of legal areas ranging from services regulation to intellectual property and immigration and impose both substantive and procedural requirements. Crucially, as legally binding agreements they all limit a state's sovereign choices. In this regard while they may differ from EU law in scope and enforceability, they do not in substance: the portrayal of EU law as limiting sovereignty and trade law as merely guaranteeing free

---

[80] GATS Article XVI.
[81] GATS Article XVII.
[82] Cp Bartels, above n 59; with P Koutrakos, 'What does Brexit mean for the UK in WTO?', 12 July 2016, <https://www.monckton.com/brexit-mean-uk-wto/> and P Eeckhout, 'Brexit and trade: the view over the hill', 16 June 2016, <https://londonbrussels.wordpress.com/2016/06/16/brexit-and-trade-the-view-over-the-hill/>. See further the contribution by G Messenger (Ch 11) in this edited collection.

trade is a fallacy. Trade agreements much like EU law contain commitments by a state to apply certain rules and refrain from passing others.'[83]

Thirdly, the impetus for the UK to conclude trade deals with the EU and with other parties is directly related to the limitations of the WTO regime. The UK economy is heavily reliant on services, and it is this area where the WTO regulatory regime is least developed. A default to WTO rules would therefore provide no sure foundation for market access or national treatment for the UK service sector. To the contrary, the UK would be dependent on specific commitments being made by other WTO members. Thus while some hard-line Brexiteers may view default to the WTO with equanimity, this is not a view generally shared by those in the service sector.

Fourthly, there is a tendency or temptation to regard conclusion of free trade agreements between the UK and the EU, and between the UK and other countries, as a self-evident economic good, which will be beneficial to the UK economy. There are indeed foundational economic arguments concerning gains for all parties from freer trade. We need nonetheless to be cautious in this respect. This is in part because of the procedural difficulties of negotiating such deals. It is in part because a beneficial substantive outcome for each party is not preordained. The parties to a FTA negotiate because they believe that their state will benefit from trade liberalisation. They negotiate to secure optimal benefits for their own country, and difficult trade-offs between the parties explain the protracted discourse prior to securing agreement. The difficulties of attaining the optimal economic outcome for one's own state are exacerbated when there is an imbalance in economic power between the negotiating parties. Thus, even if the UK is at the front of the queue for a FTA with the USA, which is doubtful, the US negotiators will target access to those parts of the UK economy, such as banking and financial services, which they believe provide the best opportunities for US firms within those sectors.

Fifthly, the practical reality is that, post-Brexit and prior to conclusion of a comprehensive trade deal, anyone seeking to do business in the EU will continue to be bound by EU rules if they wish to sell goods or services into the EU. The real difference in a post-Brexit world is that the UK will have no seat at the table and hence no voice when the relevant regulations are being drafted. This may well be true even when a comprehensive trade agreement between the UK and the EU has been duly ratified. Much will depend on the terms of such an agreement, but firms may well decide that it is simpler to comply with EU product standards if the EU constitutes an important part of their export market.

Sixthly and finally, there is a paradox underlying Brexit insofar as it relates to the balance between the economic and the social in our political ordering.

---

[83] H HESTERMEYER and F ORTINO, 'UK Trade Policy Post-Brexit: The Beginning of a Complex Journey', *King's College Legal Studies Research Paper*, 2017-04, pp 4–5.

Part of the rationale for the Leave vote was a reaction to the perceived negative effect of globalisation on certain communities. It was felt, moreover, that the balance between the economic and the social within the EU was too heavily weighted towards the former. There is little doubt that some communities have suffered, or failed to reap the rewards, from more open markets. There is also no doubt that the balance between the economic and the social within the EU has been contestable from the outset. This can be acknowledged, but it does nothing to diminish the sense of paradox that inheres in the current trade discourse. The reason is readily apparent. If and insofar as the concern is globalisation, then it is assuredly not alleviated by promise of multiple free trade agreements, which is globalisation writ large. If and insofar as the concern is the balance between the economic and the social, then it is assuredly not met through multiple free trade agreements, given that the EU provides better protection for labour and social rights than do FTAs.

## 3. SECURITY

The future relations between the UK and the EU will be shaped by the terms of the withdrawal agreement and by the content of a future trade agreement. Those relations will, however, also be markedly affected by the way in which issues concerning policing, security and the like are handled in the post-Brexit world.[84]

The UK White Paper attested to the Government's continued commitment to preserve UK and European security, and to fight terrorism and uphold justice across Europe. It spoke of the safety of the UK public as being the top priority for the Government,[85] and affirmed that the Government would seek to 'negotiate the best deal we can with the EU to cooperate in the fight against crime and terrorism'[86] when exiting the EU. The intention would be to maintain 'a strong and close future relationship with the EU, with a focus on operational and practical cross-border cooperation'.[87] There is no doubting the sincerity of the Government's statements in this regard. Translating this into a practical reality is rather more difficult.

This is readily apparent from the House of Lords' European Union Committee Report on Future UK-EU Security and Police Cooperation in a post-Brexit world.[88] The report welcomed the fact that the Government accorded priority

---

[84] See further the contributions by V Mitsilegas (Ch 10) and C Henderson (Ch 14) in this edited collection.

[85] *The United Kingdom's exit from and new partnership with the European Union*, above n 4, para 11.1.

[86] Ibid, para 11.7.

[87] Ibid, para 11.7.

[88] House of Lords European Union Committee, *Brexit: Future UK-EU security and police cooperation* (HL 2016–17, 77).

to security and police cooperation. It stressed that the current arrangements to facilitate such cooperation were 'mission-critical for the UK's law enforcement agencies', and voiced concerns that new arrangements when the UK leaves the EU would 'be sub-optimal relative to present arrangements, leaving the people of the United Kingdom less safe'.[89] It was, moreover, important that the UK remained part of the debate concerning European security after leaving the EU,[90] although the report cautioned against over being overly optimistic in this respect, more especially given that the UK Government did not wish to accept accountability mechanisms such as the CJEU. This could lead to a tension between 'two of its four overarching objectives in the negotiation – bringing back control of laws to Westminster and maintaining strong security cooperation with the EU'.[91]

The relationship with Europol and Eurojust was felt to be especially important. The future relationship with these bodies was, however, not straightforward. Evidence tendered to the committee indicated that an operational agreement with Europol akin to those that other third countries negotiated would not be sufficient to meet the UK's needs, and that a future UK-EU deal would need to go further in terms of operational cooperation.[92] There were, however, obstacles in this regard, most notably as to the role of the supranational EU institutions. Europol was accountable to those institutions, ever more so in the new Europol Regulation,[93] and this would therefore have to be resolved in negotiations between the UK and the EU. This was equally true for continued cooperation in relation to Eurojust.

Data-sharing for law enforcement purposes will be equally important in a post-Brexit world. Parliament decided in 2014 and 2015 that it would be in the national interest for the UK to participate in EU data-sharing platforms such as the Second Generation Schengen Information System, the European Criminal Records Information System and the Prüm Decisions. The House of Lords' Committee endorsed this view, regarding access to EU law enforcement databases and data-sharing platforms as integral to day-to-day policing. It was therefore vital in the national interest to find a way to sustain data-sharing for law enforcement purposes with the EU27.[94] While the House of Lords' committee advocated the search for a bespoke solution to allow continued access to such databases, it was also mindful of the fact that the two data-sharing tools regarded as particularly significant were those where there was no precedent for access by

---

[89]  Ibid, para 36.
[90]  Ibid, para 37.
[91]  Ibid, para 39.
[92]  Ibid, para 68.
[93]  Regulation 2016/794 of the European Parliament and of the Council of 11 May 2016 on the European Union Agency for Law Enforcement Cooperation (Europol) [2016] OJ L135/51.
[94]  *Brexit: Future UK-EU security and police cooperation*, above n 88, para 120.

non-EU (ECRIS) or non-Schengen (SIS II) countries.[95] The price of accessing these databases has thus far been membership of the EU and/or Schengen.

Brexit also posed serious challenges in relation to criminal justice tools, most notably the European Arrest Warrant. It was regarded as a critical component of the UK's law enforcement capabilities, and the alternative, the 1957 Council of Europe Convention on Extradition, was felt not to be an adequate substitute. A possible way forward was to follow the precedent set by Norway and Iceland and seek a bilateral extradition agreement with the EU that mirrored the EAW's provisions as far as possible. The difficulty was in relation to implementation, since that agreement was signed a decade ago, but was still not in force.[96]

There will therefore be considerable difficulties in negotiating rules to govern the future relations between the UK and the EU in the context of police and security cooperation. Deirdre Curtin provides an insightful summation:

'The likelihood of considerable "bits and pieces" looms large in particular as the UK struggles to maintain already existing levels and choices of cooperation … The UK clearly faces the future in a different position to its past one. It will move from being an engaged insider which, even in areas where it enjoyed formal opt outs in AFSJ, operated in practice as a leader, "a leading protagonist in driving and shaping the nature and direction of cooperation on police and security matters under the auspices of the European Union"[97] to a disempowered outsider.'[98]

## 4. CONCLUSION

There is much that is as yet uncertain as to the nature of relations between the UK and the EU. That is readily apparent from the preceding analysis. The way in which the UK and the EU interact now and hereafter will nonetheless be shaped by the considerations discussed above. The terms of withdrawal, the nature of future trade relations, and the way in which policing and security are dealt with in a post-Brexit world constitute the foundational architecture that will shape the way in which a plethora of other important issues are resolved. It remains to be seen whether the Conservative Party losses in the 2017 election and the resulting hung Parliament lead to change in the Government's negotiating strategy on Brexit. Political life will certainly be more precarious for a minority Conservative Government.

---

95    Ibid, paras 121–122.
96    Ibid, para 141.
97    The quote is from *Brexit: Future UK-EU security and police cooperation*, above n 88, para 27.
98    D Curtin, 'Brexit and the EU Area of Freedom, Security and Justice': Bespoke Bits and Pieces in Fabbrini above n 53, Ch 9.

# ABOUT THE EDITOR

Michael Dougan is Professor of European Law and Jean Monnet Chair in EU Law at the University of Liverpool. He is an established academic authority on EU constitutional law and Joint Editor of *Common Market Law Review* – the world's leading scientific journal for European legal studies. Michael's work has also contributed to wider public and political debates about European law. For example, he has provided written evidence to numerous Parliamentary enquiries, appeared as an expert witness before various Parliamentary committees in both the House of Commons and the House of Lords, and provided external advice to a range of Government departments and Union institutions. Michael's public engagement activities, including videos of his lectures on the EU referendum, received extensive media attention in the run-up to the 'Brexit' referendum and he continues to be a popular authority on the matter for individuals and groups all around the world.